I ♥ THE RAMONES
THE LIFE & TIMES OF THE SPEEDKINGS
NICK COOPER

Foreword by Jari-Pakka Laitio-Ramone

HUNT AND PECK
BOOKS & PUBLISHING

EARTH ISLAND BOOKS

COPYRIGHT

First published by Hunt And Peck Books, 2024

Copyright © 2024 by Nick Cooper
The right of Nick Cooper to be identified as the author of this work has been asserted by him in accordance with sections 77 and 78 of the Copyright, Designs and Patents Act, 1988.
All rights reserved.

No part of this publication may be reproduced, distributed, or transmitted in any form or by any means, including photocopying, recording, or other electronic or mechanical methods, without the prior written permission of the publisher, except as permitted by U.S. copyright law. For permission requests, contact Hunt And Peck books – info@heartbreakramones.com

For privacy reasons, some names, locations, events and dates may have been changed.

Every reasonable effort has been made to trace copyright holders of material reproduced in this book, but if any have been inadvertently overlooked then publishers will be glad to hear from them.

Book Cover and illustrations by Nick Cooper

Library of Congress Cataloging-in-Publication Data

First edition 2024

Cooper, Nick
I 'Heartbreak' The Ramones: The Life And Times of the SpeedKings

ISBN 978-1-964289-63-2 (paperback)
ISBN 978-1-964289-64-9 (hardcover)

Don't cry because it's over
Smile because it happened.
Dr. Seuss

There is no greater agony
than bearing an untold story inside you.
Maya Angelou

Take care of all your memories
for you cannot relive them.
Bob Dylan

CONTENTS

DEDICATION 11
FOREWORD 13
INTRODUCTION 27
THE ANTI-SOCIAL PRE-TEEN 35
HIDING IN THE ROCK'N'ROLL 47
THE PUNK ATTITUDE 56
FADED GLORY BOYS 61
I WAS A TEENAGE ANARCHIST ANONYMOUS 66
CRUISE MISSILES AND TERRORISM 81
MONDO MIDNIGHT 88
PARALLEL WORLD 95
A LEWD BROTHERHOOD 102
RAGTAIL & BOBTAIL 108
BEAM ME UP, SCOTTY 116
THE EAGLE HAS LANDED 122
SQUAT DELLA MORTE 129
BIKER SHINDIG 138

DESTINATION SCHNITZEL HAUS	149
GET DOWN BRASS	158
CHOCOLATES, STAGBOOKS AND ROCK'N'ROLL	163
MUSTANG MARKY	172
THE HUNT FOR THE TRAILER PARK UNICORN	177
OFF THE WRONG FOOT	182
A 2001 STATEMENT	190
MEET THE TCB-CREW	193
SUPERSONIC MILKY MAID	209
THE WILD AT HEART PISS-BOTTLE MAN	221
RAWK OVER SCANDINAVIA	235
DON HILL'S STREET BLUES	250
DUTCH COURAGE	261
LUCK WENT SOUTH	282
COLORS & SWASTIKAS	309
KABUKICHŌ COWBOYS	319
CHRISTMAN IN LA	343
THE WILD WILD WEST	351
TOO FAR NORTH	364
UNDER THE BOARDWALK	375
WINNER, WINNER, CHICKEN DINNER	386
THE TOAST OF HOLLYWOOD	396
RENDEZVOUS WITH THE END	410
WORLD FALLS APART	415
I HATE THE RAMONES	425
COMING OF AGE	431
POSTSCRIPT	438
ACKNOWLEDGEMENTS	440

DEDICATION

In line with the powerful and iconic words of the late and great Dee Dee Ramone during his induction into the Rock'n'Roll Hall of Fame: "I'd like to congratulate myself and thank myself and give myself a big pat on the back."

I boldly dedicate this book to none other than myself for being the driving force behind its creation. It was a journey that only I could start, and no one else could have accomplished what I did. Every triumph, every obstacle overcome, it was all because of my determination and unwavering spirit. This book is a testament to my resilience, my passion, and my refusal to let anyone else dictate my path. It is a celebration of my unique voice and the power that lies within me. I stand tall, knowing that everything that transpired was a result of my own actions and no one else's. So here's to me, who fearlessly blazes a trail where others dare not tread. Let this book be a symbol of unwavering commitment to living life on my own terms.

As Jack Kerouac once said: "So, therefore, I dedicate myself to myself, to my art, my sleep, my dreams, my labors, my loneliness, my unique madness, my endless absorption, and hunger – because I cannot dedicate myself to any fellow being."

The true credit for this accomplishment, however, lies not with me alone, but with the unwavering commitment to truth itself. In a world where honesty is often met with disdain, no one is more hated than he who speaks the truth.

FOREWORD

Everyone is well aware of the iconic impact that Chuck Berry's "Johnny B. Goode" had when it hit the scene in 1958, forever altering the course of music history. Fast forward to 1976 when something similar happened: the Ramones unleashed their debut album, sending shockwaves to the world. In the period between 1974 and 1976, the band only played two shows in the United Kingdom and one in Canada. All their other shows were in the US. Things exploded in 1977 when they caused an earthquake outside North America by playing close to 30 shows in Great Britain. Next to that, they played five gigs in the Netherlands, 5 in France, 2 in Finland and Switzerland, and passed once through Belgium, Sweden, and Denmark.

It was their performances and anthems like "Beat On The Brat," "Judy Is A Punk," and "Blitzkrieg Bop" that inspired a multitude of bands to form in the years that followed, creating a new world of punk rock from 1976 on. All these bands were born out of the raw energy that the Ramones embodied, igniting a revolution in music that continues to resonate to this day.

Through the first three albums of the Ramones, a sonic revolution unfurled. One of the band's original members, Tommy Ramone, departed prematurely, only to be succeeded by Marky Ramone. However, after four more albums, destiny had other plans as Tommy made a triumphant return, taking on the role of producer for their 1984 masterpiece, "Too Tough to Die." My conversations with Tommy chronicled in my third book, "Ramones: Soundtrack Of Our Lives," shed light on this epic moment. Reflecting upon our reunion, Tommy shared, "They – Joey Ramone, Johnny Ramone, and Dee Dee Ramone- brought me back for this album. When they reached out and asked me to be the producer, I was overjoyed. Too Tough To Die presented us with a remarkable opportunity to reunite once again."

The Ramones came to an end in 1996. I don't underestimate any of their albums. But when I reflect on the albums that were really tight and fast, I wonder how long it actually took to release another truly mind-blowing album from the band themselves or any of its members after "Too Tough To Die." Well, it actually took until 2001, 17 long years! It was when Marky Ramone & The SpeedKings unleashed the album "No If's, And's, Or But's!" (aka Legends Bleed) to the world. Give it a listen, and you will understand why I'm feeling this way. Marky, Nick Cooper, Dee Jaywalker, and Stevey Jay joined forces with the talented Tony De Block at Midas Studios in Belgium and created a real masterpiece that rivals the tightness of any Ramones album since 1984.

Now, here we are in 2024, and I, of course, own every album by the Ramones as well as all the solo projects by their members. The album "No If's, And's Or But's!" stands as a vivid reflection of every era of their music, just as intense as their groundbreaking debut in 1976 or their gritty release "Too Tough To Die" in 1984. Tommy played the drums on the first three albums and Richie Ramone in "Too Tough To Die." Joey, Dee Dee, and Johnny are in all four albums. I am really happy that Marky got to play in an album like "No If's, And's Or But's!" Just moments before the album hit the shelves, Nick sent me a rough mix tape of it. I decided to write a review of it on my website, www.ramonesheaven.com, and I was absolutely blown away by the fact that Ramones fans and others alike would get the chance to experience an album that is as unyielding as it is. In my opinion, Nick possesses the same level of eccentricity and charm as Dee Dee Ramone, and he is just as thoughtful and versatile as Joey Ramone. It was a heartbreaking reality that we lost Joey eight months prior to the release of "No If's, And's Or But's!" and Dee Dee left this world six months after the release. I know how much Dee Dee would have adored "Fuck Shit Up!" - a mind-bending track, and "Manuelita" - a heartfelt tribute to the people of South America. Joey would have undoubtedly selected a few tracks from this album for his own solo releases, like "Saturday Night," and he would have collaborated with the brilliant Daniel Rey, who skillfully mastered "No If's, And's Or But's!"

CJ Ramone and Richie Ramone share many similarities with Nick and Dee Dee as songwriters. I wouldn't be surprised if someone told me that CJ wrote a song like "Burning Rubber" or "Hot Rods-R-Us," or if Richie penned tracks like "Weenie Hair" or "I Don't Care Anymore" for the SpeedKings album.

The "No If's, And's Or But's!" album is definitely one of my top 5 solo albums by the members of the Ramones, along with Dee Dee Ramone's "I.C.L.C.: I Hate Freaks Like You" (1994), CJ's Bad Chopper's: Bad Chopper" (2007), CJ Ramone's "Last Chance To Dance" (2014), and Richie Ramone's "Cellophane" (2016).

We haven't been blessed with any fresh tunes penned by Marky for over two decades. It would have been absolutely cool if Nick Cooper had taken Marky Ramone under his wing and taught him the art of songwriting, as Nick wrote most of the killer tracks for The SpeedKings. After The SpeedKings, he rocked out with The Misfits and The Osaka Popstar and has, for example, recorded an album with Teenage Head. He has been tearing up stages with his band Marky Ramone's Blitzkrieg for over 15 years now, but this group only released three new songs. Marky didn't write any of those songs. That's why I'm crossing my fingers that Nick would step in and give Marky a friendly kick in the ass, so they could co-write some infectious tunes. With the Ramones, Marky actually recorded a couple of songs that he wrote.

In the early 2000s, Marky was on the road with Nick and the SpeedKings. During that time, he was a completely different person. He was so down-to-earth. The collaboration between the two of them started when they first toured together in The Buckweeds! final European tour (2000). The last time they performed together was back in 2003. Just the other day, I was revisiting an interview I conducted with Marky at his house, alongside my buddy David Kelly, for my book "Rock In Peace: Dee Dee And Joey Ramone." During that conversation in April 2004, I asked Marky, "What are your current plans with the SpeedKings?" Marky's response was straightforward and to the point. He said, "No more touring with the SpeedKings. I really enjoyed being part of the band; it was a blast.

I have to say, Nick Cooper is an incredibly talented songwriter and frontman, and I genuinely wish him all the best with the band."

I had the pleasure of spending a lot of quality time with Marky, both in various cities across different countries and at his own home. I had the honor of being a guest singer for three of his bands: SpeedKings, Tarakany (Russia), and Ramones Mania (Germany). And through these experiences, I witnessed the many facets of Marky as a drummer and as a fantastic friend and human being.

Now, I sincerely hope to see Nick Cooper once again get on stage, playing his classic tunes. Maybe he could write a few new ones together with Richie Ramone and CJ Ramone. When I saw Nick perform, I witnessed he exudes the same determination and uncompromising attitude as Johnny Ramone. And just like me, Nick has hardcore punk roots running through his veins. In the 1980s, Finland, alongside the US, was at the forefront of the hardcore punk scene, birthing numerous influential bands like Kaaos, Rattus Riistetyt, Lama, and Terveet Kädet. It created a friendship that now lasted for over two decades.

Since 1995, I have been doing Ramonesheaven.com, the most extensive and comprehensive Ramones website. Additionally, I have written three books dedicated to the Ramones, and I've had the privilege of attending almost 80 Ramones shows in 20 different countries. The Ramones ensured that punk rock would never fade away.

I say "Cheers!" to Nick Cooper, my friend. The Ramones changed his life in a very personal way, just like they changed mine. We are here to keep the legacy alive! I am happy that Nick is around and finally wrote his book. I am sure Ramones fans will enjoy it, and new fans will be made.

1-2-3-4! Hey Ho, Let's Go!

Jari-Pekka Laitio-Ramone
Kauhajoki, Finland
May 2024

PREFACE
2003 - Welcome to my Theatre of Hate.

I am a wordsmith junkie with a deep obsession with books. From a young age, I harbored aspirations of becoming an author. Back in my rebellious teenage years, when punk rock was just starting to make waves, I took on the role of an editor for my own fanzines. They may have been rudimentary, naive, and rough around the edges, but they allowed me to express my thoughts on paper. It's all about the act of creation. There's something truly magical about holding a physical publication in your hands, feeling the texture of the paper, and inhaling the scent of freshly printed ink.

At one point, I made a solemn vow to write a book. Countless times, I sat down and began crafting those initial pages, but for some reason, I never found the fortitude to see it through. There was always something else that seemed more urgent, more captivating, or perhaps just another attractive piece of skirt crossing my line of sight. Distraction kept me from becoming an author.

The desire to pen my own book resurfaced in the aftermath of the breakup when I felt a deep sense of betrayal and disappointment. I yearned to unleash my raw emotions with fiery words. Bold sentences, written in capital letters and punctuated with exclamation marks, seemed like the perfect outlet for my anger. However, I had to confront reality and prioritize my responsibilities. The disbandment of the SpeedKings forced me to face the bottomless depth of uncertainty and reclaim control over my life.

For years, I had relied on the band as my sole source of sustenance. Although parting ways seemed like the right decision, it meant returning to a mundane existence. Back to the monotony of everyday life, like a prisoner on a chain gang. I came from nowhere and went straight back there. Thrust back into the depths of obscurity. I lacked the fame and reputation to forge my own path and certainly wasn't a virtuoso on the guitar. My options were limited. This aspiring rockstar needed to find employment swiftly.

But with all the desperate need to be liberated from the shackles of life, the burning desire to express myself through writing remained, but on the grounds of the harsh reality of life, I had to find a way to survive in the real world. The music industry had chewed me up and spit me out, leaving me with nothing but shattered dreams and a tattered sense of self. It was time to dust off my resume and pound the pavement in search of a job that would put food on the table and keep a roof over my head.

As I started this new chapter of my life, I couldn't help but feel like a lost soul in need of redemption. The world seemed vast and unforgiving, like an empty stage waiting to be filled with the pounding rhythm of my words. But before I could take center stage and command attention with my prose, I had to pay my dues in the nine-to-five grind.

So, with determination in my heart and a hunger for success burning in my veins, I set off on the arduous journey of finding a job. It was time to trade in my guitar pick for a pen and let my words become the anthem of my survival. The clock was ticking, and I had to make a name for myself in a world that seemed determined to keep me down. It was time to prove to the world that this boy had what it took to rise from the ashes and claim his rightful place in the spotlight.

The whole band thing had been an escape from corporate life in the first place. The years prior to playing music full-time led me to Tokyo, Japan. I worked my way up in the manufacturing division of Pioneer Electronics and ended up as a general manager. For seven years, I slaved my ass off for the top man and company politics, which threw me into a catch-22 situation. "I'd rather die on my feet than live on my knees" sounded like a great line in a blockbuster drama, but fifteen minutes after those heroic words, I found myself on the sidewalk with all my career stuffed in a cardboard box.

The furious energy of rock'n'roll became the perfect remedy to give the middle finger to the corporate world. It felt like the ultimate form of resistance. It felt so damn good, and everything was going smoothly until I outlived the band and found myself back in the real world. The raw power of rock music was like medicine, allowing me to rebel against society's constraints and express my frustrations. But as time went on, the thrill faded, and I was left facing the Spartan realities of life once again.

As I searched for a way to make a living, writing a book was not exactly at the forefront of my mind. And to make matters worse, the unexpected bombshell of a divorce blindsided me like a freight train. Suddenly, I was caught right in the middle of a tempestuous shitstorm. Financially strapped with no income or job, I found myself entangled in bitter battles over child custody and burdened by the looming darkness of alimony payments. It felt like dark clouds were constantly hanging over my head, ready to unleash their torrential downpour.

Scattered among the relics of my past, amidst scrapbooks filled with memories, tattered band shirts that once held the sweat and energy of countless gigs, and the crackling sound of vinyl records spinning on a turntable were photographs capturing moments frozen in time. These treasured possessions, accumulated over the years, now lay forgotten in dusty cardboard boxes within the confines of a dim and musty attic. Buried beneath a heap of miscellaneous possessions I had amassed over the years.

Time has a way of speeding by, slipping through our fingers like sand in an hourglass. Racing by at a pace too swift for me to truly comprehend. It's as if the years have sprinted ahead, leaving behind a trail of fleeting moments and faded dreams. Yet, amidst the chaos and clutter, a spark reignited within me – the flame of my writing ambitions flickering back to life.

From the depths of silence, my creativity surged forth once more. The words that were once penned with youthful exuberance found their voice again, echoing through the corridors of my mind. They demanded to be heard, to be released from the confines of those dusty boxes and shared with the world.

In the midst of it all, my dormant passion for writing has reawakened, like a long-lost melody finding its way back into my soul. As I make a start on this new chapter of my writing journey, I am fueled by a sense of purpose and determination. Each word I write is a defiant act, a rebellion against the notion that time can steal away our passions and bury them beneath layers of forgotten memories.

Just as rock music has the power to transport us to another time and place, igniting our souls with its raw energy and emotional intensity, my words seek to do the same. They become the soundtrack to the stories I weave, resonating with readers and stirring their emotions.

So here I stand among the remnants of my past and the untapped potential of my future. With every sentence I craft, I carve out my own path, defying the passage of time and reclaiming my voice.

The journey ahead may be filled with ups and downs, obstacles, and triumphs, but I am ready. Armed with my pen as my guitar, I will continue to strum the chords of my stories, creating a symphony of words that resonate deep within the hearts of those who dare to listen.

Guess what? I've actually written a book. No, not the one I had in mind. Not the book I always planned to write. It all started with a chance encounter that rekindled a friendship that hit rock bottom somewhere in the mid-eighties. My high school buddy, the one with whom I formed my very first band, found himself in a devastating situation. Most of his supposed friends had abandoned him. You know how it goes; you truly discover who your real friends are when you're facing adversity. Those so-called friends scurry off like derelict rats from the sinking vessel. To his astonishment, I showed up at his doorstep and pulled him out of the darkness, out of the abyss. Well, at least I did my part.

Our casual chats soon evolved into writing sessions and exchanging emails. Old memories transformed into captivating stories. Memories of ours on which we intended would never see the light of day. It was more of a therapeutic exercise, really. But what started as a hundred pages quickly ballooned into five hundred. As we delved into old cardboard boxes, we unearthed forgotten treasures, precious material that deserved more than just therapeutic musings. It was too damn good to stay hidden in the shadows. We realized we had a book on our hands and needed an audience to rock it.

After three months of teasers and relentless messaging in a newly formed Facebook group, we managed to generate enough interest to sell out the first print run of the book. Can you believe it? The demand went through the roof! We sold out even before the official release date. It was like our words were resonating with people, striking a chord deep within their souls.

This journey has been nothing short of extraordinary. It's as if we're explorers on an epic adventure, defying the odds and captivating audiences with our raw and powerful narratives. We've embraced our recollections, refusing to conform to the rules of literary storytelling. Our words are like guitar riffs, shredding through the monotony of everyday life. That's how you make waves, Rock 'n' roll style.

Here I am; I don't feel like an author but rather a storyteller. And this book, this labor of love, is just the beginning.

"FADED GLORY BOYS - Resonating Echoes of a Less Than Glorious Past" surfaced in the Belgian and Dutch punk scene and swiftly attained cult status as readers identified deeply with the tales of small-town life. It struck a chord with countless individuals who saw their own reflections in the little stories. These writings served as a catalyst, urging people to reestablish connections with long-lost companions or locate those acquaintances who had seemingly vanished into thin air many years ago. Remarkably, some presumed to be deceased were revealed to be very much alive, while others may have departed this world, but now, thanks to the book, they are forever etched in our collective memory, never to be forgotten.

Writing a book turned out to be a wild ride, even more exhilarating than I had anticipated. It's like living the rockstar life without the exhausting toll of being in a band. Unlike the unpredictable singer who is always either fashionably late, too high, or too wasted, I don't have to worry about dealing with their antics. There's no need for me to help the bass player unload their massive 8x10 Ampeg cabinet, and best of all, the guitarist isn't constantly cranking up the volume to 11, drowning out everyone else with ear-splitting feedback. And let's not forget about the drummer - thankfully, they're not as much of a handful as my previous experience with Marky, hahaha.

I am now a writer, and as I rummage through these boxes, I uncover forgotten treasures. It's time for me to finally share the untold tale of the SpeedKings. I've been putting off writing this book for far too long. When my first book was published, it seemed like so many memories of the SpeedKings had slipped away. It was as if my mind had blocked it all out. But bit by bit, those memories started to resurface. Every photograph and newspaper clipping sparked new stories, and I couldn't help but burst into laughter, rolling on the floor. However, there were also moments that ignited anger within me.

In an attempt to relive that moment of the breakup, I can vividly recall the piercing words that escaped my lips, "I HATE THE RAMONES!" It dawned on me that this would be the perfect title for this story. With this bold proclamation, no one could ever accuse me of exploiting the Ramones' name for mere publicity. Admittedly, adding "I HATE" to the title might repel numerous diehard fans, but I couldn't care less. This is my personal declaration, and as I reflect on how Paul Cook from the Sex Pistols boldly emblazoned "I Hate" atop a picture of Pink Floyd on his t-shirt, I find immense pride in carrying on the spirit of punk rock tradition.

Recently, I've been engaging in conversations with various individuals, discussing a particular idea. During one of these discussions, Jari-Pekka Laitio-Ramone posed an intriguing question, asking me if I truly despise The Ramones. Now, I don't necessarily believe in the concept of hate, but let's be honest: it does have a certain ring to it. It serves as a powerful catalyst, enticing people to delve into the depths of this book. And guess what? Mission accomplished. By capturing their attention, I am successfully drawing the reader into the narrative of my journey.

The Ramones never quite hit the mark for me when it comes to my favorite bands. However, there's no denying their immense importance and influence in the birth of punk music. The foursome sparked a fire in the hearts of kids all over the world, inspiring them to form their own bands. The Ramones had a unique style and image that became instantly recognizable, almost like a trademark. It's ironic how, today, major fashion chains effortlessly sell their band t-shirts to the masses who may have never even witnessed their mind-blowing live performances. It's as if those who once shunned punk music are now unwittingly transformed into walking advertisements for these leather-clad hoodlums from Forest Hills.

I despise the Ramones, and my hatred for them goes beyond just a casual dislike. It's a personal declaration, one that may not hold any significance to anyone else but myself. I come from a place that is often overlooked, a forgotten corner of the world where nothing exciting ever happens. You know those small, insignificant towns you drive through occasionally? The ones that make you wonder who in their right mind would choose to be born there? Well, that's where I'm from.

Growing up in Kuurne, Belgium, my hometown, was far from glamorous. It's a far cry from the vibrant art scenes of New York or Los Angeles, devoid of any sense of fashion or cultural significance. In fact, there wasn't much to boast about at all. We had one measly grocery store, a butcher shop, and a handful of cafes where pigeon racing dominated conversations alongside the weather. Hardly the stuff of rock 'n' roll dreams.

But it wasn't just the lack of excitement that bothered me. I couldn't help but feel that my place of birth was holding me back, like an anchor dragging me down. In a world where your background and upbringing can make or break you, I couldn't help but feel like I started at a disadvantage. The absence of opportunities and exposure to art and culture left me feeling isolated and disconnected from the rest of the world.

As I drove through those forgotten corners of my hometown, I couldn't help but wonder how different my life would have been if I had been born somewhere else, perhaps in a bustling city filled with inspiration and creative energy. Maybe then, I would have had a chance to pursue my passions and break free from the banal existence that surrounded me.

So yes, my hatred for the Ramones may seem trivial to some, but it represents so much more than just a band I dislike. It's a symbol of the limitations and frustrations that come with being born in a place that offers little in terms of growth and opportunity. It's a defiant anthem, a rallying cry against the constraints of my upbringing, and a reminder that I refuse to be defined by the circumstances of my birth.

Can you blame me for wanting to escape from that cramped prison? To free myself from the constraints of middle-class values and the suffocating grip of the local church. It was like staging a daring jailbreak, a rebellion against the norms that imprisoned my spirit.

My escape from the confines of my hometown catapulted me into a whirlwind three-year journey with Marky in the SpeedKings. During this time, I experienced moments that were beyond imagination - moments of sheer bliss and moments of utter despair. It was like being caught in a turbulent, rollercoaster relationship. The highs were manic, sending me soaring to the heavens, while the lows seemed bottomless, plunging me into the depths of darkness. I had to learn how to navigate through the constant mood swings, akin to a toddler's tantrums, all while belting out Ramones cover songs.

Do I not validate myself for growing to despise the very institution that had become my musical sanctuary? As the years passed, The Ramones transformed into an impenetrable fortress, guarded fiercely by a legion of fans who worshiped their heroes with unwavering devotion. There was no room for dissenting voices or alternative perspectives. It was a black-and-white world - you were either a devout follower or an outright detractor. There was no middle ground, and when I had to choose, I found myself gravitating towards hatred rather than love.

The Ramones, once my comrades-in-arms, had become a symbol of conformity and rigidity. Their music, once an anthem of mutiny, had been co-opted by a fan base that brooked no dissent. It felt suffocating, stifling my creative spirit and smothering my individuality. The institution that was once a haven for misfits and rebels had transformed into a monolith of unyielding idolatry.

So now, as I reflect on those tumultuous years spent in the SpeedKings, I find myself torn between conflicting emotions. The memories of the exhilarating highs and soul-crushing lows are etched deep within me.

Once again, let me make it clear that I am not someone who harbors hatred. This statement is more of a symbolic expression of my personal sentiments. Out of all the members of the Ramones, I have had the closest connection with Marky, so my words don't encompass all of them. In fact, they don't even solely pertain to Marky himself. "It is what it is," he would always say, and I concur. However, there is a valuable lesson I wish to impart. It's perfectly fine to enjoy a band, but it's important not to become too familiar with your idols. Just like you and me, they are mere mortals made of flesh and blood. They have their virtues, but they also possess flaws and can be unsympathetic at times. They eat, sleep, take a dump like any other human being. Unfortunately, I have had the unfortunate experience of witnessing more of their less glamorous side. Have you ever been through it? Well, I certainly have. Perhaps a bit too much… I cut my throat with the glass shards of my broken heart. This is why I feel compelled to declare it boldly and unapologetically…

I HATE THE RAMONES!

I HATE THE RAMONES!

I HATE THE RAMONES!

I HATE THE RAMONES!

I HATE THE RAMONES!

CHAPTER 1

Introduction

My legacy is that I stayed on course… from the beginning to the end, because I believed in something inside of me." – *Tina Turner*

From the very beginning, my journey of self-development has been fueled by creativity, imagination, and an unwavering passion. Even as a child, I yearned to leave my mark on the world. However, my path was not without its challenges. Battling with asthma, I found myself sheltered and protected by my mother. But in the depths of my mind, I found solace, where my thoughts, dreams, and secrets thrived.

While some may seek companionship in their endeavors, I viewed others as mere obstacles standing in the way of my ambitions. It's not that I'm a control freak, but rather, I crave complete control as a means of experiencing true freedom. My insatiable curiosity led me to explore the world around me, always seeking new adventures and pushing boundaries. Books, magazines, and television became my sacred wellsprings of knowledge, shaping my worldview. I became steadfast in my beliefs, forming solid opinions and unwavering principles. My father instilled in me a sense of competitiveness, urging me to strive for greatness. On the other hand, my mother's attempts to limit me only fueled my desire to break free from constraints. Meanwhile, my grandfather's boundless imagination inspired me to dream big, while my grandmother provided a solid foundation of love and support as the cornerstone of our family.

INTRODUCTION

As an only child, I often found myself indulging in the luxuries granted by either parent. Whether it was through the nurturing embrace of my mother or the granting of my desires by my father, I had grown accustomed to getting what I wanted.

Everyone tends to believe that the era they grew up in is special, but for me, growing up in the early seventies was truly extraordinary. The development of music during that time was something else. It was a time when rock and roll had just been born in the late fifties, and the cultural revolution of the sixties was still strongly felt. However, it was clear that another change was on the horizon. Growing up in the early seventies gave me a front-row seat to witness the birth of an iconic era in music. The emergence of New Wave and Punk completely shook the foundations of the music industry, and it opened up a world of possibilities for me. Punk showed me that I could take matters into my own hands and do things myself. It was as if the concept of DIY was tailor-made for me.

Instead of spending endless hours studying, practicing, and experimenting, I could simply go out there and give it a shot. No one cared if it was perfect or not; the act of doing it was enough in itself. This approach resonated with my personality perfectly. It was liberating to embrace imperfection and just focus on the sheer act of creating. The punk movement taught me that I didn't need to wait for validation or approval from others. I could forge my own path and create something unique. The raw energy fueled my passion and pushed me to explore my own creative boundaries. In a world where conformity seemed to be the norm, punk provided an antidote. It was my wake-up call. Soon enough, I found myself immersed in the chaotic world of punk music, joining my very first band. It was an intense experience, and I knew deep down that this was where I belonged. However, I wasn't the sole driving force behind the band; I was just a part of it. Fast forward two years, and I found myself at the helm, steering the ship towards a new, politically inspired direction. This shift opened up a world of exploration, introducing me to different genres and allowing my signature style to take shape. While it may not have been entirely groundbreaking, every element fell into place, aligning perfectly with my vision of how things should be. Most importantly, I became the captain of my own destiny. I had found my voice.

There was a time when I thought I could purchase every single punk album that graced the shelves of our local record store. But as the number of incredible bands grew, it became increasingly impossible to possess "every" punk record. Decisions had to be made. The burning question was: should I lean towards the British punkwave or embrace the American counterpart? Each side claimed to be the pioneer of this groundbreaking music genre. London had a certain appeal due to its proximity, making it an obvious choice. However, New York City had an allure that was raw and unrefined. It didn't take long for me to be captivated by the likes of the New York Dolls, Patti Smith, Ramones, Blondie, Dead Boys, Runaways and other seminal acts.

I was just like countless other kids, going through the same emotions and transformations. It's safe to say that we all had dreams of getting up close and personal with our heroes. And in the world of punk, that dream wasn't entirely out of reach. Punk music shattered the barriers that separated idols from their fans. However, for most fans, the opportunity to truly connect with their favorite bands was limited to a brief conversation or an autograph. To become intimately acquainted with them was a privilege reserved for only a select few. And to actually play music alongside one of your idols? Well, that was something truly exceptional.

And there I stood, effortlessly stumbling upon musicians who were the epitome of idolization. It wasn't a result of meticulous planning or calculated maneuvering; it simply unfolded before me. Sometimes, all it takes is being in the perfect place at the perfect time and seizing the fleeting moment. The ability to seize opportunities is a skill that eludes many, whether due to fear or a lack of audacity. They hesitate to dream, to inquire, to speak up, and as a result, momentum slips through their fingers. But not for me.

The moment I confided in someone about my love for girl bands and how I had learned to play Runaways songs, little did I know that it would lead to an extraordinary chain of events. That person simply called Joan Jett in the dead of night, and to my astonishment, a few weeks later, I found myself strolling along the sandy shores of Waikiki Beach in Oahu, Hawaii, alongside Joan herself. Two days later, we shared the same stage on a Kaneohe military airstrip in the vast expanse of the Pacific Ocean.

INTRODUCTION

Imagine my astonishment when a friend from Los Angeles informed me that she had collaborated with none other than Wayne Kramer of MC5 fame to create a rendition of one of the songs I had written.

Once upon a time, when I found myself engaged in a project for a renowned London café racer motorcycle shop. Little did I know that this endeavor would lead me down an unexpected path. Imagine my surprise when, not long after completing the commissioned work, I stumbled upon a photograph in the press. And there, in all her glory, stood Amy Winehouse, posing in a t-shirt adorned with the very design I had created and brought to life.

Then, in a moment of sheer desperation, when my local punk band found themselves without a drummer, I mustered up the courage to reach out to the drummer of the Ramones via email. Against all odds, one month later, he showed up at my doorstep, ready to jam and prepare for an upcoming European tour.

If you were to meticulously plan and plot every single one of these occurrences, perhaps you might strike gold once. But here's the thing – it wasn't an ingeniously crafted masterplan at all. It was simply a series of unexpected situations that presented themselves, and I seized every opportunity that came my way. The result? People started gravitating towards me instead of me chasing after them.

I found myself jamming in a band alongside one of the legendary Ramones for a good couple of years. It was a wild ride, filled with ups and downs, and it's a tale that simply needs to be shared. But let me make one thing crystal clear - this isn't just another Ramones story. It's no unauthorized biography. No, this is my personal rock and roll odyssey, an integral part of my own history. The famous and not-so-famous characters who appear in this story are just players on the stage of my life. And while everything I recount is true, others may have perceived it differently. I challenge them to pen their own version of events. Some have already tried, but they conveniently left out a whole lot of truth. However, I must confess, even I have never let the truth get in the way of a damn good story.

The tale isn't about making me appear admirable. Marky Ramone, always one to speak his mind, would say, "It is what it is," and he's damn right. As I reflect on the characters within this narrative, I can confidently declare that we were once friends. Certain friendships have endured and flourished, growing even tighter with each passing year. With some individuals, years may have separated our paths, yet the instant we reconnect, it feels as though we were never apart. On the flip side, there are interactions that haven't stood the test of time. It's a damn shame, really. Life is too short to hold onto grudges.

My French buddy Thomas Goze, living in NYC, shared an intriguing tale with me. It all went down at the release party for the Ramones Raw DVD. He went over to Marky to get some SpeedKings stuff autographed. Standing alongside Marky was John Cafiero, who started asking about the SpeedKings. With a smirk on his face, Marky replied, *"That was one hell of a band, even better than the Misfits. But let's just say there was an asshole among them."* It didn't take long for Thomas to connect the dots and realize that Marky was referring to me. Emboldened by curiosity, he dared to inquire about the identity of said asshole. Marky coolly lowered his shades and uttered my name, *"Nick,"* his voice dripping with discontent. And Marky is not the only person feeling this way. Obviously, I rubbed a bunch of people the wrong way. And you know what? I'm fine with that. After all, everyone is entitled to their own damn opinion. As Henry Rollins once told me, *"Opinions are like assholes, everyone's got one."* So here I am, proudly embracing my status as an opinionated asshole, giving you two works for the price of one.

Over the years, as I moved from place to place, countless documents and photographs were lost in the shuffle. Two decades later, memories also begin to fade, but I am incredibly fortunate to have friends who have stepped in to help fill in some of the gaps. Together, we stumbled upon a few treasures along the way. We recorded hours upon hours of shows and life on the road on video. The proof is right there for all to see. The visual evidence doesn't lie. So, if you've ever heard a rumor or a story, this is the place where you can witness it all from my chair. This is what really went down.

Let me take you down to memory lane. That's where all this heartbreak begins…

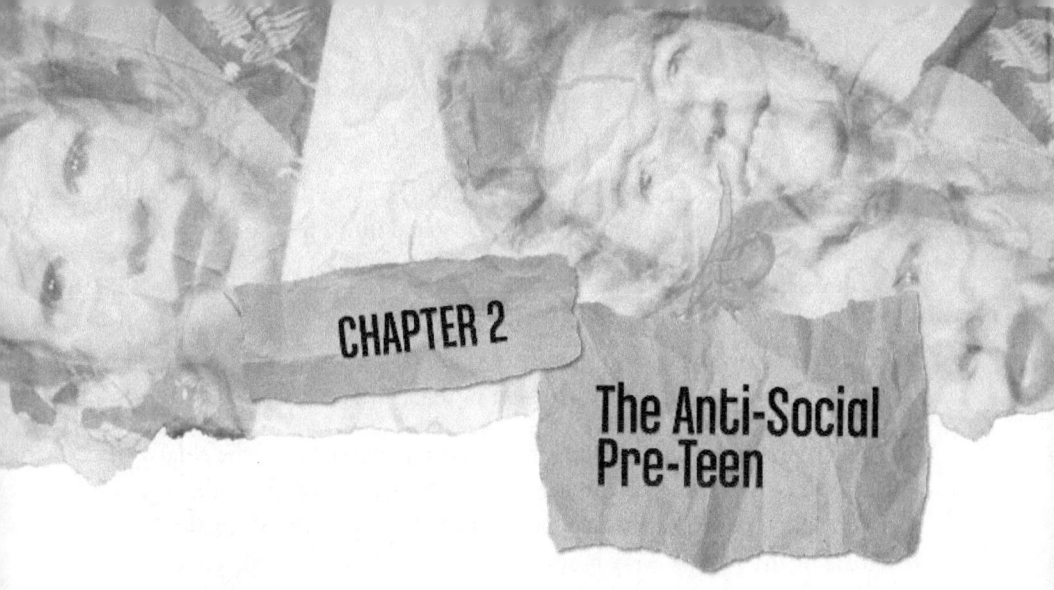

CHAPTER 2

The Anti-Social Pre-Teen

"Anti-social behaviour is a trait of intelligence in a world full of conformists." - Anonymous

I came into this world as Nico Marcel Leo Decock. Now, that's not exactly the most rock'n'roll name you'll find in the annals of history. While folks who speak Dutch might associate the word "cock" with a rooster, in the English-speaking realm, being called DE-cock, pronounced The-Cock, would likely conjure up images of some pornstar stud. Hung like a horse. If a name had the power to shape and determine a person's destiny, then mine would have pointed me straight toward the tantalizing buffet of the adult flesh entertainment industry. However, such a moniker would have set expectations too high for me to fulfill. The Cock suggests a certain… shall we say, impressive endowment hiding within my jockstrap. But hey, life had other plans for me, and it was time to separate fact from fiction. I did not come into this world destined for that particular cradle of debauchery. I was made to rock and roll; that rocking and rolling was my destiny that ran through my veins. My mom looked like one of The Ronettes, and my dad could have been in The Bee Gees. So here I am, Nico Marcel Leo Decock, defying the expectations that my name may have set.

Ten years before my birth, specifically on September 30, 1955, James Dean tragically met his demise at the age of 24 while driving his Porsche

550 in Cholame, California. I often pondered whether a spirit could wander for a decade before being reincarnated into a new form.

On September 30, 1965, The McCoy's' song "Hang on Sloopy" held the top spot on the music charts, Robert Wise's classical musical romance "The Sound of Music" dominated the box office, and the United States formally commenced its involvement in the Vietnam War.

I witnessed the flicker of life in the retirement facility of the elderly in Kuurne. A multitude of Kuurne locals first witnessed the light of day within its very walls between the years 1952 and 1968. With the joint efforts of the former Mayor and the congregation of the Sisters of Our Lady's Hospital, this place became a haven for both the elderly and orphaned from 1895 onwards. In 1952, a building was constructed adjacent to the Primary School, which was intended to serve as a maternity ward. However, in late 1968, the birth center was closed, and with its closure, it was soon transformed into a sanctuary for rest and a convent.

On one fateful day in our little town, Kuurne, when I was just eighteen years old, I found myself on the verge of a brutal beatdown by a pack of intoxicated locals who questioned my true origins. It was at that moment that the retirement home came to my rescue, saving my sorry ass. Being born within those very walls made me the epitome of a true local, an authentic Kuurnian. The nuns who had brought me into this world at that very place ensured my undeniable connection to Kuurne, making me untouchable by those doubting, intoxicated retards.

My parents tied the knot a year before I was born when they were twenty-one and nineteen. My grandfather, lovingly known as "Pop Rail," dedicated his time to working on the railroads, while my godfather, Grandpa Leo, made a living as a sales representative in the world of household linen.

As I recall perfectly, in the beginning, we resided with my mother's relatives until the construction of our own house was completed in Sente Katherina. Surprisingly, this village was even tinier than the miniature town of Kuurne. In anticipation of this relocation, I had to attend a preschool in the vicinity of our current residence. As per my mother's recollection, I only attended school on approximately three occasions. It appeared that I harbored intense emotions towards the teacher at this preschool. "The one wearing glasses is an absolute jerk," I boldly declared to her. I still find it hard to believe, but my mother took my word for it, and that was enough for her to decide against sending me back there again. Thus, it marked the unequivocal end of my association with the preschool instructor. Exit preschool.

In 1967, we finally made the big move, and I had the chance to finish my last year of kindergarten at Sente Katherina. It was a much better environment there, and even more so because I met my very first love interest. At that young age, I didn't fully grasp the complexity of that short-lived yet intense passion for someone. It wasn't just a simple crush that drew me to her, but it was the fact that her parents owned a newspaper annex toy store. I suspect the twelve-year-old girl and her friends saw me as a foolish little kid, and the idea of attraction between the opposite sexes wasn't really on their radar yet. But hey, she was in sixth grade, and even at such a young age, I had already figured out that an older, more experienced woman could offer me far more exciting opportunities than the whiny little kids with pigtails in my own grade.

Back in those days, there was a clear division between boys and girls. Even the Sente nuns seemed to consider the "boy kindergarteners" as part of the girls' group, since we were all mixed together in the same classrooms. Nonetheless, everything changed on September 1, 1971. That morning, as I stepped onto the girls' playground, a man in a beige dust jacket appeared - Master Noel. He was in charge of the first year of study, and we trailed him like little chicks as we made our way from the girls' classrooms, which were on the left side of the parish church, to the boys' school on the right side. It was like taking a step back into sexual segregation. It wasn't until 1975 that coeducational education became the norm. The Catholic congregation of Sente was not ahead of the rest of Flanders in this regard. Despite my dislike for kindergarten, I actually found primary education to be quite enjoyable.

Now that I reflect on my upbringing in the rebellious era of the 60s and 70s, I find it quite intriguing. As a child born after the ravages of war, I was constantly reminded of the Second World War by my wise grandparents. They would often regale me with stories of their courageous resistance against the German occupiers. The war may have

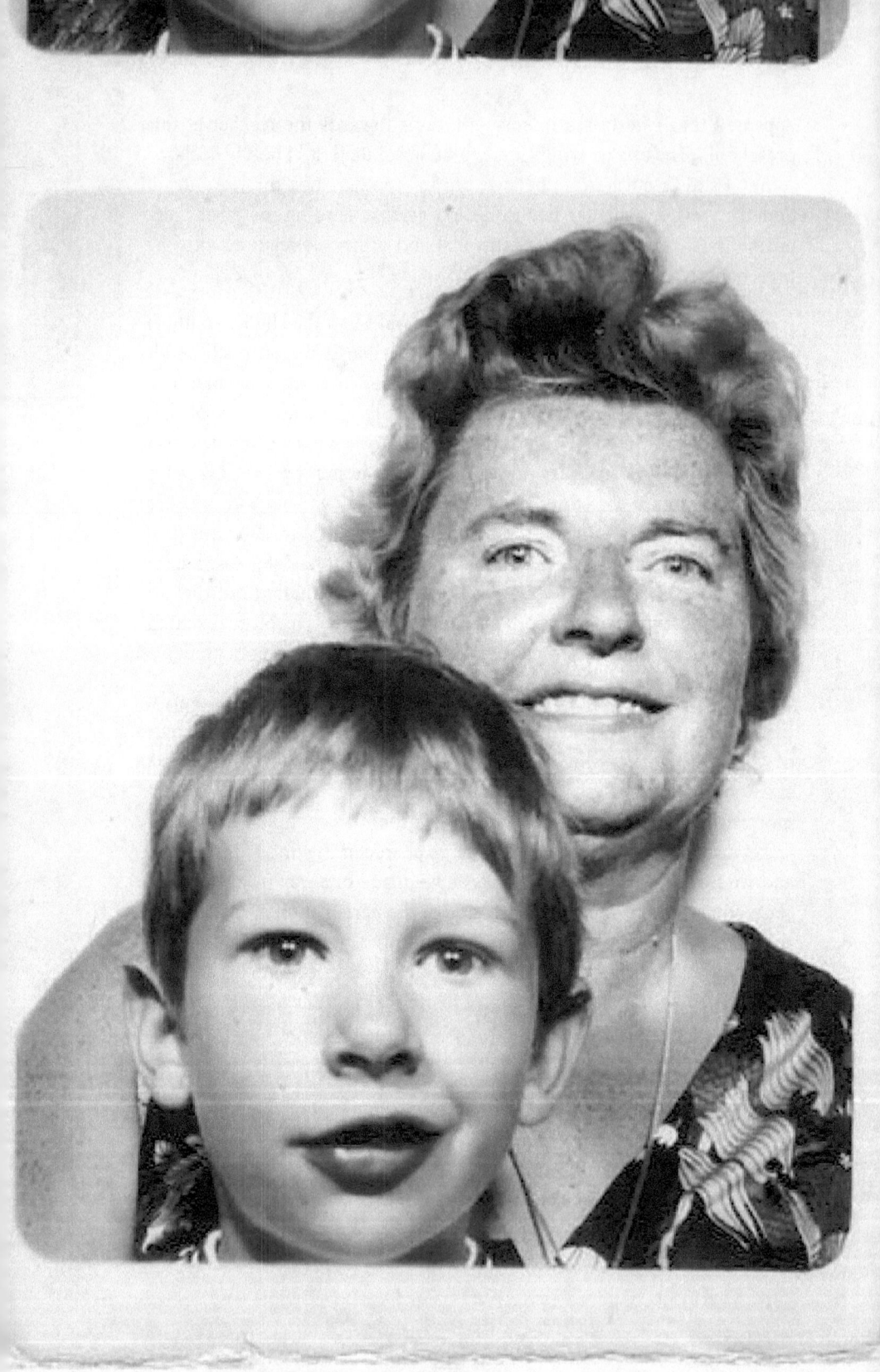

been a distant memory for them, but its impact lingered in their hearts and words.

In stark contrast to the hardships they endured, my generation enjoyed an abundance that was unheard of during their time. My grandparents, with a mix of nostalgia and pride, would emphasize how fortunate we were to live in a world filled with opportunity and prosperity. It was constantly reminded to us to appreciate the present and not take our privileges for granted.

All in all, growing up in that era shaped my perspective and taught me to see the world through a different lens, with eyes unclogged by bitterness and complaints. What my grandparents experienced throughout their lives was taught to me, and that instilled in me a deep sense of gratitude and resilience. I understood that progress comes with its own set of challenges and sacrifices, but it also brings forth new possibilities.

Those revolutionary years, the 60s and 70s, hold a special place in my heart. These were my wonder years, filled with an electric energy that resonated with the changing spirit of rock music. The era was alive with bold ideas, cultural shifts, and a thirst for change. It was a time when society was reimagined, boundaries were pushed, and voices were amplified.

Back then, life wasn't about mere likes or followers. It was more than that, something more meaningful. It was about embracing the unknown and carving our own path, finding the purpose, and living it. We didn't have smartphones or social media to distract us, and our playground was the great outdoors, where imagination ran wild and possibilities were endless. We didn't need virtual reality to escape because we had music, art, and the company of like-minded souls who understood the power of rebellion.

But looking back, I realize that each generation has its unique journey, a specialty that sets them apart and gives them meaning. It is a circle, but the experience is different and unique every time. The world may have evolved since then, but it doesn't mean it has worsened. It has simply transformed into something different, with its own set of challenges and triumphs. As I am reliving those experiences in a different landscape of time, I carry the lessons from my teenage years in my heart, embracing the adventure that defined that era.

I remember TV held a prominent spot in my daily routine, as it dictated the rhythm of my hours. Faint recollections of "Little Sandman," a children's show that signaled bedtime for my peers and me, still linger in my mind. The world was transforming, and the monochromatic TV screen brought the news and events from corners of the world and time directly into our living rooms. Sometimes, I question whether my memories of the first moon landing are genuine or if they were shaped by subsequent viewings, creating a false sense of familiarity. Nevertheless, television was steadily gaining ground. In the 1960s, communal viewing with neighbors was common, but by the 1970s, each household boasted its own TV antenna perched on the roof. Occasionally, the picture would flicker when a motorcycle zoomed by. To counter this, my father erected a towering mast in our garden adorned with multiple antennas. Beneath the TV set, a rotary dial allowed us to "zap" between different channels. In those days, children served as human remote controls, eagerly fulfilling this task with enthusiasm.

We used to spend most of our time out in the open air, embracing the freedom that came with not having cell phones or video games. Our playground consisted of the garden and the streets, where we unleashed our imagination and indulged in endless adventures. However, there was one exception to this outdoor escapade - Wednesday afternoons. As the clock struck four, all outdoor activities would come to a halt, and we would eagerly make our way back home. It was time for our beloved ritual - watching television.

Those Wednesday afternoons were a sanctuary for me and my peers. It was the time when we could immerse ourselves in a different world. For a moment, we forget about the real world.

"Uncle Bob" had a weekly TV show that was the absolute favorite broadcast to the kids of my generation. He kept us glued to the screen. Uncle Bob had the appearance of a plump leader of the Boy Scouts, exuding a tacky campfire vibe as he enthusiastically taught countless individuals from Flanders the art of playing the acoustic guitar. It was all about the tight-knit bond we shared, creating a sense of unity that made us feel like a family, reminiscent of the one in the TV show The Forest

Rangers. Back in our younger days, we were oblivious to the fact that the authority figures, like the watchful eyes of churchmen, closely monitored Uncle Bob to ensure our shenanigans were nothing more than innocent mischief. As safe and uneventful as it may have been, being part of a collective drew us in with an irresistible magnetism. We were hooked. The feeling of belonging gave us a ticket to good, clean fun.

I can't help but entertain the thought that this was my initial step towards embracing rebellion in the future. There's only a limited time one can endure this kind of crap before breaking free so far for Belgian TV. Dutch TV shows were a lot less obedient. In those days, television was different. The absence of streaming platforms and cable TV meant that our options were limited, and we shifted towards the Dutch TV channels. Boy, did they know how to captivate us! Shows like "Bonanza," "Catweazle," and "Zorro" transported us to a completely different world filled with excitement and intrigue. The Belgian Radio and Television (BRT) couldn't hold a candle to the entertainment offered by our neighbors to the north. So, we tuned in to the Channels of The Netherlands, eagerly awaiting our favorite programs.

Among the masses of shows, one series stood out as the highlight of my week - "The Six Million Dollar Man." This show, with its futuristic concept and gripping storylines, had me on the edge of my seat every time. I was mesmerized by the bionic adventures of Steve Austin, a man with superhuman abilities. As I watched him leap tall buildings and accomplish daring feats, I couldn't help but dream of having such extraordinary powers myself.

I vividly recall the night before the BRT was set to begin broadcasting in color. I was filled with excitement and anticipation. The announcement on the screen had me eagerly awaiting this transition. The shift from black-and-white to color images held such promise. However, my disappointment was immense when January 1, 1971, arrived, and the picture remained monochrome. It took me some time to realize that broadcasting in color required a color television, which infuriated me and saddened me more. I had to wait even longer for TV programs to be shown in vibrant hues. As I watched TV, the six years of my elementary school days seemed to pass by in a flash.

Compared to my school friends, my life was filled with the wild and daring spirit of my grandparents. They were true adventurers, always seeking new experiences. In every major vacation we had, I had the incredible opportunity to travel abroad with them. While many of my classmates were limited to trips to the beach or forced to endure youth camp with their flimsy cardboard suitcases, I was immersed in a world of excitement and luxury. My mother, fiercely protective of my well-being, deemed the Boy Scouts too untamed for me and refused to let me join. Traditional summer camps were also out of the question, as she believed they posed too many risks. Even the local daycare playground was off-limits. While other kids spent their days frolicking and making memories, I was confined to either playing at home or at my grandparents' house. Although I was secluded from the typical social life of a child, I was bestowed with the incredible gift of exploring foreign lands.

Every time, I eagerly anticipated the two-week journey abroad. We would board a plane, heading towards Spain, Italy, and even Romania once. Our family never opted for car or caravan vacations. No, we were modern and adventurous, soaring through the skies to reach our faraway destinations. Back then, tourism hadn't reached its current peak. The beaches of Spain and Italy were not yet swarmed with people, and Romania was still under Ceausescu's dictatorship, hidden behind the Cold War's Iron Curtain. The military airport we arrived at during that era made a lasting impression on me. As a child, it was quite intimidating to undergo a strip search. In those days, I adored gumballs, but in that country, the military personnel had never encountered those sweets before. As an eight-year-old, I was treated as if I were an enemy of the state. The presence of cold steel from Kalashnikov machine guns sent shivers down my spine. And let's not forget the fear that our concealed dollars would be discovered; those were the currency that opened doors in every Eastern European country under communist rule. Romanian people pleaded for jeans, nylon stockings, and real chocolate throughout our vacation. At the time, I didn't fully comprehend it, but those beautifully dressed girls in every hotel lobby had traded their bodies and souls for a taste of Western luxuries.

Traveling by plane back in the day was a whole different ball game compared to the present. Flying in those days was like stepping into a time machine, where the rules and norms were a far cry from what we know today. It was a surreal experience. Lighting up a smoke in the cabin was not just accepted but almost expected. The air was thick with the scent of tobacco, blending with the roar of the engines to create a unique atmosphere that can only be described as a smoky symphony. And if you were a curious kid with an adventurous spirit like me, then you could boldly make your way to the cockpit, where the captain and co-pilot would welcome you with open arms. It was an awe-inspiring sight, with rows of dials and switches. The pilots themselves were like modern-day heroes, guiding the metal bird through the skies with sheer confidence and skill like a superhero from a comic book. The words "hijackers" and "terrorists" were not yet etched into the aviation world's vocabulary—it would take some time before they crashed onto the scene.

But alas, those were simpler times, when the threat of hijackers and terrorists was nothing more than a distant nightmare. The thought wouldn't even cross my mind. It wasn't until much later that these dark forces would infiltrate our collective consciousness, forever changing the way we perceive air travel.

It may have been a different era, but it was one filled with wonder and innocence—a time when flying was an adventure in itself.

Through my travels, I experienced a profound shift in my perspective of the world, and little did I know that the world within my own mind was even more vast and boundless. Growing up as an only child without siblings or many friends, I found solace in my own company. Socializing was never my forte; I preferred the solitude of my own imagination. Within the depths of my mind, I conjured up the most extraordinary adventures, taking on various roles like a true thespian. Playing alone allowed me to have complete control over every aspect without any need for accountability. I became a master at forging my own path and overcoming obstacles in my own unique way. It was as if I had perfected the art of rebellion, always finding a way to do things on the sly. I may have appeared innocent and sweet to others, but deep down, I followed my own desires without any regard for societal norms, hence my destined mark in rock'n'roll. This rebellious spirit gradually awakened within me, and it became a part of my very essence. I was a rebel without a cause, as if it was tailor-made for me, defining who I truly was.

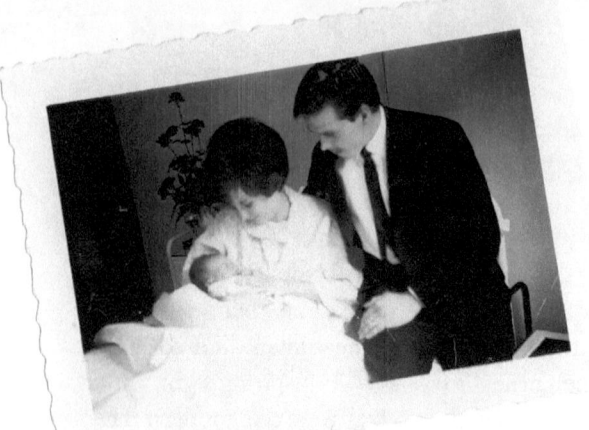

Birth of a Rock'n'Roll star
September 30, 1965

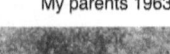

My parents 1963

My mom really did look like she was in The Ronettes

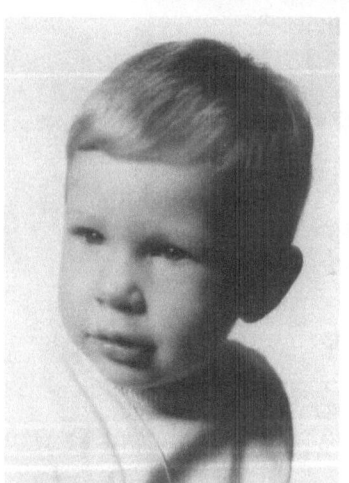

Still innocent 1966

Holidays in the Sun 1972

Me and my beloved grandma Elisabeth
Photobooth 1972

Posing in grandpa Leo's garden in front of the legendary Vergaene Glorie rehearsal shack - little did I know in 1973

Highly fashionable Schoolpicture 1973

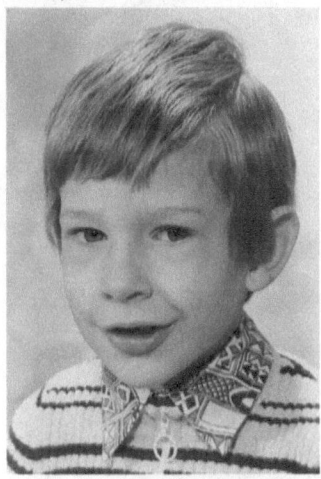

At the toystore 1974

Trying to look like Mr. Cool alongside my parents 1975

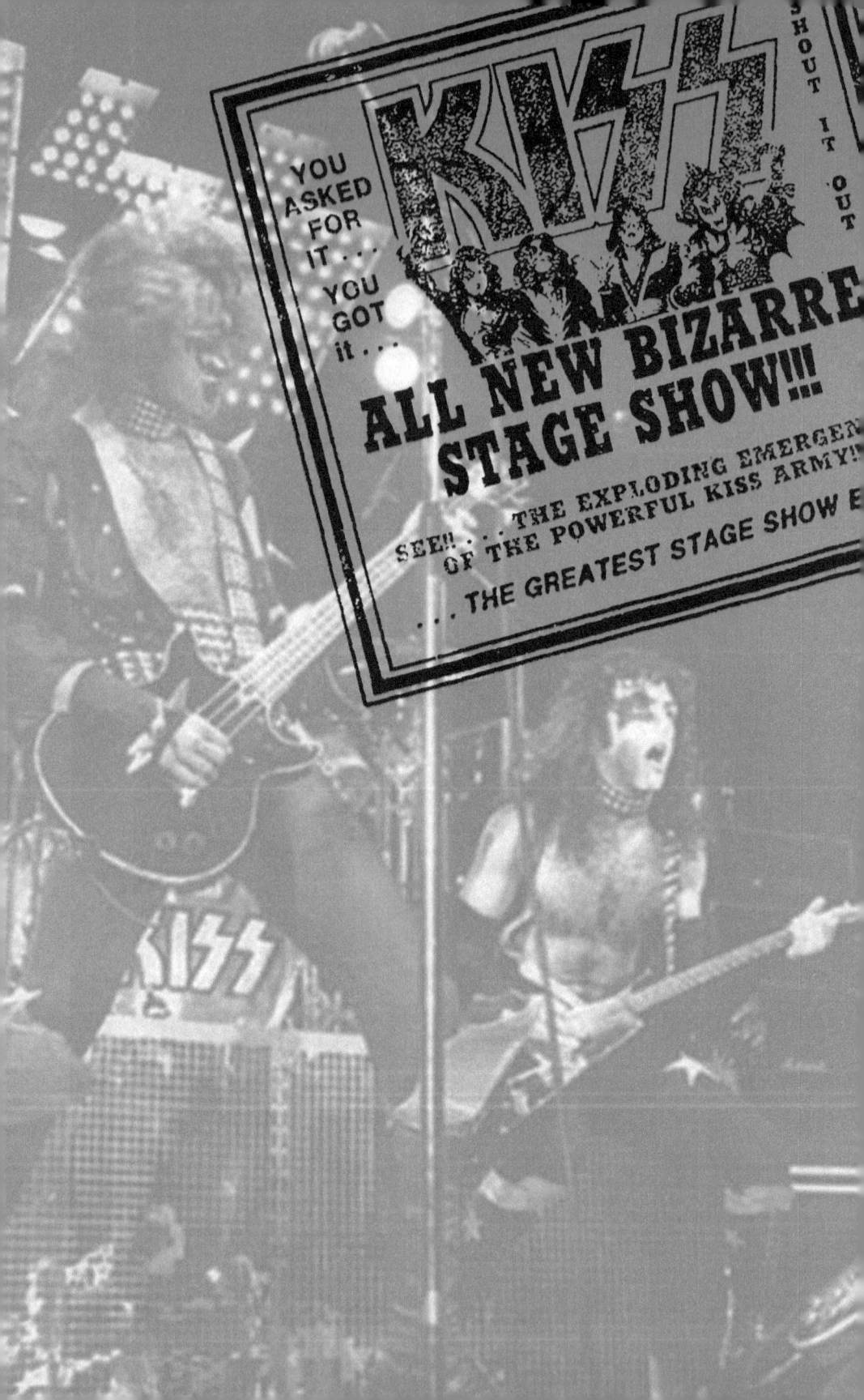

CHAPTER 3
Hiding in the Rock'n'Roll Closet

"Hide nothing, for time which sees all and hears all exposes all." - Sophocles

Becoming a fan of Punk is not something that happens overnight. It's not as if you suddenly wake up one day and find yourself enamored with a new genre of music. It's a gradual process, an evolution that takes place over time. It's a result of being influenced by various sources from different angles. The media, including radio, TV, and magazines, as well as the people around you, such as parents, family, and friends, all play a role in shaping your musical preferences. They push you in a particular direction, guiding you toward the rebellious and raw energy that Punk embodies. They are the DJs of our lives, curating a playlist of experiences that gradually mold our musical taste, like a journey, a transformation, where you slowly but surely become captivated by the essence of Punk rock.

Punk is not just a genre of music; it's a way of life. It's a mindset that challenges the status quo and defies conventions. It's about breaking free from societal norms and expectations and embracing individuality and self-expression. Just like the blistering guitar riffs and pounding drums of a Punk rock anthem, Punk culture hits you with its fierce and unapologetic energy.

My initial foray into the world of music was guided by technology. It was a tiny cassette recorder that revolutionized my existence. Through this device, I had complete control over what I listened to. By simultaneously pressing the Play and Record buttons and placing the microphone against the TV speaker, I could capture my own recordings. This marked the beginning of my journey into the world of music production.

However, there were some challenges along the way. Sometimes, I would start recording a little early and record the presenter's introduction. Other times, I would be a few seconds too late and end up missing the beginning of a song. And if my arm grew tired during the recording, the cassette recorder would accidentally tap against the TV, resulting in an intrusive click that disrupted the entire recording.

Despite these obstacles, this primitive recording method ignited a passion within me. It was raw and imperfect, but it was my ticket to a world of musical exploration.

The cassette recorder became an extension of myself, a tool that allowed me to capture the essence of my musical journey.

Through this humble device, I plunged into a wild adventure, discovering new sounds and experimenting with different genres. It was a gritty, immersive experience that shaped my understanding of music and paved the way for future endeavors.

Who would've guessed back then that I would end up professionally laying down tracks in countless studios, starting from the humble beginnings of sound recording? Who could've imagined that I'd eventually become the head honcho, the Chief Operations Officer, of one of Europe's largest recording studios? Of course, being the biggest and most renowned also meant dealing with the most notorious reputation and the habit of conveniently forgetting about paying salaries. But as fate would have it, my destiny didn't lie within those walls. Thankfully, I managed to see through the whole charade before it was too late. Still, there was something undeniably magical about working in the very place where legends like The Scorpions, Manowar, and countless iconic hits from the eighties were brought to life. It was as if every corner of that studio pulsated with an enchanting energy that fueled my own musical journey.

After the initial rush of excitement from capturing every single moment on tape, the recordings began to take on a more discerning approach. It was the songs themselves that started to shape my musical tastes and preferences. The explosion of neo-rock'n'roll, Teddy Boy, glam, and pub rock had ignited a fire within me. Bands like The Rubettes, Mud, Showaddywaddy, The Sweet, and Slade… their glitz and charisma drew me in. It's no wonder that my love for (hard) guitars, paired with catchy vocals and lyrics, can be traced back to those early influences. As the months went by, I painstakingly built up my very first music collection, with cassette tapes piling up faster than I could count.

But not everything made its way onto the airwaves. Every Sunday afternoon, we faithfully tuned in to watch the family program "Inside/Outside" on TV. It was a time when foreign bands would come on and perform live before the era of music videos. I'll never forget the day Steppenwolf graced the stage in 1970 or '71 – it was like an electric shock to my young senses. The moment they started playing "Born to be Wild," a surge of adrenaline shot through me, causing the hairs on my arms to stand on end. I watched in awe as these rugged rockers, clad in leather pants, exuded an air of nonchalance and arrogance. The sound of Harley Davidson mufflers filled the air, adding to the raw energy of their performance. It was a different kind of music than what I was accustomed to, and it spoke to me in a way that nothing else had before.

Soon after that, my fascination with vinyl records took hold. The allure of those smooth, grooved discs was irresistible to me. However, there was one problem - we didn't have a record player at home. It seemed like a cruel twist of fate. Despite the fact that my parents appeared effortlessly cool in old photographs, they weren't exactly avid music enthusiasts. They had married young and had to grow up too fast, burdened with the responsibilities of a family at the tender ages of nineteen and twenty-one. It's amazing how being thrust into the monotonous world of routines at such a young age can change a person. Unfortunately, my parents were on a dead-end road when it came to nurturing my musical interests.

Luckily, I was blessed with other relatives who shared my passion for music. Every Wednesday, without fail, I would hop into the white Fiat

Cinquecento with my mother and grandmother to visit Auntie Emma and Uncle Jozef.

Auntie Emma, the sister of my grandmother, had two daughters. Deborah, being the youngest, was my mother's cousin. However, due to the significant age gap between my mom and Deborah, more than ten years, she felt more like my own cousin. While my trusty tape recorder captured everything, Deborah became the embodiment of the "voice of a generation" for me. When you're just ten or eleven years old, a sixteen-year-old teenage girl is like meeting your idol. And Deborah played that role flawlessly, leaving a lasting impression on me.

She was a subscriber to a popular teen magazine. Her bedroom walls were covered in posters, creating a chaotic mix of genres. It may sound strange or even crazy, but there, side by side, were Ozzy from Black Sabbath and the smooth crooners. It seemed that in those days, it was perfectly acceptable to love heavy metal (or what was commonly called hard rock at the time) and also be a fan of crooners. I can't say for certain if this was true, but Deborah insisted it was. And I was more than happy to believe her. As I looked around her room, I couldn't help but admire the eclectic collection of artists on display. The cheesy crooners shared the spotlight with rugged rockers, wearing striped spandex pajama pants or skin-tight leather suits that seemed ready to burst at the seams. At the time, I was oblivious to the fact that both the flamboyant crooners and the otherworldly rockers were overshadowing ancient Greek principles. Everyone fell for the allure of the heterosexual charm that was lavishly poured upon them. However, as time went on, reality revealed itself to be quite different.

In 1976, Deborah reached the age of seventeen, just as the local heartthrobs faded into obscurity and were replaced by a rowdy troublemaker from a neighboring town. Jan, a no-good rocker who could pass for either eighteen or nineteen, held Deborah's heart captive. However, Jozef and Emma, wary of Jan's unpredictable nature, were skeptical of his intentions from all angles.

As a well-behaved individual, I had the privilege of earning the unwavering trust of my uncle and aunt. They entrusted me with the responsibility of being Deborah's chaperone whenever she ventured out with the troublemaker. Eventually, I found myself in the peculiar position of being considered both sensible and dependable, earning the title of a virtuous young man. Deborah and the mischievous rebel swiftly embraced my presence because I excelled at keeping secrets under lock and key, and my ability to exercise discretion was generously acknowledged by this dynamic duo on multiple occasions.

In the late spring of 1976, I found myself standing alongside the local Bonnie & Clyde right outside the doors of the Community center in Harelbeke. The poster on the wall featured a band called KISS from America, but I had no clue who they were. Little did I know that this particular Saturday would later be etched in my memory as something truly extraordinary. At that moment, all I felt was the rush of being in a place where I shouldn't be. The significance of this being KISS's first European tour, a band that would go on to define heavy rock, completely escaped me. It would take decades for me to realize that a piece of rock history was being written right there in front of my eyes.

One thing I do remember is Deborah, my companion for the day, generously handing over $5.00 for my entrance ticket. Back then, I didn't fully grasp the magnitude of spending so much money on a sixth-grade kid like me. However, looking back, it was an investment well worth it. The value of my discretion during numerous unforgettable events was truly priceless.

KISS kicked off that evening with their thrilling anthem, "Detroit Rock City." Little did I know at the time, but that song would soon become an essential part of my ever-growing record collection. As the lights dazzled and their iconic makeup transformed them into larger-than-life rock gods, something inside me shifted. This concert was a far cry from what it would eventually become, but when you're just twelve years old, everything feels monumental. Everything seemed larger than life. The room, packed to the rafters with five hundred people, felt like a massive arena with thousands of fans. The adrenaline coursing through my veins sent me soaring to new heights. It was in that exhilarating moment that I realized I had stumbled upon something truly unique. Something that set me apart from my parents and their everyday experiences. Something that would ignite an insatiable passion within me for those six strings. Electric guitars possessed an otherworldly temptation that captivated my very being. I can vividly recall spending the following summer months ruthlessly thrashing a few tennis racquets into oblivion, all while headbanging like a madman.

That unforgettable night also brought about a seismic shift in Deborah's world. The familiar faces of local celebrities faded into the background, making room for the likes of KISS and Judas Priest. But there was more in store, a surprise that awaited me. In his worn-out matte blue Ford Escort, Jan whisked Deborah and me away to a venue that exuded a Tirolean vibe. Jan had a penchant for hanging out with hardcore bikers, and he had somehow managed to befriend some of the notorious one-percenter Outlaws. On a particular October evening, they had brought none other than AC/DC to the Antwerp province.

The venue itself resembled a massive Austrian chalet, with lederhosen-clad revelers and Oktoberfest vibes infiltrating every corner. The air was usually filled with the clinking of earthenware beer mugs and the merry sounds of drunken citizens swaying from side to side and front to back. But on that night, everything shifted. The heavy motorcycles took center stage, overpowering the usual festivities. The scent of gasoline and motor oil mingled in the air, momentarily eclipsing the aroma of sizzling sausages and sauerkraut. Lederhosen was pushed aside as sweat-soaked bodies with long hair, denim-clad legs, and leather vests claimed the spotlight. Dirndls made a place for fishnet stockings, leather miniskirts, and tiny T-shirts showing buxom cleavage that you could drown in.

It was in this setting that Bon Scott took the stage. He appeared in skin-tight jeans, complete with a mandatory "bulging crotch," his bare torso exposed, and his long, unkempt hair dripping with grease. His voice pierced through the air like a primal scream, leaving KISS looking like mere Boy Scouts in comparison. The singer's raw and powerful presence left an indelible mark on me. KISS entertained the crowd with a dazzling fireworks display, but AC/DC seemed to come from a different realm entirely, a place where people thrived on violence and mayhem. They resembled a ruthless gang of mercenaries, ready to conquer the world. Just as Angus ignited the set with his guitar intro, Bon Scott emerged onto the stage, holding an imaginary hand grenade. With a cocky grin, he pulled the pin using his teeth and nonchalantly tossed it into the audience. And then, without missing a beat, they launched into their first song: "LIVE WIRE!" The energy in the room was pulsating with the raw force of their loud onslaught.

Throughout that night, there was an unmistakable sense of danger lingering in the air. However, the moment these Australians took flight, the atmosphere transformed into something explosive. The chaos erupted when the Federal Police stormed into the hall, causing everyone to scatter desperately towards the nearest exit. At that moment, I realized I was too young and out of place amidst the turmoil. Both Jan and Deborah were determined to escape as swiftly as possible, aware of the consequences we would face if we were apprehended. There would be no way to justify this madness back home. But believe it or not, we escaped and no further cockerel.

When, not long after, I first listened to "Never Mind The Bollocks," it wasn't shocking. It was empowering. It was a reminder that music has the power to transcend boundaries and ignite passion. KISS and AC/DC may have paved the way, but The Sex Pistols took the torch and set the world ablaze with their uncompromising sound and unyielding attitude.

Johnny Rotten evoked in me a strikingly similar energy, an almost identical rawness, and an unsophisticated manner of connecting with the audience. It was crystal clear, an instantaneous realization. This was the path I yearned to follow. Creating music, strumming the guitar, unleashing screams, and staking my claim on the stage. However, as they say, "It's a long way to the top if you wanna rock and roll." That truth would become evident in due time.

In just a little over 12 months, the realm of music completely rocked my existence. As my pubescent body began sprouting its first signs of maturity, so too did my musical tastes begin to take shape. But alas, it didn't take long for me to realize that Deborah's open-mindedness clashed with the rest of the world's narrow perspectives. Suddenly, everything had to fit into neat little boxes, and everyone seemed hell-bent on limiting their own horizons. It was as if the concept of 'both-and' was obliterated from existence, replaced by an unforgiving 'either-or' mindset. Punk was not to be confused with Hard Rock; you were either one or the other. A choice had to be made, and there was no room for wavering. The suffocating grip of close-mindedness became institutionalized, rendering anyone who dared appreciate both Hard Rock and Punk as nothing more than a counterfeit. God forbid you displayed a poster featuring both Johnny Rotten and a local crooner girl on your wall - that would surely invite ridicule and scorn. Nothing less than a crime against the laws of conformity.

When it came to choosing my musical path, punk seemed like the natural choice for me. However, deep down, I had a secret love for those hard rock records that had slipped through my fingers. The truth was, I never quite vibed with those long guitar solos. That's where punk had the upper hand over hard rock back then. Even at that young age, I knew in my heart that I wanted to be a guitar player. However, my inherent laziness held me back from fully mastering the pentatonic scale. Punk rock offered me something more than just rebellious music; it sparked my creativity, much like the striking and provocative artwork of Jamie Reid, the graphic designer for The Sex Pistols.

My introduction to music was like the opening riff of a hidden melody. It had to be done in secret, quietly slipping into the Chopper bar on Saturday afternoons with Jan and Deborah. The Chopper bar had always intrigued me, capturing my imagination with its untamed energy. I had driven past that gritty haven of hard-rock bikers countless times in my parent's car, but stepping foot inside was beyond anything I could have dreamed of. Yet, it happened. Jan and Deborah would go there to knock back cheap beers, and I'll be honest, I was scared shitless when I stood among those tough-as-nails characters. In my recollection, the atmosphere was dimly lit, soaked in the lingering scent of spilled beer. After spending an afternoon in that joint, we'd emerge smelling like a smoky barbecue feast. That unique aroma clung to our clothes, a signature scent of that era. When I first began mingling with the punk crowd, frequenting the Twenty-One club and performing with my very first punk band, Vergaene Glorie, openly admitting my love for hard rock wasn't exactly a brilliant move. It seemed like punk and hard rock were destined to be arch-rivals from the start. The Chopper, the hard rock lion's den, suddenly became forbidden territory for me, and I had to keep my true musical tastes under lock and key. My punk comrades were completely oblivious to the fact that hidden away in my closet was a collection of Hardrock records. At least, I believe they were. Maybe now, it's time to break free from the confines of that metaphorical closet and embrace my true rock 'n' roll identity.

Sunday
DEPRAVED SCHOOLBOY REVEALS ALL!

AC/DC SHOCK PROBE

"Dirty Deeds Done Dirt Cheap"
Their new album
OUT NEXT WEEK

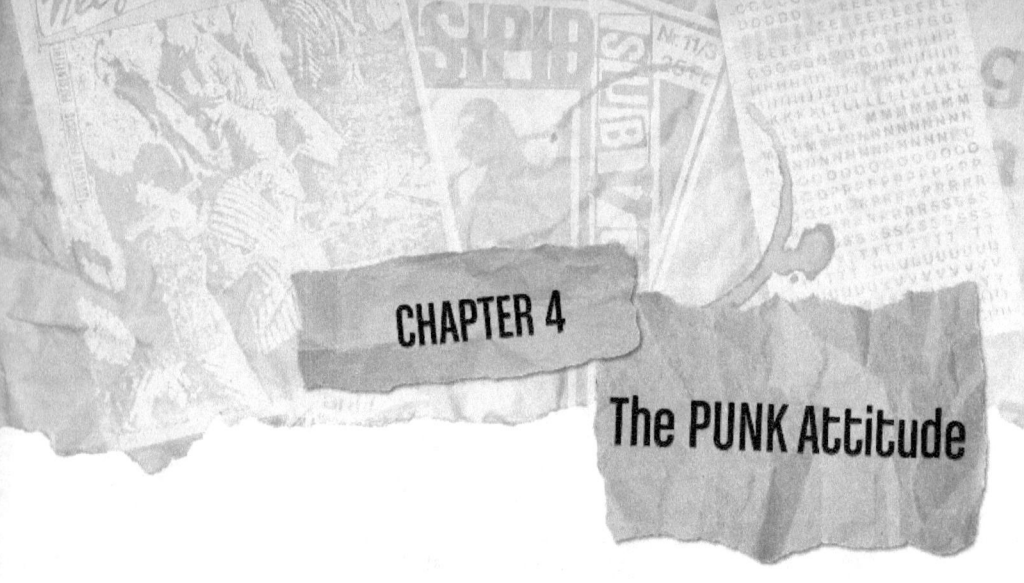

CHAPTER 4

The PUNK Attitude

"Punk is about being an individual and going against the grain and standing up and saying This is who I am." - Joey Ramone

Did I transform into a Punk the moment I was introduced to my first punk record? I highly doubt it. Reflecting on my past, I now understand that Punk is a concept far more expansive than the mere word itself. I would even venture to say that my punk-ness existed long before I even became aware of the term. It possessed an existential quality for me, transcending time and space. Punk-itude is timeless. It was only when society bestowed a label upon it that it became confined to a specific era, fashion, and musical style. What a travesty. This implies a reduction of the true essence of punkitude. What other word could encapsulate the entirety of its meaning—its defiance, rebellion, nonconformity, unique perspective…? To me, all these elements embody "punkitude." Even the whole DIY (do-it-yourself) ethos is an integral part of it. Isn't that a sentiment that has resonated throughout history? Or was it merely a label someone attached to it in the mid-'70s?

I despised school, especially kindergarten. My expressions lacked manners, and political correctness was not in my vocabulary. Thankfully, the concepts of #MeToo and being "woke" were still foreign to society. I vented my frustrations to my mother, referring to my teacher as "the four-eyed bastard." Admittedly, my finesse could have used some refinement, but my disdain for school was crystal clear. It was a pure embodiment of the "I HATE SCHOOL" attitude, fit for a punk song or an anthem of rebellion. Perhaps I was ahead of my time, as kindergarten appeared infantile and senseless to me. I often questioned why I wasted my time there, surrounded by toddlers who soiled their pants and incessantly whined. The only reprieve was being pursued by older girls, but even that couldn't salvage the experience.

I was nearing the end of my final year in kindergarten in Sente, and as per tradition, it was time for the annual school party. It was the kind of celebration that the school put on to show off how successful they were at molding us little rebels. But let's be real; it was all just a facade. The school management saw it as an opportunity to milk parents for their hard-earned money, enticing them with fancy vouchers and selling them worthless raffle tickets. They didn't care about us kids. They just wanted to line their pockets and hand out worthless junk disguised as tombola prizes to parents who were already getting wasted on bottom-shelf booze.

Months before the school play, we started preparing. This year's theme was centred around the majestic animal kingdom. To my surprise (or rather disappointment), I was assigned the role of a tree alongside a few other unfortunate souls in the class who were also deemed as "losers." The shy, introverted kids were transformed into delicate lilies, while the teacher's pet snagged the role of Doctor Frog. Of course, it was to be expected. My dreadful Nazi sympathizing teacher, who seemed to have a fondness for favorites, handpicked her beloved capo.

But here's the thing about favorites: their likability often surpasses their actual talent. And this time was no different. The little brat turned out to be utterly useless. Being in cahoots with the enemy doesn't guarantee you an Oscar nomination, after all. My audible sigh must have caught the attention of Ilsa, the guard who seemed to be trapped in a perpetual concentration camp persona. She sneered at me as if to say, *"Ah, there are some who think they can do better!"*

"Oh, Jawohl Fraulein!" I croaked sarcastically, making my way to the impromptu audition. And just like that, I became her favorite doctor. She barely addressed me as "Herr Mengele," emphasizing her disdain for my role.

THE PUNK ATTITUDE

However, my rebellious spirit was yet to reach its full potential. My cousin Deborah had graciously lent me her nursing attire, a pristine white lab coat completed with a doctor's bag adorned with a bold red cross. To complete the ensemble, I added a pair of goggles and flippers. As I made my grand entrance onto the stage at the Sente parish hall that fateful Saturday evening, the atmosphere seemed to shift, mirroring the transition of seasons. The trees transformed into a tapestry of autumn hues while the lilies burst open in full bloom, as if in sync with my audacity and the uproarious laughter that erupted from the audience. With my alter ego, Doctor Frog, claiming the stage, I reveled in the fact that I had defied expectations. It didn't matter that I had been assigned this role; what truly mattered was that I had proven my ability to seize control of my own destiny. My performance was a testament to my unyielding spirit and unwavering determination. No force, whether it be the miserable Frau Bastard or even the pint-sized capo, would ever stand in my way.

The rush of being on stage, commanding attention, and pouring my heart out ignited a fire within me. It was a feeling that enveloped me, warming my soul and leaving me craving for more. Fast forward thirty years later, I found myself at the Key Club on Hollywood Boulevard in Los Angeles. As the final notes of our set echoed through the venue - I leaped backward into the awaiting arms of the crowd. The adrenaline coursed through my veins as I surrendered to the chaos around me. At that moment, everything seemed to blur together, a whirlwind of sensations. A stunning Californian beauty named Miranda had left me breathless with her intoxicating French kiss, leaving me dazed and disoriented. Like she tried to tongue the life out of me. The world spun around me as I struggled to regain my senses. As I tried to steady myself amidst the chaos, a familiar face caught my eye. CC Deville of Poison winked at me, a silent acknowledgment of our shared journey and the trials we had overcome. In that brief instant, all the sweat, tears, and sacrifices flashed before my eyes. The memories of my humble beginnings as Doctor Frog seemed lightyears away in comparison to this larger-than-life moment., shooting me a playful wink. It was in that fleeting instant that I realized just how far I had come since my humble beginnings as Doctor Frog. I couldn't help but marvel at the distance I had since those early days.

My debut as Doctor Frog marked the beginning of my true punkitude. And let me tell you, it never left. Punkitude became my way of sticking it to the system I had to endure. Whether it was within my own family, at school, at work, or even among my acquaintances and friends, I refused to conform. Sinatra, an unlikely champion of punkitude, sang about it in "My Way". He crooned, "Regrets, I've had a few, but then again, too few to mention… I did it MY WAY!" The fact that the Sex Pistols and Sid Vicious later embraced this sentiment only solidified its power.

Living with punkitude, or "doing it your own way," hasn't always won me popularity points over the years. But it has definitely revealed who my true allies are. Many of the people I used to associate with turned out to be nothing more than Chrissie Hynde wannabes—pretenders. They stuck around as long as they could benefit from me, hitching a ride on my success and using me as a stepping stone. Once they had gotten what they wanted, they would spit me out like yesterday's garbage. It's the epitome of punkitude. Not fitting in, being the outsider—that's what it was like at those first punk gigs, right? SPITTING! So, thank you for bestowing upon me this honor!

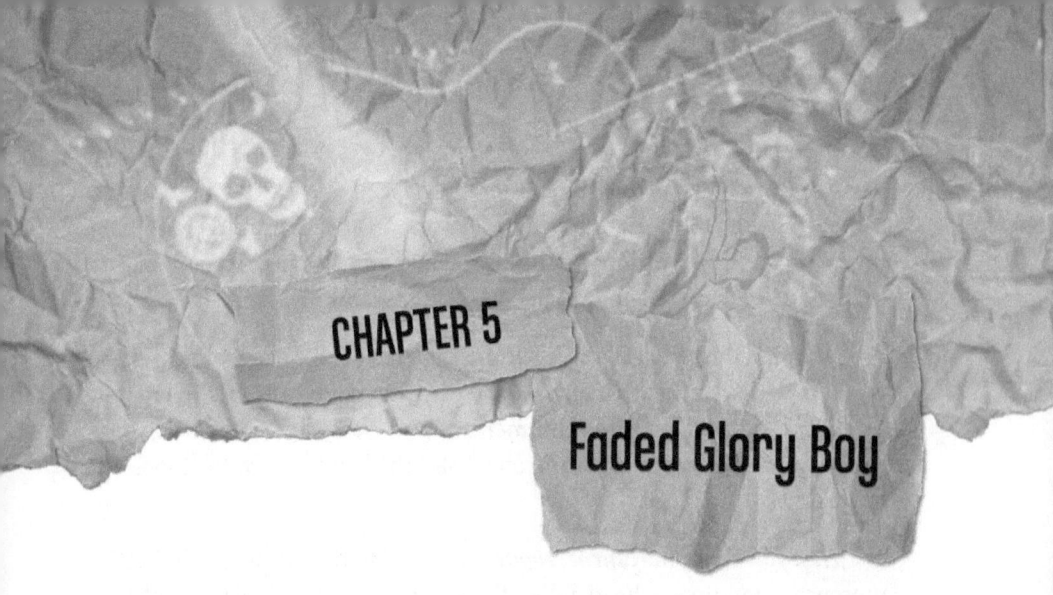

CHAPTER 5

Faded Glory Boy

"Glory is fleeting, but obscurity is forever." - Napoleon Bonaparte

Monday morning would greet us, and the bustling market stalls would await us in the center of Courtrai. Whether it was a day off from school or a well-deserved break, I can't quite recall. The details fade into my memory. In the front seat of the car, my mother and godmother would sit side by side, ready to go on their customary Monday market adventure. As for me, I found myself nestled in the backseat of my grandma's white Fiat Cinquecento, consumed by a single mission: to acquire the ultimate studded belt from the Graffiti shop, a punk boutique that exudes edginess and defiance.

It was 1980, man. I was working with a tight budget, which means I've gotta scrutinize each item like a rockstar studying their setlist. I was touching, feeling, and sniffing everything to make sure I didn't make the wrong choice. The studded belt that I've got my eye on? It's gotta have square studs, none of those round ones. And it can't just be one or two rows of studs, oh no. It's gotta be the real deal with three rows. That's the only way to rock it. One row is for girls, and two rows are for new-wavers, but three rows? That's me, baby.

I ain't going for a bullet belt either. That's too much of a hard rocker move. See, knowing exactly what you want is a damn good quality to have. But when you're only 15 and scraping together every penny, buying something becomes an adventure. I gotta navigate through all the options, carefully weighing each one against your limited resources. So there I am, determined to find the belt that screams my name.

I scanned the racks, my eyes hungrily devouring the array of belts that awaited my selection. Finally, I find it. The perfect embodiment of punkness. Its metallic studs glimmer under the dim lighting, promising to add an extra edge to my wardrobe. I slid the belt through the loops of my jeans.

"Hey, you are from Kuurne, right?" I glanced to the side and behold his presence. Standing a head taller than me, clad in red plaid Scottish bondage pants, a parachute shirt, a worn-out black leather vest, sunglasses, and a belt adorned with studs. Three rows. Of course! This is Tony. He recognizes me and assumes I am the one who posted that advertisement to kickstart a punk band. All I could manage was a nod of confirmation. Truth be told, I don't actually live in Kuurne but rather in Sente Katharina – a forsaken desolate parish adjacent to Kuurne. Visiting the Kuurne Market Square already feels like traveling in my world, but being acknowledged in Courtrai surpasses even my wildest dreams. *"We really need to have a chat. I reside in the big community blocks. Come visit me this afternoon."*

On that fateful Monday afternoon, I found myself standing in front of the apartment buildings on Red Cross Square, clutching my mother's bicycle. Determined to locate him, I scan every bell on both buildings until I finally come across his name. I rang the bell, stepped into the elevator, and within moments, I was transported to a dimly lit corridor. A door creaks open, and I am greeted by a middle-aged woman who, as it turns out, is Tony's mother. Without hesitation, she ushers me inside and directs me towards his bedroom. *"Just go straight ahead,"* she said.

The tiny room was incredibly cramped and narrow, barely leaving any space to move around. Right beside the single bed stands a record player, its presence demanding attention. Adjacent to it is a large bin overflowing with records, a treasure trove of punk albums. Against the wall, a replica Fender Stratocaster in obligatory black, complete with a red pickguard, leans confidently. A beat-up amplifier accompanied it, ready to unleash its sonic power at any moment. But amidst this rock 'n' roll haven, the focal point is Tony, the man I had the pleasure of conversing with earlier that day in the heart of Courtrai. Compared to myself, he appeared much older, perhaps eighteen, nineteen, or even twenty. His mere presence commanded respect, a stark contrast to my daily encounters with mere "kids" at school. I hardly know anyone who wears Scottish bondage trousers or dons black leather vests.

"I've recently started putting together a band with a couple of friends. You mentioned you play the guitar?" he asked, casually dropping The Damned's 'Machine Gun Etiquette' LP onto the turntable. I nodded in agreement, but my response was drowned out by the thunderous blast of Love Song erupting from the speakers. We listened to a few more tracks before he abruptly stopped the record and thrust the guitar into my hands. *"Why don't you give it a go?"* Panic and embarrassment washed over me, threatening to consume me entirely. It was only about a year ago that I was strumming away on a tennis racket, and it was my grandparents who gave me an acoustic Flamenco guitar as a present. Though the spirit of Flamenco doesn't quite flow through my veins, I decided to invest my hard-earned money, the very money I had saved up for that studded belt, into a replica Gibson "Black Beauty." I purchased it for $125.00 from the local organ store. It caught my eye in the shop window as I sat in the backseat of my grandma's white Fiat, passing by—it was fate. That guitar was meant to be mine.

Perched eight stories above the Red Cross Square, the act of playing an electric guitar resonates with a distinctiveness that sets it apart from the mere strumming of a tennis racquet. Being the lazy soul that I am, I haven't mustered even the slightest effort to learn a single chord. But as they say, in a world of blind musicians, the one-eyed guitarist reigns supreme. And that's exactly what I am – an unlikely king in the eyes of Tony. Lacking any experience with a tennis racquet himself, he is instantly swayed by the dissonant, atonal cacophony that emanates from the guitar. *"Holy shit, you've nailed it! We've found ourselves a guitarist!"* he exclaimed, fully convinced.

"Come on over next Saturday. Tom is gonna be here too. He just lives around the corner. We'll listen to some records and then take you out and let you meet some more friends."

And thus, on a fateful Monday afternoon, I was recruited to wield the six-string. Perhaps my ad had been prematurely published, and I hadn't quite mastered the elusive tennis rocket chord setting on my electric guitar. Nevertheless, I pedaled home on my mom's bicycle with a sense of satisfaction coursing through my veins. In the realm of Sente Katharina, I stood alone as the embodiment of punk. It seemed that there were two additional punks dwelling in Kuurne, and if we were to expand our horizons to encompass Greater Kuurne, our triumvirate would be complete. As they say, all good things come in threes. However, the talents and abilities of Tony and Tom, my newfound comrades, remained a mystery to me. Yet, when you're bursting with euphoria at the prospect of shredding in a punk band, such trivial details become inconsequential. They hold no significance in the grand scheme of things.

I couldn't wait for the weekend to arrive, eagerly anticipating its arrival as I spent my days practicing my guitar. During this time, my trusty mini-20-watt Marshall amp was on the verge of exploding. While my mother may have been relieved that the weekend was approaching, she secretly hoped that I would relocate all my musical equipment out of the house. But no matter what unexpected musical mishaps may occur, I knew that the Red Cross Square was where I needed to be, ready to receive any necessary first aid. It's where all the rock 'n' roll casualties gathered. The arrival of spring filled me with a renewed sense of energy and passion, as if nature itself was awakening deep inside me.

My first band VERGAENE GLORIE (FADED GLORY) back in the beginning of the eighties.

CHAPTER 6
I was a Teenage Anarchist Anonymous

"We started off trying to set up a small anarchist community, but people wouldn't obey the rules." - Alan Bennett

My first punk band had a short lifespan of only two years, and despite our lack of musical talent, we didn't shy away from hitting the stage frequently. We even caught the attention of Punk Etc Records, which fueled our hopes of securing a spot on their upcoming compilation album. Fate, however, had a different plan in store for us. Vergaene Glorie never made it onto the coveted K7 compilation, and it wasn't solely because we disbanded in the summer of 1983 but rather due to a series of unfortunate events leading up to our split.

Firstly, the recording studio where we were supposed to lay down our tracks got raided by the police. I can't confirm if this was true or not, but a phone call shattered our dreams and postponed the recording session to a later date and just when a new date emerged, we found ourselves without a drummer. It was a huge setback, and we were forced to reschedule once again. It seemed like a cruel twist of fate, a sequence of coincidences that conspired against Vergaene Glorie's chance at recording for this compilation. The frustration gnawed at me relentlessly.

I yearned to release something, regardless of whether we were truly prepared or not. The odds seemed stacked against us, but I remained determined.

Despite the problems and challenges that plagued us, I firmly beheld my dream and refused to let go. The universe may have conspired against us, but I was not willing to surrender. I was dogged in my persistence to make it happen, no matter what.

During the summer of 1983, my girlfriend and I decided to dabble in new or rather different musical directions. I had no intention of quitting Vergaene Glorie, but the other band members had a different plan in mind, and before we knew it, we were facing an unexpected split. It was a messy breakup, accompanied by a fair amount of animosity.

Experimentation meant an evolution for me, but it also reflected the metamorphosis in the music scene around me. The old '77 punk style transformed into what we called 'hardcore.' The bands started playing more aggressively and at a much faster pace. At times, it felt like a race for speed. Meanwhile, punk music was being infused with a multitude of different influences. Noise, experimental, industrial, metal... even folk...

Because I was politically inspired, I gravitated towards anarchist bands like Crass and Poison Girls. It had something thrilling, even dangerous, and above all, it distanced itself from the drunken, meaningless babble of a portion of the so-called party punk scene. If you had never sought solace in endless drinking yourself, at least this offered a sense of direction.

In addition to the anarcho bands, there was the rise of the "punk poets." It was a revolutionary act for punk as they showed that performing went beyond just making music. You could convey a message without relying on musical notes or chords. These poets were the rebels of the literary world, using their words as weapons to challenge the status quo.

John Cooper Clarke, with his sharp wit and gritty delivery, was like the Mick Jagger of poetry. Although he might not have considered a comparison with Mick Jagger a compliment. He would captivate crowds with his rapid-fire verses, painting vivid images with his words. Clarke's words were like a sonic assault, hitting you right in the gut and leaving you breathless.

Patrick Fitzgerald, on the other hand, had a softer approach. His poetry was like a haunting melody, weaving tales of love, loss, and agitation. His performances were like intimate acoustic sets, where every word carried weight, and every pause held suspense.

And then there was Attila The Stockbroker, the punk poet with a political agenda. The king of agitprop. His gigs were like a riotous protest march, rallying against injustice and oppression. Attila's words were like a rallying cry for the disenchanted youth, urging them to rise up and fight for what they believe in. His poetry was like a Molotov cocktail, exploding with anger and passion, igniting a fire within the hearts of his listeners.

These punk poets shattered the boundaries of traditional literature and brought their rebellious spirit to the forefront. They proved that poetry could be a weapon, a means of expressing dissent and challenging societal norms. They gave back the meaning of poetry, the meaning which was lost with the distance of time. With their powerful metaphors and raw, unfiltered language, they created a new form of artistic expression.

At the outset, we were primarily immersed in the realm of punk poetry. We belted out lyrics laden with emotion, singing over a backdrop of sound fragments. If you were to peruse the extensive list of works I borrowed from the library, you would discover that I listened to every sound effects record multiple times, ranging from the sounds of cars to the speeches of Hitler and Mussolini.

We created basic audio recordings using pots and pans, a Casio VL-1, and a cassette recorder. To craft the lyrics, we utilized photocopies and cut-and-paste techniques to form collages. And that marked the genesis of my new band, -XXX-. The name was inspired by an article that described the pseudonyms used by unknown authors in libraries. Our focus was on the message we wanted to convey rather than the identities of the individuals delivering it. Hence, we became known as the -XXX-, or as we preferred to be called, 'Anarchist Anonymous.' Armed with our collages and pamphlets, we bombarded fanzines in Belgium and the Netherlands, causing the word to spread quickly.

Creating authentic music, however, remained a burning desire of mine. My girlfriend was determined to master the drums and began pounding away on an ancient oil barrel. The barrel had been neglected for quite some time, particularly ever since Vergaene Glorie had envisioned using it as a raw industrial rhythm. Before long, we managed to acquire a proper drum kit, and once again, the magnetic pull of guitar strings drew me in. Sadly, our lack of musical proficiency limited us to mere sound recordings, and she eventually transitioned to singing, partly because I had a profound fondness for bands fronted by powerful female vocalists. To be fairly honest, to become a skilled drummer simply wasn't in the cards for her, so the decision was swiftly made.

It was just another ad in the newspaper that instantly connected us with a drummer from our area: Benny. He wasn't your typical punk but a hardcore rocker with an insatiable desire to make music. He possessed not only a drum set and boundless enthusiasm but most importantly, he had a car. A fiery orange Ford Taunus. At that time, Benny and I were both eighteen years old, while Iskra, our youngest member, was merely fourteen. Since we couldn't find a bassist right off the bat, we made the bold decision to kickstart our musical journey as a trio.

-XXX- gave me total freedom and complete control. Iskra was my muse, my love, while Bennie served as the hired muscle, allowing me to disregard anyone else. Every melody, every set of lyrics, and every artistic concept originated solely from the depths of my being. No incessant nagging, no need for justification or explanation. That sensation of unmitigated control has forever remained ingrained within me. As it turned out, Bennie proved to be an invaluable asset because his musical skills were truly remarkable, and he took our performances to new heights. In his presence, I rapidly honed my own ability as a musician, and despite her youthfulness, Iskra managed to deliver a remarkably mature vocal performance.

In no time, a series of gigs followed in local youth clubs, and things began to escalate rapidly. In just under a year, our band was itching to unleash something onto the world. At the same time, the punk scene in the Netherlands was exploding with raw energy. Bands like The Ex, Morzelpronk, Svatsöx, Nitwitz, BGK, Amsterdamned, Frites Modern, and countless others left an astounding mark on my soul. Their influence was amplified by the mighty force that was De Nieuwe Koekrand, arguably the greatest fanzine ever to grace the Low Countries. It was like the Dutch equivalent of Flipside or MaximumRocknRoll.

One by one, a succession of Dutch bands made their way into the bins of the record stores, with a common thread tying them together: the recording studio. In the middle of this vibrant scene that was painted before us through the craft of our destiny, there was a name that stood out, radiating an almost mythical appeal - Joke's Koeienverhuurbedrijf or translated to Joke's Cow Rental Company. It was an unconventional name that held a certain enchantment. The Netherlands, known for its picturesque windmills and delectable cheese, now boasted a cow rental company where the most cutting-edge punk records were produced.

Benny's bright orange Taunus served as our ticket to head north from Belgium. The three incognito Belgians seamlessly blended into the Amsterdam scene.

I called the studio on the phone, and together, we managed to arrange a few days for recording an LP. Our financial situation at the time was tight, with a budget of approximately $375.00 for a total of three days of studio time. So, to make up for our tight budget, we came up with the idea of performing some gigs in the Netherlands both before and after the recording sessions. This way, we hoped to recoup some of our studio budget.

Little did we realize that our Dutch escapade was about to transform into an exhilarating journey. In those days, touring meant traversing both physical and metaphorical borders. The concept of free passage within Europe was non-existent back then. Just a week or two before our departure, I found myself at the customs office, surrounded by all our gear, meticulously preparing a Temporary Admission Carnet. Every instrument and every cable had to be painstakingly listed on a stack of carbon copy forms. Then, an apathetic customs official would thoroughly inspect everything. This process entailed unloading our entire cargo, presenting it for scrutiny, and finally obtaining a stamp of approval on the paperwork. With this crucial document in hand, we were granted permission to transport our declared equipment across the border, under the strict requirement that it must return the same way it came. Any attempt to sell or trade anything across the border was strictly forbidden, as both the Belgian and Dutch tax authorities were relentless in their pursuit of every last penny.

We had planned the tour in collaboration with a French band, and whether deliberately or unknowingly, their carnet was improperly stamped. The situation took a drastic turn at the Dutch border when the French band's arrogant demeanor, combined with their loud and boisterous behavior, only worsened the already chaotic administrative situation. As a result, they were politely instructed to turn back and obtain the correct paperwork. However, there was an alternative solution on the table. We could make a deposit. The amount requested was a whopping $500.00. However, it may not seem like much in today's world, but back then, it was practically an entire month's average income. And you have guessed by now who was completely broke? That's right, our French companions. In the end, I had to sacrifice all of our studio funds and whatever meager savings we had left on our bank cards.

That night, we kicked off our first Dutch live show. Everything went flawlessly. It marked the very first occasion where we graced the stage in a foreign land, and for an 18-year-old like me, it was brimming with road trip vibes. We crashed at the humble abode of one of the event organizers, and as the sun rose on a brand new day, we set our sights on Wormer. In those days, Wormer was the definition of cool, even cooler than Amsterdam. The alternative scene in Wormer birthed legends like The Ex, alongside a plethora of other bands. The average punk who ventured into the Netherlands would always end up flocking to Amsterdam as they would be uncontrollably lured by its notorious coffee shops and questionable joint dealers who would happily rip you off. But we went the extra mile, immersing ourselves in the serene Dutch meadows and rustic farms where the real action was. It was all destination Wormer for this anarchist bunch.

The studio, situated in the very same spot, was a squatted abode once belonging to a law enforcement officer. It became a haven for the burgeoning punk movement in the Netherlands, housing renowned bands such as The Ex, Negazione, and Neuroot.

-XXX- had the incredible opportunity to lay down tracks in this legendary studio. Now, here's a wild twist: Joke, the engineer's girlfriend, was in on the whole operation. To keep nosy neighbors from catching on, they cleverly disguised the studio as a "cow rental business." Can you believe it? The local farmers didn't bat an eye at the peculiar cover story.

In fact, there was a rumor floating around that not one but two people actually showed up looking to rent a cow. Talk about bad timing! Turns out, the demand for cow rentals was through the roof, and all the bovines were already spoken for. The cow business was booming! Rock 'n' roll, baby!

But before we could kick off the recording process, something else was about to happen. Upon our arrival, the studio stood empty, devoid of any signs of life. Not a soul in sight. In those days, smartphones were nothing but a figment of our imagination, so we had to rely on good old-fashioned methods, which was, a telephone booth. After locating a telephone booth, we managed to get in touch with Dolf, the studio owner. However, our lifeline wouldn't arrive until the following day, leaving us with no choice but to set up camp outside the studio on that sweltering August day.

Our presence didn't go unnoticed in the quiet street lined with modest workers' houses. A Volkswagen van sporting a French license plate and an orange Ford Taunus with a Belgian registration plate caught the attention of every passerby. Yet it was the rowdy gang of punk kids, blasting their car radios at full volume, that truly stirred up chaos in the neighborhood. Their relentless noise pierced through the air, driving some of the neighbors to the brink of absolute madness.

So, determined to make the most of the situation, we made a quick run to a nearby store to stock up on beer. With our spirits held high, we anticipated a night filled with laughter and revelry. In accordance, the preparations were with the stage was set for an unforgettable evening ahead.

Out of nowhere, the Royal Military Police and a Tactical Mobile Unit van abruptly halted right outside the squatted residence. They swiftly collected our identification cards and engaged themselves in a flurry of phone calls with some kind of command center. But they didn't bother providing any further explanation at that moment. It wasn't until half an hour later when we were summoned to pack up and leave, that we realized something was amiss. The plan to head to Amsterdam was abruptly shattered by the uniformed ones' ulterior motives.

"Leaving" didn't simply mean hopping into the van and driving to Amsterdam as we had anticipated. No, it turned out to be a cruel twist of fate – we were being forcefully expelled from the country. With both police cars tailing us, we drove southwards. At first, we naively assumed that they would only follow us for a few measly kilometers. Little did we know that their determination knew no bounds.

Exit after exit, we anxiously contemplated refueling or even stopping altogether in hopes of evading our pursuers. But it was all in vain. They lurked, patiently waiting for us to finish refueling before urging us to resume our course on the highway. It became an endless cycle, and each mile produced an anxious tear of sweat across our forehead. The miles stretched on, and still, they clung to our tail like leeches.

This cat-and-mouse game persisted until we finally reached the Belgian border.

We stumbled back to our home in the early morning, utterly drained and devastated from a restlessly cruel night. With heavy eyelids and aching bodies, we mustered the strength to dial the studio's number, explaining that the Dutch fascist machine had thrown a wrench in our plans. We rescheduled for the following day and determined that this time around, luck would be on our side.

As the sun began to peek over the horizon, we found ourselves crossing the Dutch border once again. By midday, our equipment was set up in the recording space, ready to unleash our anger. The clock seemed to race against us as we feverishly laid down tracks for half of the songs by evening. There was no time to waste – we opted for a raw approach, recording the drums and guitar live, sans bass.

The next day held the promise of completing our album. The remaining songs awaited us. With adrenaline coursing through our veins, we poured every ounce of grit into this final session.

We blasted through the album mixing process in just a blink of an eye. In what seemed like no time at all, the finished masterpiece lay proudly before us. Our debut LP consisted of twelve tracks. However, we hit a roadblock when we realized we had zero funds to press it onto vinyl. So, with our hands tied behind our backs, we were forced to get creative, "The First Steps" was released on a cassette tape instead. We cobbled together the artwork using a trusty Xerox machine and painstakingly hand-colored each of the limited 50 copies. It was a true labor of love. The era of DIY cut-and-paste work, which had its roots in the creation of fanzines, proved to be our saving grace once again.

Out of the 50 cassette tapes, probably only 15 of them got sold, and the remaining unsold ones were forgotten and left languishing in a trash bag through the years that went by.

Although the complete album didn't make it to vinyl, an offer came in from England to include two of the songs on a compilation LP called 'Rot In Hell' by Rot Records. This compilation already boasted renowned artists such as The Varukers, Oi Polloi, and Resistance 77. The decision was a no-brainer. -XXX- was ultimately pressed onto vinyl.

Fast forward twelve years and the compilation also made its way onto CDs, thanks to a licensing agreement with Cherry Red Records.

-XXX- was never meant to have a long-lasting existence after that. I decided to pursue my studies at Ghent University. Iskra, on the other hand, still had to complete her high school education. It seemed like we wouldn't cross paths for many years to come. Iskra simply vanished from the picture, leaving no trace behind. However, thanks to the wonders of social media, I managed to reconnect with Bennie through Facebook.

Due to relentless relocations, my very own -XXX- tape vanished without a trace, leaving only the original master lock hidden ed away in some forgotten moving box. The tapes eventually landed in the possession of a friend who owned a recording studio. But alas, a series of chaotic events surrounding his own relocation caused the tapes to vanish into the depths of a dusty cardboard container once again. After the passage of countless years, they miraculously resurfaced unscathed, defying all odds. The four decades that had slipped away had left no mark on these tapes. We managed the arduous task of digitizing the damn thing, and finally, the album found its rightful place: the pressing plant. Forty years after its original recording, my cherished vision of a vinyl LP became a reality. Complete with a vibrant cover and vinyl in shades of yellow and pink, paying homage to the fluorescent markers of the past.

Listen closely to the voice of an anonymous anarchist...

During my days of scouring record stores for the latest tunes during the -XXX- era, I stumbled upon a game-changing medium that would redefine my perception of the punk movement as a whole. Initially, like many others, I viewed it solely as a "musical" phenomenon. However, my world expanded exponentially when I came across fanzines, revealing a much grander and captivating universe. At first, there were only a handful of local fanzines available, which led to publishing my own.

As I delved deeper into the world of fanzines, I realized that they served as a powerful platform for self-expression and the exchange of ideas within the punk community. These independently crafted publications became a vital source of information, connecting like-minded individuals. Creating my own fanzine allowed me to contribute to the punk subculture. Embracing the DIY ethos, the fanzine scene was not without its challenges. Limited resources and distribution networks meant that reaching a wider audience was an uphill battle.

My very first fanzine went by the name of "Subvert!" and I took inspiration for the title from a Zounds song. 'Subvert!' It couldn't have been any more crystal clear to me. This British band had a single released by Crass Records, and while on their European tour, they made a stop at our local youth club. I can still vividly recall walking into the venue and catching sight of some punks with orange-dyed hair. Wow, Zounds appeared so effortlessly cool! Well, at least that's what I initially believed. As it turned out, those individuals were actually the roadies, as the genuine members of the band, who were somewhat older than expected, took to the stage.

I witnessed plenty of amateurish and haphazardly photocopied materials circulating, and it dawned on me that there had to be a better way. That's when I delved into the realm of collage art. Back in the early 1980s, desktop publishing was out of the question for home use. We didn't have access to personal computers, so I had to rely on old-fashioned cut-and-paste techniques using snippets from newspapers and magazines or even creating my own drawings. To enhance my creative process, I quickly acquired a lightbox and raster sheets, allowing me to push the boundaries and unleash my imagination. One of the hottest trends at the time was rub-off letters, which added an extra layer of flair to my artwork.

It was a constant cycle of trial and error, but that's how I honed my skills and found my artistic angle.

My insatiable thirst for visual expression led me to embark on a year-long journey into the world of Publicity Graphics at the Academy of Arts. However, it quickly became apparent that I wasn't exactly the poster child, as I refused to conform to their expectations. I vividly recall my initial task, which involved creating a typeface. But to hell with that! I had enrolled in the academy primarily to exploit their state-of-the-art equipment: the drawing board, the light box, the enlarger... I was determined to carve my own path.

In the end, they begrudgingly allowed me to pursue my unconventional methods. I didn't harm anyone in the process; instead, I injected unexpected hues into the studio, breathing life into the stale atmosphere. I refused to succumb to the pressure of becoming just another run-of-the-mill cookie-cutter designer, whether they appreciated it or not.

Subvert 1 and 2 burst into existence, and I joined forces with the bass player from Vergaene Glorie to create a split issue. He pioneered the very first and most successful sinful fanzine in our hometown. In the year 1983, the inaugural edition of Noisy Neighbours emerged, however, it also marked the end, as my studies demanded more of my time, making it impossible to continue.

When the -XXX- vinyl album made its debut, I knew it was time to resurrect those rebellious rants. And so, alongside the record, the "Anarchist Anonymous" book was conceived, bringing together all the long-lost gems that had vanished into thin air.

Finally, they were saved from the clutches of oblivion.

-XXX- was the first band I recorded with. We went down to Amsterdam to record in the legendary studio of Dolf Planteyd, Joke's Koeienverhuurbedrijf.

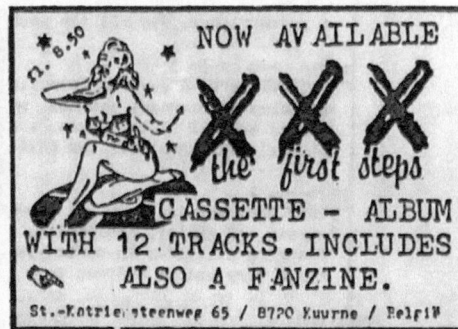

Organizing shows and punkfestivals at the local youth club Reflex.

Getting into the world of fanzines and self publishing.

-XXX- collage styled imagery with the anarcho punk message.

EXPLOITATION STARTS 'RIGHT HERE'

tits and cunt mean lots of money
and that's what really counts
tenderness has lost its romance
it's time to change your stance
human flesh is not for sale
this isn't a bloody stock-farm
page three love birds always smile
but can't you see through the lies
a womans body is a business de...
exploitation starts ... RIGHT HERE !
exploitation exploitation

CHAPTER 7
Cruise Missiles and Terrorism

"Everyone's worried about stopping terrorism. Well, there's really an easy way: Stop participating in it." - Noam Chomsky

Coming of age in the early 1980s was a whirlwind of exhilaration and intensity, with the world spinning in a frenzy around us. As the clock struck midnight on April 3, 1979, Christian Democrat Wilfried Martens stepped onto the stage of power, taking the oath as the leader of his inaugural government. Little did we know, this would be just the beginning of a rollercoaster ride through the political turmoil. One government after another toppled like dominoes, each collapse sending shockwaves through society. The reasons for this sudden turmoil were plentiful, from unemployment rates soaring to unprecedented heights, the crushing weight of a mounting public debt that hung heavily over our heads, and, in between it all, tensions within our communities reaching a boiling point, ready to explode at any given moment.

After the elections of 1981, Martens made a dramatic shift in direction. They teamed up with the Liberals and implemented extreme measures to revive the economy and break free from the shackles of political turmoil. At the start of 1982, the Belgian franc experienced a significant devaluation of 8.5 percent. Not only this, the government put a halt to the automatic indexation of wages and implemented substantial cuts to government spending.

We stood there like mere spectators as the Martens administration focused solely on the economy. While the entire nation grappled with economic stagnation, a separate realm emerged, rife with turmoil and violence. It was as if we were witnessing events unfold in a parallel universe. It all felt unreal.

Terrorism, which was once confined to Germany and Italy, was making its presence felt in Belgium as well. The Justice Department was thrown into a momentary state of panic when news broke about neo-Nazis infiltrating the state security apparatus. And as if that wasn't enough, the Gang of Nivelles committed a string of brutal robberies, while the left-wing CCC launched their own series of attacks. The situation grew increasingly worrisome. And then, out of nowhere, a bomb exploded at the Liège courthouse, claiming the life of an innocent individual. It was later discovered that the perpetrator behind this heinous act was a lawyer with twisted, extremist right-wing beliefs.

The onslaughts fortified the machinery of oppression. The funding allocated to the national police surged, which led to significant upgrades in their equipment. However, their true allegiance did not lie with our country. The gendarmes had transformed into a powerful entity within the state, poised and prepared for a coup.

In December of 1984, the CCC, also known as the Combatant Communist Cells, executed a total of 14 attacks throughout Belgium. They orchestrated simultaneous explosions at five different points along a NATO pipeline. The following year, in November 1985, they set off bombs in different banks and Bank of America, becoming the group's final target on December 4, 1985.

Although primarily focused on attacking banks and businesses. There was never the intention to harm civilians. Unfortunately, despite their efforts, two firefighters lost their lives, and a total of 28 individuals sustained injuries during these acts of terrorism. It was on December 16, 1985, that the four key members of the CCC — Bertrand Sassoye, Didier Chevolet, Pascale Vandegeerde, and Pierre Carette — were apprehended while enjoying hamburgers at a Fast food restaurant. Subsequently, on October 21, 1988, the Assize Court in Brussels handed down life sentences to the aforementioned individuals.

Throughout history, it has become painfully clear that the apprehension of radical left-wing CCC leaders was not a mere coincidence, while the Nivelles gang's perpetrators managed to elude capture. It was as if the authorities had set their sights solely on combating left-wing terrorism, leaving the investigation into the brutal acts of banditry at a complete standstill, whether intentionally or unwittingly.

Even today, the enigma surrounding the Nivelles Gang remains shrouded in mystery, and it still captivates the minds of those who delve into the dark recesses of 1980s history. The reign of terror began in 1982 with a daring heist targeting an arms dealer. From there, a series of violent robberies unfolded, with Delhaize supermarkets serving as the primary targets. What struck observers was the disproportionate amount of violence unleashed during these crimes, given the relatively meager haul obtained each time.

After a thunderous and confusing two years, a deafening silence descended upon the Nivelles gang. However, in the autumn of 1985, a wave of new violent robberies emerged that were enveloped in mystery and were never brought to light. It seemed that the perpetrators sought not only material gain but also aimed to instill sheer terror into their victims. Unfortunately, the investigation came to a grinding halt and left many questions unanswered. The alleged involvement of the gendarmerie in the gang received little attention and remained largely unexplored. The internal rivalry among the different police forces further hindered progress in solving the case.

In an attempt to dispel rumors of a massive cover-up, a parliamentary commission of inquiry was established in the late 1980s. However, instead of providing closure, it only served to amplify rumors further. The investigation into the Nivelles gang that failed to make any significant progress caused quite a stir as people were left wondering and speculating, leading them to come up with all sorts of conspiracy theories. One theory even suggested that Prince Albert, who was not yet king at the time, was involved in the gang's activities. In fact, several articles circulated linking the prince to the infamous Pink Ballets - rumored secret illicit parties involving influential individuals and underage participants. Even the former prime minister was said to have some connection to these scandalous events. The lack of a breakthrough in the investigation left many questioning the truth behind these allegations and wondering if there was more to the story than met the eye. It was a situation that fueled suspicion and curiosity, which cast a shadow of doubt over those in positions of power.

Back in those days, the Eastern Front beyond the Iron Curtain played a pivotal role in shaping the strategic mindset of Western Europe. The powers that be, which included the security services and the political elite, were constantly warned of the looming threat of the Red Menace. However, despite this rightward shift in politics, the government displayed a singular focus on suppressing left-wing activism. It seemed as though the right-wing faction could get away with anything, while the police forces not only turned a blind eye to the extreme right but even viewed them as loyal allies.

In the turbulent era of the 1980s, the Cold War was still tearing through the world with an unstoppable force as the East and West engaged in a relentless arms race. Fueled by the tension caused by the Russian SS20 missiles stationed in Central Europe, NATO made a bold move known as the double decision in 1979. On the one hand, they strategically positioned 464 medium-range cruise missiles and 108 short-range Pershing II missiles in various Western European nations. These missiles had the capability to unleash devastating nuclear warheads upon their targets. However, in a surprising twist, NATO also extended an olive branch to the Eastern Bloc, offering them an opportunity to engage in negotiations aimed at reducing the alarming stockpile of deadly weaponry. The stage was set for a high-stakes showdown between superpowers, where every move had the potential to shape the fate of nations.

The choice to deploy nuclear missiles in Europe sparked widespread protests across all the nations involved. In Belgium, the resistance reached its peak during the powerful anti-missile demonstration on October 23, 1983. While the exact number of demonstrators remained uncertain, it can be inferred from ticket sales and bus rentalsamong other factors, that approximately 400,000 people participated. Despite the overwhelming outcry, the Martens government remained resolute and proceeded with the placement of twenty cruise missiles at the Florennes Air Base.

I 'HEARTBREAK' THE RAMONES

As we neared the year 1985, the date of May twenty-nine etched itself into the annals of soccer history by marking a day of darkness and sorrow. It was a day that witnessed the unfolding of a tragic event at the Heysel Stadium in Brussels during the European Cup final between Liverpool and Juventus. In a grievous oversight, organizers had unknowingly placed Italian and British soccer supporters alongside each other, setting the stage for what would become a devastating clash.

Tensions simmered, and chaos erupted even before the match commenced. Giving in to their aggression, the British supporters hurled stones towards the Italians, which surely ignited a hostile atmosphere that was destined to escalate. The charged atmosphere reached its breaking point when the crowd surged forward by putting immense pressure on a wall that ultimately gave way under the strain. In the ensuing pandemonium, countless individuals were trampled upon, and their lives tragically cut short.

The security forces found themselves rendered utterly powerless in the face of chaos. Even the emergency services who bravely stepped onto the scene to bring order were met with a barrage of aggression from the hooligans. The result was devastating, as 39 lives were lost, and countless others were left injured and shattered. The blame was swiftly placed on the dilapidated state of the stadium and the disorganized efforts of both the gendarmerie and police. As the uproar ravenously increased, the Interior Minister defiantly refused to step down, which added fuel to an already raging fire.

We came of age in the midst of this backdrop. As teenagers, we sought to find our political footing and aligned ourselves with either the left or the right. In my high school, conservative right-wing ideologies ran rampant and dominated the landscape of thinking.

In the depths of my parents' bedroom closet, I stumbled upon my father's army bag, which held his military uniform. Curiosity consumed me, and I couldn't resist extracting the battledress from its confines. To my astonishment, it fit me like a second skin. Emboldened by my newfound attire, I reached for my mother's eyeliner and carefully traced it along my eyes. As I boarded the train to Brussels, I found myself surrounded by friends of my parents. Their voices were filled with outrage as they discussed the audacity of a young teenage boy who was adorned with makeup sitting before them. My father, who was burdened by the weight of societal expectations, couldn't help but feel a tinge of shame.

It became clear to me that blending into the anonymous sea of protesters was far easier than hiding amongst the few hundred individuals attending the Days of Anarchy. These annual events were marked by impassioned speeches and performances by engaged punk bands and always culminated in fierce clashes with local fascists.

In retrospect, it all seems like a tale of folklore. The left- and right-wing supporters swaying and twirling in a chaotic dance. Meanwhile, the police and gendarmerie acting as partial referees are caught in the middle. It was a day to remember in Ghent, where I sat captivated while being held in a trance as Pierre Carette took the stage in the university auditorium. After his speech, we exchanged a few words, knowing little that our paths would cross again under different circumstances. It was a surreal moment when his face appeared on the television screen during the prime time News. The authorities had taken him into custody as one of the leaders of the CCC terrorist group.

Forty years ago, the focus was not on climate change, as it was a future threat that was yet to unfold in the decades to come. While previous generations fought for social security, we rose up to champion the ideals of independent thinking and individualism. Today, rebellion has been reduced to mere piercings or tattoos on one's face. Society seems to revel in the confusion of gender fluidity by turning it into a leisurely pursuit. Personally, I couldn't care less. Be whoever you want to be. It's all good with me. Live and let live.

But the spirit of freedom and rebellion has been suppressed by the suffocating grip of political correctness, which is on the verge of outlawing humor and satire altogether. How absurd is that? Nowadays, you're only deemed acceptable if you take offense to everything others say. Because then, you can spearhead a movement, complete with a catchy hashtag, and bask in the validation of countless thumbs up on Facebook or hearts on Instagram. As I reflect on those formative years of the early 1980s, I can't help but acknowledge the undeniable intensity and slight tinge in the air. It was a time of risks and uncertainties, yet the threats were more discernible and easier to identify. The metaphorical wolves lurking in the shadows were not as elusive as they are today.

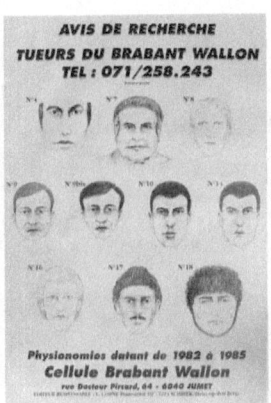 

Belgium in the Eighties. The Nivelles Gang terrorized supermarkets and killed 28 people in cold blood. The mystery never got solved.

The CCC left wing terrorists blew up a number op Capitalist institutions and military targets. It didn't take long to find them.

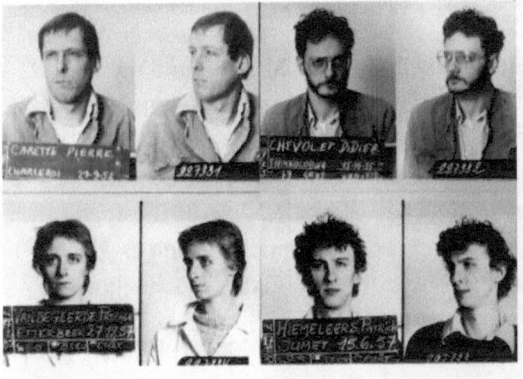 

The Belgian people don't want cruise missiles on their territory.

CHAPTER 8

Mondo Midnight

"Night Time is the Right Time" - Ray Charles

When my fascination with music ignited in the late 1970s, I found myself immersed in a new era of sonic revolution. The confines of classic rock were shattered by the explosive emergence of Punk and New Wave. This new music defied any convention. Gone were the days of complacency, where radio stations spoon-fed us a steady diet of middle-of-the-road muzak. The airwaves crackled with a new and authentic rebellion as FM rock became a profanity, synonymous with the mundane, soul-sucking tunes that were force-fed to appease the masses. We were provided with the perfect soundtrack for our defiance.

Looking back, I realize how fortunate we were to witness such a pivotal moment in musical history.

The era I found myself in was absolutely extraordinary. The span of twenty years that had elapsed since the day I was born was filled with remarkable transformation. In 1978, if you magically find yourself traveling back in time by twenty years, you would find yourself in the year 1958, rocking out to the legendary Bill Haley & The Comets, right in the heart of the Rock 'n' Roll era. And if you were to venture back fifteen years, you would be transported to a world where the Rolling Stones reigned supreme. Going back a decade would bring you face to face with the mind-expanding psychedelics, as well as the sexual and spiritual revolution of the May '68 revolutionary days.

After my musical journey gave birth to my first punk band, I experienced significant growth with my -XXX- collective. I took the leap and released my very own debut album. However, my pursuit of music had to take a backseat to my studies. Although I still strummed the guitar occasionally, there was a standstill in activities from mid-'84 until the end of '85. During this period, I immersed myself in listening to an array of music, but I wasn't actively playing in any band. That all changed when I discovered The Sonics. Their garage rock sound resonated with me instantly. It effortlessly blended the raw simplicity of Punk, which was characterized by its three-chord structure, with the captivating melodies reminiscent of '60s music. The "Nuggets" album became my gateway to exploration, which ignited an intense hunger to create this type of music myself.

The time had come to assemble a new group of musicians. It didn't take long for me to find Edward, a bassist who had a connection to a vocalist named Hazel. Together, we formed a musical alliance by using Edward's bedroom as our headquarters for new projects while my mother's room transformed into our dedicated rehearsal space.

The moment we stumbled upon a golden jockstrap labeled The Midnight Men in a racy catalog, we knew right away that we had found our name. It had the ring of an American comic, perfectly aligning with our vision and purpose. Instantly, it became clear that this was the moniker we were destined to adopt.

In just a matter of weeks, we had our gear set up and were ready to rock in the studio. We wasted no time and started laying down tracks for our demo. And let me tell you, it didn't take long for word to spread. The buzz surrounding us caught the attention of BOOM! Records, who wasted no time in snatching us up.

JP VAN, the owner of the record label, was immediately captivated by Hazel and the rest of the group when he first laid eyes on us. He fell head over heels for Hazel but understood he had to take the band along in his crush. Before we knew it, our music was featured on several of his compilation albums.

But I wasn't satisfied with just being part of some compilation LPs. My ambition pushed me to reach newer heights. So back we went into the studio. Our blood, sweat, and tears poured into every note as we recorded our very first LP, 'Mondo Teeno Experience.' While we were in the process of recording that album, we had the fortunate opportunity to collaborate with a skilled local guitarist who added some cool guitar solos. Admittedly, I had never quite mastered those solos myself, primarily due to my own laziness. However, as we laid down all our tracks, it became glaringly apparent that our songs needed that extra touch of brilliance. Enter Dee Jaywalker, the guitarist who lent his talent to our project. Little did anyone know at the time that ten years later, he would step into the spotlight and become the second guitarist for the SpeedKings, emerging as if out of thin air. It's pretty funny how life has a way of throwing unexpected curveballs, steering us down a road we never could have anticipated. It's even more mind-boggling to realize that the course of history can often be determined a decade before it unfolds. Our record found a home with 'Punk Etc Records,' who once again resurfaced. Unlike my previous band, who unfortunately missed out on being featured on their cassette compilation, we were not going to let this opportunity slip through our fingers.

By crafting a cunning sell-ourselves-strategy and weaving a captivating bullshit narrative around the band, we managed to capture the attention of quite a few labels. We invented a story larger than life. And when we finally laid down tracks for a new six-song demo and shared it with the coolest garage rock record labels. Lucky for us, their response was immediate. We were inundated with offers. It was almost overwhelming, considering we had only recorded six songs.

'Shakin' Street' from the UK unleashed 'Love Generation' as a 7", accompanied by an eye-catching album cover created by Robert Williams. The B-side of this release featured the covers 'Bad in Bed' by Wayne County and 'Scratch My Back' by The Damned. However, due to copyright complications, the song 'Scratch My Back' had to be omitted from the single. The red vinyl record made Single of the Week in UK's New Musical Express.

Across the pond in California, the notorious record label 'Sympathy For the Record Industry,' owned by Long Gone John, dropped 'Teenage

Gangbang' in the charts, complemented by a stunning sleeve designed by none other than the legendary illustrator, Coop. Meanwhile, all the way down under in Australia, 'Dogmeat Records' was determined to launch a single, as was Estrus in the US, but we had no tracks left.

The demo had also roused the interest of two vinyl geeks. In the Greek city of Athens, Dimitri and Greg established their very own independent record label called "Wipe Out Records." Both of them were die-hard collectors of sixties punk music, and they happened to stumble upon a fascinating tale about a super rare 7-inch record that we supposedly released in a ridiculously limited quantity. This record was just impossible to find. The truth was that I myself had fabricated this urban legend and even went as far as creating counterfeit covers using photocopies. This record never actually existed.

Nevertheless, "Wipe Out Records" was adamant about immortalizing this mythical single along with a collection of vintage demo recordings on an LP. And so, "Midnight Confidential" was born. This LP was set up as a radio show, expertly curated and presented by the legendary New York garage DJ known as Mad Louie Biondi.

The LP received a great response in Greece, leading to an invitation to perform in Athens. However, our reception in Belgium was far from warm, as we were dismissed as nobodies. In contrast, in Greece, the audience embraced us wholeheartedly.

Timothy Gassen's book, "The Knights of Fuzz," shed a spotlight on our band, which gave us extensive recognition. According to Gassen, "While they still need to mature, this band might become one of my favorites by the next print of this book."

And then, one day, we found ourselves at a crossroads when a real and lucrative record deal was presented. A team of seasoned professionals in the management and booking business swooped in to handle our affairs. But sadly, it all went downhill from there. The essence of our band crumbled in no time. The rawness and playful spirit that had once defined us was smothered. As the focus shifted towards contracts and money, the band lost its way. The soul that had ignited their journey was lost in the sad, sterile confines of an expensive recording studio. It was time to hit the brakes once again, to reassess and recalibrate.

The Midnight Men - end of the eighties
Riding the wave of he Belgian Garage Boom.

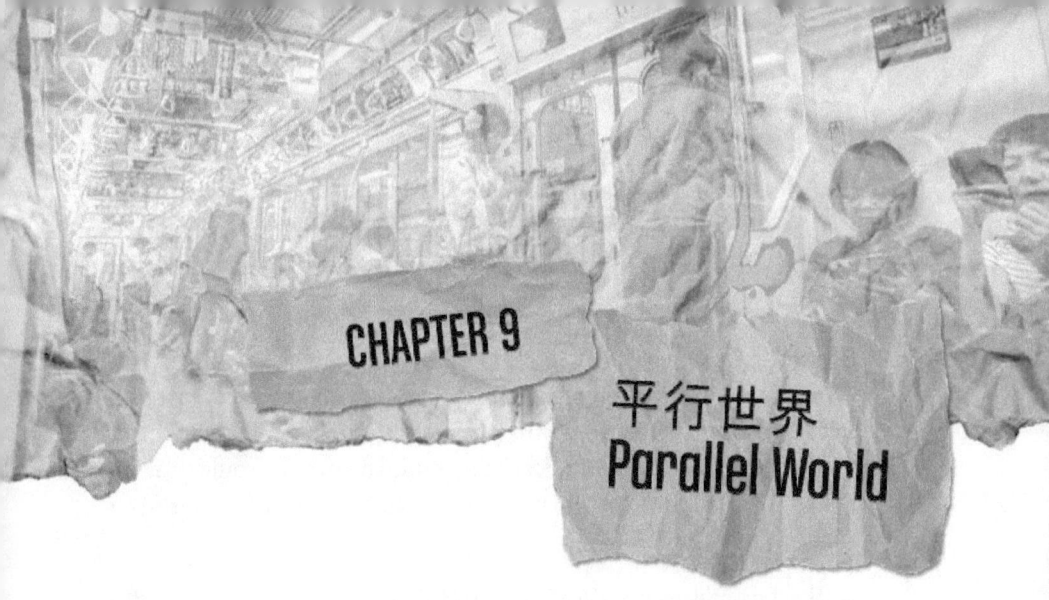

CHAPTER 9

平行世界
Parallel World

"I was bitter. She was sweet. And in a parallel universe, we were bittersweet." - Dominic Riccitello

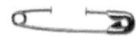

Ghent, the city where I initially started my pursuit of psychology studies, became the breeding ground for the more radical thoughts that nourished my anarchist spirit. It was a place where alternative bookshops thrived, offering a never-ending supply of captivating literature. Fanzines occupied every corner, their presence embodying the subversive undercurrent that flowed through the city. The punk cafes pulsated with the energy of live performances, providing a weekly dose of exhilaration. And within the confines of my campus, I found allies in the fight against societal norms. Ghent was more than just a city; it was a fortress of resistance.

After a less than stellar debut year, I switched to bachelor studies in the field of Labor Law following the mandatory return to Courtrai. The freshmen I found myself surrounded by were, to put it mildly, mentally lagging behind by at least a year. They had just been released from high school, after all. Adding to this disappointment, Courtrai itself lacked the activist spirit that I had come to know and love in Ghent. It was a period of relative calm in terms of political action and engagement.

As the end of my studies drew near, the daunting prospect of entering the workforce loomed over me. But before that, there was still the obligatory military service to contend with. I belonged to the last generation that would be completing this obligation. The sight of the hands and broken rifle emblem on my jacket was far from a badge of honor for our armed forces.

My godfather, who had a close relationship with an important government minister, attempted to exert his influence. However, I still received my summons letter for the physical examination. Despite this, I held onto the hope that my medical background of asthma would provide a way out. I was directed to the military hospital by a referral letter from my doctor.

In the hospital room, I found myself sharing accommodation with three aspiring militiamen. All three of them were eager to escape as soon as possible. However, one of them sat there, filled with despair, as he longed to become a soldier but faced a potential medical obstacle. We gladly appointed him as the room supervisor, and he radiated happiness at the responsibility and the small amount of power that came with it.

However, his happiness was short-lived during the first-morning room inspection. There is nothing more disheartening than being in charge of three little shits who have no desire to cooperate. The beds were left unmade, we were consistently late, and he took the blame.

In the end, everything went smoothly over there. Well, almost everything. The only downside was the food situation. Can you believe they served hot soup and ice cream cones at the same time? It was like a cruel game of choosing between slurping your soup and licking your melting ice cream off the tray or enjoying a "nice" cold treat only to follow it up with spoonfuls of cold soup. Talk about a culinary dilemma!

On the third day of my stay, after enduring multiple medical tests, I received a summons to the front office. They handed me a paper with an official stamp, which turned out to be my ticket back home. Just like that, my three days of soldiering were abruptly cut short. As I glanced around, I witnessed my asthmatic comrades gasping for breath while undergoing the testing procedures. Meanwhile, the conscientious objectors put on an act, pretending to be mentally disturbed and dragging themselves through the hospital corridors like zombies. But not me. I managed to slip through the cracks and escape to freedom. I stood outside as a young man who didn't have to become a soldier.

With my military hurdle running behind me, it was time to embrace professional life. The call of duty led me to join a service organization that catered to employers.

There's no environment more captivating than being thrown into the lion's den. The place I found myself in was the stronghold of the Courtrai Catholic entrepreneurial elite. It felt like I was playing the role of an undercover spy, blending in with them while knowing deep down that I didn't belong. The thought of "it's easier to destroy when you are on the inside" echoed in my mind day after day.

Those years were filled with excitement and opportunity. I gained valuable professional experience, but in the midst of it all, I couldn't resist indulging in immature practical jokes. One instance that comes to mind is when I tampered with the telephone switchboard. During lunchtime and in the evenings, the automatic answering machine kicked in. Taking advantage of this, I swapped out Vivaldi's melodies that greeted callers with the roaring intensity of Slayer's "Reign in Blood." Even Sister Superior from the neighboring convent had her routine disrupted when she called for her payroll records, being unexpectedly serenaded by Satanic metal. It took weeks for anyone to discover my mischievous alteration.

My name is Haas, and ironically, heavy metal wasn't even my cup of tea. But that's who I became in that moment - the torn in the side causing chaos within the confines of a seemingly orderly world.

As I immersed myself in the countless parties, my senses were captivated by the sights and sounds that surrounded me. It didn't take long for me to discern who was involved in romantic entanglements, and interestingly enough, it seems that the more devout the group, the more wild and outrageous the festivities became. This was a time long before the #metoo movement, a time when the mistreatment of women in the workplace knew no bounds. Even the seemingly respectable individuals, fueled by a few glasses of alcohol, would engage in conversations and actions that were better left hidden from their dutiful wives and innocent children eagerly awaiting their return.

In the early 1990s, I made the decision to leave behind this whorehouse and transition into the corporate world. I found myself taking up the role of a human resources manager.

The region I lived in was famously dubbed the "Dallas of Flanders." Back in the eighties, the TV show Dallas had left an indelible mark on society, becoming the pinnacle of success in the working world. In this area, there was an insatiable hunger among workers to put in overtime hours and receive under-the-table payments. This meant that companies could dodge taxes and social security contributions. Although it was illegal, it had become a widespread practice during the 80s and 90s. The company I worked for followed suit, just like all the other businesses in the vicinity.

Every month, the workers were compensated for their overtime work in cold, hard cash. To make this happen, the company needed to have the exact change ready. So, like clockwork, I was entrusted with a mission to visit a local bank that was in on the covert operation. I would walk into the bank carrying a plastic supermarket bag , filled with cash. Usually, it amounted to several hundred thousand dollars. Before I knew it, I had become a bagman for the Industrial Dallas of Flanders.

During my time in "Dallas," I spent my evenings pursuing a master's degree in law at Brussels University. This experience not only expanded my knowledge but also provided me with unique opportunities. With my newfound academic education and specialized experiences, I decided to venture beyond the confines of my home province and took on the role of General Manager of Corporate Affairs & HR at Pioneer, a prominent Japanese electronics corporation.

Within just one year, I faced the daunting challenge of restructuring an entire factory. Little did I know that this would lead to a tumultuous series of events. The employees went on strike, turning the situation into a full-blown crisis. The atmosphere became charged with tension as riot police, water cannons, and horsemen entered the scene. The sight of burning car tires and pallets sent billowing clouds of black smoke into the air. In the midst of this chaos, I found myself thrust into the spotlight as the company's spokesperson, appearing on national TV news.

After weeks of intense negotiations, I successfully resolved the conflict and managed to restore order. The settlements we reached went down in Belgian social history as significant milestones. The high-ranking executives in Tokyo were pleased with my achievements and rewarded me with an opportunity to study at Tohoku University. This marked a turning point in my career, propelling me to new heights.

In the years that followed, my career path took me to various corners of the globe, including Thailand, Mexico, the United States, and numerous European countries. Each destination presented its own set of challenges and adventures, shaping me into a seasoned professional with a wealth of diverse experiences. My journey from a small province to becoming a key player in the international arena has been nothing short of extraordinary.

The Japanese business world, however, felt like a complete joke. In my role as buchou, the head of an international division, I had the audacity to request a seat by the window, hoping to indulge in the breathtaking view of Tokyo's skyline. My colleagues regarded me with a mix of disbelief and amusement.

"By the window? Are you kidding?"
"No, I just love the view. It's a great spot."
"But… are you not aware of the 'madogiwazoku,' the 'man-by-the-window'?"

Little did I know that this coveted spot was reserved for those who were on the verge of jumping out of it. It seemed that in Japan, taking things literally was more than just a quirk. Working in this country, "lost in translation" was nothing in comparison with the challenges we faced as Westerners. It took me quite a while to fully comprehend the nuances embedded in the language and culture, often leading me to make a fool of myself. However, amidst the chaos, my punkitude kept me afloat, acting as my lifeline.

In the end, it all boiled down to a twisted game. Every morning when my working day started, without fail, I opted for the entrance reserved for mere visitors, where a magnificent Ferrari Formula 1 car was proudly showcased. Meanwhile, my boss strolled in through a discreet side door for staff only. The moment he caught sight of me deviating from the norm, his anger ignited like a raging inferno.

But I had a secret weapon up my sleeve. Whenever I jetted in from my homeland, I made sure to bring along a hefty supply of exquisite Belgian beer. And when I graciously presented this liquid gold to the higher-ups, their eyes sparkled with delight. Suddenly, as if by some miraculous intervention, permission was granted for me to ascend to the uppermost echelons of corporate power.

That hallowed floor, strictly off-limits to my boss, became my playground. The Senior Executive Vice Presidents and even the President himself reveled in my presence. It was as if I possessed an irresistible charm that captivated their souls. With my staff pass acting as my VIP ticket, I had the freedom to roam wherever I pleased, choosing the floors that were forbidden territory to him.

In this cutthroat world, where power and status reigned supreme, my stash of amber elixir became my golden ticket. It transformed me into an embodiment of popularity and influence. As I navigated through the corridors of power, defying all odds and rewriting the rules of the game.

Just remember, sometimes it takes more than just skill and dedication to rise to the top. It takes audacity, a touch of defiance, and perhaps even a little liquid persuasion.

When we went on a business trip, my boss had a peculiar fondness for visiting onsen, those natural hot springs that Japan is known for. But I, on the other hand, had no interest in joining him. I wasn't about to sit alongside him, submerging myself in lukewarm water while showcasing all my tattoos. I knew he wouldn't be ready to see me as anything other than a Yakuza member. So, instead, I concocted an excuse, telling him that I needed to put in more work on our presentations. However, the truth was that I sneaked out of the hotel to immerse myself in the local music scene at a nearby live house. It didn't take long before I found myself not just indulging in the music but actually playing it, as I stumbled upon an old Mosrite guitar.

Unfortunately, my time in Japan came to an abrupt end when I found myself facing a divorce. The years of constantly striving for success and the unrelenting demands of the mother company had left me utterly drained. As a result, I made the decision to retreat back to Belgium, vowing never again to be subjected to the authority of a boss. Thankfully, the severance pay I received was substantial enough to sustain me for a few years. These years became a precious gift, allowing me to fully dedicate myself to my passion for music and go on tours that served as a much-needed source of revitalization. In hindsight, I referred to this period of my life as an extended sabbatical on my resume, for it truly provided me with the opportunity to recharge and rediscover my true self.

Back home, I decided to start my own screen-printing business. The combination of music and merchandise seemed like the perfect recipe for a peaceful and creative life. However, as time went on, I realized that my heart wasn't truly invested in the monotonous grind of being a small business owner. So, in 2015, I made the tough decision to call it quits and dive back into the corporate world.

Surprisingly, the transition back into that life was much smoother and faster than I had anticipated. With just one job interview, I was back on my feet and ready to take on new challenges. It seemed like I still had what it took to succeed in that environment. But as time went on, I started feeling suffocated by the confines of Courtrai and its surroundings. It no longer felt like home to me. In fact, I began to question whether I was even welcome there anymore. Eventually, I found solace in leaving the city to those who would never escape its grasp.

The Campine area became our new sanctuary, and my family and I found a beautiful home nestled in Italy. There's a saying that goes, "live hidden, live happy," and that's exactly what I intend to do. My parents worked tirelessly in a factory their entire lives, instilling in me the belief that I should strive for something better. "You have to have a better life than us," my father would often say. While I may have taken a different path, I am still proud to embrace my working-class roots.

Still wondering sometimes whether I was a working-class hero or a working-class zero.

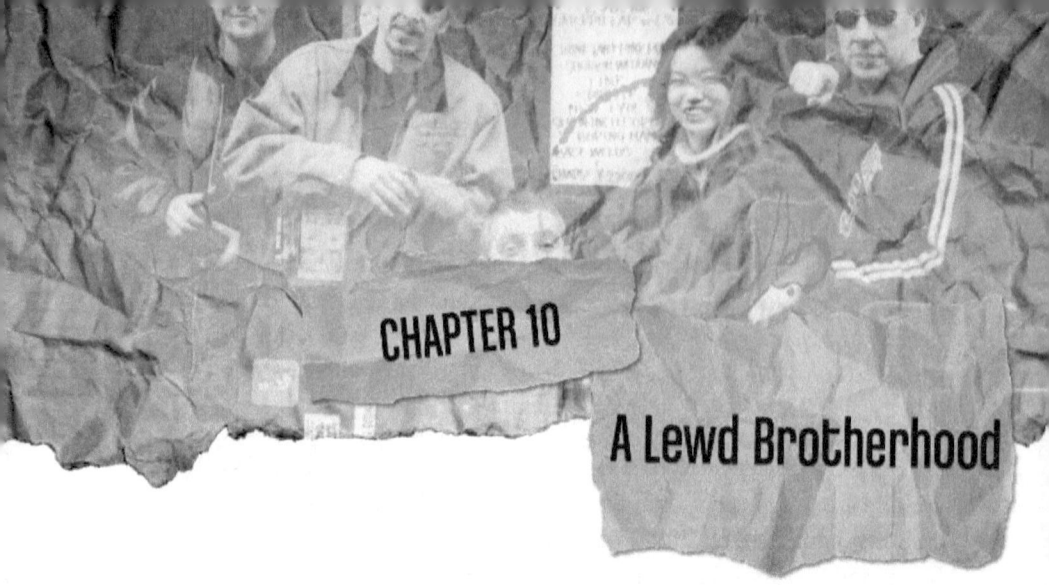

CHAPTER 10

A Lewd Brotherhood

"I don't think there's one thing I've ever said on the radio that would have been found indecent or obscene." - Howard Stern

"Hey, Buckwheat!"

Agent Mulder and Dana Scully strolled across a vast expanse of rural America; the sun cast long shadows on the field. Suddenly, their leisurely walk was interrupted by the unexpected appearance of a local farmer, a rugged redneck who exuded an air of skepticism.

Buckwheat, Buckweeds... Hmm, not a bad choice for a bunch of misfits. The new band name held its ground against Popface, the band I had just joined and started jamming in an empty swimming pool. Truth be told, that band didn't take a liking to me right off the bat. A meek and wimpy drummer who was more interested in his high school sweetheart and a guitarist who was just too darn temperamental. But with the bass player, it was an instant connection. Carlos, later known as Manny Montana, was a pimp from the infamous TV show "Hill Street Blues." He was a French-speaking guy born in Toulouse and was residing close to my hometown... a rough-and-tumble village southwest of Courtrai.

After just two practice sessions, Popface became a thing of the past. Manny wasted no time in finding a new drummer by scouring the local newspaper. And entered Ronny, from a god-forsaken town where the inhabitants were at the rock bottom of society. We not only secured a drummer, but he had a rehearsal space conveniently located behind his regular haunt. Without hesitation, we made the decision to bring him on board.

To inject some much-needed energy into our new band, I reached out to Jimyh Anti, a person who embodied the essence of vibrant color. We decided to bestow upon him the moniker of Jim Darky, and with this addition, our journey took flight. In a mere two months, we managed to compose an entire setlist together, both ready to take the stage and hit the recording studio.

Luckily, Manny and I possessed a burning ambition that propelled us to move forward. As we meticulously laid the foundation for our journey, Ronny found himself entangled in the chaos of his failing marriage, yet he managed to find solace on the stage in our rehearsal room. Ironically, we found ourselves a drummer who possessed the rarest quality of punctuality.

The top floor of the youth center undergoes a radical transformation, transforming into our very own recording studio. Equipped with a modest four tracks, it may be basic, but it serves its purpose of capturing the essence of our sound.

With lyrics that once thrived in an era untouched by the #MeToo movement, we proudly christen our debut record as "Ribbed for Her Pleasure." While some may label it as sexist in today's world, we view it as a homage to the extraordinary power and allure of our female counterparts. It would go on to become The Buckweeds' trademark, an emblem of our unapologetic celebration of femininity, beauty, and desire.

Manny and I shared a remarkable bond as it marked the beginning of a lewd brotherhood that would last for years. Strangely, or maybe not so, Ronny and Jimmy forged an unbreakable drinking buddy alliance that would reach the expiry date soon enough. Their boisterous fraternity clashes head-on with the rapid-fire creativity that flowed between Manny and me. Marginal Man and Darky made their exit, which paved the way for the arrival of Curtis Blow, a fellow soul from my Midnight Men days. Meanwhile, Manny introduced a new acquaintance, who, by the audacious standards of adult films, went by the name of Cunni Cox.

I adopted the stage name CQ Cooper. CQ was bestowed upon me by my British clients, who, for some reason, deemed it necessary that I purposely write my name differently than intended. Perhaps they thought the slight hint of "cock" in my name was a tad too fussy and preferred that I mask it with a touch of glamour. On the other hand, Cooper was an homage to the enigmatic and charismatic Special Agent Cooper from Twin Peaks, a television series by David Lynch that holds an unrivaled place in my heart.

In just a matter of a few months, we were reimagining our songs, creating new ones, and settling into the recording studio. We worked tirelessly to produce our 'Cool Songs to Shag On' album with lightning speed. Smokin' Troll Records, an independent label that was based in Wales (UK), became the first to release our masterpiece. With summer fast approaching, we wasted no time in planning a tour that would set the stage on fire.

But little did we know at the time that tour management was in Manny's blood. After our musical collaboration, he effortlessly established Teenage Head Music, a thriving business that specialized in organizing tours and selling merchandise. Thanks to his French connections, we were able to conquer France, a country notorious for being difficult for non-French bands to tour in. France was an essential stopover when traveling from the northern parts of Europe to the south. Without it, the 1,000-kilometer stretch between the Belgian border and the Spanish or Italian border feels like a desolate desert that only drains your finances and energy reserves.

Touring throughout Europe solidified the group's reputation as a powerhouse live act. The combination of hilarious lyrics and the band's impeccably executed set has proved to be a hit formula that left audiences in awe.

If I had to say one word that would truly encapsulate the essence of the group, it would be "attitude." The Buckweeds had an unwavering commitment to their obnoxious spirit that urged the fans to defiantly raise their middle fingers in defiance. This act of defiance became the trademark for our band, and that graced us on the cover of our latest CD, titled "What's Wrong With Attitude?" It was released under the American label "Fandango."

Our notoriety reached far and wide, and we caught the attention of numerous international bands. It wasn't long before we started receiving requests from acclaimed acts such as The Queers, Teen Idols, and Snap Her, all from the US, The Registrators hailing all the way from Japan, and our Northern Neighbors, The Apers and Travoltas from Holland. They all wanted to join forces with us on stage, drawn by our goofy but undeniably appealing presence.

The thrill of it all was somewhat dampened by my relentless pursuit of a professional career. With all this going on, I was toiling away for a few years, which eventually led to the expansion of my horizon to join Pioneer Electronics Corporation, the renowned Japanese electronics behemoth. In 1998, I was sent to Japan for extended periods of time on a regular basis. But as they say, necessity is the mother of invention. It was during this time that Manny and I concocted a brilliant plan for an epic adventure in Japan. Oh, and did I mention that I also formed a local band in the vibrant district of Ikebukuro? We called ourselves "The Salary Men From Hell" as a tongue-in-cheek nod to the typical office workers in Japan known as salarymen. Our intention was to rebel against the rigid corporate regime by creating a punk band with three talented Japanese musicians. Through our music, we managed to connect with several other Tokyo-based bands, and before we knew it, a caravan of Belgian and Japanese artists had formed, ready to join forces on an unforgettable tour together.

While staying in Belgium and getting ready for our upcoming Japanese Buckweeds Tour, we decided to immerse ourselves in the studio. It was there that we embarked on recording our tour CD, aptly titled 'Don't Worry It's Only Punkrock.' Not only would this record feature our music, but it would also showcase the talent of three incredible Japanese bands who would be joining us on our wild journey. In true Buckweeds fashion, I had a bold idea for the album's opening track – the Japanese national anthem. To my surprise and astonishment, the Japanese anthem during World War II was considered highly controversial and considered completely inappropriate. And guess what? Yours truly, being the joker that I am, ended up choosing that very anthem for our intro. Yeah, talk about a major faux pas.

As we made our way back from Japan, we made a pit stop at 'La Zone' in Liege, hands down one of the most badass venues in Belgium. Our lineup for the night included a Motörhead cover band from Liege and the wild El Guapo Stuntteam as our supporting act.

The Motörhead tunes were so damn tight that if you close your eyes, you'd swear you're at a legit concert with Lemmy himself. El Guapo Stuntteam, a bunch of misfits we would later tour with, took over the stage. Their secret weapon, Captain Catastrophe, jumped headfirst into the crowd and set everything ablaze. We stood there, completely awestruck and beaten. It was truly a sight to behold. But damn, it made me wonder. How the hell were we supposed to top that? How could we possibly outdo these guys?

In Japan, we decided to purchase authentic Japanese schoolgirl uniforms for ourselves. When it was time to take the stage, we confidently donned our outfits, which consisted of white knee socks, a blue pleated skirt that barely reached our thighs, a crisp white blouse, and a stylish blue debardeur, and to complete the look, each of us wore a vibrant pink wig. This was our moment, and boy, did we make an impact!

Even before we hit the first chord, the audience erupted when they saw us come onstage. They were absolutely ecstatic to see us up there, ready to rock. The energy in the room turned into a lunatic frenzy. We barely had the chance to catch our breath before diving headfirst into our first song.

But here's the thing - the crowd couldn't contain themselves. It was as if they were possessed. The front rows surged forward, reaching out for us with reckless abandon. And in the blink of an eye, we found ourselves being stripped down to our very underpants.

It was a wild ride, to say the least. For sure we have never experienced this before. What happened in La Zone stays in La Zone, but I can assure you the audience kept begging for more.

The Buckweeds couldn't care less for what others were thinking. Rocking out all over the globe.

Japanese tour flyer 1999.

Joe Queer and me hanging out after a show at the Lintfabriek, Kontich Belgium.

CHAPTER 11

Ragtall & Bobtail

"Fame attracts lunatics." Elton John

The Buckweeds came into existence during a time of explosive pop-punk revolution. The triumph of Green Day opened the floodgates for numerous bands to embrace this genre. Manny and I were die-hard enthusiasts of bands like Screeching Weasel, The Queers, The Vindictives, and The Teen Idols, just to name a few. The music's energy, infectious melodies, and relatable lyrics resonated with us like nothing else. It was our secret recipe for pure magic.

We poured twenty years of musical influence into our act and left no stone unturned. Holding nothing back, we allowed our goofy personalities to shine both on stage and in our lyrics. It was our way of celebrating the beauty of life in our early thirties. We believed it was the perfect moment to revel in the most precious thing: the incredible women who graced our lives.

While some may perceive our lyrics as being sexist and offensive, it was all intended to be a massive joke. We were far from being the sexist pigs. The key was always the self-deprecating humor, which made everything amusing. How else could you possibly interpret a song that boldly proclaimed, "How can I say I love you when you're sitting on my face"? Moreover, we couldn't care less about sexual orientation. Sure, we were staunchly heterosexual, but we had no qualms about belting out

"Why Ain't I Gay?" in a playful cover of the Village People's YMCA. This pop-punk vibe we embraced was heavily influenced by bands like The Nobodys, The Pink Lincolns, and Pansy Division. We played with words, put on exciting performances, and aimed to mock everything that loomed in our sight. No holds barred.

The best part was that both men and women adored our band, and we never found ourselves in sticky situations that required bailing out. However, we were often seen as a motley crew. As riff-raff and a ragtag and bobtail bunch.

Manny proved to possess an innate talent for orchestrating tours as if it was woven into the very fabric of his being. While other small bands were content with playing in their local area, he pushed us to expand our horizons and explore all of Europe. Not only did he ensure we crossed borders, but he also secured month-long tours for us, setting us apart from the rest. This allowed us to cultivate a strong live reputation and uncover a network of clubs that eagerly welcomed us whenever we rolled into town. Manny's expertise in tour management elevated us to a whole new level. It was as if Manny had beautifully planned the symphony of our success that led us from one exhilarating gig to the next, each one building on the triumphs of the last. His skillful navigation of the music scene transformed our band into a force to be reckoned with.

It not only connected us with numerous bands and their record labels who were eager to collaborate with us but also opened doors to new opportunities. As the 90s drew to a close, it just so happened that we crossed paths with the Norwegian band The Wonderfools. And together we did a series of shows across Europe. Our intention was to capture the attention of the German Radio Blast label in the hopes of securing a record deal. Although that dream never materialized, it didn't dampen our spirits. We had already caught the attention of Smokin' Troll, a cool UK punk label, which was more than enough to keep us going strong.

The Wonderfools, on the other hand, were far from being a perfect match. Right from the get-go, we could sense that we wouldn't mesh well. The Buckweeds, on the contrary, were always open to befriending anyone who treated us with fairness. But these Norwegians had such an inflated sense of self-importance and didn't even bother hiding their disdain for us despite the fact that we were the ones making it possible for them to perform. So, no matter how talented they were or how cool their songs may have been, in my eyes, their attitude rendered them completely finished. Manny and I were well-versed in playing this game, you know. We always had a saying: "Learn the game, play the game, and win the game." And let me tell you, we knew exactly how to play it. When we arrived in Barcelona to perform at Sala Magic, we knew we were in for a hell of a good time. Barcelona was like a second home to us, and we were bound to come across many familiar faces. While we were backstage, the Wonderfools proudly announced that they had scored an interview with some big-shot music magazine. Just another opportunity for them to look down on us because only "important" bands get interviewed, and we clearly didn't make the cut.

Two stunning beauties sauntered into the backstage area, and the Wonderfools made it clear that they wanted us to leave. This blatant display of disrespect called for some sweet payback. We couldn't predict how it would unfold, but we knew the opportunity would present itself. As we made our exit, I slyly whispered to one of the girls, *"These guys are so damn dull. Why don't you join us later?"* She responded with a polite smile, but her expression revealed that she saw us as nothing more than a motley crew of nobodies.

Meanwhile, we found solace at the bar, relishing in our own amusement. Half an hour later, the Vikings took the stage as our opening act. The girl I had spoken to earlier approached me and exclaimed, *"Oh my, you were right! Those guys are complete jerks. They had nothing interesting to say. Utterly boring."* My instinctive response was to slap her with an "I told you so," but instead, I offered her and her friend a round of shots. Slowly but surely, they succumbed to the intoxicating effects. We continued to engage them in conversation until it was time for us to hit the stage.

"We'll definitely check you guys out," one of them said, giggling.

As the lights dimmed and the crowd erupted in anticipation, we took the stage at Sala Magic for a homecoming show. The energy in the air was electrifying with raw power. As the first chords reverberated through the venue, the audience's excitement reached a fever pitch.

With a mischievous grin, we embraced our role as provocateurs and gave them what they had been asking for: the finger. The crowd responded by slamdancing, shouting defiantly, and thrusting their middle fingers high into the air. It was a middle finger salute to everything and everyone that had ever tried to hold us back.

In the thrilling magic of the throng, I caught sight of two girls who seemed both shocked and intrigued by the spectacle before them. Their mouths hung open in disbelief as they witnessed the unapologetic display of defiance unfolding on stage. Sensing an opportunity to draw them further into our rock and roll world, Manny and I unleashed a series of suggestive songs dedicated solely to them.

As the music washed over them, their inhibitions melted away like wax under a flame. They became one with the roaring rhythm, their bodies moving in sync. Before long, their own middle fingers joined the sea of raised hands.

As we left the stage, sweat-soaked and adrenaline-fueled, we knew what we had accomplished.

After the concert, they swarmed around us in the backstage area. *"You guys were incredible! That was an absolute blast. Why the hell did we have to waste our time interviewing those idiots?"* It was a total victory for the Buckweeds. Meanwhile, the Wonderfools were probably questioning their own foolishness. They didn't want to stick around and headed off to the place where we were all crashing. At Sala Magic, the party continued, and we sweet-talked the two women out of their underwear. They were completely into our wild and lewd behavior.

After a grueling stretch, we stumbled into the room where everyone was sound asleep. Our reckless entrance jolted them awake, their eyes flashing like bolts of lightning. *"Oh, for fuck's sake, keep it down! We're trying to get some sleep!"* they exclaimed in annoyance. Manny and I couldn't help but burst into laughter as we pulled out the interviewers' G-strings from our jeans pockets. *"Hey, the girls send their regards!"* we shouted triumphantly. We made it clear that if they ever needed someone to handle those interviewers again, we were the ones for the job, showing them how real gentlemen handle such matters.

From that point on, the Wonderfools despised us for the remainder of the tour, and we never shared a stage with them again. Good riddance.

The Bucky Boys were no strangers to this type of boy scout mischief. It was just another day at the Buckweeds office for us. We had a knack for finding ourselves in peculiar predicaments, almost as if we were magnets for the unconventional and bizarre.

During another crazy journey through Europe, our path led us to the city of Nuremberg. We were at a notorious venue known as K4, but what awaited us inside was far from what we expected. The atmosphere resembled a gathering of neo-Nazis, with skinheads making up a staggering 95% of the audience. It was a sight that sent shockwaves through our heads.

Ironically, it was during this time that we happened to be sporting our band shirt adorned with the iron cross symbol. Originating from the rebellious era of the 1960s, the iron cross had become an emblem of defiance embraced by American surfers and hot rodders immersed in the kustom kulture. Its significance was far from political, as many of these all-American kids had fathers who valiantly served in World War II. The legendary Ed Roth even offered these iron crosses and German helmets to his army of ratfinks.

Compelled by the philosophy behind this symbol, our shirt proudly displayed the words "B.F.F.B.," which stood for "Buckweeds Forever, Forever Buckweeds." It was a cheeky nod to our irreverent nature. To add an extra touch of irony, we chose to print this design on baby blue and baby pink shirts to bring about a playful vibe that contrasted with the skull of a laughing surfer gracing the back.

As soon as we erected our merchandise booth, the crowd of baldies swarmed around it like flies on buffalo chips. Each and every shirt was sold out that night, and it seemed like we had become their beloved companions for the evening. Perhaps they had arrived with the intention to disrupt the show, but they were led astray. And in their foolishness, they fell right into our cunning trap.

I have vivid memories of the support band that opened for us, the marginal El Guapo Stunt Team. They were absolutely terrified to step onto the stage, their fear evident in the air. I can't deny that I felt a similar unease, but at least they saw me as one of their own. Their set was cut short by the uproar from the rowdy skinheads demanding the Buckweeds to take the spotlight.

The rebellious salute of our raised middle fingers as we took to the stage was met with applause. Our infamy was spreading like wildfire as it gained momentum with every passing moment. Perhaps I should take solace in the fact that only a fraction of my introduction could be heard over the deafening roar of the crowd. *"Hey, ladies and gentlemen, we are the Buckweeds, and we are here tonight to rock for a cause close to our hearts, the Children's Cancer Hospital. We wish a speedy recovery to all you bald kids out there!"*

Nervous as hell, we raced through our setlist, leaving the audience begging for more. Within all the chaos and excitement, one moment stood out above all else. It was when we revealed our cover of DOA's "Let's Fuck!" to the crowd. The room exploded into a frenzy of headbanging and fist-pumping as if they had been waiting their whole lives for this exact moment.

As we rushed back for not just one but three encores, the crowd erupted with thunderous applause and screams of adoration. It was a surreal experience. "Let's Fuck" resonated long after we had gone.

After the gig, they were eager to hang out. It felt like being in another dimension. Stupidity can be quite entertaining. There was this adorable and cute skinhead girl, accompanied by her hulking monster-size boyfriend. His expressions ranged from a foolish grin to the fierce glare of a pit bull. These are the kind of crazy individuals you definitely want to avoid crossing paths with, and he was one of them. When they finally departed, another girl approached me and revealed that the sweet little skinhead wanted to meet me. *"I'm not ready to meet my maker tonight,"* I responded. However, she assured me that the monster boy *would be gone.* "She's my roommate, and we can take a taxi to our place." I'm not sure if skinhead stupidity is a contagious virus, but somehow, I found myself instantly infected by it. I bid farewell to Manny and the rest of the band, hopped into a yellow taxi, and off we zoomed.

The apartment we entered was massive, but its condition was in disrepair. Three girls shared the space, and I was personally chosen by the adorable one. *"Mmm, I've been eagerly anticipating getting my hands on you,"* she whispered. My anticipation instantly skyrocketed. Her phone illuminated, and when she answered, it was the imposing brute on the line. He wanted to come over, but she professionally brushed him off. Fortunately, my proficiency in the German language allowed me to understand her response. After hanging up, I noticed the word "pornstar" plastered all over her screen. *"That's what I aspire to be when I grow up,"* she clarified upon seeing my perplexed expression. As for expectations, mine were now reaching new heights. *"Why don't you make yourself comfortable, you cheeky devil."* I was still taken aback by her straightforwardness, but who am I to question it?

I headed towards the restroom, but as soon as I flicked on the light switch, I was confronted with a shocking reality. The walls were plastered with explicit images, each stallion adorned with a Hitler-esque mustache. It all felt so surreal, like stepping into a twisted alternate reality. Suddenly, a sliver of rationality returned to me, and I realized that I had ended up in the wrong place entirely. There was no way I could trust the girl who had assured me that her dangerous boyfriend wouldn't show up. If he were to barge in and catch us in the act, I would surely meet my maker. It was time to vanish into the cover of night, disappearing like a ghost.

In her chamber, she had created an atmosphere that was both comfortable and filled with romance. Well, at least as much as you can expect from a Nazi-inspired boudoir. *"I'll be back in a sec. Just need to grab a pack of cigarettes,"* I declared as I made my way out of the belly of the beast. The air in Nuremberg was chilly, but I knew I would survive to see another day. By the way, I don't actually smoke, and it's quite possible that SS-Nazi Barbie is still waiting for a wild encounter. Once again, it was just another day at the Buckweeds office.

CHAPTER 12

Beam Me Up, Scotty!

*"Madness has no purpose. Or reason.
But it may have a goal." – Spock*

August 6, 1996. Exactly 51 years after the devastating A-Bomb obliterated Hiroshima, The Ramones took to the stage and delivered their final performance. Just a few months earlier, they made a stop in my hometown at a gritty club named "De Kreun," which ironically translates to "moan." A humorous twist of fate. However, I found myself lacking the desire to attend the show. It's summertime, and after working away in Tokyo for too long, I craved a much-needed break. Regrettably, six months later, they officially disbanded, and I realized that I'd missed my last chance to witness their raw energy live on stage.

Time flies by, and the years slip through our fingers like sand. We watched as the world transitioned from the fear-ridden era of 1999 to the dawn of a new millennium in 2000, anxiously anticipating the chaos that was predicted to ensue. Yet, to our surprise, nothing happened. It seemed as though we had held our breath for naught. But it was not the chaos that awaited me in the new millennium.

I remember that phone call vividly, the one that changed everything. It was Dirk, the manager of De Kreun, reaching out to me. Little did I know that this seemingly innocuous stone thrown into the pond of my reality would create waves I could never have fathomed. The impact of

I 'HEARTBREAK' THE RAMONES

that call would unravel a series of events that would be beyond my imagination.

The Buckweeds were like my ride-or-die crew. We've been tearing up stages and putting on killer shows, and more importantly, we've got an album in the bag that kids really loved. We were the bunch of rebellious, foul-mouthed renegades who relived their wildest teenage fantasies of rock 'n' roll, debauchery, and all the finer things in life. And now, Dirk wanted us to open for none other than the legendary Marky Ramone and his band, The Intruders.

After The Ramones called it quits back in '96, Marky and Dee Dee briefly formed The Ramainz, but eventually, Marky ventured into creating The Intruders, showcasing his drumming genius once again. It was like a dream come true to be considered for such an opportunity. Opening for a punk rock icon like Marky Ramone is like sharing the stage with a living legend.

We were so ready to let loose our raw energy on that stageleaving the audience in awe. We would give it all our best. Crank up the volume, pounding the bass, shredding the guitar like a lightning bolt, and belt out the lyrics as if there would be no tomorrow.

January 23rd. We have a knack for rocking out, and we do it often. This club knows how to treat us right, so there's absolutely no reason to turn down this opportunity. Was I impressed by the chance to open for a Ramone? Nah, not really. I've always considered Tommy as the true heartbeat of the Ramones, while Marky was just a hired gun. Sure, Marky may have stuck around longer and played on more albums, yada yada yada, but in my eyes, he could never overshadow Tommy's impact. Let me set the record straight: I didn't see Tommy as just any Ramones drummer. He was the heartbeat of that band, the one who laid down the original rhythm that made their music come alive. Still, even if we were opening for some other lousy band, we'd bring our A-game and give it everything we had. No holding back. So, let's bring it on!

The night was alive with the unforgiving energy of the packed club. Despite the cold winter night, the heat radiated from the stage as we prepared the crowd for Mark. We set the stage ablaze, and The Intruders were killing it, and the kids were absolutely eating it up.

The evening's most extraordinary individual turned out to be a peculiar redhead with goggles, a plump and short individual who was bluntly giving an aura of filthiness. His name was Scotty, presumably derived from his assumed Scottish heritage. He was an obnoxious and vulgar character who unexpectedly took to the stage during The Intruders' performance. Engaging in a rather bizarre striptease act, Scotty captured the attention of everyone present. Despite Ben, the lead singer of The Intruders, attempting to prevent him from reaching the microphone, Marky seemed to derive immense pleasure from the spectacle, making no effort to intervene.

As the act progressed, Scotty acquired a banana, likely discovered in the backstage area. With great enthusiasm, he began to lick and suck on it, evoking imagery reminiscent of a scene from an adult film. Gradually, he shed his clothing until he stood completely butt-naked, with the banana making its way from his mouth to his posterior, inserted slowly as if performing an unconventional magic trick. Observing this perplexing display, those in the front row instinctively took a step back as they were uncertain of what may transpire next.

To the astonishment and revulsion of the audience, Scotty proceeded to remove the fruit from his rear with an assortment of simian-like noises. Displaying a complete lack of inhibition, he then went on to consume the banana in the most grotesque manner, even extending an invitation to a couple of girls to join him in this unusual gastronomic scene. With his mouth still full and ample banana remaining, he enthusiastically smeared the remaining morsels across his face. It elicited a mixture of shock and disgust from the audience.

A spectator extended a bottle of beer to Scotty, which, unfortunately, also found its way into the Scotsman from behind. As it emerged, he emptied the contents of the bottle and employed it to take a leak. Shortly after, he downed the piss-filled bottle. Just as he was about to elevate the performance and reach for the microphone once again, Ben forcefully ejected him from the stage. The audience was left stunned as their jaws dropped in amazement.

After the show, we all gathered for a friendly hangout. Ben and Johnny from the Intruders turned out to be pretty cool dudes, and Marky took on the role of a rock'n'roll godfather, commanding the flock.

I 'HEARTBREAK' THE RAMONES

In the dimly lit backstage room, Scotty stumbled in, completely intoxicated, and collapsed onto a plush armchair. The sound of his snores filled the air as Warren and I seized the opportunity to release our mischievous creativity. Armed with a black sharpie, we began to doodle on Scotty's face and transformed him into a sinister Nazi clown straight out of a B-movie. Marky, observing the spectacle, leaned back with a smirk stretching across his face. It seemed that Scotty had a penchant for engaging in outrageous acts from time to time. This Scottish rebel had a long history intertwined with the Ramones.

Warren recalled an incident in Amsterdam, where he found himself strolling through the scandalous red light district alongside CJ. Scotty decided to shed his inhibitions, dropping his pants right then and there. In front of a prostitute seductively perched in a crimson-lit window, he shamelessly indulged in instant masturbation. Unbeknownst to her, patiently waiting for her next trick, it was clear that this encounter was not going to end with Scotty splurging his hard-earned cash on the voluptuous blonde.

On a different occasion, they grant him permission to ride along with the band on their tour bus. Scotty, being Scotty, only had a small amount of luggage. Although it may seem like he's packed enough clean clothes, it turned out that his bag was filled to the brim with stag magazines and barely contained a couple of socks and underpants. Once inside the tour bus, he practically took up residence in the lavatory, always accompanied by his beloved literature. Every time he emerged from the bathroom, he would shamelessly lick his fingers clean, leaving very little to the imagination of the other passengers.

Things took an interesting turn when Warren, their tour manager, mentioned that they needed to do some laundry. I offered up my house, just a few miles away from the club, with a laundromat they could use. We all headed over, grabbed some drinks, and had a great time. But then, Mr. Nice Guy Johnny started getting a little too handsy with my wife. It really rubbed Marky the wrong way, and Warren warned me that this was becoming a serious problem. Johnny just can't keep his hands off any woman around him, and it was starting to piss off Marky in a way that Johnny couldn't even comprehend yet.

Meanwhile, Marky informed me that they require a backline for the final part of the tour, and The Buckweeds were more than willing to lend a hand. The Intruders would make use of our equipment for the rest of the tour, while I would personally retrieve our gear in Germany a week later.

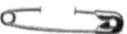

When the phone pierced through the silence of the night, I couldn't fathom who could possibly be reaching out to me. To my amazement, it was a member of the crew from the venue where we just rocked the stage.

"Hey, guys! You left one of your own behind! Can you swing by and pick him up?" I furrowed my brow, scanning the living room to ensure everyone was present. *"Nah, we've got everyone here. Who's still lingering over there?"*

"That ginger-haired, goggle-wearing, Hitler clown dude. He's part of your crew, right?" It suddenly dawned on me that they must have mistaken Scotty for one of our own. *"Nah, he's not with us. See ya!"*

In a matter of moments, the folks at the venue unceremoniously deposited Scotty and his plush armchair on the cold concrete sidewalk outside the club. Beam me up, Scotty!

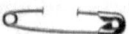

On January 30th, I encountered them in Munster, Germany. They were performing at Gleis22, a cool club that The Buckweeds have rocked before. As I stepped into the backstage room, a hard-to-ignore tension filled the air. Warren filled me in on the wild escapade that went down earlier. The audacious Johnny had gotten himself entangled with a young German fraulein who happened, as the unconfirmed story goes, to be very young, and her furious daddy came knocking for justice. Somehow, they narrowly escaped the clutches of trouble, but Marky has had it up to here with Johnny's reckless antics. It began to feel like a pressure cooker: The steam rises, and one day, it will just reach boiling point.

The final performance of this tour was insane. The German crowd was going wild, with a frenzy of pushing and shoving happening right at the front of the stage. In the chaos, I found myself in the middle of it, trying

I 'HEARTBREAK' THE RAMONES

to fend off two aggressive guys. Just when it seemed like it was getting out of control, Marky rose from behind his drum set and made his way to the front of the stage, and screamed at the top of his lungs, *"He's one of us, you motherfuckers! Back the hell off!"* It was a moment of pure solidarity that saved me from further harm. It never ceases to amaze me how people's attitudes can shift when they see you're part of a crew. But hey, who am I to argue with that?

Our backline performed admirably. Marky accompanied me on a stroll and offered a glimpse into the events of the previous week. As an impartial observer, I provided a listening ear for him to release his pent-up frustrations. I absorbed his words, attempting to offer some rational advice. He acknowledged my support, affirming, *"You're a true friend. It's been an honor playing alongside you and your band. I can't thank you enough for lending us your equipment. It truly saved us. Let's make sure to stay connected."*

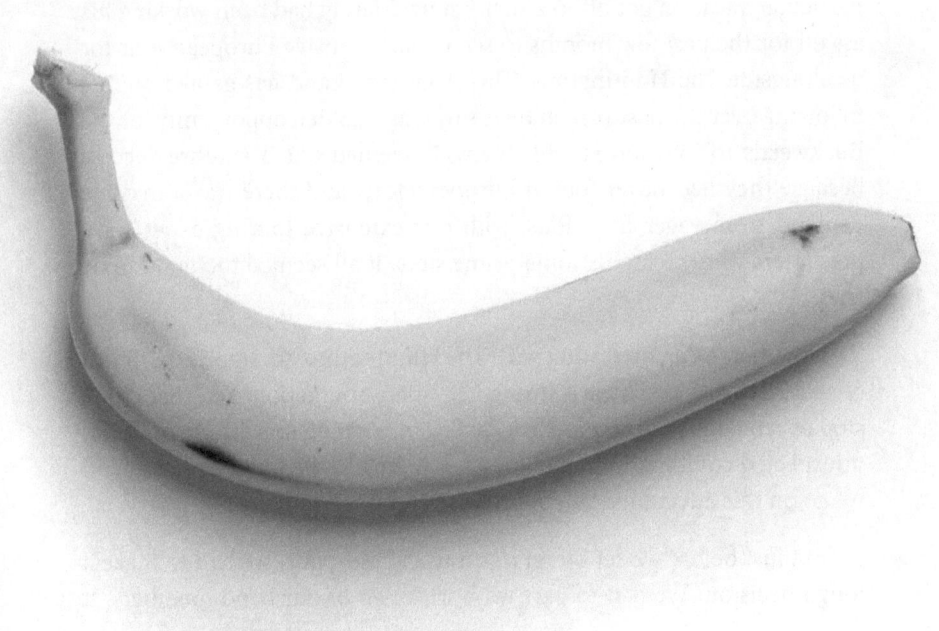

CHAPTER 13

The Eagle Has Landed

"You cannot soar with the eagles, as long as you hang out with the turkeys." - Joel Osteen

Summer had arrived, and Manny, both our families, and I took a well-deserved break in the sunny South of France. Our bond as friends had grown so strong that we now spend our vacations together. However, this particular vacation got off to a rocky start. Manny had been working his ass off for the past few months to secure an extensive European tour for us alongside The Huntingtons. This American band has gained quite a following over the past year, and we saw it as a golden opportunity for the Buckweeds to join forces with them. It seemed like a surefire success because they had never toured Europe before, and there was a massive demand from eager fans. Plus, with our extensive touring experience, promoters were giving us some prime slots. It all seemed too good to be true.

Now, here's the interesting part: The Huntingtons are signed to "Tooth & Nail Records" and have a strong Christian orientation. Yet, that didn't stop us rebellious porno punk rockers from teaming up with them. It's an unexpected combination, but hey, who doesn't love a bit of irony? So, off we go on this adventure, full of promise and uncertainty.

But just before we set off on our musical escapade, we had to make a tough decision. We had to part ways with two of our band members. It was a necessary move to ensure that we were heading into this tour with the right energy and chemistry. Sometimes, you have to let go of certain elements to make room away from negative vibes.

A couple of months earlier, Manny and I recruited two dudes from Ghent. Their names were Xavier and Steve. Xavier was a top-notch freeloader who only wanted to get paid for jamming with us. The problem was that we didn't have a drummer at the time. So, what the hell were we supposed to do? And then there was Steve, a friend of that asshole Xavier. He could shred some sick, scorching riffs, taking our "Zeke & Speedealer" level to new heights. But everything good comes with a price. Stevie had some serious screws loose in his head. He ended up getting arrested in Ghent for harassing and messing with underage Turkish girls. And since X-man was associated with him, he was shown the door, too. We thought we could manage without a second guitarist. We've been through that crap before. But on the eve of our tour, we were left without a drummer, and damn, that hit us hard.

On the front porch of Manny's cottage in the deep south, we sat down and carefully combed through a roster of drummers. The list consisted of names that had an irresistible international appeal. Our undeniable reputation as a powerhouse live band had garnered us enough respect to attract some heavy hitters. The drummer from The Queers showed genuine interest, but alas, their hectic touring schedule didn't align with our desired dates. This same unfortunate circumstance seemed to repeat itself time and time again with each potential candidate on our carefully curated list.

It wasn't until the notion arose to shoot Marky an email that things started to change. It was a simple equation: a "no" was already guaranteed, but a "yes" was within reach. It was either this or no touring at all. We didn't have much faith in this desperate attempt, but when you're desperate, you're willing to explore any avenue that might lead you out of the darkness. The response came in just a matter of days. The email sat there, unopened, as Manny and I stared at it, consumed by mixed feelings and the fear of the message it might contain. We were hesitant to unveil its contents, bracing ourselves for the inevitable "Thanks but no thanks" that awaited us inside.

Little did we realize that our correspondence had ignited a fire in someone else over in Brooklyn. Lady Marion, the wife of Marky, had been yearning for a European adventure for quite some time. And if he hadn't already agreed with her persuasive charm, it was only a matter of time before she convinced Marky to go out and jam with those charming and sympathetic European lads. The offer on the table was more than reasonable: three economy-class plane tickets and a cool thousand dollars. We didn't bat an eye at the cost. It seemed like a fair deal, and we were confident that we would quickly make up for it.

The moment the news broke that Marky would be joining us on drums, the entire tour itinerary was turned on its head. The Huntingtons went from being the headliners to the supporting act, and promoters made venue changes to accommodate a larger crowd. European clubs were eager to welcome "The Buckweeds featuring Marky Ramone." In just one simple email, our tour had taken an unexpected turn.

UPS swiftly delivered a practice CD to New York City to allow us to fully immerse ourselves in the final days of our now stressless vacation. The email notification brought immense relief and eased our stress. Manny and I wasted no time and immediately got down to business. With just a week left before the tour commenced, I made my way to Kick Backline Gear to collect a top-of-the-line DW drum kit. Thanks to Marky's endorsement deal, we gained instant access to the finest equipment available. We were completely prepared for an entire week of intense rehearsals leading up to the start of the tour.

When Marion, Mark, and Warren touched down at Brussels National Airport, they were happy to hear that the drum kit was already assembled and waiting for the first band rehearsal. Thanks to a connection with the local brass band, we were granted permission to utilize a classroom in the local municipal elementary school for an entire week. The rehearsals were no walk in the park. It was a full-time commitment, like punching in for a nine-to-five job. We kicked off each day at 9 a.m., running through the set a total of eight times every single day. As the days passed, we started living and breathing every beat until it was perfected, striving tirelessly to perfect every note and rhythm.

No one in that small-town brass band could have possibly imagined that the legendary drummer of The Ramones, an esteemed member of the Rock'n'roll Hall of Fame, would grace their humble classroom with his presence, leaving behind a lingering odor for an entire week.

As someone who may not have been the biggest fan of The Ramones, I must confess that I couldn't help but be consumed by the sheer magic of Marky's drumming. There's something about the gritty, greasy New York City accent shouting *"1-2-3-4"* and launching into the electrifying anthem of "Blitzkrieg Bop" that sends shivers down your spine. It's an absolute sensation, one that cannot be denied. It consumed me, leaving no doubt in my mind that I was in the presence of someone extraordinary.

We've got a whopping 25 gigs lined up, and Manny and I were feeling primed and ready. Marky had become the ringleader. He was a force to be reckoned with. We'd never experienced this level of intense rehearsal before, but in just one week, it whipped us into shape. Mark was an absolute pro, leaving no room for error. He was aiming to snag quotes for each show. Seven was the bare minimum he would settle for. His true expectation? Nothing short of eight. If we found ourselves stuck in a rut with a couple of lackluster sixes in a row, we better believe he'll be packing his bags while shouting, "I'm outta here." The message was loud and crystal clear.

Live at La Machine a Coudre, Marseille France
September 6, 2000

The bouncer at the door Machine a Coudre, Marseille. He owned a great record-store, Sabre-Tooth, just around the corner of the club.

The heat on stage and in the club was unbearable.
The band was close to fainting.

CHAPTER 14

Squat Della Morte

"I hope to die before I get old" My Generation – Pete Townshend

The Huntingtons made their way to Europe. Mikey and his wife Jenny were accompanied by Mike, Josh, and Cliff. This band gained quite a following in Europe, yet they left us with a peculiar impression, like a batch of undercooked potatoes. We couldn't get a grasp of who they truly were. They come across as friendly, but I couldn't help but question their authenticity. It seemed that their transition from headliners to support acts wasn't well-received. Sometimes, when you think highly of yourself, it only diminishes your stature. I always attempt to find the silver lining in people, but there are always undeniable signs and signifiers that raise doubts.

We started our journey in Germany. The first shows that followed were nothing less than electric. The energy was high, the crowds were wild, and the shows were tight. The presence of this Ramones drummer made us push our own boundaries. Powerhouse Marky undoubtedly elevated our game to newer heights, both in terms of our performance and our reputation. The tour schedule was on point and lined up with precision.

Our merchandise was selling like hotcakes, flying off the shelves faster than we could replenish them.

After Germany, we were to be heading to Switzerland, ready to showcase our spirit. Italy, France, and Spain were next on the agenda, promising even more thrilling adventures.

08/25/2000 Lehrte (DE) - Zytanien Festival
08/26/2000 Stuttgart (DE) - Che
08/27/2000 Troisdorff (DE) - JKZ
08/28/2000 Ibberburen (DE) - Scheune
08/29/2000 Geneva (CH) - Usine
08/30/2000 Munich (DE) - Backstage "Free & Easy"-Festival
08/31/2000 Vicenza (IT) - Ya Basta
09/01/2000 Montpellier (FR) – Camping ground
09/02/2000 Toulouse (FR) - Show B
09/03/2000 Palafrugell (ES) - La Bobilla
09/04/2000 Madrid (ES) - Rock Palace
09/05/2000 Madrid (ES) - Alien
09/06/2000 Marseille (FR) - Machine à Coudre
09/07/2000 Milan (IT) - Crossroads
09/08/2000 Genova (IT) - Festival
09/09/2000 Tulle (FR) - Le Salamandre
09/10/2000 Paris (FR) - Café Montmartre
09/11/2000 Courtrai (BE) - Kreun
09/12/2000 Bochum (DE) - Blackout
09/13/2000 Munster (DE) - Gleiss 22
09/14/2000 Cologne (DE) - Underground
09/15/2000 Tilburg (NL) - 013
09/16/2000 Rotterdam (NL) - StardumbRumble 2000 Festival
09/17/2000 Sint Niklaas (BE) – Kompas

From the moment they stepped onto the stage, it was evident that our fears had come true. The Huntingtons may be a talented live band, but their attitude left much to be desired. Well, not all of them, to be fair. It was Cliff who was the real troublemaker here. Right from day one, he acted like a whining, entitled brat. He carried himself as if he were the king while the rest of the Huntingtons put up with his childish behavior. Thankfully, Mikey and Jenny tried to keep their distance and refused to be dragged down by his nonsense. They knew we wouldn't stand for this kind of shit on tour.

Mike and Josh were more sympathetic to our cause, but being the newcomers, they felt like they had to tread carefully. Meanwhile, Cliff thought of himself as someone who earned some kind of special privileges just because he had been in the band longer. Little did he realize that his actions had turned him into the laughingstock of this entire tour. What a stupid American.

I could see the sinister thoughts lurking behind Warren's nerdy glasses. He was Marky's sidekick and tour manager and always ready to stir up trouble. Without wasting any time, he concocted a story about an Austrian Schnitzel House. It must have been Cliff who mentioned his craving for an authentic schnitzel at some point. Well, they say to be careful what you wish for. And so, the quest for the legendary Golden Schnitzel began.

As we arrived in Switzerland, we were met with the stern gaze of Swiss border control, who never seemed too thrilled to see bands like us rolling in. There's always a hassle when it comes to dealing with merchandise and paying VAT. Thankfully, we've learned a thing or two from Joe Queer. Well, to be accurate, he learned his lesson the hard way. The Queers had all their merchandise confiscated, and we sure as hell didn't want to make the same mistake. So, just before reaching the Swiss border, we decided to stop and book the cheapest room we could find at a Formule 1 hotel. That room served us as our makeshift warehouse, where we could stash anything that wouldn't be able to cross the border. We'd later swing by and pick it all back up after our show in Geneva.

The Usine stood before us, a colossal concert hall that dwarfs the smaller German clubs we've played. I had my doubts about filling this massive venue tonight, but regardless of the outcome, one thing was certain: they serve incredible food there. It may seem like a given that any place should offer decent food, but when you're constantly on tour, that's not always the case. Touring is a relentless assault on your stomach and intestines. Too much grease, too many fried foods, and an abundance of canned goods that you wouldn't even give to a dog. Yet, as musicians, we survive on it. So when we come across a place that serves anything remotely decent or even great, we indulge ourselves without restraint.

The only downside is that indulging in such delicacies leaves you feeling sluggish and weary. And tonight, as expected, the hall felt overwhelmingly large for our performance. Despite a turnout of a couple of hundred people, the one-thousand-capacity venue looked depressingly half-empty. It was at this moment that we collectively decided to let the Huntingtons close out the evening. Cliff felt a sense of redemption wash over him and reclaimed his honor on this stage.

Tonight was going to be one hell of a night. As the Huntingtons took the stage, Warren and Manny prepared some props to inject some serious adrenaline into their performance. With a couple of newspapers tucked under our arms, we sauntered onto the stage and took a seat on the drum riser. The crowd was perplexed, and even the Huntingtons themselves had no clue what was about to go down. But when we started flipping through the papers like we were reading some groundbreaking news, some people caught on to the joke.

We kicked it up a notch by grabbing brooms and sweeping the stage with gusto. Suddenly, it clicked for more people - they realized we were pulling off an epic prank. Josh and Mike were practically doubled over with laughter while Mikey tried to keep his focus on the singing, albeit with a struggling smile. And then there was Cliff. Oh boy, he was not amused. When I started twirling the broomstick dangerously close to him, his anger began to boil. But I didn't stop there - I pretended to strum that broom like a guitar, striking a Status Quo-worthy pose right next to him.

But that's not all. While Cliff was seething with fury, Warren and Manny snuck up behind him like stealthy ninjas and swiftly yanked down his pants. Payback time for Cliff. It may be some weird and wild practical joking, but the audience is loving it. Laughter filled the air. It was a night where rock 'n' roll met mischievous behavior and laughter, leaving everyone in stitches.

Once we wrapped up our Swiss performance, we made our way back to our cozy, little hotel room in the warehouse. It was time to gather our merchandise before embarking on our next adventure at the Backstage Festival in Munich. The memories of that festival are a blur, lost in the chaos of the moment. However, what I do recall vividly is the anticipation of what awaited us the following day as we set our sights on Italy.

Ya Basta in Vicenza turns out to be an even larger venue than the Usine. It was an old factory that had been squatted and transformed into a self-managed social center. Known for its anarchist record label and hosting concerts, this place had quite the reputation. However, as I stepped inside, it still looked and felt like a massive dump to me.

As the day dawned, the sun radiated its warmth upon us. We arrived in our van, parking directly beside the stage. The hustle and bustle of a beer truck unloading at the bar set the stage for what lay ahead. The promoter shared that tonight's event expected an impressive turnout of approximately three hundred individuals. The night's lineup commenced with a local band, paving the way for the Huntingtons, and finally, we will take the stage as tonight's headliners.

When the doors swung open a couple of hours later, the initial crowd of three hundred multiplied into a steaming horde of eager fans, totaling over a staggering thousand. And the numbers kept growing as more enthusiasts joined the ranks. In the blink of an eye, the venue was bursting at the seams, packed to the rafters with bodies energizing and ready to rock. The air crackled with a tantalizing energy, charged with raw excitement. It's evident that this gathering was no ordinary affair. As the opening band took the stage and launched into their set, a sudden announcement reverberated through the venue: the bar had completely run dry. Sold out. A wave of shock ripples through the crowd, but it quickly transformed into a roar of approval. This place was no stranger to intensity. A beer truck with God-speed made its way to replenish the depleted stash, a clear sign of how woefully underestimated the sheer magnitude of attendees truly was. It was clear that this event was not for the faint-hearted but for those craving an unapologetically primitive experience.

Right before the clock struck 11, we stormed onto the stage. The crowd was already in full swing, fueled by their pre-show libations. The resounding chants of *"Hey Ho"* grew louder and louder, creating an electric atmosphere. It was one of those moments where you just knew that the stage was about to explode.

As I reached for the microphone to start singing, four wild and unpredictable Italian girls latched onto my feet, shoes, and pants. I was instantly immobilized, anchored to a single spot on the stage. They refused to let go, their grip unyielding until the end of the show. I was literally nailed down, unable to move an inch.

All around me, I witnessed a frenzy of jumping bodies, euphoric dancing, and fearless crowd surfing. The mosh pit was chaotic and rowdy, an explosive display of raw power. These were the kind of shows that make your heart race, no matter how exhausted you may be. The adrenaline coursing through my veins pushed me into overdrive, propelling myself and the band through each song with renewed vigor.

It's moments like these that remind you why you fell in love with music in the first place. The thrill and intensity of primal power of rock 'n' roll. As sweat drips down our faces and our voices merge with the collective roar of the crowd, we realize that shows don't get better than this.

We needed a few moments to chill in the backstage room. As we stepped inside, we witnessed the Huntingtons, completely awestruck with their jaws dropped to the floor. Our performance completely knocked them out. Without any objections, we snatched their leather jackets and made our way back onto the stage for a Ramones medley at lightning speed. The crowd went absolutely insane when they caught the sight of us as if we were the legendary band straight out of the concrete jungle of NYC. Bodies blended together in a sea of movement during our five-song encore. I watched as they swayed back and forth, surrendering themselves to the music. I thought to myself, "This is a night to remember!". But I had not even the slightest clue of how things would turn out. And when I pulled all the strings of my guitar in the feedback finally it's all over. It's a wrap! *"Goodnight!"*

We were burning up, drained of energy. That's why we are out on this tour. It's a high like no other, surpassing any drug-induced euphoria you can fathom. The promoter barges into our backstage sanctuary. I flashed a grin and hollered at him... *"Damn, what a show! Loved every second of it!!"* But his expression told a different story, devoid of any joy. The deafening roar from the crowd abruptly faded, and the thunderous chants of *"Hey Ho Let's Go!"* fell silent... Something had gone horribly awry and was hitting me hard in the gut.

The promoter's eyes welled up with tears as he relayed the tragic news: an 18-year-old Italian kid had just lost his life during the encore. It was an apparent heart failure, possibly caused by a lethal dose of drugs. Trapped in the middle of the massive crowd, he had no means of escape. And so, he perished while standing upright, his body devoid of any space to even collapse. In the distance, the wailing siren pierced through the air, adding to the already overwhelming sense of despair.

Numbness consumed me as if I had been struck by a bolt of lightning. As we made our way into the hall, a haunting emptiness hung in the air. The vast space felt desolate and abandoned. The ambulance stood there, dwarfed by the enormity of the hall. Its red and blue lights continued to flash, casting an eerie glow over the scene.

And there it lay, the lifeless body in between the sea of discarded syringes and medical waste. Not even a sheet covered it yet, leaving it exposed to the harsh reality of its demise.

In a dramatic entrance reminiscent of a scene from a blockbuster film, the carabinieri storm in, their Fiat cars revving with authority. The atmosphere was thick with tension and uncertainty. The promotor was visibly concerned and warned me that this was not good news. We were all trapped, unable to leave until the arrival of a magistrate who would initiate the investigation. It is only at his discretion that we would be granted our freedom.

When Warren approached me, I noticed that Marky & Marion were nowhere to be found. He informed me that upon receiving the news, they reacted swiftly. Taking a practical approach to the situation and chose not to get involved and instead made their escape by squeezing through a gap in the fence. From there, they hailed a taxi and bolted off to the hotel. Meanwhile, we were left stranded here and left to endure the uncertainty and anxiety.

The atmosphere was charged with tension. Many of the volunteers who were involved with the squat were also unable to leave. Things took a turn for the worse when some squatters began complaining that this situation was reasonable enough for the authorities to shut down the squat. *"Screw your squat, you idiots! What about this kid who might not live to see tomorrow? What about his girlfriend, his parents...?"* My comments were met with complete disdain. I retreated to the safety of the van. The hostility became so intense that I could feel myself on the verge of a physical altercation. The crazy thing was that my words seemed to have deeply offended people. Years later, I still stumble upon posts on certain websites where individuals are actively calling me an asshole. It's almost like a backhanded compliment. Every now and then, I catch a glimpse of that kid again, lying on the freezing floor. I hope you enjoyed every moment, Hope you had the time of your life, kiddo!

The following day, as we hopped into the van and hit the road from Vicenza, Marky, and Marion pounced on us with questions about the latest happenings. Boy, oh boy, we should've stuck around! But what was really grinding my gears was how the Huntingtons were acting. All they cared about was whether their precious name would be spelled correctly in the newspaper. Talk about hypocrisy! These guys were parading around with a bunch of holy bibles crammed into their suitcases, but it seemed like compassion and charity were nowhere to be found. Hallelujah! Praise the Lord! They sure know how to put on a show.

Spain I presume.

La Spezia
September 8, 2000
Oh What a show!

Germany no doubt!

CHAPTER 15

Biker Shindig

"Life should not be a journey to the grave with the intention of arriving safely in a pretty and well preserved body, but rather to skid in broadside, in a cloud of smoke, thoroughly used up, totally worn out, and loudly proclaiming, 'Wow! What a Ride!" - Hunter S. Thompson

We were just a few days into our journey, and we already had a casualty under the belt. I couldn't help but wonder what challenges lay ahead. It seemed like trouble was always lurking around the corner. This time, it came in the form of a fuel distribution strike in France. Our carefully planned logistics were now thrown into disarray, putting immense pressure upon the crew. Determined to stay one step ahead, we managed to refuel right before entering the French border, hoping that it would be enough to sustain us for the next couple of days. Undeterred by this obstacle, we continued to push forward, crossing borders as we made our way towards the vibrant city of Montpellier.

This upcoming venue was a complete enigma to us. Someone had booked us, but the information we had was minimal at best. The sense of mystery intensified as we arrived at the designated location and found ourselves in the middle of nowhere. All that surrounded us was swampy fields. However, our concerns were alleviated when a beat-up car pulled up shortly after our arrival. A couple emerged from the vehicle and instructed us to follow them into the barren wasteland. We follow them on a ten-minute ride along rough, unpaved dirt roads until we finally reach a deserted camping ground that resembles something out of the Manson Family commune. The lodging consisted of tents, cabins, and dilapidated buses, forming a makeshift lodging. The outdoor stage, though small and improvised, stood in contrast to the massive stages we've performed on in recent halls.

Marky and Marion despised it immediately. *"We're not gonna stay here. We don't wanna sleep here. Get us to a damn hotel."* they demanded. I left it to Warren to handle the promoters, and luckily, everything went smoothly. The strange duo went quickly to find themselves a hotel nearly while we started our preparations to get ready for the soundcheck.

One hour later, we receive an invitation to the most extravagant feast. A grand buffet awaits, filled with mouthwatering barbecued delights and the intoxicating aroma of fresh herbs. The air is permeated with the scent of delicious wine and the enticing fragrance of freshly baked bread. It was a culinary experience fit for champions!

As we indulged in this extravagant meal, the promoters joined us at the table. They could sense our apprehension, fearing that our hidden gem of a location may go unnoticed. But they reassured us with laughter and words of encouragement, assuring us that there was no need to worry. And they were absolutely right.

As night fell, we lost track of the number of heads in attendance. This show was sold out. We revealed our set upon the French airwaves. The sound system was a bit rough around the edges and lacking in quality, but none of that actually mattered. Everyone was caught up in the moment, having the time of their lives.

After the show, the celebration continued with an abundance of wine and top-notch weed making its appearance. Lost in a haze of euphoria, someone pulled me into a vintage school bus. The makeshift bed inside felt surprisingly soft, yet my intoxicated state prevented me from caring too much. As I surrendered to the embrace of sleep, psychedelic dreams awaited me, like an avant-garde concert for my mind.

Our next destination was Toulouse, where we geared up for a gig at Show B. This one had been on our radar for a while, and we were beyond excited. The show was being hosted by a buddy of ours, so we knew it was going to be just great.

Gildas Cosperec, the editor of Dig It! Magazine and promotor of the show, later wrote: "When it comes to the live show, it took off at full throttle, leaving the audience in awe and crashing against the walls with sheer force. It's felt as precise as a Swiss cuckoo clock, with riffs that exploded like fireworks. Leading the charge was none other than Marky, driving the machine with unparalleled intensity. There was no time for breaks between songs, as the former drummer of the Ramones launched into the next one without skipping a beat. 1-2-3-4, Manny and Nick responded with deadly precision down to the millimeter. This was an ultimate well-rehearsed and unstoppable force. As the night drew to a close, they uncovered a powerful medley of Ramones covers. Marky stood out, commanding attention, and delivered a spectacular performance from behind his drum kit."

The Toulouse afterparty raged on until the break of dawn. Luckily, the Spanish border wasn't too far away, and we even managed to squeeze in a visit to the Salvador Dali Theatre Museum in Figueres. Marky wasn't very intrigued by art, though. It was the first time I'd noticed this about him, but it became more apparent as we explored the old towns of various European places. Maybe it's different for Americans, where history only stretches back a little over two hundred years.

Our quest for La Bobilla proved to be quite the challenge. Palafrugell, a village on the Catalonia coast, became a maze as the directions led us to some industrial wasteland. To our dismay, we ended up at an abandoned warehouse that bore no resemblance to a venue whatsoever. Adding insult to injury, the place was completely deserted. There wasn't a single soul expecting us here. The situation worsened when our repeated attempts to reach the promoter went unanswered. Our calls went unanswered and left us feeling stranded and frustrated.

Finally, we received a call from an unfamiliar and unlisted number. To our astonishment, the person on the other end informed us that we had arrived a day too early. Our performance is scheduled for the following day. It was hard to believe that Manny made a mistake in our carefully planned itinerary. He was known for his exceptional organizational skills, and he carefully arranged this entire tour. To double-check, we contacted the Rock Palace in Madrid to confirm their expectations for the following day. They verified our scheduled performance, which meant that someone made an error for today. In situations like these, it doesn't matter that a problem has arisen; what truly matters is finding a solution.

Fifteen minutes later, the promoter arrived. Surprisingly, the promoter turned out to be a young man in his late teens. Initially, I doubted whether he would approach the situation professionally. However, both he and his girlfriend displayed an incredible level of determination that proved my initial judgment wrong.

"My uncle owns a pizzeria downtown. Let's go there. We'll treat you and the entire crew to dinner - all you can eat." The young promoter suggested, "In the meantime, we'll brainstorm and come up with a plan."

This was somewhat reassuring. Going on tour can be quite costly. Finding accommodations and covering food expenses can take a significant chunk out of our earnings. Having a day off may seem like a relief, but it also means losing out on potential income. Luckily, we didn't have to worry about food expenses for today.

I watched as the youthful pair settled into a secluded corner of the eatery. They were on their phone throughout, continuously scrolling through extensive contact lists. Meanwhile, our food transported us away from the impending challenges, while the wine enhanced our sense of ease. It's a game of chance. Sometimes you win, sometimes you lose.

An hour passed, and we were completely stuffed with food, and the alcohol hit us hard. The couple we met earlier informed us that it was time to head back to the club. So we got our thing and did a soundcheck.

"What do you mean by setting up and soundcheck? There isn't going to be a show tonight, right?" I asked in confusion. "Don't worry, just come with us," they replied confidently.

We had no idea what to expect, but if they were willing to let us perform tonight, it meant we'd be getting paid, and they'd provide us with a place to crash. Who are we to argue? We go along with it.

A few moments later, we arrived at the venue. It was already open, and a group of about a dozen young people were busy setting up the sound system while our crew unloaded our equipment. It was around the time we would have started our show, but instead, we were preparing for a soundcheck. As we played a couple of songs, we noticed people starting to arrive. By the time we finished, some twenty minutes later, there was a line forming outside the club. I've never witnessed anything like that before. In just a few hours, these youngsters have managed to rally a couple hundred of their friends.

Just after midnight, it was finally our turn to take the stage. The energy in La Bobilla was explosive, to say the least. Whether it was announced or not, the kids in Palafrugell were ready for a good time, and they got it.

It wasn't every day that I witnessed promoters going above and beyond, but these individuals took it to a whole new level. They didn't just walk an extra mile; they went the distance of an entire marathon and then some. Their dedication and commitment were truly extraordinary.

The adrenaline rush we experienced from this performance filled us with an immense surge of energy that propelled us forward as if we were effortlessly gliding through the back-to-back shows in the heart of Spain's capital. We graciously allowed the Huntingtons to take the spotlight as the headliners of these gigs.

The strange location and deserted situation had also surprised some fans who would become long-time friends. Anna and Alfredo recall: "When we learned that Marky Ramone was playing with a band called the Buckweeds in a town about 100 kilometers away from home, we decided to drive all the way to see them. They were on a European Tour with The Huntingtons, the American band that had recorded one of the very first Ramones tribute albums, Rocket to Ramonia, a couple of years before. As soon as we got there, Palafrugell, in Girona, Catalonia, we noticed there was nothing around to confirm the show… no posters, no signs on walls. We didn't even know if the venue really existed, La Bòvila, and nobody seemed to know what it was or where it was. Eventually, someone told us about a place a few minutes away from the town where "sometimes" and "some people" had "parties." There we went; we drove along a dirt road for a while until we found a building that seemed abandoned… nobody around, absolute silence. There were four of us, and the two guys stepped out of the car to see if there was any sign of life there. The girls waited for them inside the car. One or two minutes later, they came back running and shouting *"open the doors!"*. Luckily, we did, as two huge Dobermann dogs were chasing them; in fact, we just missed them!

We fled but went back after some time, and the dogs seemed to be gone. After ten minutes wondering whether that could be the place, we saw a van approaching, and decided to ask for some directions. The doors opened, and to our surprise, Mr. Marky Ramone, yes, a Ramone in flesh and blood, got out of the van…"

During our time in Madrid, our crew was fixated on unraveling the complexities of a very ingenious scam. It was evident that the Ramone brand carried substantial worth, and more often than not, Marky possessed the savvy to capitalize on it. Occasionally, there were fleeting moments when we had the chance to ride in the slipstream. Among those moments, the pinnacle of excitement was the infamous Hardrock Cafe scam. Whenever we touched down in a new city during our tour, one question would inevitably arise: *"Does this place have a Hardrock Cafe?"* If the answer was affirmative, I knew exactly what to do. I'd search for their phone number and make the call.

"Is this the Hardrock Cafe? Would you be so kind as to get me the manager, please?"

Moments later I got connected to the manager's office.

"Hello, this is Nick Cooper speaking. I am calling you on behalf of the management of Marky Ramone of The Ramones. We are in town for a show tonight, and I wondered if you guys could cater to us tonight. We will be bringing over some merchandise."

It always did the trick. Well, almost always. The Madrid branch was the stingiest of them all, but everywhere else, they fell for it without hesitation.

Whenever our group of hungry musicians arrived, usually consisting of eight to ten of us, the routine kicked off. We would charm the manager, snap some photos, trade merchandise, and then make our way to the table where we could indulge in a lavish feast. Except in Madrid, where we were only offered cocktails, there seemed to be no limit to what we could order elsewhere. However, Amsterdam took the cake when it came to Hard Rock Cafés. Not only did they invite us back for desserts after our performance, but our evenings of excessive indulgence always ended with a generous $50.00 tip for the waitress. A mere pittance compared to what we had raked in.

The undeniable excellence of Amsterdam, particularly the exceptional manager named Pilar, became abundantly clear when I returned to the city months after our tour. As I entered the restaurant, I made it a point to inquire about Pilar's whereabouts and promptly presented her with a collection of cherished photographs from our previous visit. To my astonishment and delight, I was once again lavishly pampered, completely free of charge. This extraordinary gesture served as a testament to the unrivaled hospitality and unwavering commitment exhibited by Amsterdam and its remarkable staff, epitomized by the incomparable Pilar.

Our return to France was eagerly anticipated, particularly in Marseille, where we had established quite a notorious reputation. This Mediterranean harbor city carried a violent reputation, with the streets ruled by the mafia. It is within this gritty environment that we found ourselves immersed in a raw and exhilarating atmosphere during previous shows. We could hardly contain our excitement at the prospect of arriving at La Machine A Coudre, aptly nicknamed "The Sewing Machine." The club's intimidating black bouncer happened to be a close friend of ours, and he also happened to own the finest record store in town.

I couldn't help but wonder if they named this place the Sewing Machine as a nod to the iconic NYC venue, The Knitting Factory. But honestly, who gives a damn? This joint was teeming with the wildest creatures of the night. Marseille would raise its proud middle finger in approval. The club was jam-packed with a sea of bodies. Our support band, the Christian horde, kept the energy up for a mere twenty minutes. The crowd didn't mind their premature exit. Everyone scrambled outside, craving a breath of fresh air. Meanwhile, inside the club, condensation drips from the ceiling, creating a surreal atmosphere of tears.

That day, we were stoked to hit the stage. We were halfway through this tour, so we've amped up our set and played with military precision, leaving no room for hesitation. But damn, it's scorching hot up there. Suddenly, in the middle of a song, I saw Manny's world go dark. He blacks out for just a few seconds. And before he even hits his knees, I witness his eyes snap open, hitting every note without missing a beat. This was not a journey for the faint-hearted. It takes guts and resilience to rock this hard.

An hour passed by, and we resembled individuals who spent a considerable amount of time submerged in a steaming hot tub. We socialized with our eccentric weirdo acquaintances outside the establishment. Having undergone the chaotic ambiance of a city overrun by the mob, we now find ourselves eager to venture back into the depths of Italy once more. This time, however, our destination was embraced by a different kind of alliance—the most infamous motorcycle gang in the world. The Crossroads Club in Milan serves as the headquarters for the notorious Hells Angels. I must retrieve my cherished Lyn Lyn, City of Sin sweater, for this occasion. Donning an "81" support patch will grant us entry into their realm.

It was clear that The Huntingtons were completely out of their element when it came to the venues we performed at. As a band with Christian inspiration, I can't help but think they're used to playing only all-ages shows and church dances, and I'm pretty sure my assumption isn't too far off. They seem pretty terrified if you ask me. But that fear doesn't dissipate once we realize that the Hells Angels have their own set of rules on their home turf. Tonight was an exclusive biker night, and punks are strictly prohibited. And there's no room for negotiation on that.

Once inside the club, my support patch granted me an introduction to the local chapter president. He warmly welcomed us, and it felt genuine and sincere. This wasn't some phony reception. We were even allowed to use their office to catch up on some much-needed communication with our loved ones back home. And in the meantime, we discovered that Italian biker cuisine is an absolute delight. It was a real treat for the taste buds, no doubt about it.

It was clear as day that we were the main act tonight. The crowd was wild, and when we reached the Ramones medley, I made a spontaneous decision to have Sheena portray a Hell Angel instead of her usual

145

headbanger self. The rowdy bikers, I went absolutely nuts for it, loving every moment. Manny was having a blast during the show, but as a trio on stage, we each have our roles to fulfill. However, Manny was slacking off on his backing vocals, and I shot him a skeptical glance. Come on, buddy, I can't carry this whole performance on my own. Yet, Manny completely disregarded me. Completely.

After our performance on stage, I delivered a swift kick to his ass with my sneaker. As he spun around, his eyes blazed with anger. Within the confines of the backstage room, he retaliated by landing a punch right on my nose. Reacting instinctively, I swung my gold top guitar and struck him squarely in the face. In an instant, chaos ensued as we found ourselves locked in a fierce brawl.

The backstage room, more accurately described as a pantry, was stocked with the whole booze stock but also boxes filled with new drinking glasses. Seizing an opportunity, Manny grabbed one of those boxes and began hurling glasses in my direction. The sound of glass shattering reverberated throughout the room. The impact against the wall shattered us into countless fragments. Some shards collided with me head-on, leaving me with bleeding cuts and bruises. Curiously, Marky stood by and observed without intervening. It appeared as though he derived some twisted pleasure from the unfolding spectacle. After what felt like an eternity, when the dust settled and we found ourselves standing amidst the wreckage, Marky broke the silence, "Did anyone get this on film?"

But we must return to the stage for the encores. My body was drenched in blood. A few of the Hells Angels who witnessed the scene wore smirks on their faces. This was pure entertainment. It's what will earn us the reputation of being as tough as nails. The Huntingtons have never witnessed anything like this at their tame church gatherings.

As the night wore on, Manny and I found ourselves seated outside, completely drained from this relentless tour. We may be best friends, but we never anticipated becoming blood brothers. It's funny how things can reach a breaking point out of sheer frustration. Our anger wasn't directed at each other, though. No, it was the incessant pestering from some of the Huntington crew that's been getting to us, especially that annoying Cliffy, and the constant whining from Marky, which we were not used to dealing with. However, sitting there on the curb, we managed to regain our sanity. Soon enough, we find ourselves back on the same page, ready to conquer Geneva together.

Genova is a town that bears some resemblance to Marseille, with its own unique charm. Just like Marseille, it is a harbor town that carries a similar questionable reputation. Our presentiment for the upcoming show at the Fitzcarraldo was obvious, and we were eagerly awaiting the chance to reunite with our Italian friend who fronted the incredible band, The Manges, hailing from the city of La Spezia. Kicking off the night, a local band called the Warriors took the stage, and instantly, we were hit with a sense of déjà vu reminiscent of our experiences in La Machine A Coudre. The venue itself was sweltering, making it challenging to find comfort in such intense heat. However, the memory of how the crowd responded lingers vividly in my mind, and I can confidently say that this show ranks among the absolute best of the entire tour.

The Spanish Connection: Dolores Cubero, Anna Piella Castells, Alfredo Cordero, Marky, Manny, Me and Xevi Zoroa

Mr. Cabdriver take us to
the Hardrock Cafe!

The Hardrock Cafe Madrid.
Only cocktails are for free. Bummer!

In the Hardrock Cafe Amsterdam, we got treated like royalty.
Restaurant Manager Pilar was the best!

CHAPTER 16

Destination Schnitzel Haus

"I'd say I'm a good cook. I have a lot of German recipes that I can make schnitzel, meatballs and things with cabbage. I love cabbage." - Heidi Klum

The turmoil in France caused by the strikes at fuel distribution centers became a constant source of headaches for us. We've managed so far by crossing borders and refueling in neighboring countries. However, when it came to our journey from Marseille to Italy, we had to get inventive. There wasn't enough gas to make it to the Italian border. Thankfully, we found a solution by renting a van. Rental companies are required to provide the rented vehicle with a full tank so we can reach our next gig.

As we traveled, we came up with a clever idea. We purchased plastic bags typically used for transporting wine and filled them with gasoline on our way back to France. This way, we could refuel our own vans again. Of course, we had to pay the fine for returning the rental van with an empty gas tank, but it was a small price to pay to keep the show on the road. Problem solved.

We held on to high hopes of reaching our upcoming French shows, praying that the fuel blockades would disappear any day now. In fact, for our show in Tulle, we even negotiated that part of our payment would be made in fuel. Who would have ever imagined such a bizarre turn of events?

Solving problems became our specialty, no doubt about it. We didn't rely on any fancy tour managers or booking agents to handle things for us. We took matters into our own hands, even though it meant carrying a heavy burden on our backs. But you know what? We thrived under the pressure. If anything went wrong, there was no one to blame but ourselves. As the tour went on, it became clear that Marky had never experienced anything quite like this before. I started to wonder if even the Ramones had to deal with things on this level. Regardless, Marky was initially annoyed and unsure of how we would keep things going. But as time passed, he came to realize that we had everything under control. Taking care of business became our trademark, a key factor in our future success. It remained a key factor in the tours to follow.

Warren, who joined Marky and Marion on this tour, brought a wealth of experience with him. While he was a valuable asset, it was Manny and I who truly worked our magic behind the logistic scenes. Warren, however, proved to be an essential member of the team. He had an uncanny ability to anticipate Marky's trouble before it even hit us, whether it came in the form of unreasonable demands or unattainable expectations. Not only that, but Warren had a razor-sharp wit and a knack for sarcasm that kept us entertained throughout the journey. He particularly enjoyed poking fun at the Huntingtons, making it clear that he was firmly on the side of the Buckweeds gang. Marky had a knack for teasing Warren, always poking fun at him. When you're on the road for weeks, privacy becomes a luxury. You get to know each other's best qualities, but also the flaws. Marky had a voracious appetite that couldn't be tamed. He would devour anything that caught his eye without a second thought. Warren, tired of his food disappearing, resorted to writing his name on every item in his luggage and in the trunk. But to no avail, the food continued to vanish.

One day, Warren caught Marky red-handed, munching on a chocolate bar in the front seat of the bus. Frustrated, he snatched it away from Marky's grasp and exclaimed, *"Marc, my goddamn name is written all over this! How could you possibly eat it without noticing?"*. Marky, with an air of indifference, simply replied, *"I can't read!"*. And just like that, the case was closed. In a bizarrely charming way, Marky managed to escape any consequences for his insatiable hunger. He always got away with his gluttonous behavior in a way that was oddly endearing.

Warren wasn't the only one who fell victim to his practical jokes. Marky enjoyed playing tricks on Marion as well. She always kept a watchful eye on him, which wasn't always to his liking. So, whenever he spotted an opportunity, he would try to escape her gaze.

One day, while we were on the road, nearing the city where to perform that night, he said to me, *"Nick, she wants to go to the hotel."* Marion, who had overheard our conversation, retorted, *"Marc… 'SHE' has a name, you know."* Unfazed, without even a hint of a smile, he responds with a straight face: *"Nick, the crackhead wants to go to the hotel."* Once again, he managed to get away with it. It sounded heartless, downright cruel, and asshole-ish, but I have to admit that, from what I observed and felt, there was an unbreakable bond between those two. Somehow, their way of coexisting must have worked, and it still does to this day. In the world we live in today, that kind of connection can be considered a remarkably strong marriage. I have to give them credit for that.

Back in France, we made our way to the Bar Salamandre in Tulle. This place felt more like a quaint countryside café, definitely not big enough to host our gig. But hey, it's a welcome pit stop between the South of France and Paris, where we're headed next. So, instead of having a day off, we settled for this small joint. It was to come with a small fee, but at least we'll have a roof over our heads and plenty of grub.

The crowd tonight was mostly made up of locals, and there were not a whole lot of die-hard punk fans in sight. We were just another one of those events that the regulars saw as a way to pass the time. They were tolerating us as long as they didn't have to give up their daily dose of cheap booze. As soon as we stepped foot in the bar, you could feel the tension in the air, ready to explode. And when we finally hit the stage, it was clear that this place was too cramped, too rowdy, and just too damn intense for the folks from this backwoods region. That's when things started to get dicey. Manny later recounted, "There was this lunatic who whipped out a massive Bowie knife with an eight-inch blade—I kid you not—and just started slashing and stabbing at random. Some poor guy got sliced open." And just like that, the show came to an abrupt end. Cue the arrival of cops and ambulances, and all hell breaks loose. Time to get the hell out of Dodge. The road was calling our name once again.

Our next destination brought us to the city of Paris, the City of Light. We made our grand entrance at the Café Montmartre. The streets of this metropolis proved to be chaotic and challenging, resulting in a fashionably late arrival. Unfortunately, we missed the load-in time and soundcheck, leaving us scrambling to catch up with the support band already rocking the stage. What's more, there isn't even a stage here. We will be performing at ground level, right alongside the audience. It's not ideal, but it's a clear indication of the laid-back French attitude. They couldn't care less. We should be grateful they've allowed us to perform at all. I can't help but reminisce about last year when we played on a boat floating along the enchanting River Seine with the Buckweeds. As we rushed through our set tonight, I found myself yearning to be back in that magical setting. But that's just how it goes sometimes. No use being a crybaby! Vive la France!

And so, we find ourselves back in our homeland, with a pitstop in Paris. We touch down in Courtrai, where we make a special appearance at the famous Popcenter record store and rock the stage at the Kreun Club. It was at this very venue that our adventure began, as we had the chance to open for Marky and The Intruders. It feels like destiny has come full circle.

Tonight, it was a homecoming match, and we refused to let anyone else steal the spotlight. It was time to celebrate with our loyal friends by our side. But that's not all – we have a surprise in store. Joining us on stage is none other than KPW, the mastermind behind the International 1-2-3-4 Ramones Compilation. He graciously invited us to contribute a song to this record.

Speaking of legends, KPW was a renowned Belgian musician. His journey as a musician began in 1977 when he picked up the bass for one of Belgium's pioneering punk bands, The Misters. Rumor has it that he was one of the lucky few to get his hands on the very first Ramones album when it hit the streets of Belgium. Needless to say, he's a true Ramones aficionado. We couldn't be more honored to have him join us on stage. Besides, the club also brought sweet memories to him since he got married there. What better place to rock out, right?

The pitstop In Belgium was nothing more than a fleeting moment. After spending a single night back home with our kin, we still had two

I 'HEARTBREAK' THE RAMONES

more legs to conquer on this adventure. In just a matter of days, we'll be setting our sights on the Netherlands, but first, we attack the Germans in our rock'n'roll blitzkrieg. The memories of the Blackout Club in Bochum are a bit hazy, but the place where we landed on day two of the German invasion holds a special place in my heart. This is the Gleiss 22 venue in Munster, where I formed an alliance with Marky during the Intruders tour. I had come to pick up the Buckweeds' backline, and little did I know that this place would feel like a second home to both the band and Marky. When you perform in the same venues multiple times, you start to make local friends, and seeing them at each show adds to the sense of belonging. The Munster Hall was no different. As we prepared for our last show in Germany, the familiarity of the surroundings became a home away from home.

The joke about The Schnitzel House was starting to lose Its edge. Cliffy Huntingtons was now convinced that we were playing a prank on him, and we couldn't come up with any more material to keep the story going. However, as we cruised down the German autobahn, we suddenly found ourselves stuck in a frustrating traffic jam. Our tour bus attracted a lot of attention, and we started making silly faces at a kid sitting in the back of a Volkswagen Beetle. Poor kid was squished between two not-so-attractive aunts in the backseat while his parents were upfront. With the traffic crawling along, we decide to have some more fun. The Huntingtons are in the lead van, and we're following closely behind. I step out of our car and make my way towards their vehicle. I had a little surprise for Cliff – a pornographic VHS tape we discovered backstage at our previous gig. We kept it on hand, knowing it would come in handy someday. Cliff was actually excited to receive this unexpected gift. As I walked back to our van, he eagerly tore off the wrapping, only to realize that it was an unholy present. In disgust, he hurled it out of the window.

Just when we thought this hilarious adventure was coming to an end, I witnessed the German kid stepping out of the vehicle to retrieve the tape. He swiftly picked it up and made his way back to the family car. In a matter of moments, screeching brakes pierced the air, and the car door swung open, revealing an enraged, beet-red-faced German who shouted at us while angrily tossing the tape in our direction. It seems the explicit anal backdoor education movie was already a part of his personal collection. Cliff glared at us with utter disgust and bellows, *"You guys deserve this!"* But then, as if by some divine intervention, on our right side, we glide past a massive eatery named... you guessed it... The Schnitzel House! It was as if the heavens themselves had come to our rescue. A sign from above, a stroke of luck bestowed upon us by the rock gods themselves. We've been saved by a higher power.

Last show in Germany. The Underground in Köln has always been a pleasure to visit. It was one of those venues that knew how to run things smoothly, with its very own restaurant and band apartment. And here's the kicker – the numerical code to the lodging is "4711," which practically screams, "Look at us!" 4711 happens to be the most iconic Kölnisch Wasser or Eau de Cologne there is.

We take the stage by storm, absolutely owning the place. The weather was on our side, enticing us to spend most of the night outside in the courtyard. The devout Christians of the Huntingtons had already said their bedtime prayers and were peacefully asleep. However, Chris and Josh were busy defying the Christian norms and thawing their icy restraint. Their curiosity for German female fans knew no bounds. Warren and I playfully goad them on, pushing them to be more and more outspoken. They were so ready to reveal their uncensored thoughts. Two German bombshell beauties joined in the fun and decided to play along, teasing them with glimpses of what lies beneath their panties. It's pure comedic gold. It's an uproarious spectacle. Those Catholic boys turned as red as roses, leaving them blushing into the night, unable to escape their embarrassment.

The Netherlands was just a stone's"thro' away from the German border, and our itinerary was slowly reaching its conclusion. We found ourselves in the Batcave room at Tilburg 013, an intimate hall with a limited capacity. 013 was a venue that hosted many international touring bands. Being scheduled in the Batcave was a special treat. It's not too small, but definitely not too big either. Tonight's show promises to be jam-packed, with the fans standing just inches away from us. This proximity always adds an extra layer of excitement to the experience. It was at this club that I met Bram van Schaik, an influential Dutch reporter. "For years,

I've always had a soft spot for small venues. Small venues may not have the glitz and glamour of large arenas, but they hold a certain magic that can't be replicated. There's something about the intimate atmosphere that brings out the best performances. And that's exactly what I experienced at the Batcave in 013, Tilburg. It was like being in a gritty underground sewer, but in the best way possible. You were practically face-to-face with the band, feeling every chord and beat reverberate through your body.

I'll never forget that day, September 15th, 2000, when I stepped foot into the Batcave to see The Huntingtons for the very first time. Alongside them were The Travoltas, a Dutch band that has always held a special place in my heart. But there was another band on the lineup that caught my attention – The Buckweeds from Belgium. Little did I know at the time, but they had a hidden gem behind their drum kit – none other than Marky Ramone himself.

It was mind-blowing to think that this legendary drummer, who had played in front of 45 thousand people at the farewell concert of The Ramones in Buenos Aires, was now gracing this obscure venue with his presence. The energy and passion he brought to that small stage was electrifying. Even though I don't remember much about the actual concert, I do recall a moment when he walked right past me on his way to the backstage area. It was a surreal experience, witnessing a rock 'n' roll icon up close in such an unconventional setting", he wrote about that night in Tilburg.

The following day, we will be sharing the stage with some Incredible bands. They were all there, present and ready to rock. After the gig, we hit the road and made our way to Rotterdam, where we would be spending the night at the Stardumb headquarters. These guys were the epitome of Dutch punk multitaskers. They not only run a record label but also publish a fanzine and perform in multiple bands. They have been true friends of the Buckweeds for quite some time now. In fact, one of them even stepped in as our drummer during a previous tour. Rotterdam feels like a home away from home to us, and we are always welcomed with open arms.

Since we don't have to go anywhere, we've got plenty of time to chill and check our emails. The busy Catholic crew had already claimed all the available computers, so all we could do was wait until they were done.

Finally, when we got our chance, Warren realized that their email account hadn't been closed. We've got instant access to their inbox. We couldn't help but crack up as we read through all the polite back-and-forth messages between the Huntingtons and well-behaved kids. And wouldn't you know it, a request for a gig comes in. It's an invite to some lame Christian dance. Warren decided to respond: "Hey! Where the hell do you get the nerve to ask us to play your pathetic church dance? Don't you know we're currently on a Church Burning Tour in Europe with the infamous porno rockers, the Buckweeds? When we return to the United Satanic States, we'll come pay you a visit. Rest assured, we'll tear your head off and shit down your throat. Your loyal servant of Satan, Cliff Huntington." We burst out into laughter and practically piss ourselves from laughter. We couldn't wait for the Huntingtons to discover our prank.

In the meantime, we head over to the festival spot. That's where we linked up with some other Italian buddies of The Retarded who were gonna kick off the show. We get wasted before we hit the stage, feeling the buzz in our veins. As the first song's opening riff blares through the speakers, I attempt to balance on two monitors in front of my mic stand. But hey, even I can't defy gravity. Those monitors gave way, and I came crashing down, hard, flat on my back. But that ain't gonna stop us. We're here to rawk and that's exactly what the audience will get. The setlist was ingrained in our souls after weeks of nonstop touring. We play without hesitation, lost in the moment. After all the previous shows, it's become like second nature to us – we eat, sleep, breathe the setlist.

And now we found ourselves at the final performance. We've returned to Belgium, ready to rock the house one last time. It was a bittersweet moment, knowing that this incredible challenge is coming to an end. Marky, Marion, and Warren were catching a flight back to the US, leaving Manny and me to reflect and plan for the future of this band. The whole experience was nothing short of amazing. Marky didn't back out due to a lackluster performance. In fact, we could tell he was hungry for more, ready to sink his teeth into what was coming next.

Chilling with the Huntingtons. Jenny gives her best smile.

Me hanging out with Chris and Josh Huntington.

After the Montpellier show on an abandonned campingground. The best food we had on the whole tour. Warren Cohen front right.

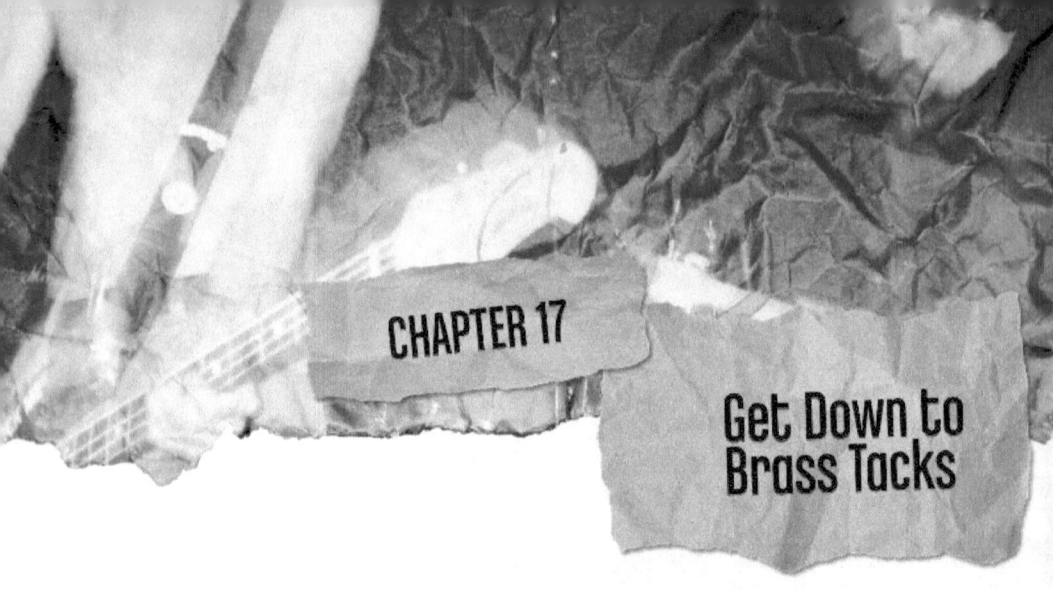

CHAPTER 17
Get Down to Brass Tacks

"Birth, and copulation, and death; that's all the facts when you come to brass tacks." – T. S. Eliot

Once we returned home, the day-to-day reality of the "normal" life replaced the exhilarating whirlwind we had experienced on the road. It had been an absolute rollercoaster ride that left us breathless. While we were no strangers to long tours, hitting the road with Marky took things to a whole new level. The attention we received was overwhelming. The crowds kept on growing larger, but so did the stress and expectations. Manny and I had been at this for a few years now, like two peas in a pod. Without even uttering words, we'd know what was going on in each other's minds, and most importantly, everything that we were doing was synchronized; nothing we said or did was a surprise. However, the aftermath of the fistfight in Milan hit me harder than I expected. It was a blow that was difficult to swallow, and I believe Manny felt the same way. Deep inside, something had been shattered, and even though we moved forward, I couldn't help but wonder if things would ever be the same again. Bad blood is a peculiar thing. Once it seeps between two people, it's unlikely to dissipate on its own. as the days turned into weeks, we tried to bury ourselves in distractions, hoping that time would heal the wounds that had been inflicted.

The ultimate surefire guarantee that everything would fall Into place came from the multitude of projects that had been established. Manny, who was rapidly rising in the ranks as one of Europe's top tour promoters, managed to secure coveted opening slots for The Buckweeds on tour with the American Heartbreak in both Belgium and Holland. Conversations with Marky gave a strong hint of potential tours in Japan and Down Under, where we would join forces with the Japanese Sheena & The Rokkets and Teengenerate. Additionally, a South American tour was well within our grasp. With all this, we were resolute in conquering new territories in Europe. Our sights were set on Slovenia and Greece, among other uncharted lands, fully confident that they would succumb to our irresistible rockin' attitude. Things were pacing up, and we were experiencing things for the first time. It was then that Marky expressed the desire to release a full-length album. It would give us a valid excuse to travel far and wide. However, before Marky could come back to us, the Buckweeds, with assistance from one of our pals at Stardumb on drums, would open for The Hookers EU tour.

Just when you think everything is going smoothly and nothing can go wrong, disaster strikes. It's like fate is relentlessly chasing after us. Manny was accompanying The Hell Suckers and Jack Black on their tour, and in early October, in some random bar in France, a guy accidentally collided with Manny. This simple collision led to an altercation, which resulted in a severe injury – a triple fracture in his arm and elbow. It's a devastating injury that required a few months of rehabilitation. In just a matter of seconds, all our plans, hopes, and dreams went down the drain. Our world, yet again, crumbled into pieces. We'll have to put everything on hold, and unfortunately, Marky wasn't much of a support. One would expect him to be understanding, but instead, I encountered an impatient individual who lacked compassion. It left me with tons of conflicting emotions. He literally placed me in a situation where I had no good options – trapped between a rock and a hard place. Add to that the lingering animosity and tension between Manny and me, and we took a detour down the path of destruction.

Marky was adamant about replacing Manny, and I didn't want to hear that. I was aware that it would disrupt our momentum. It was a heartless move, but plain and simple. And ringleader Ramone, well, he couldn't care less. All he cared about was keeping the band on the road. The show must go on, right? Time is money, and Manny's recovery was draining Marky's cash flow. I found myself caught in a dilemma. As for Manny, he didn't have a say in the matter. Circumstances forced his hand. Conflicting emotions began to surface within him. Even though he couldn't perform, his booking activities were off the charts. He could conduct business from the comfort of an easy chair, and his sense of urgency shifted away from the band. He may not have had a choice, but he made one anyway.

We had numerous discussions about it, and he was aware of the challenges I was facing. The desire to hit the road again was consuming me, and the possibilities that awaited me alongside Marky were infinitely more captivating than without him. Deep down, I knew very well that Marky could be a real pain in the ass, and that wasn't going to change. In fact, if anything, he would become an even bigger pain in the ass. However, I was lost in my own delusions. When you have tunnel vision, reality becomes distorted to the point where you fail to see that you're sacrificing friendship and compromising your integrity.

Looking back, I now realize that Manny was absolutely spot-on. I should have made a swift exit. I appreciate the offer, but I failed to recognize the hidden dangers lurking ahead. In no time, I found myself entangled and unable to escape. It was like being ensnared in a treacherous web of enticing commitments. Similar to Robert Johnson, who famously traded his soul at the crossroads. All for the sake of rock'n'roll.

In an instant, the animosity surged to the forefront once again. Manny and I lost touch, and I found myself regrouping with Demon Ramone. He was eager to hit the road with the circus once more, and our top priority was finding a new bass player. Manny may not have been the most technically skilled musician, but he had his act and his shit together. In other words, he was reliable. He knew the songs, he had a creative flair, and, most importantly, he could put on one hell of a performance. However, that alone wasn't going to cut it for his replacement. We needed someone with a well-known reputation and fame. Marky wouldn't settle for anything less. One of the first names that came up was Glen Matlock. His fame from his time in the Sex Pistols would be the perfect addition to the Ramones legacy. I suppose I was tolerated because someone had to handle the shitwork in the end. The star quality would be provided by others.

Star quality came with a hefty price tag, and let me tell you, it wasn't some cheap bargain. When you have Marky by your side, decisions could shift in the blink of an eye. The ultimate deciding factor was always boiled down to how much money would be left after expenses were accounted for. What amount of cash would be left to line his pocket? He had this grand idea of assembling an all-star cast, but in this particular moment, it just wasn't feasible. Marky had fallen from the heights of the renowned Ramones to a mere amateur status with the Intruders. The Ramainz, his attempt to create a band with Dee Dee, didn't quite yield the same level of fame as The Ramones themselves. Now, you can argue all day about who actually picked up whom. Did I pick up Marky, or did Marky pick me up? Honestly, it doesn't really matter in the grand scheme of things. The fact of the matter is we both benefited from the situation. Today, I firmly believe that I set him on a new path that would define his future success. Now, I must admit this may come across as an exaggeration, but I do believe I helped him shift his thinking and mindset. Regardless, he certainly didn't need me to become one of the greatest punk drummers ever and let's not forget about his business instincts, which were undoubtedly supported by Marion. Anyway, I'm convinced that the formation of a special forces line-up began around that period. However, when we examined the so-called "business case," we realized the need for a change in our approach. Time to change stripes. We made the decision, at least for now, that any bass player would suffice as long as he or she possessed the skill to play and rock it out. It was time to search for a capable, hired gun to join us.

CHAPTER 18

Chocolates, Stagbooks And Rock'n'Roll

"He spoke like a man who'd been born in a barn and raised by a pile of porn magazines." - Mimi Jean Pamfiloff

To make this work, we decided to seek out a band member from Belgium. This would allow me to commence rehearsals and begin recording demos. Marky possessed a very impressive ability - with just a simple tape, he could, in an instant, grasp and adapt to new songs within a matter of days. Without hesitation, I posted an advertisement on various message boards and music magazines. It didn't take long before the floodgates opened, with applications and inquiries pouring in. At this early stage of our development, we couldn't divulge too many details about the band, as we didn't want to create unrealistic expectations prematurely among potential candidates. The advertisement read, "Drummer (US) and guitarist/vocalist (BE) seek a dedicated and tight bass player. We require someone with 20% punk rock musical skills and 80% attitude. Please apply…"

Stevey Jay emerged as an early contender among the applicants, recounting his experience with a mix of excitement and uncertainty. "I remember receiving a swift response the day after I sent my email, informing me that the renowned US drummer featured in the advertisement was none other than Marky Ramone," he reflects. "However, beyond this fragment of information, I remained largely in the dark. Time passed with no further communication, and I began to believe that the notion of joining forces with this legendary musician was simply beyond my reach."

Stevey's initial enthusiasm slowly waned as his doubts crept in. He resigned himself to the idea that this opportunity was far too grand for someone like him to get his hands on, and the silence from the other end only reinforced his belief that his dreams of being in a band with the iconic drummer were just wishful thinking.

As the flood of applications continued to pour in, Marky and I found ourselves hesitating and pondering over the best course of action to take. I have to confess, deep down, I was clinging to the hope that Manny would make a miraculous recovery. Subconsciously, I still refused to accept the cruel reality that our plans would never come to fruition again.

After encountering a couple of unsuccessful bass players during the initial interviews, we decided to reach out to Stevey. Just when he had mentally let go of the possibility, fate intervened. My phone call was jolting him out of his complacency. The sudden resurgence of hope engulfed him.

A few days later, we arranged to meet at the buffet at the Ghent railway station. Perhaps I chose this location because it felt like neutral territory, but more likely, it was simply a convenient midpoint between our respective residences. Stevey, who was working as a trainee technician for national radio at the time, arrived wearing a puke-ugly canary yellow sweater. Little did he know that his fashion choice almost jeopardized his chances of joining the band. Nevertheless, our engaging conversation and the strong connection we felt that night made me completely overlook the questionable garment. Lucky Steve! Our meeting had erased any doubts or insecurities, and with renewed determination, he seized the opportunity with both hands. He knew that this was the break he had been waiting for.

Shortly after we commenced our rehearsals, my teenage cousin, who had been taking drum lessons for a year, displayed remarkable progress. Joining us proved invaluable in helping Stevey master all of our songs. Surprisingly, our new member quickly familiarized himself with the songs in just two sessions, and we even managed to improvise and create fresh material. Before we knew it, we were prepared to record new demos.

Stevey conjured up the killer riff for our song "Girls and Gasoline." He had scribbled it down on a beer coaster during a rowdy night of heavy drinking. Although the lyrics he came up with were total crap, the song itself was breathing pure rock and roll. I arranged the song in the studio, and when he laid down the bass track, much to his astonishment, I had already recorded scratch vocals. The inspiration for this particular track struck me after I watched the 1973 road movie "Badlands," which was based on the true story of Charlie Starkweather and his girlfriend Caril Ann Fugate's murderous rampage back in 1958. Little did I know at the time that this song, crafted with Stevey's infectious riff and my lyrics, would become one of our signature pieces, forever ingrained in the SpeedKings' story.

Four months had passed, and the time had come to reunite with Marky once again. Throughout those months, our collaboration with Stevey had proven to be rock-solid, which allowed us to venture into some trial performances. The concept of SpeedKings was still in its infancy, and we had yet to find a suitable name for what we considered to be a passion project. In order to keep things simple, we decided to go with the Marky Ramone Group - a name that had been embraced by many bands before us. Little did we know at the time that Marky would later raise concerns about this name and its implications on the legacy of the Ramones. However, this realization only came after our initial kick-off show.

Stevey showed up a day ahead of schedule, crashing on my couch in the eerie Bruges "haunted house." The next morning, we made our way to Brussels to pick up Mr. Ramone from the National Airport. By noon, we were back at my place, ready to grab some lunch. Stevey, being the well-mannered lad he was, had a special gift for Marky. He figured Americans had a soft spot for Belgian chocolates, so he brought two boxes along. In the blink of an eye, Marky devoured one box completely. Then, he dove into the rest of the lunch spread on the table. "I couldn't believe how quickly this guy could eat," Stevey recently confessed. "He wolfed down anything within arm's reach. If you had told me he hadn't eaten in three weeks, I would've believed it." It was a display of insatiable greed that I had witnessed before and would see countless times again.

During the lunch break, Marky casually asked if any of us had weed. Now, Marky isn't exactly what you'd call a pothead, but he went off on this whole tangent about "aroma therapy" that was just mind-blowing. According to him, only losers smoke cannabis. True connoisseurs simply appreciate the pleasure of the therapeutic scent. As I observed Steve getting completely hypnotized by Marky's mumbo jumbo, I couldn't help but feel like I was watching some surreal scene unfold right before my eyes.

But believe it or not, the thrill of one unexpected event after another was far from over. I had assumed that after a lengthy flight, a two-hour car ride, and a raucous lunch, Marky would be completely exhausted. But man, I assumed wrong; he was still full of energy and ready for more. He insisted on going out to find a stagbook store. Now, Bruges is conveniently located near the Dutch border, where sexual morality is a bit more relaxed compared to Belgium. So, without hesitation, we set off to cross the border into the Netherlands. In a quaint tourist spot just across the border, we had no trouble finding what we were looking for. In fact, there were numerous adult shops scattered about, and we decided to choose the largest one, with proportions resembling that of a supermarket. I figured that if it couldn't be found here, it probably couldn't be found anywhere else.

Stevey and I were casually hanging out but more interested in Marky's exploration of the aisles than roaming through the bins ourselves. Suddenly, the guy behind the counter approached me and exclaimed, *"Hey, isn't that one of the Ramones?"* I quickly corrected him, informing him that he was mistaken. *"Nah, that's just a doppelganger. Everyone asks me, but I always have to disappoint them,"* I explained. However, my attempts to convince him proved futile. He was too clever for that and gave me a cheeky wink. We both burst into laughter. *"Next time, I'll bring David Bowie along,"* I quipped. Meanwhile, Marky had stumbled upon a treasure trove of literature. The cashier couldn't contain his laughter as Marky seriously claimed, *"These are some magazines for my buddies here."* As we walked out the door, I caught a glimpse of the shopkeeper still doubled over with laughter. The guy just barely choked. With a stash of stag books in the trunk, this bunch was ready for it.

The countdown to the try-out shows was just a fortnight away, and our to-do list was a mile long. As we geared up for our upcoming tour and recording sessions, it was extremely crucial for us to have some kick-ass promotional photos. So, we found our way into an abandoned industrial lot next to a railway station to seek the perfect surroundings for our raw and edgy imagery. There, the remnants of a forgotten era, an old gas pump, a forsaken truck, and heaps of scrap metal provided us with the ideal setting for the shoot.

The photographer happened to be Vito d' Agostini's father, who would later join forces with Marky and me on the first European SpeedKings tour. And we had no clue that we'd soon be on the hunt for yet another bass player. Nevertheless, we eagerly snapped away, experimenting with various angles, trying to capture the specific look we were after. Marky was always pushing the boundaries so he decided to climb atop a crane for a shot from a worm's-eye view. The perch proved to be anything but stable, and in a split second, he lost his balance and tumbled from his lofty position. It just goes to show that even being a renowned drummer from New York doesn't guarantee the perfect balancing act. Even the most seemingly invincible can stumble and fall. We brushed off the dust and helped Marky back to his feet.

Finally, with only a limited time on our clock, we were able to begin working on the set with the real band. As mentioned before, Stevey had primarily rehearsed using tape, and we had done some impromptu sessions with our temporary drummer. He had the daunting task of learning over twenty songs for our live performance. I recall his pleasant surprise when he discovered that our rehearsals were disciplined and precise, devoid of any nonsense. With our ongoing studio recordings, we had to choose between rehearsing or recording. In the end, Stevey dedicated four full days to recording sessions with us.

He vividly remembers a particular incident. On the day we first arrived at the recording studio with Marky, it was drizzling outside, and he appeared to be dealing with a congested nose. As we approached the entrance and pressed the doorbell, he attempted to clear his nasal passages by forcefully blowing his nose with the hope that the mucus would land on the ground. However, due to an unexpected gust of wind, his bodily fluid ended up splattering directly onto his wild and voluminous, unruly hairdo. Frantically, he tried to brush it out of his sleek, jet-black hair. Just as he was doing so, the front door swung open, revealing the studio owner's wife extending her hand in greeting. In a panic, Marky instinctively wiped the sticky substance on the front of his worn-in leather jacket. The sensation was undeniably repulsive and disgusting.

The recording session flowed with ease, but the start of the third day took an unexpected turn. We were hit with the devastating news that Jeffrey Hyman, known as Joey Ramone, had passed away. It was a surreal moment, coinciding with Stevey receiving a collection of photographs of Joey from Lynne Cameron, one of our dedicated fans. Strangely enough, Joey's presence seemed to envelop us as we continued our session. His spirit and love for rock remained apparent in our sessions, which created a unique and otherworldly atmosphere and cast an ethereal presence upon us. During the span of the intense four-day recording session, we managed to establish a significant foundation for what would eventually evolve into our debut album, "No ifs, And's, or Buts." The amount of work accomplished during these days was immense.

One week had passed, and it was time for our first live show. It seemed ironic that our debut performance would be as the headliner at a festival. Despite its remote location, the venue was packed with enthusiastic Ramones fans who had turned up in droves. Stevey, always one to add an element of surprise, had invited his friend, a skilled fire eater, to kick off our performance. The crowd erupted in applause as the last flames illuminated the dark night. As the cheers subsided, Marky took to the stage and dedicated the show to Joey, his beloved bandmate who was no longer among us. The fans roared in appreciation, setting the stage for an explosive performance. The atmosphere was charged with electricity.

Ahaus, located in Germany, came second to Brussels as the epic finale of our three thrilling debut performances. The venue boasted a much larger capacity than the previous night, and it was bursting at the seams with eager fans. Stevey claimed it was the least exhilarating show out of the three, but I beg to differ. While it's true that Germany brings a different vibe compared to Belgium when it comes to rock concerts, I still felt an incredible energy in the air. I'm convinced that Stevey felt it, too. Otherwise, why would he be standing on the edge of the stage, passionately shouting at the crowd and igniting their spirits? As I gazed at him from across the stage, his eyes were ablaze with fervor and determination. Marky also caught onto this, and we couldn't help but burst into laughter, for we both anticipated Stevey diving headlong into the crowd, shouting, "It's time to party, Motherfuckers!"

After completing three trial performances, we were left with a multitude of thoughts swirling in our minds. These shows not only showcased our strengths but also laid bare our vulnerabilities leaving us no choice but to confront them head-on. With Marky spending considerable time in Europe and myself having an assignment in Mexico, we made the decision to rendezvous in the heart of Los Angeles. Like the Three Musketeers, our paths diverged once again. Each of us departed in a different direction. Marky returned to the streets of NYC while Stevey resumed his boring day job.

Debut show at the Dudstock Festival
April 28, 2001 Dudzele, Bruges Belgium

Hanging around before showtime at Magasin 4, Brussels, Belgium

Second show - supported by the Ewings and Bumpers
April 29, 2001 Magasin 4, Brussels, Belgium

April 29, 2001 Magasin 4, Brussels, Belgium

The bald guy in the front is Les who would become the SpeedKings tourmanager on the first EU Tour in 2001

CHAPTER 19

Mustang Marky

"Mustang is meant to be driven so that one can enjoy the hell out of all of it." – Caroll Shelby

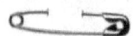

I hopped on the flight to Monterrey, Mexico, where I had to carry out a consultancy assignment. Torn between a corporate job in the business world and rocking out while traveling the world was never easy. But being able to spot opportunities, connecting dots between things that came my way, and making the most out of every situation has always been my strong suit.

Upon arrival at the airport, I was asked to press a button at customs that would either display a green or red light. If it showed green, you could simply proceed. However, if it turned red, you would undergo a thorough inspection of your luggage, and if luck wasn't on your side, the customs officials exposed you to a strip search.

Monterrey, the sprawling metropolis of Nuevo Leon, holds the title of Mexico's second-largest city. It was in this urban landscape that Pioneer established its South American manufacturing site. However, I must admit that the industrial area didn't quite resonate with me. And to make matters worse, the scorching heat of the season only intensified my distaste for the surroundings. Thankfully, my business affairs in Monterrey were swiftly concluded, letting me break free from the oppressive heat. On the evening of May 4th, I bid farewell to Monterrey, and I boarded the evening flight destined for the city of Angels. I was supposed to meet Marc and Marion there. On Saturday, May 5th, the Misfits were going to perform at the Palace Theatre, which, by the way, was the same venue where the Ramones had their final show. Marky was brought in as a special guest that night to play a series of Ramones songs.

This would be the perfect moment to brainstorm together about how we were to proceed with the band. The European tour with the Buckweeds and the first shows with the Marky Ramone Group had made it clear to us that we had something good in our hands, but it all still needed to take shape. Marky and I wanted to make plans, but Marion's presence was just as important. Even though she was the silent figure in the background, the cliché of a strong woman behind every man held true here, too. She also had a say in what was to come. Besides, it was always nice to see Marion. We had gotten to know each other much better on the European tour, and she turned out to be someone with a lot of common sense and her feet firmly on the ground. When you get lost in daydreams because you want to play as much rock 'n' roll as possible, having someone like her around is essential.

When I arrived at the Grafton Hotel on Sunset Boulevard, I attempted to check-in, in my tailored suit, which was accompanied by my briefcase and pilot's case. I appeared far from someone belonging to the hip in-crowd of this electric city of Los Angeles. The girl behind the counter gave me a look of a certain disdain. Her contempt only grew when she couldn't find my name on her list, and she made no effort to hide her mockery. *"Are you sure you booked with us? You're quite unfamiliar here. Undoubtedly, you must have made a mistake. It happens more often."* The smirk on her face left little room for doubt. She didn't want anything to do with me, and I was clearly wasting her Friday evening. The calmness that filled the lobby only intensified things. It was evident that I was disturbing her in her divine state of idleness.

But I wasn't going to let her brush me off so easily and insisted that she check again. In the meantime, she started sighing in irritation, with her eyes darting in every direction. When it came to customer satisfaction, she definitely wasn't going to be winning any awards. I could tell that she was just moments away from calling a security agent. But I was in a good mood and was relishing her annoying attitude. I wanted to make her sweat. After all, Marion had given me the coordinates for this hotel, and I was certain that she had taken care of everything. I could bet my life on it.

"Sir, you're not on the list. You don't have a booking here. I'm going to have to ask you to leave," she said, her voice taking on a harsher tone and increasing in volume. A colleague emerged from the adjacent office. They say strength comes in numbers, but they clearly didn't account for my charming self. I had, however, saved my trump card until the very end. After all, a cat doesn't immediately devour a mouse but plays with it a little. And that little game had gone on for long enough.

"Perhaps you should take a look under the names Marc Bell or Marion Flynn. They assured me that a room has been arranged for me."
"Ooh, you mean Mr. Marky Ramone from The Ramones?"
"That's right, that's who I mean. I'm a band member, and they assured me that my room would be ready as soon as I arrived. It's a shame to hear that the hotel couldn't make it happen. I had hoped for a different reception. I had a long flight, and this back-and-forth hassle is wearing me out."

As I stood at the counter, the conversation seemed to drag on forever. But just as quickly, I was whisked away to my room. An upgrade, finally. And what did you expect? My tailored suit was stashed away in the closet, and before you knew it, I found myself standing under the warm rain shower. I was ready for a night on the town, ready to go and hang out with Marc and Marion.

When I woke up the next day, the sun had already been up for a few hours. I delighted myself with the breakfast on the terrace by the pool, and it was pretty clear that the ladies at the front desk were looking at me differently. "Oh, simple souls, I may be a nobody, but I revel in your ignorance. You have brought this upon yourselves."

Marky was feeling extremely pumped today. Later in the afternoon, we had to practice with The Misfits, and Marky asked me to arrange a car. "Which car do you prefer?" I asked him. He said he didn't really mind the car, but I knew he would prefer a Mustang convertible if possible. There was a car rental company right across the street from our hotel. My European driver's license and credit card quickly got me the requested

Ford. As soon as I tossed the keys to Marky, they were immediately thrown back to me. *"You drive. I'm riding shotgun,"* he said, and before I knew it, we were cruising through West Hollywood. The weather was gorgeous; the sun was warm, and a gentle breeze filled the air. How much more California dreaming could one ask for? And believe it or not, as I turned on the car radio, The Eagles slapped me in the face with their Hotel California. The majestic palm trees witnessed us along the boulevard.

"CBGB's! You are a long way from home!" Jerry Only's voice booms across the parking lot of the Palace Theatre. With a wide grin, he greeted us and introduced us to the crew. Dez Cadena from Black Flag and Robo were already sound-checking with Doyle. Rise Above exploded loudly from the PA system. It was time to go over the Ramones setlist. They decided to play a total of 7 songs together. It was clear that everyone was on the edge. I ain't hanging around for the rehearsal. Tonight, I was ditching the front row, and from the backstage area, I made up my mind to catch the show. I was confident that everything would go off without a hitch. Marion was all ready and waiting for me at the hotel. We had plans to grab lunch together in downtown LA and then go on a thrilling hunt through the city's thrift stores in search of some killer vintage finds. And then rendezvous with Marky later in the afternoon.

In the hotel, I was being treated like royalty. *"Sorry, I really had no idea you were one of the Ramones. I wouldn't have recognized you. We see so many people here, and I definitely didn't expect you to be in a three-piece suit!"* There's dumb, and then there's extremely dumb. The attractive young lady was even more foolish than I could have imagined. This is the epitome of idolizing famous individuals, and yet I'm not even famous. Me, in the Ramones? Give me a break. It was an insult to both the Ramones and me while Miss Universe continued to babble on relentlessly.

"You have a show tonight, right? Can I be so bold as to ask if I could possibly be on the guest list? I'm a huge fan! If you're up for it, we could hang out afterward. I'm off tonight." I tell her that I'll see what I can do. NOT! Or wait, maybe I can get you on the guest list for the support band, The Impotent Sea Snakes. I saw them earlier at the rehearsal. I absolutely adored that band. Years ago, I played their LP on Posh Boy until it was worn out. These guys were hilarious. They mixed arrogance and humor in such a way that it would annoy and insult just about everyone. I

chuckled the first time I played "Pope John Paul Can Suck My Dick" and "I Wanna Fuck Your Dad." However, I had never seen them live before. Earlier in the backstage area, I caught a glimpse of them all dressed up. They were like a horde of rampaging barbarians mixed with vaudeville drag queens. You gotta love them! I hope the reception desk Barbie will share the same feeling.

As we returned to the venue that evening, I witnessed the crowd lining up and jostling each other at The Misfits' merchandise booth. The truck carrying their merchandise was bigger than the one housing their musical instruments. Everyone in the parking lot and inside the venue were donning the same black, Crimson Ghost t-shirt. It was almost eerie. The Misfits were throwing a wild party tonight. The setlist consists of no less than 44 songs. They kicked things off with the most popular Misfits tunes: Static Age, Teenagers From Mars, Attitude, Angelfuck, and Skulls… not one popular tune was left out. After 20 Eyes, they picked up the pace with five Black Flag songs. Keith Morris tore through Nervous Breakdown, and in the feedback of Six Pack, the next Misfits classics come to life: Violent World, Horror Business, Bullet, We Are 138. Marky was eager to take Robo's place. The crowd went wild for the seven Ramones songs. Sheena, Sedated, and Blitzkrieg Bop eventually made way for Michael Graves, who took on the last Misfits songs. It was Saturday night, and what better song to close the set with than Saturday Night?

CHAPTER 20

The Hunt For the Trailer Park Unicorn

"You weren't born to be perfect. You were born to be a unicorn, but that is pretty much the same thing." – Anonymous

The day after the Palace Theatre show, Marc and Marion made their way back to the concrete jungle of New York City. And me? Well, I wasn't quite ready to spread my wings and fly home just yet. Fate had led me to connect with Jadelyn Hunter, a wordsmith extraordinaire residing in the heart of Marion, Illinois. With my burning literary ambitions, the stars aligned us for an adventure, and I decided to pay her a visit for an entire week. And so, I boarded the interstate flight towards Marion, Illinois, with a pitstop in St. Louis. But here's the kicker: the journey to Marion involved boarding a pint-sized jet. Picture this: a minuscule aircraft with only a solitary seat on each side. As we prepared for take-off, the pilot kindly requested that we distribute our weight evenly across both ends of the plane. Talk about a thrilling start!

As I touched down at the local airport, a surge of excitement coursed through me. Finally, I arrived at my destination and proceeded to retrieve my rental car. Prior to my arrival, I had made an online reservation for a Ford Cougar equipped with a manual transmission. Opting for a manual transmission had always been a no-brainer for me, as it simply was the prevalent choice in Europe, and it's what I was most at ease with. Additionally, I believe it injected a certain sporty vibe into the act of driving. However, as I made my way towards the car, a disconcerting realization dawned upon me. The people in the States are not as well-acquainted with manual transmissions as our European counterparts. This became abundantly clear when I attempted to enter the vehicle. To my dismay, it soon became evidently clear that this particular car has been adapted for use by individuals with disabilities. The configuration was completely unsuitable for my needs and made it impossible for me to operate.

Thankfully and very rarely, fortune smiled upon me as there were no other passengers eagerly awaiting their assigned vehicles. Without delay, the helpful staff swiftly reassigned me to another car that aligned with my requirements and preferences.

Miss Hunter extended an invitation for me to meet her in the heart of Carbondale, a few miles away from Marion. Cruising through this region of the Midwest was an adventure in itself. The landscape reminded me of scenes straight out of the National Lampoon movies. It's as if I had been transported back in time as I passed by burger joints and fraternity houses. There are moments when I couldn't help but feel like I stepped right into an episode of Twin Peaks. As I pulled into a parking spot on Main Street Carbondale, I caught sight of my date waving at me, clearly waiting. Perhaps she doubted I would actually show up, thinking this was all just a playful prank.

It was awesome to encounter her. We began conversing enthusiastically while deciding to grab a bite before anything else. We hadn't solidified any definitive plans for the upcoming days. In all honesty, I assumed we would simply stay at her place. However, she seemed hesitant about this idea. *"I currently reside in the local Kay-Lou Courts trailer park, and I don't want my neighbors to have any wild thoughts and assumptions about me going on a blind date with a foreign guy. Can't we just find a place in a nearby Motel and go from there?"* It was a kind request I couldn't resist but imply. And so we made our way to the Super 8 Wyndham Motel on Vernell Road. But not before passing by the Trailer Park where Jadelyn needed to gather some clothes for the upcoming days. As I waited for her, I could see why she insisted on not staying there. The intense and piercing stares I received from some of the people gave me the creeps. It felt like something straight out of a B-movie. Trailer Park thrash at its finest. Anyway, an hour later, we finally checked in at the motel. There weren't many travelers around and the room was spacious and clean, equipped with all the modern amenities. But hey, it's all about the company, right? I was more than cool with it. Being in a touring band took me to much stranger places than this, so I wasn't complaining. I knew we were going to have an amazing time. I really enjoyed the short stories she had sent me, and I was excited to dive deeper into her mind and exchange writing ideas. But before we started our get-together, we were missing one crucial thing – comfort food and, of course, the obligatory and some much-needed booze. After check-in, we hopped back in the car and headed to the nearest liquor store to stock up on our supplies. Over time, the days flew by in a whirlwind of deep conversations and occasional moments of exhaustion. Whenever we woke up from our alcohol-fueled dreams, we made our way back to the liquor store to stock up on more supplies. On the way there, I caught sight of a pawn shop displaying an electric Gretsch guitar in its window. Intrigued, I decided to take a closer look, but deep down, I knew there was little chance that this would be the instrument I truly desired.

Two days before I planned to depart, we engaged in a conversation about tattoos in general, as well as my own personal ink. The Hunter girl spontaneously decided that a mark on her skin would only enhance her inspiration, and before I could fully grasp the situation, she snatched the yellow pages from the hallway of the motel. Flipping to the tattoo business section, she started at the letter A, and as soon as she stumbled upon a Marion address, she tore out the page and headed straight for the phone. Only minutes later, she returned to the room and announced that I would be driving her to the tattoo artist later that evening. In my mind, getting a tattoo could never be just a hasty, spur-of-the-moment decision. However, it seemed that she perceived this so much differently. Preparing herself for a session of getting inked, she believed it was an absolute necessity to procure a bottle of vodka in order to conquer her fear of the tattoo gun. I knew there was no chance of dissuading her from this notion, but I chose to let it slide as I am confident that a seasoned tattoo artist would never permit an intoxicated individual to sit down in their chair.

As the navigation voice guided us toward the address listed in the Yellow Pages, we found ourselves in a neighborhood far removed from the city center or any business district. Instead, we were surrounded by modest middle-class homes, and we stopped in front of an unassuming house. It was hard to believe that this could be the place we were looking for. It didn't resemble a parlor at all. Nevertheless, Jadelyn confidently pressed the doorbell, and within moments, a tall, gaunt man wearing a tank top and dirty jeans opened the door. *"Just come around to the back,"* he instructed us before promptly closing the door again. As we made our way around the house, he had already reached the porch and waiting for us. In the middle of that porch, a worn sunbathing chair appeared; being the center of attention, we guessed it to be the tattoo chair. *"This is where the magic happens,"* he chuckled, revealing a smile with several missing teeth. The guy didn't seem that old, but his teeth told a different story. I wouldn't be shocked if this was a crystal meth smile. Jadelyn burst into laughter, tightly gripping the bottle beside her. *"Hey, you've got yourself some liquid candy,"* the man eagerly remarked. As she handed him the bottle, he took a massive gulp. I couldn't believe my eyes. It felt like a surreal moment as if a hidden camera crew was about to emerge from the shadows. I wouldn't be the least bit surprised!

"What kind of design do you want, my love, and where would you like it?" he asked with a mischievous glint in his eyes. *"Hmm, I think I'm going for a unicorn. Yeah, that's right, a unicorn. That's totally me! And I want it right here."* She pointed to a spot just above her pubic area while pushing down her jeans. *"Well then, why don't you get rid of those jeans, young lady, and take a seat in my chair!"* This whole scene started to become more and more bizarre. It felt surreal like it wasn't actually happening. I was left speechless as I found myself perched on a barstool in the corner, observing the unfolding wild spectacle. The artist and his canvas began to knock back shots of vodka, and I watched as they both quickly became intoxicated. She was lying down, wearing nothing but a tiger-print G-string, and he confidently started working his magic. I hear the buzzing of the tattoo gun as it jumps into action in his trembling hand. Each moment of pain was met with a sip of liquid courage. He took his time, and his free hand wandered more and more direction g-string until he both tattooed and shamelessly fingered her. Midway through the session, the sunbathing chair toppled over, finally giving up and sending them both crashing to the ground. Believe it or not, they were actually enjoying this chaotic experience. I tore my eyes away and accepted the beer he offered me. Over an hour later, Jadelyn and I made our way back to the

Super 8 Motel. Her tight jeans haphazardly pulled up over the newly inked and bruised area.

"Oh my fucking God! I am absolutely ecstatic! My very first goddamn tattoo!" Shouting with excitement, she couldn't contain her joy. Back at the gritty Motel, exhaustion finally took its toll on her, and she succumbed to a deep slumber fueled by alcohol. As I watched her sleep, I couldn't help but wonder if this was all just a dream. But no, reality hit me hard - I was wide awake, fully aware of the momentous occasion that had just taken place. Eventually, fatigue caught up with me as well, and I drifted off into my own restless sleep. When I rose from my slumber, she emerged from the restroom, proudly displaying her inked artwork. *"Isn't it simply breathtaking?"* she exclaimed as if it was a museum masterpiece. I found myself gazing at a misshapen creature that bore no resemblance to a majestic unicorn. Even a Gremlin or ET would fare better on their worst days. However, who was I to disrupt her blissful reverie? My eagerness to depart from this place grew, yearning to return to the familiarity of the airport, board a plane, and escape back to the realm of normalcy. And back at the trailer park, without a doubt, Jadelyn would now reign as the queen of trash.

"Oh, that's awesome, you're from Belgium," the lady behind the check-in counter at Marion Municipal Airport exclaimed. *"Is this your first time flying?"* I couldn't even process what she said. I found myself in some kind of bizarre dream. How on earth did I end up here? Did I sail? Swim? If someone told me I was magically transported here, I might actually buy it. The Midwest couldn't get any more bizarre than this.

But my struggle was far from over. Even reaching JFK Airport in the midst of a raging storm preseneds its own set of obstacles. After the flight captain instructed the crew to prepare for landing, we waited anxiously for what seemed like an eternity. Finally, a voice crackled through the intercom, delivering the news with an air of stoicism, *"Welcome to Bozeman Yellowstone Airport."* We had been redirected to Montana due to the treacherous weather conditions. "CBGB's, you are still a long way from home." After onboarding and endlessly waiting at the counter, long after midnight, the other stranded passengers and I were dumped at the local Ramada Hotel. The $20,00 food voucher was a welcome gift, but there was no place to spend it.

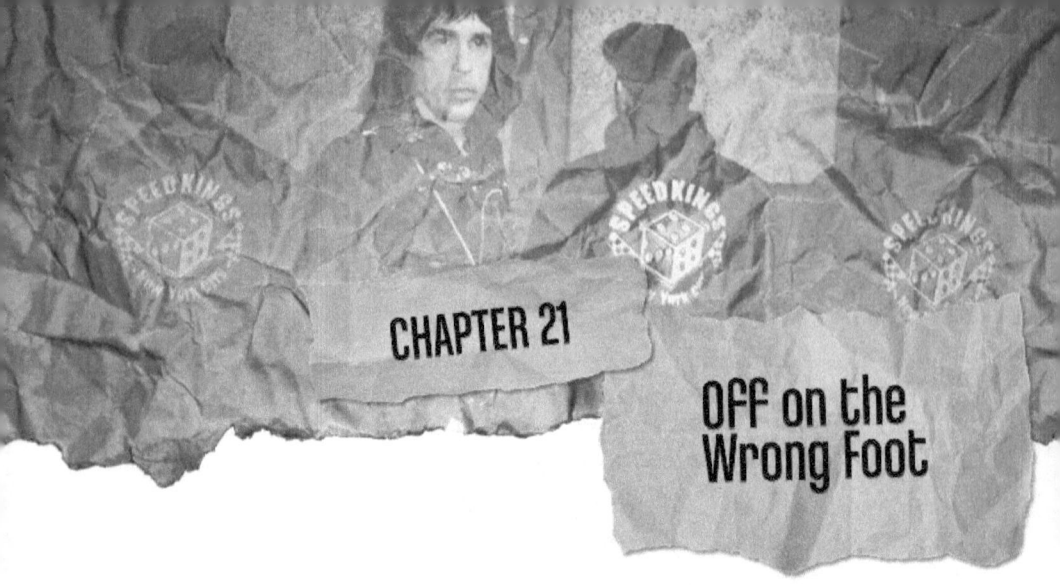

CHAPTER 21

Off on the Wrong Foot

"If you start off on the wrong foot, the footer you go, the wronger it gets." - Hank the Cowdog

One day late and a dollar short, I finally got back home, still confused as to what had just happened and how it happened. Back in Los Angeles, Marky and I finally had the opportunity to sit down and hash things out. The performances we had in Belgium and Germany shed some light on our situation. We realized that we really had something special going on, but we hadn't reached our full potential just yet. If we truly wanted to create a powerhouse rock'n'roll band, a mere trio wouldn't cut it. We needed to expand our lineup and bring in additional members to create a tight-knit force. We had a clear understanding of what steps were necessary to propel this band forward and set it on the path to success. We urgently needed to fix the little room there was for me to concentrate on lead vocals while simultaneously playing the guitar. Enter an additional axe slinger. I reached out to my friend KPW, who had previously been a member of the Misters. However, despite his deep admiration for the Ramones, he regretfully declined the offer. His heart bled as he explained that he had recently joined a well-known Belgian band, although it lacked the seminal punk essence that came with playing alongside the drummer of the Ramones. Nevertheless, this new venture guaranteed him a stable income as a musician, and I couldn't fault him for prioritizing financial security over our uncertain endeavor.

I 'HEARTBREAK' THE RAMONES

Once again, I was on the lookout, venturing into the familiar realm of hiring. It is in this vast expanse that I stumbled upon Dee Jaywalker. Ah, Dee, a familiar face from my hometown, a regular at the Twenty-One club, and a member of various local, even talented bands. He may have been confined to the limitations of our dead-end city, but his talent shone through. What set Dee apart was his eclectic taste in music and it extended far beyond just punk music. Armed with his Gretsch guitars, he effortlessly unleashed some mind-blowing and mean rockabilly tunes. It was a stylish touch that perfectly complemented the raw, gasoline-infused direction we were taking with our sound. But it wasn't just his musical prowess that made Dee the obvious choice but also his ability to quickly grasp and master our set was a stroke of luck. In hindsight, who else could we have possibly chosen?

Dee and Stevey were an ill-fated duo, like two puzzle pieces that simply didn't fit together. In fact, Dee's presence and his nasty remarks brought a level of discomfort to Stevey that I failed to notice. My mind was too preoccupied with other matters to pick up on the underlying tension between them. While Marky was back in the States, wooing Jerry Only from the Misfits to earn some quick buck, he also pushed me into organizing more shows.

The festival where we made our debut had caught the attention of organizers from another, even larger festival, and they offered us a prime slot. On top of that, four other festivals had expressed interest in having us on their line-up. One of them was none other than the legendary Holidays in The Sun festival in Morecambe, UK. We had all the gigs booked, and Stevey, Dee, and I were pumped to rock. But just before our five-date festival tour, while I was enjoying a vacation in the South of France, Marky called me with an unsettling calmness in his voice. "I'm backing out of the shows." It sounded downright placid, and I was completely floored by his message. It couldn't be true. Our name was plastered on posters all over Europe, adorning every wall. And now, with one simple phone call, this guy pulled the plug on everything we had worked so hard for.

"*Just because...*" That was the pathetic excuse I had to work with. And now I had to clean up Marky's mess. "*You'll handle the explanation to the promoters, right?*" I seethed with anger. "Just because" is not a valid reason. It's a cop-out. But in Marky's narrow-minded world, it seemed to be the only answer. He selfishly went to chase after some quick money from US shows over supporting our new band. Fine, I would deal with the festival organizers myself.

I concocted the narrative of our escape, painting the art of deception. You know, when you're offered peanuts, you act like a monkey. Everyone knew about Marky's struggles with alcohol abuse during his time in The Ramones. He was even booted from the band for years because of it. So, I called each and every promoter, spinning a tale of woe. I explained that poor Marky had been forced into rehab for "issues I couldn't disclose any further." Not a single promoter failed to get hold of my insinuation. In fact, my little white lie stirred up sympathy and compassion from every last one of them. Compassion for a guy who barely understood the meaning of that word. And just like that, we were off the hook.

I never revealed the truth about how I managed to salvage the situation and avoided starting off on the wrong foot. But here it is – my secret weapon of diversion. I cunningly maneuvered out of that sticky situation created by Sir Marc Bell.

The fiery blush of shame still tinged my cheeks as we stumbled through the month of August, unaware of the impending chaos that awaited us on the eleventh day of September. I can vividly recall the urgent ring of the telephone. "You need to switch on the TV. Turn to CNN. Something monumental is unfolding in New York," the voice on the other end exclaimed. Mesmerized, I planted myself in front of the glowing screen, fixated on the captivating images that unfolded before my eyes. And then it happened, captured live on camera - a second plane mercilessly piercing through the heart of the New York World Trade Center. In that moment, the world changed.

When I initially tuned in, the news anchor had casually referred to it as a tragic accident - a commercial airplane inadvertently colliding with one of the majestic Twin Towers. But now, confronted with the horrifying reality, it became abundantly clear that this was no mere accident. It was an act of unspeakable terror that would forever alter the course of history.

The moment that the second plane struck its target, the trajectory of tragedy shifted abruptly. "Ladies and Gentlemen, we are at war…" The entire world recognized this as a malevolent act of terrorism - an invasion penetrating the heart of the United States. Speechless, we stood in shock and disbelief. The mere mention of the word "war" unleashed a torrent of thoughts that surpassed my understanding. My mind immediately turned to my dear friends in New York City - Sheena, Celine, and our punk rock lawyer, Dave Stein. Oh, and Marky too. I desperately attempted to call their numbers, but all I encountered was an infinite barrage of occupied signals. Never before had I encountered such a surreal and unsettling experience.

On live television, we bore witness to the unfolding of a tragedy. People, engulfed in flames, leaping from the towering infernos, holding hands in a final act of desperation. They chose to embrace certain death rather than endure the unbearable fire and suffocating smoke. And then, as if the weight of the world couldn't bear any heavier, both towers collapsed before our eyes. The devastation was indescribable - a cataclysm that brought the entire world to a standstill.

The recording tapes of our debut album resided in the studio alongside Daniel Rey in New York. He was diligently working on the mastering process. Suddenly, "No ifs, Ands, or Buts" took on a whole new sound in this unfamiliar realm. The Al Qaeda attack had silenced the United States of America, like a stubborn child who finally succumbs to being told to stop arguing. As the world collectively hesitated to resume its daily routines, chaos ensued further. The stock exchange plummeted, air traffic came to a screeching halt, and as we prepared for another attempt to play live again, everything we had meticulously planned disintegrated before our eyes. Another tour, which I had poured countless hours into organizing, was indefinitely postponed, leaving our album unable to be released for the time being. It felt as though chaos had enveloped us from all sides.

And back at home Stevey found himself under intense pressure at his job. Although it was never explicitly stated, it was painfully obvious that he had to make the difficult choice between his career and his passion for music. In the end, Stevey made the heartbreaking call to leave the band and prioritize financial stability. My heart went out to him as I understood the sacrifices he had to make. Little did we know that just a few weeks later, the National Radio and Television Company where Stevey worked announced a restructuring and downsizing, leaving him without a job. It was then that his entire world came crashing down around him, all his sacrifices cruelly rejected. I desperately wished there was a way to turn back time and undo the choices we had made. As for our band, I couldn't help but question whether we would ever be able to get it off the ground again. The uncertainty hung heavy in the air, leaving us all feeling lost and unsure of what the future held.

Stevey couldn't shake off the curse of bad luck. He found himself caught up in a never-ending cycle of temp jobs, constantly in and out of employment. He tried his hand at further education, hoping it would lead him to better opportunities, but fate had other plans. The company he ended up in didn't last long, leaving him feeling disillusioned once again.

In a desperate attempt to find stability, Stevey ventured into the catering industry and opened his own bar. However, his lack of business acumen and attitude proved to be his downfall. The landlord suffocated him with increasing demands, the brewery mafia and gambling machine mob exerted their influence, and he found himself facing threats and extortion. When he refused to turn a blind eye to drug peddling in his establishment, things took a turn for the worse.

With his back against the wall and no way out, Stevey was forced into bankruptcy. And to make matters worse, his so-called friends vanished into thin air and left him on his own. Even his own family turned their backs on him, but the final blow came from his girlfriend. She heartlessly abandoned him, leaving him to fend for himself on the streets. Left with nothing but the rain pouring down on him, Stevey had nowhere to go.

His lover destroyed all of his singles and CDs, ripping apart every photograph. And what remained was brutally defaced, with his face scratched out in a vicious manner. It must be acknowledged that the level of punkiness captured in those pictures cannot be denied.

He confided in me, admitting that he had stopped sharing the fact that he once belonged to a band alongside one of the legendary Ramones. "No one ever believed me, and instead, they mocked me mercilessly. But what can you expect? The essence of rock'n'roll, tattoos, and all that rebellious spirit has been co-opted by the most middle-of-the-road, conformist individuals. No one gives a damn about my cherished memories."

"Although, every now and then, someone will ask me if I'm the one who played with a Ramone, speculating whether it was Dee Dee since he resided in the city of Malines. Much to their astonishment, I reveal that it was Marky I joined forces with. Once again, I witnessed the disbelief etched on their faces. Thankfully, you uploaded a few snapshots of us together, providing undeniable evidence that I was part of that extraordinary journey.

Stevey managed to break free from the toxic atmosphere and started rebuilding his life. Going through a cycle of falls and rises, he got back on track. Once again, he is working temporary jobs, but he is confident that one day everything will fall into place. *"For now, I live my life the way it comes. I paid my dues — that's what truly matters in the end.*

Index print sheet of the Marky Ramone Group promoshoot. Some of the pictures were used for the imprint and cover of the first SpeedKings album "No If's, And's of But's".

CHAPTER 22

A 2001 Statement

"if you tell the truth, it becomes part of your past. If you lie, it becomes part of your future" Anonymous

October 7, 2001. This entire adventure kicked off when Marky made a statement to Jari-Pekka over in Finland:

"I couldn't think of any better way to end this year than the release a new album and to do an extensive tour. 2001 has been a year with a lot of work but, above all, tons of rock'n'roll. I have been touring with The Misfits in the US as a special guest on their 25th Anniversary shows, and in between the dates, I have set up this new band and recorded a full-length album.

It all started when I first met Nick Cooper during the Intruders European tour in January 2000. He helped us out on some occasions, and his previous band played our support on a few shows. In the summer of that year, I agreed to help him out when his band needed a drummer for their European tour. Playing with them was a lot of fun, and I knew they had their shit together. By the end of the tour, Nick and I knew that some longer-term collaboration was getting started. I liked what I saw, I liked what I heard, and the rest is history. Here I am with my new band, The SpeedKings. There were quite a few songs there. We picked the ones that the kids loved at the shows and recorded them. My friend Daniel Rey mastered the album, and here it is, 'No Ifs, Ands, or Buts!'

2001 was a good year, but there was also a lot of sadness and grief. One of those moments was when Joey Ramone passed away. But although he is *not here anymore, the music lives on. Rock'n'roll will never die and that's why I will keep on playing it.*

This year, the Ramones have been nominated for the Rock'n'roll Hall of Fame, and we received the Lifetime Achievement Award at the NY MTV Music Awards. Dee Dee is on the road; CJ has his new band, and I and Daniel Rey played on Joey's solo album.

In my case, playing in a new band, recording a new album, and hitting the road for another tour is my way of saying thanks to all the kids and fans out there. We owe it to them for being such a loyal family through all the years. This new album is dedicated to all of them. I hope they will enjoy the songs as much as we enjoyed recording them. As for the release, I am very pleased that we made this cooperation with White Jazz Records. Their reputation for bringing great music was so convincing that they were an obvious choice. And I believe the choice came from both sides. We have a very good contact and treat each other on a friend's base. This makes our bond so strong.

I look forward to seeing all our fans out there in Europe after being away for far too long. I can promise that we have a scorching set waiting for them. After all, 2001 is the 25th Anniversary of Punk Rock, and I will make sure no one will forget about that!"

After the Canadian tour and subsequent breakup, it became clear that the album we had recorded before the US Tour would never see the light of day. The official explanation given was that I insisted on performing at least 150 shows a year, with Marky sarcastically remarking, "That's more than the Ramones ever did!" The truth was concealed when Marky shared his memoirs. The SpeedKings had suddenly never existed. I didn't really care. I had learned not to let the truth get in the way of a good story, and coming from him, it almost felt like an honor to be silenced. He is undoubtedly a talented drummer, but when it comes to storytelling, he got lost in a maze of fantasy. A world of make-believe. Nevertheless, that's entertainment. It's all part of showbiz, and while writing a book may have some dignity, promoting pasta sauce, non-alcoholic beer, and "Too Tough to Break" condoms just feels a bit cheap and tacky in comparison.

RAWK-A-HULA & WHITE JAZZ RECORDS
present the new album "No If's, And's or But's!"

RAMONES nominated for the ROCK'n'ROLL HALL OF FAME
MTW MUSIC AWARDS - RAMONES LIFETIME ACHIEVEMENT
A TRIBUTE TO 25 YEARS OF PUNK-ROCK

MARKY RAMONE
& The SpeedKings

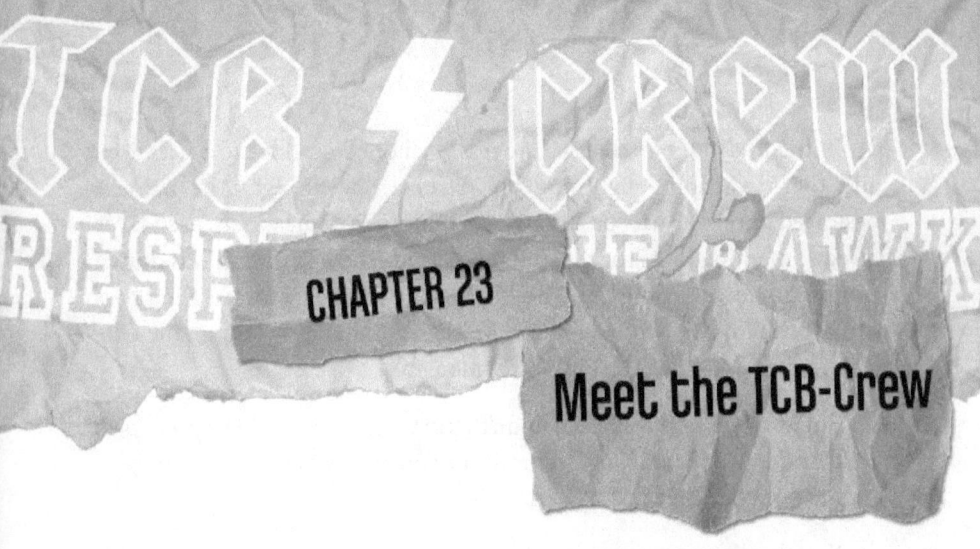

CHAPTER 23

Meet the TCB-Crew

*"I've been taking care of business (it's all mine)
Taking care of business and working overtime."*
- Bachman-Turner Overdrive

My memory hadn't erased the situation we had been in where I needed to bullshit ourselves out of planned shows. The capricious nature of Marky's decision-making was something I dreaded facing again. Telling small lies may have temporarily rescued us, but eventually, luck has a way of abandoning you. There's only so much you can get away with. I wasn't going to let it happen all over again, no more abruptly cancelling shows. It completely undermines credibility and as a new band trying to make our mark, we simply couldn't afford to have a tarnished and bad reputation. I was fully aware of the fact that flying over for just a few shows was more trouble than it was worth. However, I'm a man of my word, and dedication holds immense value to me. That's why I needed true commitment. I wasn't gonna take opportunities for granted.

The September 11th tragedy had a devastating impact on all aspects of business in the United States, including the show business industry. Perhaps Marky thought that fleeing from the US on another extensive European tour could provide some respite. And so, the plan was set in motion to organize another few weeks of touring towards the end of the year 2001.

In the midst of our creative process, we honed our idea to perfection, and that's when the lightning bolt struck: SpeedKings. The name I bestowed upon our new band carried a multitude of meanings, each layer owed something to its rock 'n' roll reputation. The inspiration was drawn from the Ludwig Company, who birthed the legendary Speed King bass drum pedal. I saw a connection to Marky, our band's drummer, the true star of our ensemble. The link was undeniable.

But it didn't stop there. I couldn't ignore the impact of Deep Purple's 1970 anthem, "Speed King." Its raw energy and feel became an integral part of our collective inspiration.

Yet, there was more to our name than just musical influences. We embodied a sound of punk-infused rockabilly. Our lyrics were a high-octane race of fast cars and adrenaline-fueled adventures. We became the unrivaled Kings of Speed, rulers of a wild and untamed world.

I started crafting the visuals that would complement the world of hotrods and loose women we were immersing ourselves in. Elliott Mattice, hailing from Syracuse, NY, had willingly stepped in to create an awe-inspiring painting for the album's front cover. With a brush in hand, he embodied the essence of a SpeedKing, swiftly translating his raw talent into a captivating piece of lowbrow art. His audacious style was and still is among the most notorious in the scene. Our first album was infused with the most outrageous and cartoonish Speedy Gonzales and Roadrunner fantasies, and our efforts paid off as we secured the record deal we had been tirelessly pursuing. It was none other than Swedish White Jazz Records, the cream of the crop of European record labels at that time. Home to legendary bands like The Hellacopters, the Nomads, and Gluecifer. White Jazz had built a formidable reputation for unleashing the best of the best in hard-hitting, raw rock music! And to top it off, the label's owner, Calle Schewen, happened to be a die-hard Ramones enthusiast. White Jazz held immense sway in the music scene as it opened doors to venues that wholeheartedly embraced our genre. Respect the Rock!

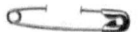

Promoters were thrilled by the concept of merging the band's image with the legendary status of the Ramones. The impact we made with the

Buckweeds just a year ago was still running fresh in their minds. This worked as a charm as the booking process went seamlessly. The demand for our performances was overwhelming, with all available dates being snatched up in just a heartbeat. In record time, we managed to secure an impressive lineup of 26 consecutive shows and travel through 10 European countries.

12/06/2001: Magasin 4, Brussels (BE)
12/07/2001: PaardThe Hague (NL)
12/08/2001: SommercasinoBasel (CH)
12/09/2001: So What, Oslo (NO)
12/10/2001: Knust, Hamburg (DE)
12/11/2001: Zauberberg, Wurzburg (DE)
12/12/2001: Musikbunker, Aachen (DE)
12/13/2001: Colchester, Arts Centre, Colchester (UK)
12/14/2001: Ramones Fanclub -party, Roma (IT)
12/15/2001: C.S. Pedro, Padova (IT)
12/16/2001: Schlachthof, Wiesbaden (DE)
12/17/2001: KSET Centre, Zagreb (HR)
12/18/2001: Estragon, Bologna (IT)
12/19/2001: Indian's Saloon, Sesto San Giovanni, Milan (IT)
12/20/2001: Mephisto, Barcelona, Mephisto (ES)
12/21/2001: Sports Hall, Girona (ES)
12/22/2001: Sala Mogambo, San Sebastian (ES)
12/23/2001: Macumba, Kerrang Christmas Party, Madrid (ES)
12/24/2001: Weekend, Sevilla (ES)
12/25/2001: Gamma, Murcia (ES)
12/26/2001: Roxy Club, Valencia (ES)
12/27/2001: ISC, Bern (CH)
12/28/2001: Shrine, Stockhol (SE) Sound Pollution meet and greet.
12/29/ 2001: Kulturzentrum Pelmke Hagen (DE)
12/30/ 2001: Falkendom, Bielefeld (DE)
12/31/ 2001: Wild At Heart, Berlin (DE)

Booking the tour was a crucial aspect of the entire endeavor. However, creating a truly successful tour requires much more than just securing dates and the crew plays a the most important role in this equation. Your strength as a band is only as strong as the team that propels you from one show to the next, building up the stage and the backline for soundchecks and performances, handling the technical aspects of sound and lighting, managing merchandise sales, and essentially doing whatever it takes to shield the band from the gritty challenges and obstacles that can arise. When you step onto that stage, you can't afford to have any shit or troubles weighing on your mind. They would only hinder your ability to deliver what the audience has paid for - a great night out and a performance never to be forgotten. It must be acknowledged that Marky always had an unwavering commitment to delivering. Regardless of how you may feel personally, once you step onto that stage, you owe it to the fans to give them everything you've got. No excuses.

Fortunately, I had a fair share of tours under my belt. However, I can't deny that I deeply longed for Manny. Sure, I somehow got the job done, but his expertise was on a whole other level. There were still certain aspects that I had to navigate through trial and error, learning as I went.

Les, the Belgian longtime friend of the Ramones whom we had met during the Marky Ramone Group trial shows, was enthusiastic about joining us as the new tour manager. This big-hearted man worked as a redcap, handling ground and flight dispatch for the Belgium National Airlines. With his expertise in efficient and effective logistics management, I was thrilled to have him on board. It seemed that even Marky found comfort and trust in Les taking charge of the caravan. In 2001, Europe also still had different currencies in each country, so having someone who could handle the financial aspects and didn't flip over conversion rates was crucial. What the best part was him honest and trustworthy which made him the perfect accountant to have by our side. Moreover, he was the mastermind behind our incredible merchandise booth. He designed it as a flight case, complete with interior lighting and lined with luxurious pink plush cloth. Putting cherry on top, he adorned it with our name, logo, and an outlined display of Marky's head. It truly was a masterpiece of artwork!

Putting together a kick-ass band was a whole different ball of wax. Circumstances made Stevey split, leaving us, once again, without a bass player. Although Dee and Stevey wouldn't have lasted in the long run, we were missing him as a crucial piece. Finding a replacement wasn't going to be the hard part; what we needed was someone who could commit to a full-blown tour. And that's when UxJx came into the picture, a straight-edge dude I knew from the scene, playing in various hardcore bands.

UxJx, short for Uniform Jantje, was a die-hard fan of Uniform Choice, the SxE band hailing from Orange County, California. Those little x's in his name symbolized the straight edge movement. It was the marks people drew on their hands to identify with the unwavering conviction. UxJx and I went way back. I knew him from years ago when I was still in the Midnight Men, and our bassist and female vocalist ditched the band one day to form Rise Above, one of Belgium's first hardcore acts. That band eventually transformed into the legendary Nations on Fire, and the leader, Edward, went on to establish Goodlife Recordings, pioneering one of Europe's biggest and earliest hardcore record labels.

I knew that UxJx had aspirations of going on tour, but when I tried to convince him, I sensed a bit of fear in him. He doubted his own abilities and believed he wasn't up to the task. However, he eventually agreed to join the road crew, which I gladly accepted. He also brought along another young kid named Tim, who had just started playing drums. With plenty of free time on his hands, he was more than willing to tag along with us. This meant that Marky would now have his own personal drum tech, and I remember how thrilled he was about that.

As I reflect on our road crew, there's one incredibly funny aspect that stands out. Marky, Dee, and I had absolutely nothing to do with the straight-edge lifestyle. We embraced every aspect of life, indulging in all kinds of food, including meat, and enjoying any kind of drink, alcohol included (except for Marky). And yes, we've had our fair share of dirty sex and the regular fornication. Ironically, our crew was the complete opposite. In hindsight, this had its advantages. We had the most sober crew ever to navigate the wild world of rock 'n' roll. While we were tearing up the stage, the backstage room remained untouched. The booze sat there, untampered with, and the mouthwatering meat that was occasionally offered to us went uneaten until we had the chance to indulge. However, we missed out on all the lettuce and tomatoes. You win some, you lose some.

During the load-in process, they were fully prepared to account for every item. They took great care to ensure that nothing was overlooked or left behind. Additionally, and luckily, there was never a need to search for anyone who may have gone missing due to the disorienting effects of multiple types of substance abuse. These kids were just perfection!

Pearl, Paiste and DW Drums productplacement at Midas Studios, Lokeren, Belgium

And that wasn't just it. A friend of UxJx and Tim, who had experience singing in various hardcore bands, somehow talked his way into the position of bass player. Unfortunately, he totally sucked at it, but since I was pretty hopeless myself, I figured that dealing with just four strings instead of six might be less of a hassle, and he would learn eventually. Hans was the typical pretty boy with a tan that made him look like he came from somewhere in the south, so I jokingly gave him the nickname Vito d'Agostini as if he were an Italian dude. That name was inspired by a Zeke song, and the tongue-in-cheek nature of the joke fit perfectly with the concept of SpeedKings.

To kick things off, we relied on word of mouth to connect us with a mysterious Eastern European dude named Tsepitch. This character happened to own a mammoth Mercedes Sprinter that he had expertly transformed into the ultimate touring machine. It boasted the perfect number of seats for our band and crew, and even had a custom-designed cargo area to house our backline equipment. But the pièce de résistance was undoubtedly the double bed bunk situated directly above our instruments. With this remarkable set-up, we were more than ready to hit the road in style! The crew donned TCB Crew shirts, representing the powerful mantra of "Taking Care of Business," a motto personally embraced by Presley during the early 1970s for his backing band. It's hard to think of a more fitting name for this exceptional crew, who are unequivocally the most devoted in the entire world!

Well, almost there, but not quite. We had to make sure Vito was ready, and let me tell you, it was no walk in the park. The whole setlist and breakneck speed we were playing at made it tough for him to keep up. He just wasn't on the same level as Manny and Stevey, not even close. They had this natural talent for self-preparation and quick learning that Vito seemed to lack entirely. It was like the Sex Pistols bringing on Sid Vicious, who couldn't hold a candle to Glen Matlock's musical skills but had that rebellious, pretty boy image that served its purpose in the band. Although, it is clear Malcolm McLaren had a hand in that marketing ploy. In our case, Vito was a necessary evil, and we simply didn't have enough time to find a replacement. Besides, he came as part of the package deal with the crew, so we had no choice but to make do with what we had. Time zooms by when you're juggling a million thoughts in your head, and in the blink of an eye, I found myself welcoming Marky back from his airport arrival. With only two days left before the tour kicked off, he had a mere day to recover from the jetlag and another day to rehearse the set with us. That second day of rehearsal was a lifeline for Vito, saving him from total catastrophe. Once the tour started rolling, there was no turning back. I'm pretty damn certain that if Marky had discovered Vito's abysmal playing skills during a full week of practice, he would have swiftly packed his bags and hit the road in the opposite direction.

On the 6th of December, the day that celebrates Saint Nicholas, the beloved old geezer who brings treats and toys to well-behaved children, we kicked off the tour in Brussels. Our destination was Magasin 4, a venue where we had previously performed a tryout show. That initial performance exceeded all the club's expectations, and we were greeted with open arms by the audience. It's quite amusing, really. Given that I am from Belgium, one might assume that we have played numerous shows in my home country. However, the opposite

is true. We have only had the opportunity to perform in Belgium on four occasions, and two of those times were at Magasin 4.

The following day, we made our way across the border into the Netherlands. Our place to be: The Hague, where we had a gig booked at a venue called Het Paard. It was an important night for us, as our Dutch distributor, Suburban Records, had organized a release party for our debut album as part of the tour. Ron, the guy in charge on Suburban's end, and I had been working together on this for a while now. We always communicated in English, so it was quite amusing when we sat down for dinner that evening and heard him talking, thinking we couldn't understand a word. We decided to have some fun with it and played along, pretending not to comprehend. Then, out of nowhere, we pulled a language switcheroo flash mob style, catching Ron off guard and leaving him speechless as if he had just crash-landed back to earth. But Ron was a good sport about it; he actually enjoyed the fact that we had taken the piss out of him.

One of the spectators that night was Bram, a friend-to-be. He recalls: "On December 7, 2001, I make my way to a small room located on the top floor of a complex in The Hague's Grote Marktstraat. This room, named "Paard op hol," pays homage to the local cultural center Het Paard, currently undergoing extensive renovations. It's the second show of Marky Ramone & the SpeedKings' tour, which kicked off the previous day in Brussels. As a journalist for Utrechts Nieuwsblad, I have a preliminary interview scheduled with Marky Ramone. Over six months have passed since the tragic loss of lead singer Joey Ramone, and I'm eager to delve into the post-Ramones era.

As I excitedly engage in conversation with Marky's friends in English, they respond in fluent Flemish. Huh! Who would've thought? Nevertheless, this initial brief exchange, particularly with Nick, forms the foundation of a punk rock connection that endures to this day. That's how it goes in this scene. There's no need for constant visits; simply knowing that you share the same musical "blood type" is enough to forge a bond.

I observed something incredible at the concert in The Hague: The crowd seemed to appreciate the SpeedKings' repertoire, even though it was unfamiliar to them. But it was only when the band launched into an unadulterated Ramones medley in the last fifteen minutes that things really started to get wild. Suddenly, the atmosphere ignited with old-fashioned chaos right in front of the stage. Young punks and heavily tattooed men, who could have easily been their fathers, pogoed furiously together. As Marky, the usually stoic drummer, exited the stage last, he uttered these words: *"This one was for Joey."* Those simple words struck a chord deep within the hearts of the fans, resonating with raw emotion."

After the gig, we barely had any time to rest. Our next performance was scheduled in Switzerland, which meant we had to cover over 600 miles to reach the Sommercasio Youth Club in Basel. The Dutch punk band Bambix was there to support us, adding great warming up that night.

But here's where my so-called impressive booking skills came into play. I had managed to secure us another show in Oslo, Norway, a mind-blowing 1000 miles further along the road. Luckily, we had the option to fly. Our crew took the tour van to Hamburg, Germany, while we boarded a plane. We would reunite with them the following day when they picked us up at Fuhlsbüttel HAM.

MEET THE TCB-CREW

The gig in Oslo was once again an extraordinary experience. It was organized by Andre Dahlman, a 21-year-old die-hard Ramones fan. "It's not a secret that I have always been and still am a massive Ramones fanatic. The second album I ever owned at the tender age of 9 was 'Leave Home,' which, in my humble opinion, is the greatest album ever made," Andy shared with me.

"I had the opportunity to witness the Ramones perform live on five occasions in Sweden, Norway, and Germany. I was so dedicated that at the age of 13 that I even ran away from home just to catch their first live show in Sweden. The Ramones meant everything to me. From the time I was 11 until I turned 18, my whole world revolved around them. I was so obsessed that once, I even counted Tommy's hi-hat strokes on 'It's Alive' and compared them to Marky's performance on 'Loco Live'... Marky won."

Needless to say, his excitement was off the charts when I reached out to him and inquired about any potential venues in Norway that might be interested in hosting The SpeedKings and Marky. Andre was heavily involved in the music scene for several years so he had an extensive network of contacts. Without wasting a second, he got in touch with the So What! Club in Oslo, a place where he had previously organized a tribute concert for the Joey after his passing. <the club readily agreed, and thus, the stage was set for an unforgettable show.

Upon our arrival at the airport, Andy was there to greet us. Technically, we could have easily hailed a taxi, but the young gun insisted on personally chauffeuring us to the venue. Actually, he wanted to be in the car with one of the revered Ramones members for a full hour. For him, it was an experience akin to having an audience with the pope himself. "If you had told me this when I was just a twelve-year-old kid, I would have laughed and dropped dead," he confessed as we settled into the old Mercedes Benz borrowed from his father for this occasion.

"The trip from the airport was absolutely epic. Marky, as a partner in crime, was riding shotgun, and we got into this deep conversation about my old man's wheels. He was throwing questions left and right, all about the engine and whatnot. Marky and the rest of the band were so chilled out it was like they were in their own rock 'n' roll paradise. However, we were running late, and I couldn't help but think they'd be pissed off about it. But you know what? Marky couldn't give a damn. All that mattered to him was finding a sex shop to score some raunchy magazines. What unfolded right before my eyes was almost unreal." Andy still feels amazed by this.

As soon as we arrived in the city center, our first mission was not to do a soundcheck but to find an adult bookstore. It must have been quite strange for Andre. He had finally met one of his idols in person. We had spent over an hour driving together, chatting about random things, and he probably expected our conversation to revolve around all things Ramones. But there we were, stepping into a grungy bookstore. Marky didn't seem too concerned about the awaiting soundcheck. He took his time, leisurely flipping through magazines. He knew we would wing it no matter what. Just as he was getting lost in the naked pages, his phone suddenly rang. I could see the panic on his face. It was Lady Marion calling. He tossed the phone *at me, urging me to answer and pretend that he was sound-checking.* "And get out of the store," he whispered urgently, *"when she hears the music playing in the background, she'll know we are in a sex shop!"* I almost choked on my own surprise.

Apparently, Marion knew Marky so well that she could immediately recognize his location just by the sound of the store's background muzak. "Marion, it's Nick here," I said in my deceptive voice. *"We made it safely to Norway. We're running a bit behind schedule. Marc is setting up right now. We'll get back to you soon."* Deep down, I knew she probably saw through my lies.

A little while later, at the So What! venue, The Graves had finished setting up, and we rushed through a quick sound check. We found ourselves in the backstage room, where they served dinner. One might expect that we had already experienced the strangest part of the evening, but then the most unthinkable happened next. Right in the middle of dinner, Marky suddenly felt the urge to take a dump. He strolled into the toilet that happened to be located in the same backstage room, leaving the door wide open. He continued chatting with all of us while taking care of his shitty business. Ah, nothing quite like getting up close and personal with your idols! It goes without saying that Andre was absolutely stoked to receive an invitation to join us on stage for a heart-pounding encore of Blitzkrieg bop. He grabbed hold of my guitar and played with an intensity that made it seem like it was the last thing on earth he would do. The most amusing part was when the show concluded, and I spotted him snatching the damp towel that Marky had used on stage. Curiosity got the best of me, so I inquired about his peculiar action. Andre nonchalantly revealed that he also possessed a towel he had taken from Dee Dee Ramone. *"One day, when science can transform DNA into a cloned human being, I'll be the lucky one with Marky and Dee Dee in my own room,"* he confessed. I couldn't bring myself to burst his bubble, but let's be real: having those two in your personal space is equivalent to wishing for a vacation in a psychiatric ward. It's no surprise that Andre was 21 at the time. Fits the bill perfectly.

The refreshing slumber at the nearby hotel revived us, but it was time for us to catch a flight back to Germany. The Hamburg Reeperbahn beckoned, calling out our names. Our crew had finished setting up for the soundcheck, and we were itching to explore downtown. Suddenly, the drummer from the support band approached me, practically begging me to use Marky's drumset. They had assumed it wouldn't be an issue, but now uncertainty filled their eyes. And truth be told, they had a valid point. Marky never allowed anyone else to play with his cherished kit. The only option left for these youngsters was to pack up and head home, their hopes crushed. I couldn't help but feel sorry for them, and I couldn't simply turn them away. So, I informed our crew that I would take Marky on a little excursion through the red-light district and treat him to dinner. In the meantime, they would allow the support band to use Marky's drums, carefully returning everything to its rightful place, hoping that Marky wouldn't notice a thing. And then, they would give me a call, signaling it was safe for us to return to the venue, ensuring we wouldn't stumble in during the middle of the support band's set. We had planned everything meticulously. This was the perfect scam.

Sometime later, we were getting ready for our performance. As Marky settled behind his drum set, I heard his voice from the back: *"Nick, some asshole played my drums!"*

Marky, an incredible and exceptionally accurate drummer, consistently delivered flawless beats with pinpoint accuracy. He never skipped a beat, always hitting the center of the Kevlar skin on his snare drum. The unfortunate drummer from the opening act, on the other hand, mercilessly battered the black drumhead in every imaginable spot except the one that mattered most—the center.

Wurzburg was the next stop, the sixth gig of the tour, and we knew it was going to be something extraordinary. The show at Zauberberg, aptly named the Magic Mountain, was organized by none other than Frank Droll, a close friend and the mastermind behind Devil's Shitburner Records. Frank was a force to be reckoned with - a bald-headed, heavily bearded man adorned with an array of metal piercings on his face and tattoos of spiders and venomous centipedes crawling up his arms. He kept those creepy crawlies as pets in his own home, a true animal lover with a taste for the dark and dangerous. Tonight was going to be an authentic, no-holds-barred rock'n'roll experience - not some watered-down phony rock'n'roll imitation. And to top it off, the venue, Zauberberg, was on the brink of destruction, setting the stage for a true demolition party. That night was an absolute riot. Frank, our incredibly generous host, decided to join the TCB crew and tag along on one of our upcoming tours.

First European Tour.
September 6, 2001 - Magasin 4, Brussels Belgium

Backstage with the Legendary King Koen and his wife Melinda.

First Euro Tour
December 7, 2001- Het Paard, Den Haag Holland
Suburban Distribution Party.

UN TRIBUTO A LOS RAMONES

MARKY RAMONE
& The SpeedKings
¡¡¡10 temas de los Ramones en directo!!!

MARTES, 25 DICIEMBRE 22:00 h.
Sala GAMMA
MURCIA

MIERCOLES, 26 DICIEMBRE 22:00 h
Sala ROXY CLUB
VALENCIA

Venta de entradas en: Tráfico, Contraseña, cafetería Habana, BBVA ticket y en propia sala
Venta de entradas en: BBVA ticket, centros autorizados y en propia sala

Venta anticipada: 2.000 pts (IVA incluido)
Venta en taquilla: 2.500 pts (IVA incluido)

www.sagamusic.org

CHAPTER 24

Supersonic Milky Maid

"A dairymaid can milk cows to the glory of God" - Martin Luther

Leaving Würzburg behind, our trusty tour van was en route to Aachen, where we were scheduled to perform at the Musikbunker. This colossal concrete bunker from WWII was about to witness a full-blown blitzkrieg. The German police were on high alert. Just moments before we arrived at the venue, our van was cornered by the Polizei. It was a nerve-wracking situation, considering our grungy punk-rock appearance and the fact that our van had Czech license plates. It was practically begging for trouble. We narrowly avoided a strip search, but the authorities were determined to inspect every inch of our van. Their hopes of finding a massive stash of drugs were dashed when they noticed the cross marks on the back of our crew's hands, which made it clear that there were no illegal substances to be found in the realm of Straight Edge.

The band and crew were in an awkward tension due to the police encounter. It could have been the influence of watching The Marathon Man on video during our drive that day, but all of a sudden, we transformed into a dodgy gang of shady Germans, speaking exaggerated and weird English. Bursting into laughter, we hilariously mimicked scenes from the film, shouting, *"Wherrrreee arrree ze diamonds?"* If anyone happened to witness our antics at that moment, they would surely have concluded that we were nothing more than a group of fools on an ill-conceived field trip.

The show flew by in a whirlwind, but I couldn't help but notice a striking German blonde who had been eyeing me throughout the entire set. As I stepped off the stage, ready to make my way to the backstage area, she intercepted me with a bold introduction. Her name was Claudia. Amidst the blaring music that blasted from the speakers, she boldly declared, *"I just wanna fuck your brains out!"* Pointing to her boyfriend nearby, she assured me that once she sent him home, she would be all mine. It seemed my opinion held little weight in this situation, just like her poor boyfriends. I couldn't help but wonder what they would call a hotwife in German. As she sauntered over to her man, I swiftly vanished into the crowd, not realizing that our paths would cross again. Little did I know her wild ride was only postponed in her mind. Claudia would return to shake things up when I least expected it.

After the kickass Aachen gig, we were on a tight schedule. The crew hustled us to Brussels Airport, where we hopped on a flight bound for London Heathrow, where a nightliner was waiting for us. Final destination: the Colchester Arts Centre. But that was just the beginning. We had another gig lined up in Rome, Italy, the day after the UK show. While we were tearing up Great Britain, our crew embarked on an overnight journey towards Italy. It was gonna be one hell of a ride.

To make things even more intense, heavy snowfall was predicted all across Europe. My mind raced with worry for our crew and equipment as they faced the treacherous task of crossing the snow-capped Alps in Switzerland. We all hoped they would make it safely. And even if they conquered the land of cuckoo clocks, Rome was nestled deep in the heart of the Italian boot.

The huge tour bus was a breath of fresh air compared to the cramped confines of the tour van. With comfortable bunk beds and plush sofas on the top deck, we had a prime view as we cruised through the streets of London.

Our night in Colchester kickstarted with a video interview that would be featured in a Ramones documentary. Backstage, we rubbed shoulders with the legendary British punk poet John Cooper Clarke and Animal from the Anti-Nowhere League. But as usual, chaos ensued. Once the show ended, we were grateful to retreat to the sanctuary of the bus, which transported us to the airport. Exhausted, we slept through the entire day until it was time to board.

In the departure hall, we caught the attention of a group of Italian Bella Ragazze who had indulged in a shopping spree in the British capital. These girls may have been prima donna babes, but it seemed that a taste of rock'n'roll was just what they needed to inject some excitement into their empty lives. When they overheard that we were heading to Rome for a live show for MTV, their interest in us skyrocketed.

Tsepitch, Les, UxJx, and Tim exceeded my expectations. From the moment we started this tour, they showcased their exceptional talent and professionalism, making them the tightest outfit I had ever had the pleasure of working with. Therefore, it came as no surprise to see them eagerly awaiting our arrival at the Leonardo Da Vinci–Fiumicino airport, their smiles stretching from ear to ear. Their journey to reach this point had been an adventure filled with challenges and obstacles that would have deterred most. But these guys persevered, refusing to let anything stand in their way. And now, we were off to our destination - Locanda Atlantide, tucked away in a dark back alley of Rome.

The crew of MTV Supersonic awaited our arrival, and as soon as I walked in, veejay Monica and I instantly hit it off. Vito and I found ourselves in the midst of an interview, creating Marky finger puppets out of the show's flyers. The interview itself, with Marky as the main guest, took on a more serious tone. I half expected Monica to fall asleep right in the middle of it. It definitely didn't have the same lightheartedness as the playful charade she had witnessed earlier.

The venue was packed to the brim, and we knew we had to give it our all since this performance would be broadcast on television. Rome and the Italian fans were beyond ready for us, and we kept the energy going with multiple encores. After the show, we hung out with some die-hard fans from the Ramones Fanclub. They graciously escorted us to the hotel in the heart of the city on their Vespa scooters. However, our arrival at the Chinese-owned hotel was met with displeasure from the triad behind the front desk. The Chinese ladies, seemingly part of some secret inbred sisterhood, gave us menacing looks. It became clear in the morning that they intended to overcharge us by doubling the room rates. Luckily, one phone call to the credit card company resolved the issue, as all payments were blocked. The anger within us started to rise, but we decided to leave without paying a cent.

I shouted at the toughest one among them as I gave her the finger, *"You should have stuck to an all-you-can-eat joint. This old dog won't be on your menu!"*

The next few days took us to Centro Social Pedro in Padova and brought us to share the stage with the Italian ska band, Shandon. A journalist, capturing the essence of our performance, proclaimed, "From the very beginning with 'Saturday Night,' it became abundantly clear that the Speedkings draw inspiration from the same well of music as The Almighty. The band played at high speed, with lyrics that delved into the really important things in life: sex, drugs, rock 'n' roll, and, of course, cars. It was impossible to overlook their iconic anthem, "Fuck Me," which is a timeless classic. Songs longer than three minutes are nowhere to be found. Instead, the rocking and pogoing are as intense as I last heard from Bad Religion in the good old days of "Suffer." There's really no need to worry about punk rock."

The gig set to take place at the Schlachthof in Wiesbaden ended up being a major setback. We departed Padova ahead of schedule, but unfortunately, Mother Nature had different plans for us. The weather conditions were already challenging, but to make matters worse, it seemed like the weather gods themselves were actively working against us. We found ourselves caught in the midst of a colossal snowstorm, rendering it impossible to reach our destination. This turn of events was particularly frustrating because we had a long night ahead of us as we were en route to Eastern Europe. It felt like we were on the brink of an all-night adventure, only to be thwarted by uncontrollable forces.

What would come next was a different cup o' tea. While touring with the Buckweeds, we had already crossed the borders of Slovenia and Croatia, immersing ourselves in a different kind of raw. One day, we found ourselves rocking out at a festival nestled in a stone quarry. It was like stepping back into the prehistoric era of the Flintstones. A raucous gathering of biker gangs on their bikes stripped down to their brutal, primal instincts. As far as drinks were concerned, beer was the only option. The culinary choices were as basic as it gets – a loaf of bread and a half-chicken. But they more than compensated with an abundance of strippers slinking their way through the sets, giving the event a truly Stone Age vibe. Armed with this raw and untamed spectacle etched in my mind, I could only imagine what awaited us at the KSET club in Zagreb.

As soon as we crossed the border into Croatia, it felt like we were transported back in time. The entire landscape, from the buildings to the roads, seemed frozen in the past. It was like stepping into a time capsule towards the forties or fifties. We had been given directions to a hotel that boasted four stars, and we were excited about the prospect of enjoying top-notch facilities. We didn't knew that in a country with Eastern European and communist roots, you have to divide the number of stars by at least four or five to compare it to Western standards.

The hotel itself was massive, a prime example of communist architecture. Sculptures and mosaics adorned its exterior, paying homage to the glorious past of the socialist movement and the comrades who fought alongside each other. However, when we approached the front desk, it felt more like we were entering a social service helpdesk rather than a hotel reception. A typical place where they give you the eternal runaround, from pillar to post.

And we hadn't even laid eyes on our accommodations yet. The harsh reality hit us square in the face as we stepped into the haven where we were going to spend the night. Tim and UxJx were assigned to share a room, but as soon as they departed to wait for us in the lobby, Vito and I seized the opportunity to sneak into their quarters using the spare key we had obtained from the front desk. With infantile grins plastered on our faces, we proceeded to completely rearrange the entire space. The cupboard was upended, defying gravity. The beds were stacked on top of it, while the mattresses mysteriously vanished into the confines of the minuscule shower stall. It was a moment of juvenile amusement that injected some much-needed warmth into the cold winter day.

We finally found ourselves with a rare opportunity to unwind and explore the old town of Zagreb. The entire group, except for Marky, reveled in the historical and cultural richness of the city. For some reason, though, Marky seemed disinterested in such intellectual pursuits, opting instead to retreat to his room for an extended period of rest. I couldn't fathom why he chose accommodations that resembled a locker room for jocks, but as he often said, "It is what it is," a phrase he used when faced with inexplicable situations.

Just like every other show on this tour, there was a big turnout. But what set this one apart from all the others we had done was the fact that the audience seemed already wasted before the show even began. People were scattered around, clutching full-sized liquor bottles in their hands. This was not a place for pussies. Damn, sure, not for the faint-hearted. I couldn't spot a single person with a simple beer bottle. Instead, whiskey and full-blown vodka bottles were being thrust in my face. The atmosphere was deafening. I mean, really loud and rowdy. The crowd looked more like a gang primed for a street fight rather than a group of people out to have a good time at a music show. It was intense, to say the least.

This performance really had Marky feeling the pressure. We had to navigate our way to the stage, pushing through the sea of people. Marky absolutely despised this. The one thing that particularly irked Marky was when fans would touch him without permission. He hated it so much that he often talked about having the band acting as a group of bodyguards to shield him from unwanted contact. Marky's unique autistic demeanor made him an easy target for those seeking to mock and ridicule him. Vito was always eager for a good laugh and loved playing pranks on others. In KSET, as we we were on our way to the stage, straight through the audience, Vito was right behind Marky, ready to strike. The mischievous troublemaker began lightly tapping Marky's shoulder and then swiftly yanking on his leather jacket. Each pull became more forceful, causing Marky's frustration to escalate, unaware that it was Vito who was behind the antics. Marky directed his complaints towards Les. I couldn't help but notice Vito struggling to contain his laughter, nearly pissing himself.

This was going to be an all-out, no-holds-barred experience. The crowd was right in our faces, and as soon as I struck the first chord, they erupted into a frenzy of wild pogoing. I was taken aback by how familiar they were with most of the lyrics, shouting along in a drunken pirate-like fashion. The album had only just been released, but it was clear that the die-hard fans had already secured their copies.

Then, out of nowhere, I was ambushed. A colossal woman stormed the stage and began to strip. The guys at the front went into a frenzy as they watched her remove her t-shirt and struggle to undo her huge bra. Her breasts were so large that they defied any attempt to fit into delicate French lingerie. As I glanced to the side, it felt like I had been transported to a dairy farm where a factory worker was about to attach suction cups to those gigantic nipples.

I felt a wave of queasiness wash over me as I watched the mammoth breasts sway back and forth, defying gravity. And then, she made her move towards me. She grabbed me from behind, and I could feel two hard nipples pressing against my shirt. Almost instinctively, my arms started to rise as if a police officer had threatened me with a 9mm Glock and demanded that I raise my hands.

Tim and UxJx were caught off guard, their faces filled with surprise. I yelled at them to get that relentless milky maid off my back, but it seemed like the two boys lacked the courage to confront her. As a result, she continued to press against me, almost pushing me off the stage, lost in an orgasmic state of ecstasy. I knew Marky was relishing this spectacle. I could picture his face, a wide grin spreading across it as he signaled the crew to hold back. However, he had another challenge to tackle halfway through the set - his snare stand had broken. The snare drum was loose and unstable, but we were in such an intense performance mode that stopping and replacing the damn thing was out of the question.

In the chaos, Tim rushed onto the stage. In the brief pause between two songs, he discarded the broken stand with a forceful throw, positioned himself at Marky's feet, and tightly secured the snare drum in place. Without hesitation, Marky counted off 1-2-3-4, and we launched into the next set of songs. Tim's swift action screamed PUNK ROCK POINTS! That night, he earned a medal for his unwavering dedication and self-sacrifice. It's interesting to note that today, he is the drummer for The Kids, one of Belgium's earliest and most renowned punk bands. Fate works in mysterious ways.

Once again, we winged it. We dominated and overpowered Zagreb, and we survived. The crowd, initially plastered to the walls, had transformed into a horde of drunken zombies. It was time for us to retreat to the hotel. As we sat in the van, a persistent car followed closely behind, honking incessantly and swinging from left to right. It turned out that some die-hard fans had made the decision to tail us all the way to the hotel. These hardcore kids were willing to spend the night in the freezing cold just to catch a glimpse of us as we departed in the morning. Talk about insanity in the East!

European Tour 2001
December 17 KSET, Zagreb, Croatia

Soundcheck at KSET.

December 20, 2001
Kerrang Show, Barcelona, Spain

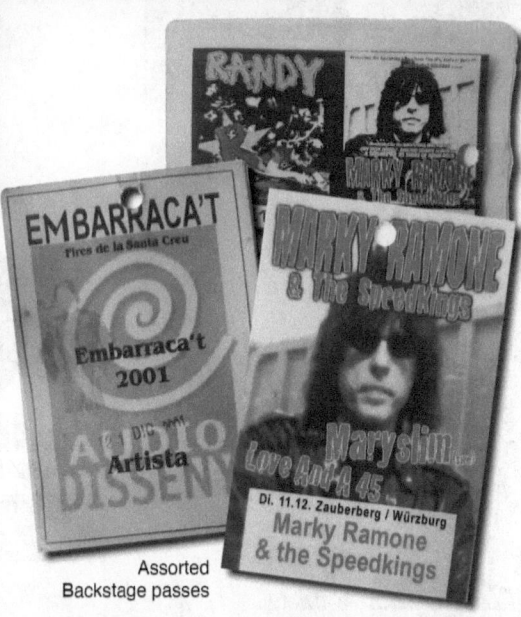

Assorted
Backstage passes

Bringing the Blitzkriep Bop into Germany.
Hagen and Aachen shows.

Locanda Atlantide, Rome, Italy - MTV Supersonic show

Stockholm Syndrome: Me with Jari-Pekka, Vito D'Agostini, Calle van Schewen of White Jazz Records, Dee Jackwalker, the bodyguard drummer from NYC and Kenny of the Cretins.

On stage at the Shrine Venue in Stockholm. Jari-Pekka counts down. My guitar is gone so I guess Kenny Bergdahl is ripping away the Blitzkrieg Bop.

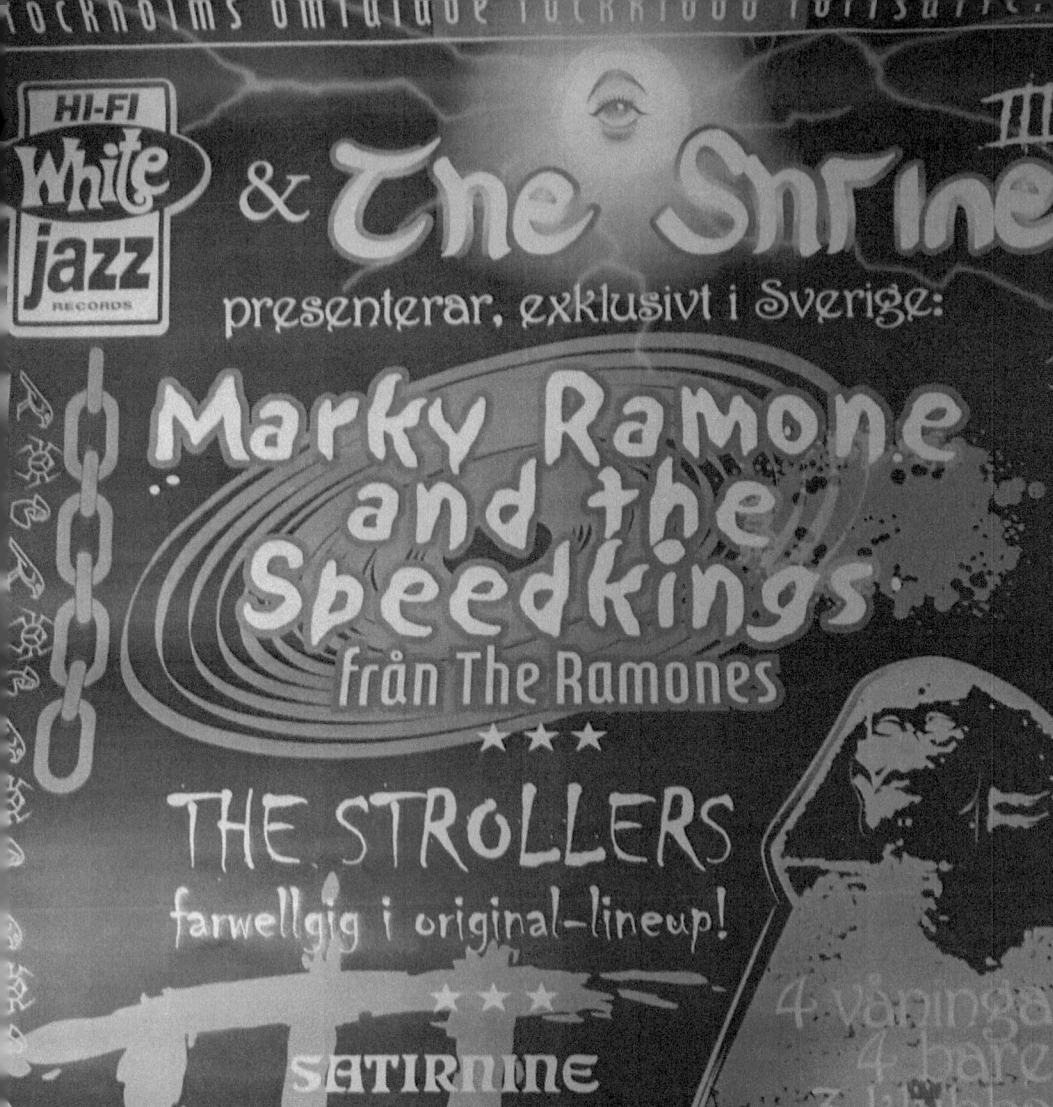

CHAPTER 25
The Wild at Heart Piss-Bottle Man

"Every time I pop, I think of my pop and pay my dues." - Mike Watt

On our journey back to Italy, we cruised through Bologna, playing at the Estragon club as we made our way to Milan, where we ended up once again at the Hells Angels clubhouse. Ready to experience another mind-blowing punkshow - "punks not allowed." The one percenters had their own set of rules, and who were we to question that? I remember that the clubhouse had one massive, authentic pizza oven. This wasn't your average pizza joint; these bad-ass bikers knew how to make a mean pie. It was quite possibly the most exquisite pizza I had ever tasted, made even more satisfying by the knowledge that it was crafted by one of these rough-and-tumble bikers.

After our incredible pasta-filled escapades in Italy, it was time to take on Spain. We had a series of seven shows lined up, and with Christmas just around the corner, it was no easy task to secure these gigs during the holiday season. However, I was determined and managed to make it happen. Finding that delicate balance between expenses and earnings was crucial, and I made sure to lock it down.

Leaving Milan behind, we embarked on a road trip through the picturesque landscapes of Southern France, heading towards our destination: Barcelona, Spain. Awaiting us like a mythical creature ready to devour our souls was the infamous Mephisto club, known for its raucous hard rock and heavy metal shows. It seemed like an unusual choice for this band, but we were ready to shake things up.

I remember our performance going smoothly, but the most memorable part for me was what went down in the backstage room. Just before we were about to take the stage, two girls managed to sneak their way in and introduced themselves as Alien Love, a Spanish heavy rock band. These girls looked like they were from another planet, with their goddess-like appearance and their tight leather pants and revealing tank tops. They were like the irresistible Spanish version of Girlschool. Accompanying them was a shady-looking guy known as CNN, nicknamed so because he worked as a cameraman for the news network.

Marky found himself captivated by the attention of the girls, who were insistent on throwing a wild party. However, Dee and Vito weren't in the mood, and the crew was still busy loading the backline. Marky, exhausted from his journey spanning over 700 miles from Italy to Spain, was longing for his bed. That left me as the only one tempted enough to venture into the back of the Alien Love van.

This beat-up old van had been transformed into a makeshift love shack, adorned with purple pillows, psychedelic lights, and a large, comfortable mattress. CNN took the driver's seat, and we fled into the dark but promising Barcelona night. One of the stops was Sala Magic, a smaller club where I had previously performed with the Buckweeds.

Inside the club, the girls were treated like royalty, and free shots of whiskey kept flowing endlessly. CNN, always equipped with a stash of cocaine, indulged in line after line. It was a true Spanish white-line fever. Surprisingly, the combination of alcohol and drugs had an interesting effect on me - I remained focused like never before. I didn't get drunk, nor did I get high.

As the sun rose at 8 in the morning, they dropped me off at the hotel just in time for breakfast. The rest of the band assumed I had taken a leisurely stroll down the street when I walked in. Ah well, what happens in the alien love van stays in the alien love van.

The day after, we found ourselves in the Basque country. This part of Spain has a completely different vibe compared to the rest of the country.

It's always felt more intense and way more violent. The show at the Mogambo was no exception. The energy was off the charts, fueled even more by a real Ramone. But despite the explosive atmosphere, it all ended up being good, rowdy fun. That is until the next morning when we discovered our van had been stolen right from the street in front of the hotel. Or at least, that's what we assumed. After making a few phone calls, we learned that during the night, someone had smashed one of the windows in an attempt to grab some valuables. The thieves ended up taking one of our cheap backup guitars but had to flee in a hurry. The Basque police, upon finding our van with a smashed window and a foreign license plate, decided to tow it away. In their minds, they saw an opportunity for the Basque terrorist group ETA to steal our van and use it for a car bomb attack. Luckily, we managed to retrieve the van just in time to hit the road again. We got a replacement window installed quickly and efficiently.

The over-popular heavy rock magazine Kerrang awaited us in Madrid. They were hosting their extravagant X-Mas party, with Marky and the SpeedKings as the featured dance act of the night. Every year, the magazine puts on a show in Madrid to honor the best-selling heavy rock artists and records. They invited us to be part of this grand charade, and the event was hosted by a typical Spanish platinum blonde with a penchant for hard rock. She embodied the type of person who is all talk but fails to deliver in the end, leaving you high and dry. Easy to wet, hard to get. She attempted to have us toss free CDs into the audience, but they vanished quicker than she could count. At that very moment, Dee and I made a spontaneous decision - we believed the crowd deserved another cheap present. Seizing her by the arms and legs, we swung her around, preparing to launch her into the outstretched hands of the testosterone-fueled rockers below. Like an alley cat, she fought back with kicks and scratches, her eyes shooting fiery glares our way. It became abundantly clear that our hopes for an exhilarating adventure had dissolved like snowflakes under the scorching Spanish December sun. Christmas Eve was just around the corner. The Kerrang babe had fled with the reindeer and the sled.

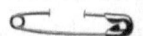

Every single day, Marky would hound Les to record the entire set on video just so he could scrutinize it later. Each member's performance was dissected and commented on without fail. However, it was Vito who bore the brunt of Marky's watchful eye. "I know that I was not the best bass player in the world. Almost daily, I got confronted with it, but I always gave it my best. Full force, always," Vito confesses. When it came to Vito, the critiques took a more cutting and insulting turn. Vito swallowed his pride and soldiered on, doing the best he could and enduring it all because he was having such an incredible great time. He simply chalked it up to Marky being an insufferable jerk: "I put up with it for a few weeks because every day was a blast, and I figured Marky was just being an asshole about it."

In Madrid, the tension between Marky and Vito reached a breaking point. When Marky pulled Vito aside, the unspoken words hung heavy in the air: *"You are just not fit for it!"* Maybe there was some truth to that. The bass was never Vito's first choice, but as a vocalist, he had belted out his heart at hundreds of gigs. He absolutely knew what touring was all about. Fed up with Marky's attitude, Vito finally snapped and declared his intention to walk away, escape the chaos, and return home for Christmas with his family. Marky fired back, acknowledging Vito's courage to speak his mind but refusing to let anyone abandon the tour. *"You have one pair of balls, and we're in this together,"* he declared defiantly. *"Let's put an end to the drama and make the best of this."*

After that fateful night in Madrid, a shift occurred, and things kinda changed for the better, and Vito regained his confidence.

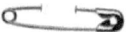

Santa Claus was in for a whirlwind of surprises, both good and bad. Little did we know, there was even more excitement awaiting us. Tony made a comeback, and it just so happened to be on December 24th, the night before Christmas. Now, any sensible person would argue that performing on such a night is simply impossible. However, as we drove into Sevilla, the sight that greeted us was nothing short of astonishing. Larger-than-life posters plastered all over town showcased none other than ourselves. We were scheduled to rock the stage at the Weekend venue at 6 o'clock in the evening, with a strict deadline of 8 o'clock so that our fans could make it home in time for their festive Christmas dinner. It was an ingenious plan, and despite Tony's previous mishaps in Girona, he had truly redeemed himself this time. The venue was packed, as no one else had dared to schedule a show on this special night.

At precisely 8 o'clock, our whole crew and our family members who had flown in for the Christmas weekend found solace in a Chinese restaurant that miraculously remained open. The atmosphere was filled with joy, soy, and camaraderie, a welcome respite after spending weeks on the road. We felt confident that our upcoming Christmas show in Murcia would be just as successful as this one.

On Christmas Day, Marky had a scheduled meeting with a prominent Spanish magazine for yet another interview. The designated location was the hotel lobby where we were staying. Marky, as usual, was taking his time perfecting his hairdo while Vito and I were just hanging out. The woman reporter approached us since we were the only ones in the lobby who had that rock'n'roll vibe. It's worth noting that the hotel and its lobby were both massive. So, we found a comfortable spot for ourselves and the reporter to sit down and commence the interview. However, it quickly became apparent that she had quite an arrogant attitude. Aside from guiding us to the interview spot, she completely disregarded our presence. It was crystal clear that she was solely interested in the Ramones angle and couldn't care less about the SpeedKings. There was no chance of conducting the initial part of the interview, and she made it abundantly clear that the SpeedKings could go to hell and fuck themselves.

Vito and I didn't need much to hatch a plan to take down the conceited bitch. When Marky entered the room, she practically jumped off the couch. I wouldn't have been surprised if she wanted to devour him whole. She was completely consumed with him, oblivious to everything else around her. In that split second, both Vito and I noticed her tape recorder, ready to capture every word from the Rock God himself. Before we knew it, the recorder vanished into thin air, and we casually walked away. About ten seats down, we discreetly hid the device under one of the thick cushions of a lounge chair. It didn't take long before Marky confronted us, shouting, *"Where's that damn recorder? You guys took it, didn't you?"* We acted as if we were from another planet. The reporter was livid, but we insisted they search their own belongings. It took nearly half an hour before we gave in, and suddenly, Vito "found" her precious tape deck. We played innocent, knowing that Marky saw right through us. He knew we were responsible, and as he wasn't exactly fond of Vito anyway, he made him the scapegoat. But it was worth it. We weren't going to get that interview, no matter what.

Once again, Tony struck gold with the turnout. The Gamma Club was completely full and sold out. We were en route to Valencia for our final show in Spain at the Roxy Club. Murcia and Valencia were not too far apart, giving us plenty of time for an extensive soundcheck.

Vito believed he had ample time to go and acquire a new punk rock haircut, and he would have succeeded if it weren't for the fact that he lost his way on the way back: "I recall being fashionably late for soundcheck because I was wandering aimlessly after leaving that sketchy barber establishment. Those winding Valencia streets all appeared the goddamn same to me. Meanwhile, Marky was seething with anger, fuming, on the verge of exploding."

The audience was a wild and crazy lot, hurling all kinds of crazy shit onto the stage. Shards of broken glass and spilled beer littered the floor, adding to the chaotic atmosphere that hung in the air. We tore through each song with lightning speed, our performance tight as hell, thanks to our tireless touring routine. That week in Spain was the turning point for me, finally making me feel like I truly owned that bass, man. It took a damn long time to get there.

Once we wrapped up our set, the place erupted like a volcano, the crowd hungry for more. Marky, in all his pissed-off glory, boldly declared, *"Fuck it, no encores tonight."* But the rest of us were amped up and ready to take it to the next level. Marky stormed off to the backstage room, leaving me behind as Nick and Dee ditched me as well. The crowd outside went apeshit, banging on the walls, demanding our return. And there I stood, alone in Marky's backstage lair, amidst the chaos and with adrenaline coursing through my veins, he revives the moment while reflecting upon it.

Nick and Dee were furious beyond belief as Marky adamantly refused to step back onto the stage. I have to confess, it was an incredibly tense situation, even by SpeedKings' standards. But hey, that's exactly what we were all about. We lived for those intense moments. We owed it to the crowd since that was exactly what they came here for.

As Vito and Marky lingered in the backstage area, an inferno of rage burned within me, seeking release. In an attempt to alleviate my anger, I unleashed a water bottle with all my might, hurling it towards the door of the room. The impact reverberated with a resounding thud, causing both Dee and myself to exchange knowing glances. We were well aware that Captain Marky would not tolerate any form of mutiny. Hastily, we made our way back towards the stage, hoping to avoid any further confrontation.

Then, the door swung open, revealing Marky's furious expression. His voice dripped with venom as he barked, *"Who the fuck threw that goddamn bottle?!"* Caught in the midst of their conversation, I overheard him assuring Vito, *"I know it wasn't you, and I know you won't betray your comrades. But someone has hell to pay!"* Marky's wrath was about to be unleashed upon whoever came in his way.

I could sense the rush of adrenaline coursing through Vito's veins. He was just as invested in this madness as I was. If it weren't for Marky's presence in the room, Vito might have been the one hurling that bottle.

Marky dashed back to the stage, saluting the cheers from the crowd, and we cranked out another wicked set of encores. "Absolute mayhem surrounded us, but damn, we put on one hell of a show. Those were the fuckin' days," Vito's eyes sparkled with pure joy.

After Spain, we trudged our way to Switzerland for a gig in Bern. I can't recall a single thing about the ISC. All I knew was that we were making our way to Stockholm, where White Jazz was throwing a release party for our album.

Even though my memories of the Stockholm show are vivid, my dear friend Jari-Pekka had his own mind-blowing saying: "December 2001 was an absolute whirlwind for me, leaving me yearning for a much-needed break to catch Marky's concert. I had been tirelessly dedicated throughout the entire fall season, especially working on my Joey Ramone book. Finally, on December 26, I embarked on a journey from my small hometown of Kauhajoki to Tampere, where the great Finnish band called Pojat was about to rock the stage.

In the early hours of the morning, I hurriedly made my way to the bus station, filled with anticipation for the arrival of a package sent by Hannu, the mastermind behind Woimasointu. The demand for the SpeedKings single had been off the charts during this tour, resulting in a lightning-fast sell-out. To meet this insatiable demand, Hannu Jokinen graciously arranged for another batch of singles to be shipped to me in Tampere.

During my journey on the ferry, I made a purchase of Salmiac Vodka for the SpeedKings and grabbed some chocolate for Marky, who has been clean and sober for many years. The next morning, I decided to reach out to Calle von Schewen, the band's label manager, who informed me that their flight had been delayed. So, I let him know that I would head to the hotel in the meantime.

As soon as I arrived at the hotel, I spotted Marky strutting in with his signature swagger, and we exchanged friendly greetings. It wasn't long before the rest of the band members rolled in, each one with a radiating aura. They revealed that they had unleashed their sonic fury on 25 mind-blowing shows in just 26 days, conquering stages across ten different countries. Their rock 'n' roll rampage had been so good. Unfortunately, Mother Nature's mother nature decided to throw a wrench in their plans, forcing them to cancel one show due to a vicious snowstorm.

In the meantime, Kenny Bergdahl, a member of the Ramones cover band called Cretins, arrived at the airport on a different flight. We all gathered together and engaged in a long but entertaining chat. Despite their exhaustion, the band members were surprisingly friendly. It was captivating to hear their stories from the tour. I gave them the salmiac vodka that I had purchased specifically for them. Calle, who believes that Finnish beer is superior to Swedish beer, also joined in and enjoyed some of it. Soon after, Peter, from Vitaminic.se, an online magazine, made his appearance. Marky joined us after taking a rest, and Peter proceeded to conduct a photo shoot.

Kenny approached Nick and asked if he could join in playing the guitar for a few songs that evening. They agreed that he would perform "Blitzkrieg Bop." A month earlier, it had been decided that I would sing a couple of songs. Nick proposed that "Blitzkrieg Bop" and "I Wanna Be Sedated" would be suitable choices for me. Following this discussion, Marky, Nick, Peter, and I ventured out for a series of interviews.

The Shrine venue sat conveniently close to the hotel, so we strolled over to make sure Marky's drums were in tip-top shape and handled some technical business. Marky had an eye for detail and made sure everything was just right. Eventually, Marky and Calle hopped in a cab to do a record signing at the Sound Pollution record store. Meanwhile, me and the rest of the crew and our buddies sauntered down the street and headed back on foot. It wasn't even a mile away. As we arrived at Sound Pollution, we noticed a pretty substantial line forming outside. And guess who I bumped into? My pals Jari 'Juki' Lehtola, Fredrik 'Freddy' Eriksson, and Iggy Pettersson. Instead of tagging along with the band inside, I decided to stick around outside with them. The bands' meet and greet lasted a solid half hour.

The band made their way back to the venue, ready to do their soundcheck. When we returned to the club ourselves, we were met with the performance of an all-female band called Satirnine. Despite their young age, these girls knew how to rock and roll. Later on, it was Maryslim's turn to take the stage, followed by the Strollers. Personally, I found their performance to be quite lackluster. They seemed to have a chip on their shoulder when it came to the SpeedKings. Blaming them for the subpar sound quality, they acted pretty poorly. One of the members of the Strollers even mistook me for one of the SpeedKings and approached me. Curiosity got the better of me, and I decided to accompany him to talk to Dee. The Strollers' member was adamant that the SpeedKings had intentionally sabotaged their sound, but it simply wasn't possible. The SpeedKings didn't even have their own sound engineer for the show.

And at long last, it finally happened. The anticipation surged through my veins as I eagerly awaited the start of the show. Nick and I had made a pact that I would only perform the "Blitzkrieg Bop" song. I purposely positioned myself away from the front row, craving the freedom to leap and thrash about when the music ignited. It was no surprise that the opening anthem from Marky Ramone & The SpeedKings was none other than "SpeedKings Ride Tonight." The energy in the venue was electrifying as they belted out lively renditions of "R'n'R Asshole" and "Manuelita" early on in their set, infectiously catchy tunes that had the crowd in a frenzy. Then came the moment I had been waiting for, as the familiar chords of "Chinese Rocks" filled the air, signaling the first Ramones song of the night. The SpeedKings flawlessly delivered their performance, allowing me to bounce joyously alongside my fellow fans. And there, on the left side of the stage, stood Iggy, Freddy, and Juki, fully immersed in the spectacle before them. At times, I found myself headbanging in unison with them, completely caught up in the raw power of the music.

The opening tracks, "California Sun" and "Glad To See You Go," set the stage perfectly for the encore. Positioned by the stairway, I met up with Juki, who had his camera ready to capture some epic shots during "Blitzkrieg Bop." The crowd was on fire, belting out the lyrics to "I Wanna Be Sedated" and "Girls & Gasoline." These songs had it all - high-octane, relentless energy mixed with moments of pure bliss, perfect for kicking back and soaking up the sun.

With his leather jacket on, Kenny made his way towards the stage, fully embodying the spirit of the Ramones. And then it was my turn. Nick graciously introduced me, praising my website as the ultimate and most comprehensive source for all things Ramones. And to top it off, he introduced Kenny from the Cretins, adding even more excitement to the atmosphere.

"Blitzkrieg Bop" was the ultimate climax of the show, leaving the crowd brimming with contentment. The SpeedKings flawlessly delivered what their fans craved, belting out a staggering 23 songs throughout the over-exciting night.

As the night drew to a close, the SpeedKings shared their hotel rooms with me and my friends. The following morning, we arose from our slumber and embarked on a tranquil journey to the airport. The car ride was a peaceful respite, allowing us to reflect on the triumph of the previous night."

Sweden was actually the first country where we experienced the exhilarating phenomenon of spontaneous boob-flashing. This captivating occurrence would become increasingly prevalent on subsequent tours. At the Shrine show, a stunning Swedish blonde on the front stage boldly discarded her t-shirt, leaving Vito and our straight-edge crew momentarily startled and flushed with embarrassment. It was an unexpected sight that momentarily diverted their attention from the euphoric spectacle unfolding in the crowd. Welcome to rock'n'roll!

We soared back from Sweden, ready for the last leg of the tour. Deutschland, the land of "Ze Diamonds," would be our way out. We were all worn out and drained, never having experienced such a challenge that pushed us to our limits. The Kulturzentrum Pelmke gig was just another stop on the tour. Nothing particularly memorable happened, except for Marky doing an interview for Tooraloo Radio. Besides the usual questions about SpeedKings and the Ramones, I could tell he was craving some downtime. "This touring is so crazy, I don't even have the time to take a shit," he confided to the radio host. Little did the presenter know that Marky's words were more than just a figure of speech. I couldn't help but remember the shithouse talks back in Oslo. And to add to that, Marky earned the title of the ultimate piss-bottle man for the tour. While the rest of us made pit stops at gas stations to pee, Marky kept on filling bottle after bottle. Life on the road is a weird thing, and you encounter more than just the wild rock'n'roll lifestyle. Unexpected things happen, like people falling ill. In Bielefeld, Vito found himself in dire need of a dentist. He had been suffering from excruciating pain for days and desperately needed a professional to alleviate his agony. The dentist managed to help him, but Vito was left feeling disoriented and dazed. The show itself became a hazy blur for both of us. However, amidst the foggy memories, one thing stood out vividly - the mosh pit right in front of the stage. It was chaotic as always, with a few obnoxious drunk punks ruining the experience for everyone else. Everything was going relatively okay until one of those imbeciles decided to throw an empty bottle of Beck's beer against the wall behind the drum kit. The sound of shattering glass echoed through the venue. In an instant, Marky leaped off his drum set, charging into the crowd with determination, and delivered a resounding earwipe to the troublemaker. The tough punk was left stunned, resembling a defeated schoolyard bully as he drifted away.

Our focus was now solely on the grand finale, New Year's Eve in Berlin. The Wild at Heart club had earned its reputation as one of the finest venues in all of Europe. Opening for us were the incredible Bones from Sweden. Those guys were beyond amazing, and I couldn't think of anyone better suited for the job. But things were about to get even better.

Lea and Uli, the club's owners, were as passionate about music as we were. Uli had set up a recording studio in the basement. Our final performance was going to be captured and preserved in the best possible way. We had every intention of releasing it exclusively for our devoted fan club.

The Alive CD finally saw the light of day some months later. In my humble opinion, it is one of the most mind-blowing live recordings I've ever come across. When you crank up the volume and dim the lights, you're transported right into the heart of the action. It took nearly 22 years for it to also be released on vinyl, and now, not just 13 but 19 tracks are available for your listening pleasure. Each time I listen to it, it catches me at the absolute exhilarating high that left me breathless after the clock struck twelve in Berlin.

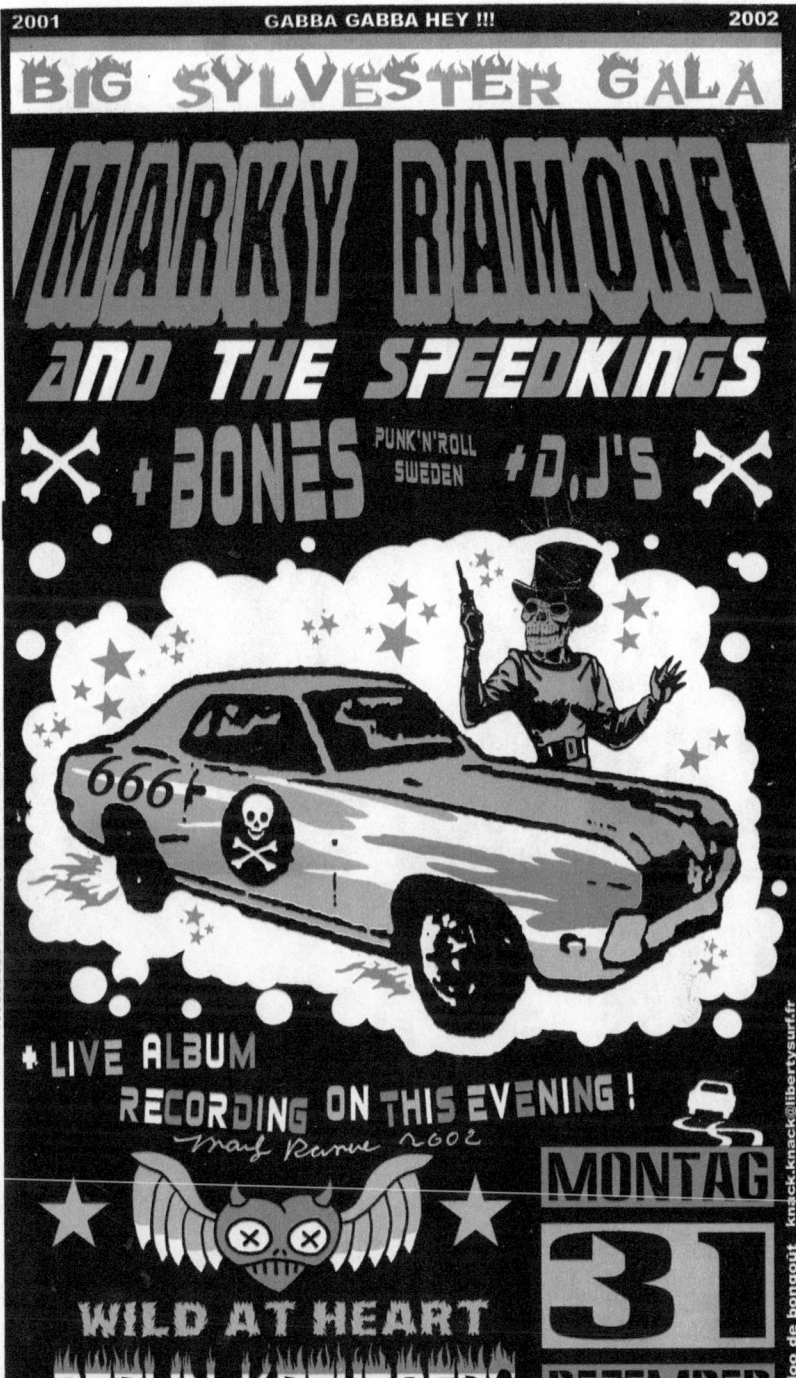

CHAPTER 26
Rawk over Scandinavia

"Don't wait till your deathbed to tell people how you feel. Tell them to fuck off now!" - Old Viking saying

The first SpeedKings appearance had been an absolute triumph. The album soared to great heights, capturing the hearts of kids all over Europe. While White Jazz took charge of the European release, Marky took it upon himself to secure a license for the US and Argentina. I was thrilled to have his support in this venture, but little did I know that it would turn out to be a disastrous decision.

As expected, the band didn't see a single cent of the advances made for both licenses. Shockingly enough, it was even a struggle to obtain a few copies of our own albums. It soon became clear that this was not an isolated incident but rather a recurring pattern of deceit. In my world, a word holds immense value and carries more weight than a mere signature on paper. When you shake hands on a deal, it should be binding, a sacred promise.

Yet, time and again, I found myself standing alone, the sole believer in these naive notions. It was frustrating to witness the lack of integrity and honor in an industry that thrived on passion and artistry. But I refused to let this discourage me. In the end, it wasn't just about the money or the fame. It was about leaving a mark on the world.

In 2002, Thirsty Ear unleashed their first album in the United States. Prior to this, I had no knowledge of their existence, and all I could gather was that they were known for their jazz releases. However, we stood out like the oddballs on their roster. It seemed as though they were uncertain about how to handle an album like ours. Unfortunately, we never received any backup or support for our release. To make matters even more perplexing, the label and Marky decided to rename the album "Legends Bleed." I couldn't help but wonder if this choice was somehow connected to the untimely deaths of both Dee Dee and Joey, but Marky's intentions remained a mystery to me.

On the other side of the world, in Argentina, Fogon Distribution released the CD under the title "No If's And or But's." This was another brainchild of Marky's, and personally, I wasn't a fan of it. However, there was no point in arguing or fighting against it. Sometimes, you just have to choose your battles wisely and let certain things slide.

For our first European tour, I connected with a dude named Hannu, who ran Woimasointu Records in Finland. I think it was Jari-Pekka who hooked us up. Hannu operated this record label as a hobby, but he had so much passion for it. He was all about keeping things simple, no contracts or paperwork. Just a "let's do it" mentality. To support the tour, he suggested we release a 7-inch record. I sent him a song that we had only recorded as a demo, one that didn't make it onto the album in time. That track was called "SpeedKings Ride Tonight." We quickly laid it down in the studio with my 18-year-old cousin on drums, and that kid absolutely nailed it. We were short on time and couldn't get Marky to do the proper drum tracks, so we made the decision to press that raw demo. On the flip side, we included a studio outtake from Hot-Rods-R-Us. The thing is, when we re-recorded that demo song later on for our second album with Marky, it just didn't have the same magic. It never quite sounded right. Marky just couldn't get into the right beat, and he didn't even manage to simply copy it.

The sophomore album we recorded remained withheld from public release to this day. I've affectionately referred to it as my rock 'n' roll pension plan, waiting patiently for the day when I can dedicate time to completing it. Within its musical depths lie some truly remarkable gems, such as the radio commercial we did for Rheingold Beer. And let's not forget the rendition of The Clycke's hit single, "Red Rubber Ball." Plus, brace yourself for the adrenaline-fueled anthem, "Son of Sam," a high-octane NYC rocker. Stay tuned, and you never know when it hits the streets.

After completing our first tour, I wasted no time in preparing for the next one. We had a mere two months before hitting the road again, and it was a clear decision to head north and conquer the Scandinavian countries. We could only hope that the arrival of Spring would bring with it less snow compared to the harsh December we had endured.

Meanwhile, Vito was out of the picture. Marky had spent an entire month dealing with him and had reached his limit. "Dee, you step up and handle the bass duties. We'll manage with just one guitar. It will make us tighter but maybe less outspoken. But for sure, it will cut down on expenses and make our travels lighter." I can't say that Dee and I saw it as a stroke of genius, but we simply didn't have the luxury of time to find another bass player and ensure they were up to par. Moreover, we couldn't afford to bring in just anyone who wasn't a top-notch musician. That could have spelled the end for the SpeedKings, and we weren't ready to throw in the towel just yet.

Preparing in just two months was a true test of my abilities, and it was House of Kicks, our Swedish distributor, who came up with the idea of bringing Thomas from Lotoma Bookings on board. I couldn't help but trust their suggestion; after all, House of Kicks and White Jazz were the powerhouses of the Scandinavian scene. So, I placed my complete faith in this guy. True to their word, within a mere fourteen days, he managed to arrange six shows effortlessly. It was a short but perfect one-week blitzkrieg through the northern region aimed at boosting our record sales.

03/31/2002: Kraakerieret, Moss (NO)
04/01/2002: Nyx, Oslo (NO)
04/03/2002: Pusterviksbaren, Göteborg (SE)
04/04/2002: Kulturhuset, Hässleholm (SE)
04/05/2002: Kammaren, Norrköping (SE)
04/06/2002: Contan, Örebro (SE)

Once again, we found ourselves teamed up with Maryslim, a Swedish band that delivered a decent performance. But let's be real, bands like that are a dime a dozen. They had this grandiose idea of themselves, thinking they could shatter gender boundaries by engaging in a steamy French kiss between the guitar player and the guitarist during their final song of the set. Honestly, it didn't even faze us. I mean, I'm all for breaking norms and embracing individuality, but it just came off as a cheap gimmick to show off how "cool" they were. Anyway, these guys were back to support us, but deep down, I knew they weren't too thrilled about it either. They were so damn full of themselves that they actually believed they were the headliner act.

On March 30th, me and Dee flew in from Brussels, while Marky made the long journey from New York, all to rendezvous in Oslo a day before the tour kicked off. As we touched down at Oslo airport, we were expecting to see Thomas, who had assured us that he had everything taken care of. But to our dismay, Thomas was nowhere to be found. No hotel booking and we had absolutely no idea how we were going to make our way from Oslo to Moss, where our first show was scheduled. We could only hope that the backline equipment was secured. Frustrated and uncertain, we checked into the airport hotel to strategize for the next 24 hours.

In a desperate attempt to salvage the situation, I reached out to Kenneth Bergdahl from the Cretins. Kenny was an incredibly cool guy we had met on our first tour, and he even played guitar on one of the Ramones' songs at the Shrine. I dialed his number, hoping that he would be available to lend a helping hand and drive the van we intended to rent. Unfortunately, my heart sank as Kenny informed me that he couldn't join us due to work obligations. I could sense the disappointment in his voice. His heart was bleeding.

But as per usual, I improvised and devised a backup plan. And this backup plan was none other than Frank. It was a daring concept, and we hadn't even considered the distance between Wurzburg and Oslo, but I decided to give it a shot. *"Just give me thirty minutes! I'll pack my shit and hop into my Volkswagen van. You cover the fuel expenses, and I want one bottle of booze each night. That's the deal!"* I was ecstatic. If that isn't unwavering commitment, then I don't know what is. However, one thing puzzled me... "One bottle of hard liquor" every night... this guy was supposed to be our driver! But I brushed aside the thought. We had a driver and would address the issue later on.

I only shared the positive news with Marky. We managed to secure a driver who would be joining us tomorrow. However, he wasted no time bombarding me with demands, insisting too speak to this Tomas guy as if I had him stashed away somewhere and could summon him at a moment's notice. The truth was, I was eager to connect with the man myself. This rocky start was far from promising.

But the good thing was that I managed to find a solution to our predicament. And in the midst of the darkness, another glimmer of hope emerged - we would have the chance to meet Andre Dahlman once again. What made it even more interesting was the fact that Andre had actually grown up in Moss, the very place where we were scheduled for our first show.

But before anything else, as soon as we opened our eyes the following morning, Frank was already there, waiting patiently in the parking lot. He looked exhausted, worn out from the chilly Scandinavian spring that was even colder than I had anticipated. To revive his spirits, we treated him to a steaming cup of coffee and a shot of warming alcohol. It was like a magical elixir that brought him back to life. With newfound energy coursing through his veins, we departed on our drive towards Moss, a mere hour away from Oslo.

When we arrived and crossed paths with Andy, his joy in seeing us was almost touchable. And believe me, the feeling was mutual.

"I had long left Moss behind me, and the last thing I wanted was to go back there. But then I found out that Marky Ramone and The Speedkings were making their way to town, and to top it off, Nick put me on the guest list; I knew I had no choice but to return. It was a conflicting experience for me to witness Marky's presence in Moss. On the one hand, I was ecstatic and couldn't fathom that this was actually happening. On the other hand, I despised it. I had to share this moment with a bunch of people who had never given a damn about the Ramones - individuals who had spit me out during my youth because of my devotion to punk music. And now, they would be at this show in Moss, pretending they had been die-hard fans since day one."

In the venue, we encountered the tongue-wagging rebels of Maryslim. They were in the midst of setting up when I approached them about sharing the backline. Their response hit me like a bolt from the blue. *"That wasn't part of the deal,"* the lead singer arrogantly declared. I was seething with anger. Not only was I furious at their reaction, but I was especially infuriated with Thomas, who hadn't even bothered to show up yet.

I could sense the impending storm approaching. Meanwhile, Marky had made his way onto the stage and was giving instructions to the drummer, dictating how the set should be arranged according to his demands. That poor guy seemed completely taken aback and pole-axed. I could see a shift in Marky's expression, and it felt like thunder was about to strike.

The lead singer of the band was on the phone, probably talking to the booking agent. After a few moments, he approached me and said, *"You can use our backline, but you'll have to pay us for its use every night."* I can't quite recall the exact amount he asked for, but it was absolutely outrageous. It nearly drove me to madness. Keeping my composure, I calmly responded, my voice devoid of any emotion, *"Why don't you guys pack up your stuff? The tour is over for you."*

I shouted over to Andy, who was nearby, *"Call The Graves. You guys are playing tonight."* With that, I walked away. The Maryslim singer wasn't as talkative and all tongue anymore. Within seconds, I found myself on the phone with that Thomas guy again. *"They were just messing with you, Nick. Of course, you guys can use their backline."* Yeah, double fucking right. If they pull one more of these petty tricks, they're out. I've had enough of their prima donna bullshit attitude.

That settled the issues with our backline. The driver and van were secured, and we had everything arranged with our equipment. But I couldn't shake this uneasy feeling. I could totally understand where Maryslim came from and how they felt about things, but this was rock and roll, and we were in it together. Regardless, they would continue to

Hotel lobby entertainment and assigning hotel rooms.

be jerks, and once this tour was over, our paths would diverge forever. I didn't shed a single tear over this, even though I knew I would miss Urrke and Bengtson. Those dudes were always a blast to hang out with, and they didn't have that stick-up-their-ass vibe like the rest of the band did.

The show was completely sold out, and Andy was having a tough time avoiding all the people he didn't want to see or talk to. I could sense the way he was feeling, so I grabbed him and dragged his ass over to the backstage area. Problem solved. And it was a major bonus for him to get the chance to hang out with the band and discuss the show in Oslo from the previous year. "If someone had told me this when I was a kid, I would have freaked out and lost control of my bodily functions. Here I am, chatting with a member of the Ramones, all alone in Moss, of all places!"

Just moments before we took the stage, Marky approached him and asked him to join us once again for a Ramones song. The expression on his face was priceless and revealed his disbelief as if he couldn't fathom the opportunity that lay before him.

"I can't recall much of the performance," he confessed. "There was simply too much going on in my mind. As I was introduced and called onto the stage, I found myself standing alongside a genuine Ramone right in front of all the despicable assholes I despised. It felt like a triumph, a glorious act of revenge, a defiant middle finger thrust directly into the faces of all those fake motherfuckers who dared to be present," he later recounted to me. Revenge is indeed a dish best-served cold.

Although our performance was well-received, there was an unsettling vibe lingering throughout the tour. The following day, we had a show in Oslo once again, with our sights set on entering Sweden the day after. Thomas, on the other hand, seemed to vanish into thin air. Despite him supposedly residing in Götebro, we struggled to come across any promotion posters or announcements for our upcoming gig. That guy was a complete disaster. On a brighter note, we had the pleasure of having another band join us for a few shows. They were called Silver, and they absolutely blew everyone and everything away! It's hard to believe they were only 18 years old, but their punk glam set was nothing short of amazing. Their Riot 1-2-3 mini album was released on Virgin Records, and they deserve it. Finally, here was a band that could show those pretentious assholes in Maryslim how to truly rock'n'roll.

I 'HEARTBREAK' THE RAMONES

A day later, we found ourselves at Kulturhuset in Hässleholm. The performance was all right, but what struck me was the encounter with a couple of die-hard fans afterward. Marky had already made his escape to the hotel, leaving us at the bar, indulging in drinks. There were a few kids lingering around, and I could tell they were buzzing on something - probably speed. The wild, piercing gaze in their eyes seemed to penetrate right through anyone they laid their sights on. One girl managed to get her hands on one of Marky's shattered drumsticks. Luckily for her, he hadn't noticed, or he surely would have charged her for it. However, she took it upon herself to continuously slap my upper thigh with it. At first, it was a gentle tap, but the force gradually intensified until I couldn't take it anymore. I snatched the drumstick from her grip and unleashed my frustration by shouting, *"You want me to shove this up your ass?"*

Bengtson, the driver of Maryslim, stood to the side, taking in the scene with a watchful eye. He was one tough, toothless motherfucker, always with a wad of tobacco in his mouth, one of those gritty Scandinavian habits. He lingered nearby, spitting out repulsive yellow phlegm, and I couldn't help but suspect that he only bathed when the moon was at its newest. He stood there, chuckling to himself. Meanwhile, on the other side, I spotted Frank guzzling down a bottle of gin. He had been an exceptional driver, but I couldn't understand how he managed to consume a bottle every night without suffering from a wicked hangover for the rest of the week. His insides must have been drenched and perfectly preserved.

But the most amusing character of the night was a girl with eyes that almost resembled those of Asian descent, accompanied by a strikingly unique feature: a single, thick black eyebrow that stretched horizontally across her face from left to right. In an instant, we christened her our very own Eskimo girl. Miss Unibrow.

Eventually, Frank stumbled into the van, completely intoxicated. Thankfully, Dee took control of the wheel, making a smart and obvious choice. To my astonishment, upon arriving at the hotel front desk, I discovered that my room had already been checked in, and I was given a spare key.

Upon entering the room, I noticed that my bed was not unoccupied. There, snoring away, lay the Eskimo girl, much to my surprise. She was clad in a tank top and a tiny Union Jack tanga. On the bedside table, I discovered a partially empty bottle of vodka. I had to gently nudge her aside to find a spot to crash. Then, I heard Bengtson knocking on my door, his laughter echoing through the hallway. *"Enjoying the room service?"* he chuckled, displaying his scumbag nature.

I awoke as the girl began to stir and toss in the bed. To my surprise, she didn't seem taken aback by my presence at all. While she may have been glad to see me, her excitement was clearly directed towards the bottle of vodka. *"Mmmm, breakfast!"* she exclaimed with a smile as she eagerly gulped down the alcohol. In her Union Jack G-string, she exuded a most stereotypical punk rock vibe. God save the Eskimo girls!

Nörkopping held an unexpected surprise. Jari-Pekka made a grand entrance accompanied by a group of friends. Despite being engrossed all Eastern weekend in his book about the Ramones, he managed to make the journey all the way from Finland. This adventure involved buses, trains, and even a ferry boat. It took them a grueling 17 hours to reach Stockholm and an additional 3 hours to finally arrive at the Kammaren venue. Witnessing such unwavering dedication left me in awe, and it's no wonder Jari-Pekka remains a loyal friend even after more than two decades.

He walked into the club with Kimmo, Turo, and Juki right on his heels. Exhaustion didn't faze him one bit, as he was determined to conduct interviews, capture countless photographs, and even document the entire event on video. His passion for the music knew no bounds.

This crew had made a bold decision to have an absolute blast, taking turns capturing the show on video and then immersing themselves in the chaotic energy of the moshpit, bouncing and thrashing the night away. Prior to the performance, Juki had confided in me about his tradition of serenading his girlfriend with the song "Telephone Love." So, when that tune finally made its appearance on the setlist, I dedicated it to both of them, igniting his excitement. Juki's enthusiasm reached such heights that mere moments later, he leaped onto the stage during "Sheena is a Punkrocker" and forcefully seized the microphone from my grasp, belting out the entire song with fervor. I must admit, it was a welcome relief to be freed from my vocal duties. To bring the show to a climactic close, we unleashed a couple of Ramones classics, and as "Gimme Gimme

Shock Treatment" reverberated through the venue, the crowd went totally nuts.

Following the performance, we discreetly ushered our comrades into our hotel rooms, where they found solace and contentment on various surfaces - be it the bed, the floor, or any other spot they deemed comfortable.

On the 6th of April, we reached the end of our week-long tour. Our destination was a badass rock and roll hotel called Contan in Örebro. Talk about convenience! The venue was downstairs, and our private rooms were just upstairs. No need to navigate through late-night traffic to crash at some random place. This place had it all. And to top it off, the week before, they hosted Therapy.

Jari-Pekka, always the videographer, was capturing everything again. He managed to get up close with Marky on stage. It was during the song "Saturday Night," which featured Celine, a mutual friend of ours. Jari-Pekka took a moment to emotionally acknowledge her presence. But that wasn't the only surprise of the night. Iggy, another good friend of ours, joined Jari-Pekka at the front of the stage and had a blast. The crowd was hyped, cheering for Jari-Pekka. That's when I decided to pull him up on stage.

What better way to introduce him and pay homage than by letting him sing "Blitzkrieg Bop"? As he shouted, *"1-2-3-4!"* the entire venue erupted into the anthem of Hey Ho Let's Go. It was an absolute explosion of energy and pure punk rock bliss. To make it even more special, many friends we had met at the Shrine show in Stockholm last December were also present. Madde and Monka, two amazing girls, even decided to join us for a while and continue the adventure.

After the gig, it was crystal clear that nobody wanted the night to come to a close. Despite the chaotic nature of this tour, nothing could surpass the bond of friendship that was forged during our time in Scandinavia. We spent the entire night chatting away, engrossed in each other's company until the realization hit me like a ton of bricks - we had a flight to catch. In a frenzy, Dee, Frank, and I took turns driving for over two grueling hours to reach Stockholm airport. Marky, on the other hand, had to make his way back to NYC. However, when we reached the check-in desk, fate dealt us another cruel blow. It turned out that Marky's departure was not from Stockholm but from Örebro instead. We had wasted precious time and effort getting him here for no reason. And to make matters worse, we were left with no time left to get him on the originally booked flight. In the end, we had no choice but to purchase a new ticket for him from Stockholm. This tour had plunged us into deep financial turmoil. Thomas, who was supposed to be there with us, never showed up and never bothered to pay any of our dues. It felt like we had sacrificed everything for this backline setup, only to be left empty-handed and penniless in the end.

Our Scandinavian Gang featuring Turo Ihalainen, Helena Peterson, Kimmo Aaltonen, Martin Östh, Fredrik "Freddy" Eriksson, Henrik & Jari "Juki" Lehtola.

Marky acts like Jim Jones. "Drink your CoolAid!" Potent energy drinks heal a sore throat.

Our youngest support band ever. Swedish Punks Not Dead!

Swedish Black Leather.

Helena Peterson joins Marky after the show.

Jari-Pekka Laitio-Ramone singing his heart out.

Andy Dahlman joins us on stage in his hometown.
March 31, 2002, Kraakerieret, Mos, Norway.

Sweet revenge after all those years!

The band and roadcrew engaged in serious conversation almost daily.

Frank insists on liquid payment. Nick does payrolling.

Maryslim - Urrke Thunman (front left) and their buddy "Sparky Macaroni".

CHAPTER 27

Don Hill's Street Blues

"We gonna napalm this whole neighborhood!" - Jesus Martinez

Radical Records, located on Dean Street in Brooklyn, released the "Ramones Forever – An International Compilation" CD that hit the shelves in late May 2002. It's worth noting that this gem is actually a condensed version of the Belgian compilation, "1-2-3-4 A Lo-Fi Ramones Tribute," which was curated by my friend KPW.

In celebration a release party was arranged at Don Hill's night club in SoHo on the 11th of June. However, a tragedy struck the Ramones family just days before the event that moved all of us. On Wednesday, June 5th, the world mourned the loss of founding member Dee Dee Ramone.

But his heartbreaking passing didn't derail the combined tribute to the Ramones, which was a record release party and a fundraiser happening that week in New York City. "Now, it's become more of a tribute than we originally intended," explained Johnny Chiba, one of the event's organizers, "the main objective of Wednesday night's performance at Don Hill's Nightclub is to raise funds for the Joey Ramone Lymphoma Research Fund, which was established at New York Hospital Cornell Medical Center following Joey Ramone's demise last year. I'm sure there are going to be a lot of Ramones fans there who will be wanting to commiserate over Dee Dee's death," Chiba said. "But we're not promoting anything of that nature. We're celebrating the Ramones, we're celebrating

Joey's life, and, in that respect, now we're going to be celebrating Dee Dee's life as well, as opposed to memorializing them."

With the incredible lineups of the artists, it was sure to be an unforgettable night, one to remember. There was Gina from the Lunachicks, Pete "Type O Negative" Steele, "Furious" George Tabb, Mike Blank from Blanks 77, and Jayne County, among others. They were all set to perform a Ramones song. The Marky Ramone Group, who contributed to the compilation "I don't wanna grow up" by Tom Waits, were also invited. However, quite surprisingly, Marky declined the offer. Even though the whole event was a fundraiser where artists were more than willing to play for free, it seemed that free shows didn't align with his agenda. However, I had the chance to fly in and perform a song. Since I had been involved in the original release in Belgium, Radical was thrilled to have me join them.

I was looking forward to this NYC trip so very much. I knew that it would be so cool to attend this show, but even cooler was the idea that I would finally meet Adrienne "Sheena" Manglos and Celine Moray, two badass ladies from NYC. These girls had actually been mentioned in one of SpeedKings' songs, "Saturday Night," where they were portrayed in a catfight. "Cee is pulling hair, and Sheena knocks you out" - that line always cracked them up. They had been die-hard fans of the Ramones for as long as they could remember, and they had a history with the boys. So, being featured in the lyrics of a song felt pretty damn cool to them. In some twisted way, Sheena had always had a soft spot for me. Maybe even more than I wanted to handle. I had a huge crush on Celine, and it was like walking on a tightrope. I was trying my best not to interfere with the bond between these lifelong friends. I knew I had to tread carefully as I had no intention of jeopardizing their friendship for anything in the world.

I was so restlessly excited that I had arrived a couple of days ahead of schedule. After having a good night's rest the very next day afternoon, I decided to spend time hanging out with Marc and Marion at their apartment. We had a ton of things to go over regarding the upcoming tours and the release of our live CD. Being in that neighborhood, right near Brooklyn Heights, always had a certain vibe to it. Marc had this incredible collection of vintage movie posters and the sickest old-school robots you've ever seen. It's hard to believe, but the guy actually has good taste. Marion whipped up some lunch, but I had to pass on the fish. My religion doesn't allow me to eat anything that swims, but Marky didn't seem to mind. I learned on tour that the dude always has room for more.

Reflecting on the memories of that apartment, the "enigma of the wig" comes to my mind. Marky has always been pursued by it. The haters took pleasure in mocking and teasing him relentlessly. Meanwhile, his loyal followers were constantly disgusted by the cruel behavior of these haters. Nevertheless, the relentless pursuit resulted in a collection of truly peculiar yet uproarious stories. One of these anecdotes immediately stands out: it was a day when two guys, ironically both named Johnny, happened to be present in the apartment. At one point, one of the Johnnys needed to use the bathroom, and Marky, being the kind and helpful guide he is, directed him to the hallway. However, the hallway presented a confusing array of doors. Opening the first one, Johnny found himself face-to-face with a hall closet. Now, if this had been Marky in that situation while on tour, he probably would have just pissed right there in the closet. But not Johnny. Unfazed, he moved on to the next door, only to be greeted by shelves adorned with…wig heads! Without hesitation, Johnny quickly closed the door and continued his search until he eventually found the actual bathroom.

This story wasn't just a standalone tale. Recently Jack confided in me, revealing something he had never shared with anyone before. As we traveled in our van, Marky would often disappear into the back bunk, situated above the instruments. He would sleep and kill the time while we journeyed down the seemingly endless road, moving from one venue to another.

"One day, as both you and Dee were snoring away the miles," Jack began, "I glanced back from the backseat and noticed Marky's hair sticking out. I couldn't resist my curiosity, so I decided to pull on a few strands. I thought that if he shouted in pain, it would mean that the hair was real and truly his own. But if he remained silent, it would confirm my suspicions that it was a wig. And guess what? He didn't even flinch. The silence spoke volumes."

Jack's revelation continued, "And then, just to add fuel to the fire, I took out my lighter and set the hairs ablaze. Oh man, the stench was unbearable. It lingered for what felt like an eternity before finally dissipating."

This unexpected revelation added another layer of intrigue to the hairy mystery. It made me realize that appearances can be deceiving, and that we all have secrets. But honestly, who gives a damn? You must be living on another planet if you think any of the Ramones could have maintained their iconic hairdo forever. Besides, isn't this comparable to them wearing their timeless leather jackets? Cut the guy some slack. I'm pretty damn sure he looks way better this way than if he were to join the ranks of the Baldies from the Warriors! Perhaps I should have snagged one of those disguises, giving myself a fresh mop of locks to steal the show that evening.

As night fell, Celine and Sheena rolled up to fetch me from the plaza before the apartment. We tore through the cityscape, from Brooklyn's gritty streets to the glamour of Manhattan, descending into Soho's heart. And surely, the nightclub was already buzzing with life when we arrived, and there I had the thrill of encountering the legendary Don Hill in the flesh.

The creme de la creme of New York's punk scene was all there, in full glory. John Holmstrom, the man behind Punk Magazine was engaged deep in conversation with a few of my buddies. Over at the bar, Wayne or Jayne, the vocalist who tops my all-time favorites list, was holding court. The guys from Radical were making introductions. Believe it or not, we were slated to collaborate on a couple of songs. Picture that! An edgy duet with the most outrageous singer of my dreams - man enough to be a woman. 'Beat on the Brat' and "Cream in My Jeans" were the songs we choose. And let me tell you, I'd have gladly taken a beating if that's what it took to seize this once-in-a-lifetime chance. Jayne lived up to any expectation as a "hostess with the mostest."

As this was a gathering of NYC punk icons, Marky not being present felt a bit awkward. But, then again, what else to expect? These were among those who were dutifully late. Among the unfamiliarly similar faces of the crowd, there was one that stood. It was a very familiar presence. It was none other than Phil Carson, the mastermind behind AC/DC's success in the United States, who showed up at the club. He had come to observe on behalf of his friend Dee Snider from Twisted Sister. Dee was once again engrossed in a new horror movie project and had expressed his desire for Marky and the SpeedKings to compose the film's title track. But Marky remained unmoved. It wasn't a matter of his persistence or dedication but rather his financial situation that stood in the way. The same can be said when we had plans to record a tribute to The Partridge Family, with a cover of a David Cassidy song. Unfortunately, nothing could sway Marky's decision.

The Partridge Family, a television series from the 1970s featuring Shirley Jones as the lead, revolved around a musically inclined family who traveled in a vintage school bus. As a child, I was completely enamored by the show. Songs like "I Think I Love You" and "I Woke Up In Love This Morning" were like anthems to me, constantly playing in my head as I lived my life. However, due to a stroke of bad luck, I never had the chance to record those songs on tape. Looking back, it feels like I missed out on a golden opportunity that could have added an extra layer of magic to my childhood memories.

Fine words, butter, no parsnips, Marky must have thought. But cash surely did. It should have been obvious to me when B-track Records struck a deal with Marky for the liner notes of their compilation CD. The record company coughed up $400.00, and I was tasked with writing the introduction under Marky's name.

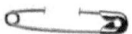

On that particular evening, the backing band killed it with their thrilling performance. The fine selection of Ramones' masterpieces was performed tight and riveting and at a great pace. But even with sonic brilliance, Pete Steele was a discordant note. This skyscraper of a man, the vocal powerhouse of Type O Negative, sauntered around wearing an army-green tee with "Lesbian" emblazoned across the front. As his turn came by, he began to complain, casting doubt on his ability to do justice to any Ramones track. Instead, he expressed his desire to perform Paranoid by Black Sabbath. Embarrassingly, the antics that he was showcasing were mimicking that of a three-year-old, and I wasn't alone in my disapproval. As John Holmstrom penned in his critique of the night: "I've never seen Type O Negative, the band that (in the words of The Undertaker) made Pete Steele "famous." This guy was a mess. He fell on the floor in front of Jayne County when he made his grand entrance. He had to carry lyric sheets for "Sheena is a Punk Rocker" and "I Wanna Be Sedated," and still he, perhaps by means of a miracle, managed to forget all the words. In fact, he had to stop the band - physically - when he got lost in the middle of "Sheena" and in the middle of "Sedated" he started falling on the floor. (He did seem to be on something.) Then he decided to sing Black Sabbath's "Paranoid" after polling the audience (half wanted him to get off the stage, the other half wanted him to stay, so of course he told both factions to fuck off.) Pete looked and sounded exactly like Jim from the "Taxi" TV show in a Tiny Tim wig. I couldn't tell if he was a pathetic loser whose life was in shambles since his band kicked him out or if he was parodying being a mess. If so, then, a perfect imitation."

To say we had a blast was an understatement. It was one hell of a night. Sheena got caught up in some chatter with familiar faces, and that's when Celine and I locked eyes, and we had our little silent agreement that was screaming louder than any sound could be. We knew it was now or never. High time to make our discreet exit, even if only temporarily. We slipped away, undetected by the crowd, and ventured out into the calm of the night.

We found our comfort on the city streets, showing a contrast to the rambunctious vibe within Don Hill. The evening air was balmy, a welcome break from the stifling atmosphere inside. And there she was, standing next to me in a rare moment of solitude. It was a treat to be alone with her, away from prying eyes. It felt like an exclusive backstage pass – priceless and exhilarating.

Our bond was raw and unspoken and needed no defining. We reveled in our shared silence, comfortable in each other's presence. But that's all where it ended - we didn't cross any lines, didn't push any boundaries. A duet without the promise of an encore. It was just us, lost in a moment that felt stolen from time.

And then we returned, finding ourselves back into the crowd unnoticed as if we'd never left. It was flawless - no awkward questions, no raised eyebrows - just us blending seamlessly back into madness. And that was perfection in its purest form.

We indulged in revelry until the break of dawn, my two companions sending me back to my apartment just as the initial rays of sunlight pierced the morning sky. I was in desperate need of some shut-eye as an upcoming crucial gathering demanded my presence later that day. On the brink of launching our live record, I had birthed the idea of the "Speed Queen." If there were Kings of Speed, then surely their female counterparts were out there somewhere, too.

The concept had barely left my lips when it was catching fire, and suddenly, there were possible queens at every turn. We made the call to stick with two. We concocted a plan: to unveil the album sporting two distinct covers - one shrouded in black, the other bathed in white. For the white rendition, a photoshoot was scheduled with Mandy, a girl who had boldly stepped into our world. She had enticed us with provocative burlesque snapshots, and we found ourselves unable to resist her. Her overall presence - the ink permanently etched into her skin, her unconventional attire, and the aura she exuded - screamed volumes about SpeedKings, hotrods, and rock 'n' roll in all its raw glory.

Mandy was the main squeeze of James Drescher, the frontman of the infamous NYC hardcore band Murphy's Law. He was more commonly known as Jimmy Spliff or Jimmy G, but his most notorious nickname was Jimmy Gestapo. It was somewhat uncanny, setting up a photoshoot with the girl who was linked to someone with such an intense alias. I could only hope that with "Gestapo" embedded in his moniker, he'd be cool with us using somewhat revealing snaps of his lady love on our album cover.

Everything fell into place without a hitch. In just a few fleeting hours, we cranked out enough shots that we had a veritable treasure pile of choices for the album cover. We weren't shackled by the confines of a single option. Truth be told, the full collection of shots are still unseen by the eyes of others, but a few of us are involved.

As for the black sleeve that eventually came into existence, I wasn't granted the chance to stage a similar photo session. Getting Danielle

Deville in front of the lens was just impossible. But fortune struck when I discovered her extensive portfolio, chock full of photos. Unlike Mandy, Danielle was a seasoned model, her experience was shining through, and she swiftly found the perfect shots for the album.

My fleeting visit to the Big Apple reached its curtain call, but I was primed and ready to dive headfirst into the graphic design of "Alive." If luck was on my side, it would be unleashed upon the world, perfectly synchronized with the launch of our upcoming tour.

The legendary Don Hill, may he rest in peace.

A memorable evening at Don Hill's with me doing two songs with Jayne County. "Creamin' in my Jeans".

The Radical Records Crew at their merch stand.

A memorable walk around the block.

The New York City photoshoot with SpeedQueen Mandy Ellis. One of the shots was used for the white fanclub edition ALIVE CD..

Texas pinup girl Danielle Deville was featured on the Black edition of the live CD.

CHAPTER 28

Dutch Courage

"Days of Dutch courage, just three French letters, and a German sense of humour." - Elvis Costello

Trying our luck on a clash against the Vikings may not have been the wisest choice, especially from a financial standpoint. While we burned down their stages, one of them managed to escape with the plunder, and we found ourselves in desperate need of something to sink our teeth into. A small tour within familiar territory seemed like the perfect solution as it minimized our travel complications. Belgium and Holland were our saving grace. Given the hilarious connection between porn magazines quests we had been on and the perception that The Netherlands was once a sanctuary for sex shops, we aptly named our endeavor the "We Have Come For Your Stagbooks" Tour.

Although our band managed to do decently as a trio, it was far from ideal. Dee, as guitarist, was absolutely irreplaceable. I simply couldn't replicate the magic he brought to the table. While he did a great job on bass, both of us felt it was a waste to confine him to that role. As soon as we returned from our Scandinavian tour, Dee and I began actively searching for a new member to join our ranks. With the SpeedKings gaining momentum, it surprisingly wasn't too difficult to find someone new. And that's when Glen entered the picture, the renowned bass player from the legendary Belgian punk band, Revenge 88. Despite going through several lineup changes since its inception in the late seventies, Revenge 88 managed to stay afloat. Glen was a true maestro on the bass, and, most importantly, he expressed genuine interest in joining us. We didn't even need to have a single rehearsal. All Glen needed was our CD to learn the songs. It reminded me of Stevey back in the day, but Glen was an even more talented musician. Both Dee and I had high hopes that he would be the perfect match for us. On top of his musical prowess, Glen exuded rock 'n' roll vibes and possessed an undeniable charm. He was definitely a pretty boy who fit right in with our image.

Marky crossed paths with Glen on the fateful day of our first-ever show together. In an instant, he bestowed upon him the name Jack. As we made our way to the debut show, Marky pulled me aside at a gas station. *"He looks alright, but he needs a different haircut and a dye job in jet black. Let him know that we'll find a hairdresser and spruce him up,"* he instructed me. I understood the significance of appearances, but it was astonishing that less than an hour after their first encounter, Marky already sought to shape Jack in his own image. To my surprise, Jack didn't object. *"You know, I've been thinking of the same idea for a while now. Perhaps this is the perfect moment to make the change,"* he responded, relieving me of any concerns. However, I couldn't be certain if he truly embraced the idea. When I conveyed Jack's thoughts to Marky, he retorted, *"Jack plays bass, and he should leave the thinking to us."* And just like that, the matter was settled. Sometimes, you don't need an abundance of words to understand your place in the grand scheme of things.

Hannu Jokinen, who had released our first 7-inch record, was absolutely thrilled with the final result. To cater to the diehard collectors, he pressed 1000 copies in three different colors. We had 300 copies on light blue vinyl, another 300 on creamy orange, and 400 on classic black. The demand for the 7-inch was so high that it sold out quickly. Hannu decided to press an additional 300 copies on green/yellow vinyl and another 300 on red/blue swirled wax.

The first ever picture with Jack (left) after Vito Jr. left the band.
Bruges 2002. Ready to start the Holland Tour.

Entrance Ticket for the first show in Holland
June 21, 2002, Willemeen, Arnhem, Holland.

Flyer for the show at Gigant, Apeldoorn, Holland
June 28, 2002.

After listening to our live recordings, Hannu was even more excited to collaborate with us on a follow-up single. That's when I came up with a wild idea: we could take four classic Ramones songs and redo the vocals in different Scandinavian languages. This would not only result in a new SpeedKings 7-inch record but also serve as a novelty item. Thankfully, our friends from Scandinavia saw eye to eye with us on that idea. Jari-Pekka Laitio-Ramone translated "Blitzkrieg Bop" into Finnish. Andy Dahlman tackled "Sheena is a Punkrocker" in Danish, Kenny Bergdahl provided the Swedish translation for "I Wanna Be Sedated," and Valgardour Gudjonsson took on "Rockaway Beach" in Icelandic. The translations were the easy part. The challenge, however, came when we had to sing in these languages. Nevertheless, we managed to pull it off, and before we knew it, 1000 copies of the "Rawk over Scandinavia EP" were out in the world. This EP stirred up quite a buzz on Icelandic television, capturing the attention of viewers far and wide. We proudly held the distinction of being the first non-native Icelandic band to unleash our powerful sound in their language. Whether considered a novelty or not, we had a fresh array of merchandise to offer while on tour, feeding the insatiable hunger of our fans for all things SpeedKings.

Setting up a couple of gigs was a breeze. Bringing Marky in was not just for the shows but also because we were gearing up to record our second full-length album. While on the road, we had been concocting new material, and I had a stash of songs waiting to be recorded and released. Dee, being a skilled songwriter himself, had some melodies up his sleeve too.

Squeezing in a few days for recording between two sets of shows seemed like the perfect plan. We knew that playing a few gigs before hitting the studio would capture that raw live energy even more intensively than usual. Plus, I didn't want to stray from my home turf for too long. You see, my dear old granddad had been in the hospital for a while now. Cancer and dementia had brought him to the point where palliative care was necessary. I wanted to be around, just in case.

To rock the Dutch crowd, we joined forces with the Grolschbusters. These guys were a wild, fun punk band from the Netherlands, named after the iconic Ghostbusters, but also paying homage to the Dutch beer, Grolsch. Their shows were like stepping into a crazy alcohol-drenched party where Jägermeister shots were always within reach. Winny Kas, a friend from just across the border and a member of our Wreckin' Crew, suggested these rockers to us. This Wreckin' Crew was a dedicated group of fans who never missed a beat, always ready to follow us wherever we went. We did have some unforgettable times together with Sniper, Daniel, and Phil, among others.

06/21/2002: Willemeen, Arnhem (NL)
06/22/2002: Buk Buk, Heiloo (NL)
06/23/2002: Het Bolwerk, Sneek (NL)
06/27/2002: WRECKIN' CREW Special, JH Quo Vadis, Heule, (BE)
06/28/2002: Gigant, Apeldoorn (NL)
06/29/2002: Poppodium Atak, Enschede (NL)
06/30/2002: De Troubadour, Hardenberg (NL)

The tour kicked off with a bang in Arnhem at the Willemeen Hall. We had the utmost pleasure of spending quality time with Bram van Schaik and his companion, who graced us with their presence. Bram was a devoted die-hard fan of the Ramones and an excellent journalist. He commanded respect from Marky, and they hit it off famously. For the past couple of years, Bram had made it a point to attend every single one of Marky's appearances in the Lowlands, and several interviews were done.

In Arnhem, another guest made an unexpected appearance. When we arrived, the girl from Aachen showed up at the club's doorstep. Claudia was flying solo this time, and she had a clear goal in mind. Personally, I wasn't interested, but Jack and I concocted a plan to introduce her to Dee. It wasn't a malicious act in any way but a way to extricate ourselves from the situation while also shifting the problem elsewhere. Perhaps we should have reconsidered, but the damage was already done, though it wasn't too severe. Luckily, Dee and Claudia hit it off right from the start. This wouldn't be the first time we encountered her in Holland, and it certainly wouldn't be the last.

The morning after, we drove towards Heiloo, a secluded village that seemed worlds away from the big city. Our destination: Buk Buk, a small but lively youth club where our music was set to ignite a fire. It was clear that this town rarely witnessed the arrival of international bands, making this night all the more special.

There we met Frank. Frank was our German buddy and driver on the Scandinavian tour who had become an inseparable part of our crew. We formed such a close bond with him and shared countless hilarious moments. The moment you laid eyes on him, you witnessed his body being adorned with tattoos and piercings; it was enough to send shockwaves through the veins of the so-called "normal" folks who crossed paths with him for the first time.

As we made our way to Heiloo, we decided to make a pit stop in Amsterdam. We knew that the tranquil countryside wouldn't ignite our spirits like the vibrant city would. So why not soak up the urban energy and indulge in some thrills before hitting the stage?

Navigating through the narrow streets, we miraculously stumbled upon a parking spot in the heart of the red-light district which was nestled alongside one of the picturesque canals. It was a fitting location for a rock 'n' roll crew like ours, with an unapologetic love for all things risqué and a wild ride on the stag books tour. Getting rid of our car couldn't have been any better than in this notorious district.

Amsterdam had transformed into a haven for tourists over time, with its reputation for safety preceding it. However, with this aura of security, incidents of pickpocketing and car break-ins still occurred on a daily basis. The moment we left the vehicle, an unsettling feeling washed over us. On the doorstep of an aged house, a group of vagabond junkies bums loitered. Their eyes were fixated on our car, and it was evident that we had become their prime target even before we had a chance to step out. Instead of assuming a defensive stance, I made the audacious decision to launch a preemptive strike. Motioning for Frank to accompany me, I approached the group with an air of exaggerated friendliness. "Hey there, guys! What's up? Isn't this just the perfect day to hang out?" I exclaimed with my tone overly amicable. The unexpected warmth in my approach left them bewildered, as evidenced by the question marks that appeared in their eyes. "See that car over there? It actually belongs to Frank," I declared, pointing toward the bloodhound standing by my side.

"I'd really appreciate it if you all could keep a close watch on it and ensure that nobody lays a finger on it or gets too close," they were caught completely off guard. "If anyone even dares to look at it the wrong way, I'll hunt each and every one of you down and kill you," Frank added with his thick German accent. I had never witnessed people agreeing so quickly to a proposition, but u don't blame them, as even I was intimidated. When we returned to the car a few hours later, they were still there. "The car's all good!" one of them shouted from across the street, giving us a thumbs up. Those junkie boys turned out to be pretty friendly, after all.

We had one final gig before getting into the studio for the recording sessions. Sneek, a town in Friesland, was our next stop. Similar to the rural Heiloo area, it seemed that not many foreign bands had made their way here. However, the Bolwerk venue, resembling an old storehouse, was surprisingly impressive. Situated just across from the river that flowed through the town, it was a sight to behold. The place was absolutely packed, and the crowd went absolutely insane when we played our Ramones medley.

Among the audience, there were some truly unique individuals. There was this one punk rocker who stood out from the rest, he dressed in a flashy garbageman workwear outfit. His enormous mohawk adorned with five or six massive spikes stood tall over all the heads. If you accidentally bumped into him, you'd be looking at some

serious injuries. Thankfully, his workwear made him easy to spot and avoided any unfortunate collisions.

The guy was all up in Marky's face backstage, but our drummer was usually into some wild and crazy freaks, so he let this kid hang around. But when this older lady with a massive set of knockers got a little too close to the Markster, he had no choice but to serenade her melons and tattoo her white breast with his signature. Judging by the expression on his face, he wasn't exactly thrilled about it. And when situations like that arose, I was the one he would call for backup. *"Nick, I think we need some alone time,"* he'd say, which really meant, *"Get rid of them! Time to kick'em out... now!"*

Since we made the return journey all the way from the northern region of Holland back to Belgium, we decided it would be best to head straight to the studio. It just so happened that the studio was conveniently located along our route. We had been to Midas Studio multiple times before, and Tony, the owner, had set up a fantastic band apartment. This clever shortcut would save us a significant amount of time on the road, cutting out the need to go back and forth. Not only that, but it would also grant us a few extra precious hours in the studio.

Tony had been my partner in crime when it came to recording for the past few years. He was heavily involved in most of our Buckweeds recordings, and that made his place an obvious choice for us. Not only was he a meticulous studio engineer, but his production skills were absolutely top-notch.

After a series of exhilarating live shows, we realized that the best approach for our recording was to embrace a near-live setup. We wasted no time and swiftly laid down several tracks. Our preparation for this record was minimal as it was more about capturing the essence of the songs that were floating around and we had rehearsed while being on tour. The final selection would come later. Personally, I had my fingers crossed that Daniel Rey would once again master the album. I believed that it would explode from the speakers like the first one did.

While we were recording "SpeedKings Ride Tonight," I couldn't help but notice that we were unable to capture the same spontaneous magic I had achieved during the demo recording, which ultimately ended up on the Finnish 7-inch record. It made me wonder why Marky had never inquired about or even thought about, who played on the actual record that was released months ago. It was a strange situation, to say the least. As a result, that particular song didn't quite come together as we had hoped. However, things took an interesting turn when he presented us with the "Red Rubber Ball" by the Cyrkle. It was a groovy sixties tune, but infusing it with the SpeedKings' signature sound proved to be quite challenging. He did put our feet to the fire.

Years later, it would hit me like a sudden revelation that the words of the song, even though they were originally meant to depict a tale of romance between a boy and a girl, turned out to be eerily prophetic of the predicament that Marky and I would find ourselves in.

> "The story is in the past with nothin' to recall
> I've got my life to live, and I don't need you at all
> The roller-coaster ride we took is nearly at an end
> I bought my ticket with my tears. That's all I'm gonna spend."

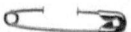

The recording days flew by in a blur, and before we knew it, we were gearing up for our only show in Belgium on this tour. Little did we know that it would also mark the final performance ever of the SpeedKings in Belgium. The venue chosen for the gig was the Quo Vadis youthclub, a cozy local café situated near my hometown. To accommodate the massive turnout, they built an enormous tent to ensure that everyone would have a spot to rock out. The ticket sales skyrocketed and promised a full house. The night would feature three bands. Captain Buerk from Paris, our Dutch amigos of the Grolschbuster, and us.

Before the chaos ensued, Marky and I took off for Brussels in the morning for a live interview on national radio. By the time we returned in the late afternoon, everything was set up and ready to go. Time was slipping away, and as I glanced at the clock, a wave of regret washed over me. I cursed myself for not being able to visit my grandpa in the hospital. The timing was just too tight, and with our show looming on the horizon, I couldn't find the time to go over to him and just sit by his side for a while. Everything was pure chaos. It felt like a whirlwind of events, all crammed into the same limited time frame. I longed for an extra hour to be added to each day, just to catch my breath.

Meanwhile, the journey from Holland to Belgium for the Grolschbuster proved to be quite a challenge. Despite thinking they were accustomed to rural surroundings; it became apparent that they were unaccustomed to navigating the smaller roads nestled among vast pastures. As the entire band and crew sat in the van, their eyes glued to the signs that would guide them to the venue, they may have indulged a bit too much in the fiery shots of Jägermeister. In the midst of their distraction, the van veered off the country road and careened into a deep ditch, toppling onto its side.

Thankfully, a helpful local farmer came to their rescue, offering the use of his trusty tractor to pull them out of their predicament. However, before this rescue mission could commence, Frank had to come into action himself. He hopped into our van and drove over to load all of their equipment, lightening the load in order to facilitate their extraction.

The commotion caused quite a stir, attracting a crowd of curious onlookers. The Grolschbusters and their crew captured the entire spectacle on video, transforming it into a captivating road movie-worthy scene.

In an effort to globalize the madness, we extended an invitation to a friend from Australia who happened to be on a thrilling road trip across Europe. We thought it would be a great idea for him to join us for a couple of days. This guy was no ordinary traveler, and he was the mastermind behind an incredibly cool radio show and music magazine called Long Gone Loser. The name alone was synonymous with badass, hard-rocking tunes. And to top it off, our friend Damo was also a talented musician, rocking out in a band known as Muscle Car. With Damo at the wheel, we knew we were in for one hell of a ride.

Damo surprised me with his extensive knowledge of Belgium. When Vito and I went to pick him up, he couldn't believe he was riding in the car with a hardcore kid who had been a part of Rise Above, a band he admired. His astonishment grew even more when we arrived at Goodlife Recordings, which was run by Edward, another former member of Rise Above who had transitioned into Nations on Fire, another one of Damo's favorite bands. It's incredible how small the world is, after all.

With his camera gripped tightly in his hand, he captured extraordinary moments that will forever be remembered in our memories. One such moment was when my mischievous daughters, Eva and Emma, aged three and five at the time, playfully smacked Marky on his butt like a pair of little troublemakers. It was an uproarious scene that left us all in stitches.

The evening of the show, the atmosphere of the event was volatile, similar to the adrenaline rush of being on a constant high.

Captain Buerk was ready to kick things off, igniting the stage and playing with the ferocity of bands like the Nobody's and the Ramones. The bassist, bearing an uncanny resemblance to Mr. Bean, added a touch of eccentricity to their performance. Though they may have been a bit rough around the edges and could have benefited from a second guitarist, they managed to start the fire.

Following them were the 'Busters, bringing a 70's punk vibe. With their unconventional use of an accordion and Scottish influences, including kilts, they defied expectations at every turn. After all, what else would you expect from a band with an album titled "Strange Blowjob." Their rendition of The Police's iconic song "Every Breath You Take" took on a whole new meaning as they cleverly reworded "breath" to "bitch," injecting a sense of obnoxious juvenile fun into their performance. The crowd was set ablaze, their excitement reaching fever pitch as the temperature in the venue soared even higher. All the people we adored were there, reveling in their own unique ways.

Finally, we had our go. Damo wrote the following about the show in his magazine: "The SpeedKings hit the stage, and it felt weird being so close to Marky Ramone. I mean, there were no bouncers, no rail in front of the stage, nothing. This was pure punk rock. The band ripped through a set of 25 songs in about 40 minutes. They played a swag of songs from their debut album, and of course, the crowd went nuts when the band broke into Ramones tunes. The encore included Blitzkrieg Bop, where friends were invited on stage to sing along. What a finale!"

The air was filled with wild energy, and it seemed as if the night would never come to an end. In the early hours of the morning, Marky, Damo, and I headed to my place to catch some sleep. We had three upcoming shows, and our departure was scheduled for the following day.

Marky puts his mark on the Dutch lady.

Bram van Schaik and his wife at Willemeen, Arnhe

Nasty spikes giftwrapped in a safety jack

50 Cent wardrobe girl.

Les gets ready to make the audience spend their hard earned cash. Take the money and ru

When I woke up, my euphoria was abruptly shattered as reality crashed down upon me like a ton of bricks. I received a devastating phone call from my mother. My beloved grandfather had passed away on the very same night. My heart shattered into a million pieces. Even to this day, I carry the weight of regret for not being there in his final moments. He was the visionary who instilled in me the belief that everything is attainable in life if you possess unwavering determination. And yet, I left him to depart this world alone. I was shattered and paralyzed. I felt a wave of sorrow that went beyond anything I had ever experienced. With a heavy heart, I drove myself to the hospital, where a nun guided me to the morgue. She lingered impatiently, seemingly oblivious to the magnitude of my pain. Finally, I mustered the strength to ask her to leave. Some people just don't grasp the depth of grief.

In that cold and sterile room, I held his lifeless hand tightly in mine as tears streamed down my face. It was a moment of raw vulnerability where I could feel his soul lingering around. At that moment, we were completely alone, left to grapple with the weight of our loss. The absence of any comforting words from my beloved New York City star was a cruel reminder that life always goes on and no matter how broken we may feel, Time stops for no one. The harsh reality was that the show did go on. On the same day of my devastating loss, I found myself back on stage with the band, going through the motions. My heart and mind were far away, consumed by thoughts of him. The funeral would have to wait until we returned from the last few shows. It was also during those performances that I realized I wanted Herr Bell out of my face for some time.

Jack showed up at my place just as Marky and Damo were engrossed in a lively conversation, munching on cheese and bread rolls. At that moment, I felt completely numb and overwhelmed with confusion. It was as if I was suppressing any hint of emotion and refusing to let it seep through. One thing was crystal clear - I wasn't going to be behind the wheel. Instead, we headed over to Dee's house, where Frank had crashed for the night. My sanity was about to be pushed to its limits. Frank, being Frank, had his van stocked with a full collection of tunes that could only be described as truck drivin', hog tossin', gun wieldin', redneck hillbilly music. It couldn't get any more bizarre than that. Both Damo and I silently thanked the Lord when one of the tapes abruptly snapped, causing the broken tape to jam the entire mechanism.

That fateful evening at the Gigant Poppodium, we followed our usual ritual. Twenty-five songs, a relentless forty-minute onslaught. The venue had hyped us up in the local press: "They are LOUD and FAST. Embrace yourselves for an exciting explosion of terrifying rawk and infectious powerpop." Once the show wrapped up, our whole crew descended upon a rock nightclub. Some obscure crustcore band was on stage, but they were met with indifference. Unfazed, Frank stumbled upon the bar's public computer and promptly captivated the crowd with his quest to verify that every adult website was still online like he felt that was some sort of duty to perform. Hell, someone had to do it, right? He gleefully introduced the Netherlands to Sky Lopez and other porn stars that fueled his fetish desires. Frank persistently bellowed, "Let's go out and meet some girls!" However, fatigue had taken its toll on most of us, leaving us too drained to prolong the night any further. Sleeping through a significant portion of the day was absolutely not an option. The hotel we were staying at happened to be situated in close proximity to a church, and the incessant tolling of the bells in the bell tower completely ruined any chance of enjoying some downtime.

The Wrecking Crew had arrived in town, ready to hit the road with us for the final two shows. The ones who were new to each other quickly became easily acquainted. The bond within the group was undeniable, as they all effortlessly clicked and got along famously. The gig at Atak in Enschede went down like any other. We did our thing, but I found myself slowly turning into a soulless zombie, desperately trying to distance myself from my own emotions. It was as if I was merely an observer, watching everyone around me move, talk, and interact while I remained detached. The weight of guilt crushed me relentlessly. I continuously blamed myself over and over again, yet I refused to let anyone on the tour down, so I swallowed my true feelings and put on a fake smile. In the end, you can't please everyone, no matter how hard you try. And in that pursuit of trying to please everyone, you end up disappointing them all. It wasn't until later that it hit me - nobody gave a damn about how I was feeling.

Damo 'Long Gone Loser' Holland tour memories with members of the Belgian and Holland Wreckin' Crew. Winny Kas, the King of Snoring, always ready to quench the thirsty and Frank Droll giving thumbs up to the endless supply of alcohol - Stagbooks Tour Holland 2002.

In the club, there was a girl who took charge of the business side of things. She was responsible for handling payments and managing logistics. From the moment we stepped foot in the place, she made it abundantly clear that she was the one calling the shots. And for some reason, she seemed to be fixated on me, constantly hovering around like a moth to a flame. Maybe she had the hots for band members, but I didn't pay much attention. Maybe I just didn't realize that playing hard-to-get only fuels the fire of attraction.

As she ushered us into her office to discuss contracts, she tried to create an atmosphere of comfort, as if we were about to spend some intimate time together. She rattled on and on in broken English, but being the nice guy that I am, I suggested that she could just speak Dutch to me. I said it in her native language, but she stared at me as if I were speaking in an alien tongue. It was as if I had unleashed some bizarre Chinese dialect. And then, out of nowhere, she exploded in anger. "Why are you messing with me?" she shouted furiously. Clearly, she felt foolish for thinking that she had a chance with some American guy she thought she could hook up with. I shrugged it off, counted the money, and signed the receipt. I definitely wasn't prepared for her sudden outburst of adolescent tantrums.

When I opened my eyes the following morning, I was greeted by the sight of eight familiar faces in the room. This wasn't anything out of the ordinary for the SpeedKings, though. We were always known for taking care of our friends and fans, and the previous night was no exception. The challenge now was to discreetly leave the hotel without arousing any suspicions from the front desk. It was quite a hilarious scene, reminiscent of those elaborate pranks where people keep piling out of a tiny car as if there were dozens of individuals crammed inside.

We were all set for our grand finale in a town called Hardenberg, where we had a gig at a venue known as the Troubadour. This joint may not have been the one on Sunset Strip, but it had its own charm. Picture this: the interior of the club resembled an old church, and when we hit the stage, it felt like we were performing in a medieval castle. The only bummer was that the turnout wasn't exactly rocking. Sadly, the crowd wasn't as massive as we had hoped. Sundays were never the prime time for a late-night show, they explained. After all, everyone had to drag themselves to work on Monday morning. But the food was out of this world! This spot wasn't your typical rock club; it was more like a fancy bar and restaurant serving up some top-notch grub. No matter the size of the crowd, whether it was packed or sparse, we always gave it our best. This gig felt like a paid rehearsal. But we didn't complain, and in the end, everyone had a good time.

As we hit the road after the show, we faced a daunting six-hour drive ahead. Frank had managed to rip out the tape from the tape recorder and flood the car with country redneck tunes once again. The music enveloped and transported me to a different world as we made our way back to my place.

Arriving home, we were greeted by the first rays of light peeking over the horizon. Exhausted and running on fumes, I could feel every ounce of energy draining from my body. It was as if I had given my all on that stage, leaving nothing behind.

On his journey back to Germany, Frank made a stop at the airport to drop off Marky. I chose not to accompany them as my own misery was providing me with enough company. With everyone gone, I found myself preparing for a funeral.

De Troubadour, Hardenberg - June 30, 2002

Some typical Wreckin' Crew Fun

The many faces of Marky Ramone.
Nobody's Monkeyboy!
Tomfoolery in The Netherlands

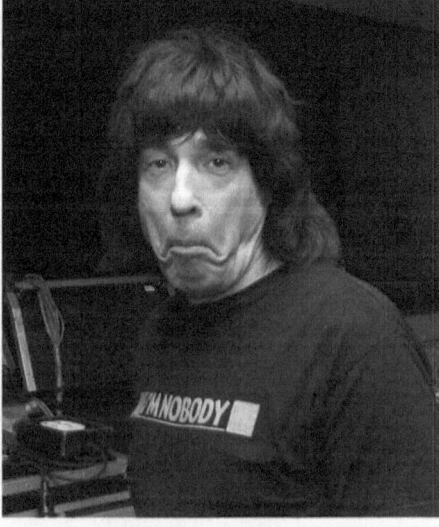

CHAPTER 29
Luck Went South

"Bad luck never lost a race." Mark Getty

After my devastating loss, it became clear that I needed a period of introspection to contemplate the meaning of life. Summer came and went, and I found a new perspective. Life is transient, for none of us are exempt from its grasp. It also made me realize that loving someone means having the strength to let them go. The pain endured by a loved one should never serve as an excuse to delay your grieving process.

But whatever the case, the show went on and the gears of booking started turning once again. After playing the High North and the Lowlands, it was time to head south. Italy, Spain, and Portugal had a completely different vibe when it came to their audience, and they were different from the rest of Europe. These countries were full of countless die-hard Ramones fans eagerly waiting. So, the chance to catch a glimpse of one of the few surviving members was an opportunity that few would pass up. At that time, Johnny was still among us, although he had retired from active band performances. His battle with cancer began in 2000, and perhaps that played a part in his decision to step away from the stage.

I had no trouble at all locking in 21 gigs. Most of the performances took place in Italy and Spain, with Switzerland, France, and Portugal serving as transit points to reach the other side.

Tony, the Spanish guy who had scored big for us by nailing down a couple of deals during our last European tour, specifically for the notoriously challenging Christmas dates, wasted no time in coming through for us again. This time, he managed to book us shows in France. Now, France ain't the easiest place to secure gigs, and maybe that's because of the language difference, but it feels like the country has this air of seclusion about it. And let's not forget about the French rock scene - it's a whole different animal. You've got these local bands that are like legends within France, selling records like crazy and filling up stadiums, all while being completely unknown outside of the country.

In the wake of Tony's arrival, Christina quickly followed suit to spread the operations of Ballistic Bookings in the city of Malaga. Collaborations like these are a godsend because they have the potential to exponentially expand opportunities by tapping into their own network. However, it is crucial that these partnerships are built on a foundation of honesty and trustworthiness – qualities that can only be learned through firsthand experience. Unfortunately, I must confess that I have gained an abundance of knowledge in this area over the years, and most of it has been far from positive. Losing trust is a blow that can only be endured once, but the repercussions are always substantial. The financial impact alone is enough to leave a lasting mark.

09/13/2002: Jux Tap, Sarzana (IT)
09/14/2002: Velvet Rock Club, Rimini (IT)
09/15/2002: Lagabbia Club, Vicenza (IT)
09/16/2002: Sommercasino, Basel (CH)
09/17/2002: Mondo Bizarro, Rennes (FR)
09/18/2002: Koslow Club, Bordeaux (FR)
09/19/2002: Sala Magic, Barcelona (ES)
09/20/2002: Dr. Slump, Castellon (ES)
09/21/2002: Industrial Coperam Granada (ES)
09/23/2002: Gruta 77, Madrid (ES)
09/24/2002: Bilbao Rock, Bilbao (ES)
09/25/002: Santa Sede, Oviedo (ES)
09/26/2002: Pabellon De O Berbes, Vigo (ES)
Days off in the South of France
10/02/2002: Thunder Road, Codevilla (IT)
10/03/2002: Blackout Rock Club, Roma (IT) - Cancelled
10/04/2002: Totem, Pisa (IT)

For this tour, I couldn't rely on our usual crew anymore. Our straight-edge hardcore kids were out on the road somewhere, doing their own thing. Les and his wife were likely unavailable, but luckily, I found my brother-in-law and his girlfriend, who were more than willing to step in. Stitch, being a young dude, had skills in guitar and bass, and he had a knack for all things technical and handy. He was like a wizard when it came to electronics and fixing things. His girlfriend, Sofie, had an incredibly outgoing personality, and as our merch girl, she could charm anyone into buying our stuff.

This South European tour felt like a strange in-between journey. We had to keep moving, constantly in motion, so that the audience wouldn't forget about us. And, of course, there were those who wanted to keep the money flowing even during our downtime. Personally, I wasn't too thrilled about it. All I could think about was the urgent need to be in the studio and work on our new album.

But then again, it was my own money that was funding this whole project. The advances we were supposed to use for important things like studio time had mysteriously vanished as if someone had no concept of basic accounting. It's simple math: profit is the result of subtracting costs from income. But some people have this twisted belief that the income is theirs to keep, while the costs are all on me. Talk about skewed logic.

In the end, greed never makes for a reliable friend. It poisons everything it touches and turn the most reliable allies into dreadful enemies leaving nothing but bitterness and resentment in its wake.

During our time on this tour, we came across some of our favorite bands who were also on the road. It's almost like we were all on a road trip together, following each other's trail. There were moments when you couldn't help but wish you were in the audience and watching their show instead of watching them from backstage. We missed out on seeing the Specials and Girlschool, even though our paths crossed multiple times. But the most unforgettable encounter happened down south when we crossed paths with Ronnie James Dio.

Ronnie, a legend in his own right, had been a part of some truly influential metal bands, with Rainbow and Black Sabbath being the most notorious. While we were touring in Italy, he was busy rocking out on his Dio "Killing the Dragon" tour. It seemed like fate had brought us together because, for at least a week, we kept bumping into each other at highway truck stops where we would stop to refuel or grab a bite to eat. Each time, we couldn't resist going over to hang out for a while. Despite his reputation as a metal icon, this pint-sized headbanger, who supposedly invented that universal hand sign of the devil, was down-to-earth and always greeted us with a warm smile. We always had a blast chatting with him.

There was just one problem. Marky didn't take too kindly to our newfound bond with Ronnie. No matter how hard we tried, we just couldn't convince Marky to join us for a photo with the rock legend. It was as if he had an aversion to sharing the frame with someone he deemed a leprechaun. But it didn't stop us from enjoying our encounters and sharing memorable moments with one of metal's greatest icons.

The adventure kicked off on a spine-chilling Friday the 13th at the Jux Tap Club in Sarzana. Matt and Livio, the guys behind Hellfire Booking and Promotion, warmly greeted us as we were ready to start the Italian leg of the tour. Livio, the guitarist of the Italian punk band, the Duffers, would be joining us as support for the upcoming shows. Marky had already arrived the night before, and we rendezvoused with him at the Al Sant Andrea Hotel. Without wasting a moment, we found ourselves in his room, ready to dive into an acoustic rehearsal session. The man was fully prepared and ready to rock. Our mission was simple yet powerful: to spread our music far and wide and touch as many souls as possible. Our mission was simple yet powerful: to spread our music far and wide and touch as many souls as possible.

Italy has always held something special for me. Since the early seventies, when my grandparents introduced me to the Italian Riviera, I fell head over heels for its enchanting climate and exquisite cuisine. It seemed like destiny when, years later, my family and I found our own little haven nestled in the serene Tuscan mountains, just a stone's throw away from the Marecchia River. Our backyard oasis is no ordinary pool; it's a charming natural lake that sits right beside our humble abode.

But of course, back then, I couldn't even dream it, not in a million years.

Returning to Rimini, the next day, felt like coming home. When I was a kid, I spent endless hours on that beach, playing with a sieve, a bucket, and a spade. And now, here I was, about to take the stage at the Velvet Club.

The massive venue sat alongside a picturesque lake, but Marky didn't care much about the view. When Stich and Sofie mentioned it, he responded with a curt "Fuck the lake!" However, this club held significant memories for him, as he had once played here with the Ramones.

As we gathered in the parking lot, we encountered a group of dedicated fans who had traveled over six hours in a camper just to witness our performance. Unfortunately, we had to prioritize the soundcheck and couldn't join their private party.

One of the opening acts that night was Senza Benza, who had previously opened for the Ramones. Marky wasn't too thrilled about crossing paths with them. He found them quite pretentious, as their performance seemed like an attempt to impersonate the Ramones themselves. Frustrated, Marky confided in Livio that they would never open for us again. Never.

Before we made our way to Hotel Villa Lalla, a flock of girls surrounded Jack and me. They eagerly requested autographs on their bellies. Being the good guys that we were...

Our next destination along the Italian trail is Bassano di Grappa, Vicenza, where we'll rock the Lagabbia Music Club during its re-opening weekend. Just the day before, The Selector graced the same stage, setting the tone for an unforgettable night. The club has undergone a stunning renovation and emanates those groovy vibes of the sixties and seventies.

Before hitting the club, we indulge in dinner at the Alla Carte Hotel. As we make our way back, we're met with a scene straight out of a time

The night we felt like cage fighters in the Lagabbia Music Club.
September 15, 2002 - Vicenza, Bassano di Grappa, Italy.

machine. It's as if a parade of punk-loving kids from the late seventies has teleported right before our eyes. Never have we witnessed such a glorious display of old-school punk attire in one place.

The opening act, The Duffers, wraps up their set with a rendition of the Ramones' classic "53rd and 3rd," inviting our roadie to take the mic. To our surprise, it was a roaring success, igniting the crowd's enthusiasm.

But as for me, during our performance, I found myself locked in a battle with one of my guitar straps. It just kept slipping off, frustrating me beyond belief. In a fit of rage, I tossed my guitar to the ground. To my astonishment, the crowd erupts with excitement, feeding off the raw energy. Dee cranks up the intensity on his guitar to fill the void left by my outburst. Fueled by frustration, I unleashed a furious kick against the cage enclosing the stage. And the kids just ate it up like candy. In the end, I found solace in belting out the vocals alone, but to be honest, the crowd couldn't care less. They were captivated by the raw emotion.

Switzerland was eagerly awaiting our arrival, but as luck would have it, we hadn't even traveled fifty miles when Marky realized that his passport was nowhere to be found. Faced with this setback, we had no choice but to turn the van around and head back to the hotel, knowing that crossing the Swiss border without passports was simply out of the question. However, it turned out that our detour was unnecessary. When we finally arrived at the border, we found ourselves in an endless line for customs control. But as fate would have it, I spotted an open gate while behind the wheel, leading our van away from the watchful eyes of the officials. No one seemed to notice our massive vehicle as we boldly passed through. *"Fuck the border patrol!"* Marky exclaimed triumphantly. And just like that, we entered the land of cheese, chocolate, and cuckoo clocks without a hitch.

The Summer Casino held no surprises for us. It was always a killer spot to make a pit stop, like crashing at a buddy's place while passing through town. We had played there before. As soon as we arrived, the local crew jumped in to lend a hand with unloading our gear.

Meanwhile, Marky was completely captivated by the whole concept of the SpeedKings Casino-style we were about to unveil. *"Viva Las Vegas!"* he declared. From now on, our future tours will embrace a more vintage vibe, channeling the spirit of the 1950s. We would suit up in sleek black attire and rock old-school bullet microphones; we were fully committed to this new direction.

Driving from Basel to Rennes was quite the journey. As we drove over there, memories of my time with the Buckweeds flooded my mind. It was during that period that I felt most creative, and Manny and I pushed each other to new heights. Being on the road with Marky reminded me of a song Manny wrote called "She Looked Like Joey Ramone." It was about a girl he went to high school with who bore a striking resemblance to the lead singer of the Ramones. What made it even more surreal was that she lived in a town called Ramonville. That song played on repeat in my head as we arrived at the Mondo Bizarro Club, where we were scheduled to perform that night. When we finally reached our destination, we were greeted by the enigmatic Madame Claude and the ever-mysterious Claude himself. They had an intriguing proposition for us - an invitation to stay for an additional show. The original performance they had scheduled had sold out so quickly that they saw fit to throw a consecutive party. It was tempting, but alas, we had already made plans for a show in Bordeaux the following day. Little did we know that Bordeaux would turn out to be a complete disaster. If only we had known, we would have gladly stayed in Rennes instead.

This time, we were just passing through because Spanish Tony of Tony Producionnes hooked us up with two shows in France. France wasn't exactly my strongest booking territory since Manny left after the Buckweeds. Actually, Manny was an excellent booker, way better than I was, and maybe it was because he was born in Toulouse, but he knew the French mindset like no other, and he made it work both ways. He earned the Frenchies' trust.

Mondo Bizarro was a cool club which was filled with the raw energy of the feeling of intense rock'n'roll. Despite its small size, it gave an aura of exhilaration that reverberated through the air. As soon as you stepped foot inside, you could feel the electricity in the air, knowing that you were going to be able to lock eyes with a wild audience.

Tony arrived accompanied by a group of individuals who seemed out of place in this rock and roll haven. They had an air of corporate formality around them, they were dressed in suits that clashed with the spirit of the venue. There was an indescribable vibe permeating the air, one that unsettled me to the core. I couldn't quite put my finger on it, but something felt off. I couldn't comprehend what Tony was trying to achieve by presenting these people to us. It felt as if he was showcasing a product to potential buyers, but I couldn't comprehend how these individuals could relate to our dirty music.

But I didn't have much time to dwell on these thoughts. The post-summer heat was scorching and delightful, and we were getting closer to a whole lot of fans who arrived early. One person in particular stood out from the crowd. We had already communicated through email, but meeting Thomas Goze in person was a different experience. He was an absolute fanatic when it came to the Ramones, and he had fully embraced our music. His infectious enthusiasm charmed me beyond measure. It felt like we were forging ties that would last for eternity.

As soon as we started playing, the audience erupted into a frenzy of wild dancing and singing along. After playing countless shows, you develop a sense of what kind of night it's going to be based on the audience's reaction to the first song. And my instincts were spot on. The venue couldn't contain the sheer number of people who showed up; it was jammed and packed. The heat inside was unbearable, and the music was so loud it busted eardrums. All these elements combined to create an explosive cocktail of energy and excitement.

If there was one special thing between Marky and me during live shows, it was the way I messed up the lyrics by adding new parts that were completely different from the original. Marky had this uncanny ability to anticipate when I would shout out something twisted, and he loved it in a strangely freakish way. I often caught him laughing behind his drum kit. He never shied away from controversy and was always incredibly open-minded. Bigotry was not his thing at all. Sometimes, these twisted lyrics led us to completely abandon the original ones and come up with something entirely new. It became the norm for us. "Girls and Gasoline" transformed into "Boys and Vaseline," and sometimes I couldn't even remember what the lyrics sheet said anymore.

In the heat of the moment, among the chaos, the lyrics slipped from my mind and left me with only nonsensical words to salvage the situation.

Young Thomas stood at the forefront as we launched into "I Don't Care Anymore." The only fragment of the lyrics I could grasp was the raw declaration, "I'm gonna tear you another asshole," while the rest became a hazy blur. However, when I saw Thomas among the crowd, he flawlessly recited each and every word. It became clear that my best option was to bring him onto the stage with me. And just like that, he became my savior. He delivered an awe-inspiring performance, not missing a single word. From his perspective, it was likely an unexpected honor to be pulled into the spotlight, but in reality, he rescued me from the clutches of embarrassment.

Tony left early and informed us that he would meet up with us in Bordeaux the following day. As is customary with our band and our devoted fans, we always make it a point to give the opportunity for young enthusiasts to join us on our adventures. Thomas had some spare time on his hands. While we checked into a cheap Formule 1 Hotel, he accepted our offer to accompany us for the Bordeaux show and was content with claiming the bunk bed in the van as his sanctuary for the night. While the sleeping pad served its purpose while we were on the road and driving, we definitely preferred the luxury of a proper bed whenever it was feasible. However, for Thomas, this humble sleeping arrangement was like residing in a grandiose five-star rock 'n' roll suite. Simultaneously, we ensured that our van received the utmost protection by enlisting the services of the most formidable security and watchdog available. If anyone dared to tamper with our vehicle, they would swiftly retreat upon discovering that there was someone inside ready to defend it.

The following day, we faced a grueling six-hour drive to reach the Koslow Club, an industrial venue in Bordeaux. As soon as we stepped foot into this goth-inspired venue, it was as we entered the Titty Twister bar from the iconic 'From Dusk Till Dawn' movie. We realized that the usual crowd that frequented this place wouldn't necessarily appreciate our style of music. There were hardly any posters or advertisements promoting the event. To make matters worse, we were introduced as the 'Markee Ramones.' Tony dropped the ball on promotion this time. In a feeble attempt to divert our attention, he led us to a seedy bar called Ghizen in the heart of the redlight district, offering us drinks and food as if that would somehow appease our rage. But it did nothing to quell our anger. Tony tried to reassure us that everything would be fine, but we were streetwise enough to sense that it wasn't. Sometimes, you just have a gut feeling about these things.

A lame and lousy show sucks the life out of you and leaves you desperate for a decent place to crash. Unfortunately, Bordeaux was not going to offer us this comfort. As soon as we arrived at the hotel, we could tell by its location that it was the bottom of the barrel. We had to wait for the usual occupants to vacate their rooms before we could even check-in. Tony, in his infinite wisdom, brought us to a shady red-light hotel known for hosting hookers and their tricks. These were the kind of rooms rented out by the hour that reeked of old men, streetwalkers, and the godawful scent of cum. Jack and I found ourselves in a cramped room with a garnish nylon pink bedspread, and we were surrounded by a collection of used condoms that hung from the trash bin. In the adjacent room, there were passionate moans of a soul desperately trying to fuck their way through the night with a toothless prostitute. While they climaxed, they surely kept us from getting the rest we so desperately needed. I kept thinking of Thomas, who was snug in his bunk bed in the van. Compared to this den of debauchery, that van was like a luxurious five-star retreat.

It had been a show that left us feeling let down, but the worst was yet to come. Life is not always a sweet melody. The next morning, we realized Tony Baloney had vanished into thin air without leaving a trace. During a previous tour, this person had managed to secure some shows at a ridiculously low price around Christmas time, and it seemed like luck was on his side. However, the truth was that he had been short on funds and had promised us the France shows as a way to settle this open debt and some additional fees to make it up to us.

But this cunning individual had other plans in mind. He orchestrated the perfect disappearing act to leave us all in disbelief. That old bastard pulled off the heist of a lifetime by taking advantage of the situation to make a fortune while leaving us high and dry. Despite getting shows for a steal, he couldn't be bothered to pay us the amount he owed. And, of course, it went without words that it had to be me to swallow the bitter pill of loss.

Even though I had an IOU from Tony, I knew better than to hold my breath. I would end up being the one stuck with that worthless piece of paper, while Tony would get away with his deceitful actions. Marky wouldn't take the lousy paper as payment.

I was fed up with this tour. Once cracks started to appear, it became damn near impossible to patch things up. The following weeks dragged on, a monotonous cycle of playing shows and selling merchandise, while this so-called marriage began to feel like a sham.

My uncertainty about how to proceed became painfully clear. Should I soldier on, or should I just end it all? I had been foolish, falling into an adventure with a deadbeat freeloader who saw me as nothing more than his bread and butter on a dreary day. He may have talent and a name that opens doors, but that didn't make him human. Instead, it made him a heartless machine. I felt used, like a cheap whore performing sleazy tricks for someone else's pleasure. It was like some twisted Loverboy affair, and I was utterly disgusted.

The tour was all right, but it lacked that energy that had fueled all our previous shows. Deep down, I knew we should have been in the studio, diving deep into our next album. Sure, the money was coming in now, but we were sacrificing long-term success for short-term gains. In the business world, that's always a recipe for disaster.

Barcelona was up next on our list, and Sala Magic was eagerly awaiting our arrival. Tony, as usual, had messed up the promotion, but this club had quite a reputation, so I had faith that enough people would show up. Miraculously, we were provided with a decent place to crash for once. The Atenas Hotel turned out to be surprisingly comfortable.

That night, we met up with David Riu Valls of the Vietcongs. David was a friend from Barcelona who had visited us during our Stagbooks tour in Holland. Little did I know then that in the coming years, he would become close with Marky and handle a lot of tour management. But let's not forget, it was me who introduced him to Mr. Ramone. Sadly, David turned out to be one of the people who would backstab me later on. So-called friends.

We were also introduced to No Picky as the support act for our Spanish shows. These guys were a riot, full of humor and coolness. The

Chillin' at the Mondo Bizarro Club in Rennes, France.
September 17, 2002.

show at Sala Magic was yet another success. After the performance, some guy approached Jack to express his admiration for the show. Jack simply brushed him off, unaware that it was Nicke Borg, the lead singer of the Backyard Babies. Ah well, you can't win'em all.

The El Duende Club in Burriana was the spot we were set to rock out at the next day. But when we arrived, we discovered that "Marky Ramone and the Intruders" had taken our slot. The Tony screw-ups just kept coming. Luckily, he managed to salvage the situation, but it was the Aloha Hotel and the chance to dive into the ocean that made up for all the chaos.

As the night wore on, two local speed freak junkies named Miguel and José hooked Jack and me up with a couple of white lines of pure energy. Marky and Dee could barely keep up with the fierce pace we set. The show flew by in a whirlwind. We were so amped up that the only way to cool off was to take another midnight swim. The enchanting glow of the full moon added to the intensity of the moment.

Venturing further south, we arrive in Granada for the Industrial Copera Festival. This time, everything is meticulously organized to perfection. The abundance of stagehands ensures a seamless experience, and the dressing rooms are pristine, complete with refreshing showers and a fully stocked fridge. The food they serve is not too shabby either.

This festival held the grand finale of a local rock contest. I was asked by the mayor of Granada himself to present the first prize to the victorious band! It was quite a moment. I distinctly recall someone scribbling down some ridiculous text about "chicas mas calientes" on a piece of paper, and when I stumbled upon it during my speech, the entire crowd erupted in laughter. It was pure madness.

But before we hit the stage, the winners of the contest took the stage to warm up the crowd for us. And then, the time came. We faced a sea of a thousand wild and outrageous fans. We unleashed our music like we were demons from hell, delivering a performance that was both scorching and filthy. And we knew that the next day would be a well-deserved break for us.

That night at the Nava Hotel, we encountered a level of female attention that surpassed our expectations. It was more than what we were accustomed to, but after all the excitement, we were in dire need of a solid night's sleep.

The Nava Hotel, being quite satisfactory, was an obvious decision to extend our stay rather than search for another accommodation before reaching Madrid. After spending eleven days on the road, we were in desperate need of doing some laundry. And since we were already in Granada, it felt mandatory to visit the Alhambra. However, we never made it there. Instead, we were captivated by the enormous painting of the Alhambra adorning the wall of the restaurant, so far for cultural discovery. It served as a substitute for the real experience. After a night filled with copious amounts of wine, we prepared ourselves for the journey to the Spanish capital.

Gruta 77 stands as one of the most renowned rock clubs in Spain, and our show there was a complete sell-out. Before we even took the stage, the local band Supa Space Rockets did an incredible job of hyping up the crowd, setting the perfect atmosphere for the explosive energy that SpeedKings would bring. And when we finally kicked off with our intro, it felt like all hell broke loose. Marky pounded on the drums with such force and speed that it became evident this would be one of the tightest performances of our entire tour.

Little did we know, Spanish television had captured the entire show without our knowledge. It wasn't until after the show, when they brought microphones into our backstage room for an interview, that we discovered we had been filmed.

As always, after the show, a swarm of kids gathered for autographs and to engage in lively conversations. However, one particular kid caught Marky's eye. This young rebel wore a leather jacket adorned with a cool Ramones logo and the word "Commando" painted across it in bold letters. Marky couldn't resist the allure of that jacket. He was determined to make it his own.

It seemed like an eternity as Marky tried to convince the kid to part with his prized possession. Perhaps it was the kid's reluctance, or maybe it was the combination of Marky's endless begging and a generous offer of hard-earned dollars that eventually swayed him. Regardless of the reasons, Marky's persistence paid off, and he finally got his hands on that coveted leather jacket.

We left the bustling capital city, venturing into the vibrant Basque country. Our destination was Bilbao, where we were scheduled to rock the stage at Bilbo Rock. However, the municipal theatre seemed unprepared for the raw energy of a punk rock show. It took some serious negotiation and persuasion before the theater manager reluctantly allowed us to unload our gear.

As we settled into the Arragas Hotel, we discovered that the Basque people had a deep-rooted connection to their folklore. Right next to the hotel, there was a charming little tapas bar where we stumbled upon a group of elderly men belting out heartfelt songs. It was their way of passing down tales from the past, a cherished tradition that resonated with us.

Despite the enchanting atmosphere, I couldn't shake off an unsettling feeling about staying in this area for too long. Our van had already fallen victim to the meddling of the local authorities, being towed away without any warning. I had no desire for an encore of such incidents in Basque Country. The next day, we eagerly sought solace in Oviedo, a city that promised a much-needed escape from the turmoil we had encountered.

We'll always remember the night we rocked the Santa Sebe Club and blew away a crowd of around 400 fans. But what really stood out were the encores. This punk chick from one of the opening bands managed to flash enough skin to earn herself a spot on our grand finale. She looked smoking hot. She is the kind of babe who turns heads wherever she goes. But here's the kicker: her voice was a complete mismatch. She couldn't carry a tune to save her life. Even a bunch of alley cats screeching in the night would have sounded better. It was a valuable lesson learned that night - appearances can be deceiving. You can't judge a book by its cover, or in this case, a singer by her looks.

The following forty-eight hours passed like a blur, fading into a haze of frenzied excitement. The Pabelon Club in Viego and Carabel

Marky and the No Picky Boys.
September 2002.

Some member are really not so picky after all.

Signing CD's and free mugshot pics.

in Palencia failed to leave a lasting impression. We performed, we unleashed our raw power, but aside from Marky's trademark full-moon duck walks, there was little worth recollecting. Marky's absurd antics nearly had us rolling on the floor in fits of uncontrollable laughter. That man never fails to deliver some delightfully foolish moves. But it was Stich's birthday that left the biggest impression. It happened just a few days before mine, and it was a celebration to remember.

And at last, we reached our final gig in Spanish territory. No Picky, true to form, was right on time when we arrived at Zulo, in the heart of La Sarte. It was mind-boggling how these guys pulled it off. They smoked pot all day and night yet still managed to deliver a decent performance and show up exactly when and where they were needed. Talk about earning punk rock points! But there was another guy who stole the show that night - a punk rocker in a wheelchair. "Put me in a wheelchair and get me to the gig," we couldn't help but point at him as we belted out the lyrics. Goodbye Spain! After the show, a couple of girls just wouldn't let up, and the sun began to rise as Jack, Dee, and I made our escape from the bar they had taken us to. Three glorious days off were waiting for us!

We decided to take a well-deserved break on the stunning shores of Biarritz. As my birthday drew near, September 30th, I couldn't help but feel a sense of strangeness being away from my real family. September 30th was just around the corner, and instead of being home, I was on the road with my chosen family, feeling like a fish out of water. We were in France, and some of the dates we were supposed to perform didn't pan out. So, we decided to take a few days off and escape to a peaceful bed and breakfast in the South of France.

During our downtime, we lounged by the pool while Marky, always the showman, flexed his muscles and did some hilarious and exaggerated bodybuilder poses. It was quite a sight to see him strutting around in his underwear, proudly displaying his abs. But hey, live and let live, right?

Eventually, we made our way to a restaurant where we planned to celebrate my birthday. However, much to my surprise, it turned out to be a party for someone else entirely. When dessert time rolled around, the menu presented a massive bowl of chocolate mousse. Mr. Greed couldn't resist indulging in this guilty pleasure all for himself. As the dish was placed in front of him, he scooped up huge mouthfuls of chocolate and

Enjoying lunch in Biarritz, France.
There is always room for more.

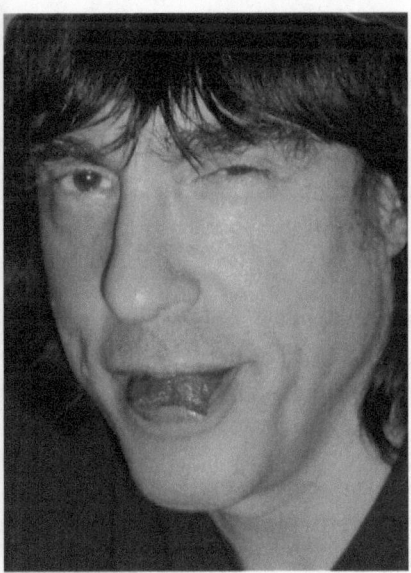

It's my party and I cry if I want to.
Marky hijacks the bowl of chocolate mousse.
The infamous shitmouth pictures.
September 30, 2002.

then let it dribble out like he was eating something dog shit. It did make for some incredibly entertaining and amusing photos, but deep down, I couldn't help but feel a pang of disappointment. After all, as Lesley Gore so aptly sang, "It's my party, and I'll cry if I want to…"

He must have sensed it, no doubt about that. Maybe he wasn't the sharpest tool in the shed, but even he couldn't ignore the obvious signs. It's funny how things turned out the next day when we all gathered for breakfast. He had some breaking news to share, and everyone was hanging onto his every word. Some people just can't shake off that feeling of excitement. *"We're going on a West Coast tour!"* he announced. The band and crew were left speechless, in complete awe. It was the ultimate achievement for us. A tour in the United fucking States of America. For the band, myself included, it felt like the pinnacle of our hard work.

Marky gave off this vibe like he was ready to step up. According to him, we had proven ourselves and were ready for the next level in the game. We had earned our place, and now things were about to change in a big way. We were done with the amateur gigs and small-time bookings. It was time for the big boys to come in.

Our time in France was absolutely rejuvenating. It felt as though we were immersed in a never-ending wave of pool parties and barbecues. Although, truth be told, having days off during a tour isn't ideal. It involves taking care of an entire crew and can end up costing quite a bit of money. However, the weather in October was fantastic, so we couldn't really complain.

Once we wrapped things up in Spain, it was time to focus on our final shows in Italy. We were relieved to have Matt and Livio by our side once again, as they had been there for us since the beginning of the tour. Their presence brought us a sense of comfort and reassurance.

The Thunder Road show in Voghera was an absolute blast. It was exactly what we needed after those days off. We were able to let loose and unwind, forgetting about any worries or stress.

South European Tour 2002
September 23, 2002 Gruta 77, Madrid, Spain
Flyer and poster

Gruta 77 - Magazine
Front and backcover.

Unfortunately, the night brought some bad news. Our show in Rome the next day had been canceled. It was a real bummer, but we soon learned that it was due to the unfortunate passing of the promoter just a few days earlier. We couldn't help but feel lucky that it was only one show that had to be canceled, considering the circumstances.

On our day off, Matt and his girlfriend went above and beyond as hosts. They introduced us to the secret world of Italian pesto, which was an absolute game-changer. At this point, we were more than ready for this tour to come to an end. The final leg of the tour took us to the Totem Club in Pisa. Unfortunately, we didn't have the chance to visit the iconic Leaning Tower. The way I had been feeling towards Marky was akin to a leaning tower itself - unstable and filled with mixed emotions. Even though I didn't want to face the harsh reality, Marky saw right through me in those last few days. He knew I was starting to see through all the lies and deception. The world was crumbling around us, and I was on the brink of blowing up our little side hustle. We needed something magical to turn things around, and the USA was just that.

Deep down, I knew I was being played, but I couldn't resist diving headfirst into the next chapter of our journey. It was my burning desire to become a rockstar ever since I was a kid, just like countless kids across the globe. And now, the doors world swung wide open. But despite the risks, knew the next shot would kill me still I had to get that fix so bad. And just then someone was more than willing to put the needle in my vein.

The Japan tour was on the horizon next, and the rest of the free world was poised for conquest. If we could pull this off, we were guaranteed entry into the ultimate, most untamed territory: South America. It was the holy grail, the place where the Ramones had witnessed their wildest and most crazy crowds, where their cars were pursued by the most outrageous fans to ever walk this earth. It felt like someone was toying with me, playing a game of cat and mouse, rabbit and carrot, and I couldn't help but be drawn to it. The allure of what lay ahead was irresistible.

Izna Rock
Tourpass

South European Tour 2002
December 21, 2001 Izna Rock, Figueres, Spain
Concert poster.

Izna Rock
Invitation and entrance ticket

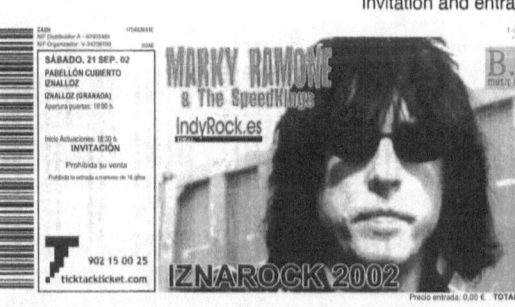

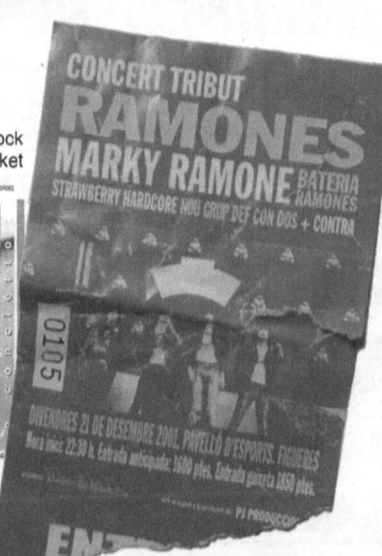

Rockin' out and meeting friends. The ideal world!

CHAPTER 30

Colors & Swastikas

*"You're just a bastard kid, And you got no name
Cause you're living with me, We're one and the same"*

Johnny THUNDERS - You Can't Put Your Arms around a Memory

I can immediately spot the familiar writing style and juvenile prose of those who possess only half-literate abilities, sending their letters to the President or any other influential figure. It's as if they truly believe that these individuals would spare a single thought for the incoherent ramblings of some fool from a forgotten corner of the nation.

When I tore open the envelope and read the letter, it was as if the writer believed that I also held significance in his life. It felt like he saw something special within me, a connection that he hoped to be potentially meaningful.

"Dear Sir,

My name is Eddy and I collect all the Belgian records. I have almost everything and I would also like to get your records with Marky Ramone for my collection and archive. I will contact you.

Sincerely, Eddy"

A piece of paper, ripped in half, hangs by a thread. A trembling hand carefully wrote along the crimson edge. The page is enclosed in a grimy envelope and stamped with precision. I nonchalantly toss it onto the table in the living room, not giving it a second thought.

I used to reside in Bruges, in a residence referred to as the "haunted house" by the locals. This name came about due to a previous tenant who tragically ended his life by hanging himself in the turret. It was in this very house that I witnessed the horrifying events of September 11, 2001, unfold on live television. As I sat there, watching the news on CNN, I saw the second plane crash into the Twin Towers during the devastating attacks in New York City. The horror is presented in real time.

Bruges, with its haunting past and eerie atmosphere, served as the backdrop for my life during that time. The house itself was known as the headquarters for the SpeedKings tours. It held a certain mystique that fascinated and intrigued me. Its dark history only added to the appeal of living there.

I was immersed in a fascinating book, enjoying the serenity of the garden, when suddenly, the sound of the bell interrupted my peaceful moment. My wife pressingly called out to me. With a sense of curiosity, I made my way to the front door with a wonder. As I opened the door, I was greeted by an unexpected sight - a wretched piece of paper, worthless and stationary, held out towards me with an outstretched hand.

"Nice to meet you Sir. My name is Eddy. I wrote you a letter."

When I laid eyes on him, the initial thought that crossed my mind was "scum of the earth." Now, I may be a bit biased, but with his unkempt, greasy locks, a sleazy mustache reminiscent of adult films, a denim jacket with the sleeves ripped off, and a beat-up moped lurking in the shadows, it was hard to conjure up a more fitting depiction. This individual embodied everything that society deems undesirable and disreputable.

Let me tell you about this guy. He was rocking a dirty, sleeveless jean jacket adorned with countless patches. But beneath that rough exterior lay a hilarious out-of-place touch of elegance - a flowered shirt. And if that wasn't enough, his arms were completely inked up with complex prison-style Chinese ink tattoos. It's safe to say that the word "marginal" doesn't even come close to describing the intense feeling I got when I saw him.

"I wrote you a letter and did not hear back from you. I just passed by and thought to give it a try. Am I coming at a bad time?"

It's that awkward feeling of honest embarrassment that prevents me from immediately showing them the door. Due to an overwhelming sense of kindness, it is not long before Eddy finds himself seated beside me in the tranquil confines of the garden.

He clung onto a tale as if he possessed the most exhaustive compilation of Belgian music records and was acquainted with nearly every individual in the Belgian and international music scene.

His torrent of anecdotes and name-dropping somewhat eluded me, but what I was truly captivated by was his vibrant Hawaii floral shirt. Like a rabbit entranced by a luminous display. And then, my gaze was drawn to the skull adorned with wings. The iconic, universally recognized symbol of the Hells Angels. The distinctive logo surpassed even the fame of Coca-Cola. So here sits a foolish person in front of me who bore a Hells Angel tattoo. Undoubtedly, he must be deranged because anyone who has such a tattoo without being a full-fledged member knows that one day it will be forcibly removed, perhaps with a cheese slicer. You'd be fortunate if your arm doesn't come off entirely. Or could it be that I am sitting here in the garden with a bona fide patched member? That would certainly astonish me. Him? No way. Or could it be that the Brotherhood inadvertently allowed this individual to infiltrate their ranks in an unguarded moment?

"You should come and visit me. I am living close by with my mom. When can you come over?"
"Oh, I will, Eddy. I will let you know."

Out of the depths of procrastination emerges more procrastination. Eddy slips from my mind, until one day, out of the blue, he reaches out to me. In an attempt to shake off this lingering feeling, I impulsively decided to take a short drive back and forth. What harm could half an hour possibly do? But what I did not know was that this seemingly insignificant choice would have consequences I never could have anticipated.

I swiftly locate the neighborhood where he resided, the social district. It was a poor area with affordable two-story buildings, erected by the local housing company. Each building consisted of both an upstairs and downstairs apartment. Just as I approached the door to ring the bell, it swung open. Standing there was Eddy, who was eagerly waiting for me, beating his elderly mother to the punch.

"It's my friend, mama. Go back inside. I don't want you to catch a cold."

He took me up to the second floor with his quick and purposeful steps. As he opened the door, a whole new world unfolded before my eyes. It was a hidden realm that Bruges could never fathom. Behind these closed doors laid a secret that remained unknown to the unsuspecting locals of this neighborhood.

The hallway stretched out before me. It was enveloped in darkness that added an air of mystery. It lead me towards the living room, but along the way, I noticed a door that concealed a bathroom, a toilet, and a bedroom. Despite the dim lighting, I made out the walls of the hallway adorned with an array of patched vests. I can't quite recall the exact number, but each one tells a story. I spotted a Hells Angels jacket that boldly proclaimed its affiliation with the notorious biker gang. Nearby, a vest emblazoned with the words "Slaves of Satan" caught my attention, while the "Property of" vest declared its wearer as someone's prized possession. Most likely worn by the Eddy's beloved.

It felt as though I stumbled into a gritty biker gang film. Each vest had a musty scent. They gaze at me with disdain and intimidation, well aware that I don't belong to their exclusive one-percenter world. The tattoo on my arm, once a mere question mark, now held new significance. Only those with the proper credentials call this place home.

As I made my way into the living room, a thrilling surprise awaited me. On two of the walls proudly displayed an impressive collection of vinyl records with a hidden music system tucked away in between. But what caught my attention were the walls themselves. They were decorated with Nazi flags, which transformed the room into a provocative shrine. If Hitler himself had possessed a passion for music, I can't help but imagine his Berlin bunker resembling this very space.

My eyes then wander to an old dresser cabinet that stood tall and ominous. The drawers were filled to the brim with relics from the Third

Reich. Large rings with swastikas gleam in the dim light. Next to them were fearsome daggers, whose blades glinted with a dangerous allure. And there, nestled amongst the artifacts of a dark past, were a few Lugers – enough firepower to assemble a small private militia.

The sight before me evoked inside of me a mixture of fascination and discomfort. It's as if this room was a time capsule that preserved a chapter of history that still resonates with raw power. The juxtaposition of music and Nazi symbolism sent shivers down my spine. It was like a paradox that both repulsed and intrigued me. I was in a state of shock and speechlessness, and I felt completely out of place as I settled into the club seat. Eddy, on the other hand, confidently took a seat in the three-seater and swiftly began to roll up a few cigarettes. This ritual was essential for him, as he smoked one cigarette after another without pause. It may sound like a small detail, but the worn-out balatum flooring clearly showed the exact spots where he sat countless times over the years. Two dark patches, resembling his "feet," reminiscent of the X marking a secret location on a pirate's treasure map.

Eddy had amassed a record collection that was nothing short of extraordinary. He unveiled albums that I've never even heard of, let alone laid eyes on. Each vinyl was meticulously encased in a pristine plastic sleeve, accompanied by carefully curated clippings from countless magazines and personal notes penned by Eddy himself. It was an admirably unparalleled archive, a treasure trove of musical history.

As time goes by, the brief moment I intended to stay stretches into a much longer period. An hour and a half slipped away unnoticed and I was consumed by the enchanting world of photo books. In that dimly lit space, saturated with the scent of nicotine, reality faded into insignificance. The cigarette smoke permeating the air was engulfing me in its larger-than-life embrace.

Eddy informed me that he was acquainted with Max Cavalera from Sepultura since he was just a 15-year-old kid, corresponding with the Belgian Haupt Sturmbahn Führer. And that's just scratching the surface. Stacks of photographs featuring Eddy alongside Lemmy and Motörhead were scattered across the grimy coffee table. He boldly asserted that he used to serve as Lemmy's personal bodyguard and chauffeur during the band's frequent visits to our shores for European tours. I was completely unfazed when he showed a collection of snapshots that showcased Lemmy and his companions alongside adult film stars. It has become the new norm, the absolute minimum I expect from Eddy. Settling for anything less simply does not satisfy his appetite for excitement.

The stories just keep pouring in. Tales of Eddy's audacity when he confronted a man who dared to lay a hand on his beloved. The two adversaries strolled towards the shoreline to fight it out. Tension mounting with each step. The scoundrel who dared to defile Filthy's woman had nothing better to do than taunt Eddy, tapping his head repeatedly with a motorcycle helmet. As they neared the beach, Eddy's patience wore thin. He reached for the dagger dangling from his belt and swiftly struck the other man. "That's the price you pay when you mess with my queen," Mr. Filthy must have thought. Later that very evening, Eddy hitchhiked his way to Amsterdam, seeking refuge with the notorious Hells Angels. In exchange for a place to hide, he immersed himself in the treacherous world of speed and cocaine while offering his services as a trusted associate. Upon arrival at Angels Place, the Amsterdam chapter stripped him of his colors and forced him to prove himself once again as a lowly prospect. Eddy's dedication to the club consumed him day and night, exacting a toll on his weary soul. While amphetamines and cocaine may keep one awake, there is always a limit for every individual, even someone as resilient as Eddy. In no time at all, he transformed into a mere skeleton of his former self, vulnerable to the two afflictions that plague those on the edge - either a wasting disease of the flesh or a debilitating bone ailment.

All skin and bones, he was driven by an insatiable desire for adrenaline, a feverish craving that propelled him back across the border of Belgium. But alas, his reckless escapades caught up to him, and the enforcers of justice had him in their clutches, bound by cold, metal handcuffs. He was no stranger to being confined. From a young age, he found himself occasionally locked away in a correctional facility.

"I went in there as a Provo, all Peace and Love! I came out with my middle finger up. FUCK YOU AND FUCK THE SYSTEM!"

I 'HEARTBREAK' THE RAMONES

I was stoked that I made the decision to come to this place, and Eddy was totally loving it, too. He's found a new partner in crime right here in his own damn Bruges. And that partner happens to be the lead vocalist of the drummer from the legendary band, the Ramones. It was like I've become a fresh addition to his life. The singles I gifted him were going to be treasured, like precious gems in his collection.

"You know Nick, look around ya. When I am dead and gone, they will put a wastebin outside the window and throw it all away. My whole life, all I ever cared for."

I can still hear the lingering resentment resonating in his words. Eddy had long abandoned his nicotine sanctuary. For years now, he's been gallivanting around, most likely propping up the bar with Lemmy. Years after his death, I stumbled upon this news myself. It's a bitter pill to swallow. The larger-than-life figure, the caricature-like station man who used to stand at my doorstep, revealed himself to be a complex individual with countless layers. To some, he was an asshole, a man to be feared. But to others, he was a role model, someone they admired. Every time Eddy entered a room, he commanded respect like a king. However, deep down, beneath his tough exterior, he was a vulnerable and sentimental soul, burdened by his own memories as he journeyed towards his inevitable end.

After dedicating countless years to the arduous task of looking after his mother, whose mind had been consumed by dementia, he found himself blindsided by the insidious presence of lung cancer. In this dire moment, his trusty dagger, which had provided solace and protection throughout his tumultuous journey, proved futile. Eddy, a warrior in his own right, ultimately succumbed to the overwhelming might of the enemy, losing the hard-fought battle that had consumed his existence. His loyal friend Pat stood by his side until the very end. He informed me that Eddy's final farewell was marked by his cremation while donning the T-shirt I personally crafted for him, a garment that had become tattered and worn from his constant wear. This revelation fills me with a profound sense of reverence and respect, as if being entrusted with such a task is a true privilege.

Eddy, for those about to rock.... I salute you! You can't put your arms around a memory.

Eddy and The Ramones. While Joey is covering the left wing, Marky and Johnny are keeping things right with Mr. Filthy.

Stepping into Filthy Eddy's world.

Eddy and Lemmy of Mötorhead were always pretty close.

CHAPTER 31
Kabukicho Cowboys

"Maybe these streets are typical of a society without modesty, morally unhinged." – Anonymous

Our first record was doing great, and talks began for its launch in the US, South America, and Japan. Given my past life in the far-eastern Land of the Cherry Blossom and my experiences of strutting my stuff on their stages, I was the chosen one to engage in dialogues with the slant-eyed record label moguls.

You may give shooting off emails a shot, but when the rubber meets the road, nothing beats the authenticity of a face-to-face interaction to seal a bona fide deal in Japan. The term 'nomunication,' an intriguing blend of cultures and languages, originates from the Japanese term "nomu," translating to 'drink,' fused with the universally recognized English term 'communication'. This unique linguistic cocktail literally stands for 'communication over drinks', with a particular emphasis on alcohol.

This term abbreviates the essence of Japanese drinking culture, where social interactions revolve around the communal act of sharing a bottle of sake or beer. Screw the deal if you decide to snub this ritual in the Land of the Rising Sun. It's no mere one-off booze fest. It's a marathon, not a sprint. The "Hai," or yes, isn't a genuine "Hai" until it echoes through multiple rounds of sake. In my time there, this rhythm was on a constant replay, and only tenacity could strike the right chord. Go too fast, and your business dreams will fade faster than a one-hit wonder.

Even in the music industry, where I thought the rules might dance to a different tune, more akin to our Western beat, the same traditional melody played on. So, we plunged into the ocean of liquor…

Roadrunner Japan's fascination was the most prominent. I perceived the record label to be straddling the line between the minor independent players and the undisputed majors of the record industry. Regardless of having a Ramone among our crew, the SpeedKings were a mere whisper in comparison to the Ramones themselves. As for Marky, his fame was not exactly in its prime. Therefore, we were comfortable with aiming for a label that was neither too diminutive nor excessively grand.

Roadrunner, *in* the end, proved to be an unfruitful endeavor. Excessive libations, endless chatter, but a glaring lack of real commitment and support. The album was already in the can, which meant they didn't have to shell out a dime for its production. It was a risk-free game for them, while all we sought was a decent advance for the licensing deal and, more importantly, a steadfast assurance and backup for a tour.

The most regrettable aspect of squandering that time was my failure to initiate a dialogue with an alternative party. People always claim that straddling two horses with a single seat is impossible, but in the contemporary corporate sphere, it's a savvy tactic, provided you're transparent about it to avoid any accusations of disloyalty, merely perceiving it as a display of intelligence. However, deciding on the next step wasn't a walk in the park.

I had the option to align with the hippest Japanese label I was aware of, 1+2 Records in Shinjuku. It would mean working with one of my personal friends who owned that label. But there was this nagging fear that Barnhomes wouldn't be capable of delivering the publicity we genuinely craved. Conversely, we were running low on alternatives. The only record labels that really held any weight were giants like EMI and JVC. The question that loomed was, how could we possibly ignite their interest in our motley crew?

Japan's societal structure is a complex web of insiders and outsiders, with identity deeply rooted in group affiliation. The concept of individuality is often deemed insignificant. Hence, being a foreigner and an individual might seem tantamount to admitting defeat before even entering the battlefield. However, there was one crucial detail I had overlooked. I may have been more of a lone wolf compared to the average Japanese Joe, but I was part of an influential pack. My employment was with a brand that was renowned throughout Japan, a fact that functioned as a master key to unlock numerous opportunities. Pioneer was a brand that commanded respect, and this association gave me an unexpected edge.

Before I could blink, I found myself scheduling an appointment with the Japan Victor Corporation. The entire spectacle was about to replay. But the previous dealings with Roadrunner had seasoned me and sharpened my skills. So, I felt a sense of déjà vu with JVC and prepared alternative strategies.

In no time, I sensed a genuine interest from their side. Despite being a major in the record industry, we moved at a pace that would put punk rock to shame. Within a few weeks, I managed to secure the license and negotiate terms for a follow-up album.

They also planned to connect us with a Japanese booking agent, and the album's launch would align with a tour, the expenses for which they'd shoulder.

It took me aback when they gave me the reins, handing over a significant amount of control. It wasn't complete control as The Clash sung about, but everything I proposed concerning the production, the packaging and what else, seemed to get their nod of approval. White Jazz had earlier set the bar high with an elaborately designed foldout digipack and JVC was hell-bent on maintaining that standard, if not exceeding it. Yuko Inoue, one of my buddies and an astoundingly talented comic artist, took charge of designing the sleeve while I managed to rope in my beloved lawyer friend from Japan, known as Miss Sosueme. The humor behind her name flew over most heads. This lawyer lass was a figment of my imagination, and her name, "So sue me," was an under-the-radar wisecrack, which I had cunningly slipped into the sleeve's credits.

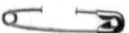

JVC was the bridge that connected us to the Booster Dragon Booking Agency. The term 'dragon' in their name immediately bestowed upon them an aura of samurai-like prowess - or at least that's how I perceived it, and even wished for it. However, for all the openness we'd experienced with JVC, the Booster Dragon was a different beast altogether. Perhaps their hesitance stemmed from our association with a leading record label - they didn't want to risk screwing things up. Trust, in Japan, is not merely a word; it's akin to sacred currency. Losing it can have disastrous consequences, something they couldn't afford. The Japanese don't revolve around the concept of forgiveness; it's an honor that forms their core ethos. So, our dragon tread lightly, as if walking on hot coals.

Anyway, it marked a break from the usual grind of grueling tours. A refreshing deviation that spared us the burdens of relentless travel. One of the key benefits was getting to do the soundcheck just once. It was like a sweet alternative after enduring torturous moments on those intense, heavy-duty tours. The venue was nestled amongst the larger 'live houses' in downtown Tokyo, yet it didn't match the huge capacity places like Akasaka Blitz.

We thrived in this setting as a band. Club shows were our thing, our comfort zone. It's a different kind of rush when you're performing for a few hundred people, so close that you can see the gleam in their eyes. There's an unspoken bond, an electric connection forged in the heat and sweat of close quarters. The energy vibrates and shoots adrenaline sky-high.

One of the high points of this gig series was the abundant opportunity we had to dive deep into the cityscape's pulse. The boys in the group were amped up, knowing I'd be their local guide. Having logged nearly a septennial in Tokyo, its secrets were as obscure to me as an open book. What's more, our stomping ground was none other than the Urga club, located in Kabukichō s throbbing core, infamous for its neon-drenched red-light reputation. We were on a crash course with a roller coaster ride of sheer exhilaration.

Booster Dragon resolved to storm the radio waves from the 26th to the 29th of November. This proposition was something we could get behind. The band was already on tenterhooks for those gigs. The ball was in Marky's court now. The man with an insatiable appetite for sushi didn't need much time to mull it over. Before we knew it, I was prepared to haul our passports to the Japanese Embassy located in Brussels. It was a matter of a few weeks before our artist visas would be in our hands, and our booking agent was adamant about adhering to the rigid paperwork process. The unholy marriage of state control and rock'n'roll. A peculiar cocktail that only the Japanese could understand.

What set our booking agent apart was the unflinching certainty that every detail would be managed with precision. The Japanese way of organizing is a head-banging, ground-shaking testament to meticulousness. There's no room for uncertainties; everything is streamlined down to the last flicker of the strobe light. Every minute, every second was accounted for, and no room was left for vagueness. One might venture to say that Japan could be the birthplace of Autism. The intense structure and precision of Japanese organization is nothing less but suffocating.

For once, completely divergent from the typical booking agents we've encountered, we had an unwavering certainty that things would pan out just fine. No lingering anxieties about logistics, transportation, accommodation, or sustenance. We were poised to receive royal treatment. It was an odd scenario, considering that agents usually view you as a gold mine to be exploited for every penny you possess. They assume the role of a king and you, merely the underling tasked with guaranteeing their compensation as if you were the cash cow. Any leftover crumbs might trickle down to your pocket, though they invariably manage to skim off the top somehow.

The outlook of our upcoming tour was promising, and it allowed me to finally focus on the core essence of our existence: our raw sound. JVC was nailing its promotional duties, and our album made its grand entrance just as we had envisioned.

Simultaneously, I had instigated discussions with Mosrite guitars. The axe wielded by Johnny Ramone was the most potent, ultimate endorsement any brand could dream of. Punk kids across the globe swore by the belief that the iconic Ramones vibe could only be born from this instrument. Without the Ramones, this guitar brand might have faded into oblivion.

The crew at Mosrite were genuinely thrilled at the prospect of collaborating with us, owing to our association with the legendary Ramones. It wasn't long before they laid down an offer that was music to our ears - three bespoke "SpeedKings" guitars crafted exclusively for us. A couple of six strings and a bass guitar. Picture us three, clad in our stark Reservoir Dogs black suits, strumming those matching guitars. Sure, it might come off as cheesy, but it would create a unified image. And I was certain, in the psyche of the Japanese audience, it would strike the right chord.

Yet Marky was the wild card in this game. Marky, the undisputed crowned champion of endorsements, did not miss this opportunity. His greed was stirred by the tantalizing prospect of a one-of-a-kind trophy. If not him, then who else was deserving of a custom guitar tailored to his every whim? Sure, he was the man behind the drums, and it was a stretch to believe that a brand would bankroll someone on a different stage. But that didn't deter him - he had already set his sights on "his" guitar. And he wanted it handed to him before we even had a sniff of ours. The back-and-forth bickering that ensued ate all our time until Marky's dreams were left unfulfilled. But so were ours. His attitude was clear - if I can't have mine, neither can you. People are strange, and the self-absorbed mentality of some truly knows no bounds.

We were all seething, yet we'd grown accustomed to swallowing such bitter pills. This wasn't a unique occurrence in our lives, nor would it be the final act. Eventually, you adapt to its taste. What used to be a joke gradually changes into stinging sarcasm and cynicism, stealthily corroding the once joyful harmony. It's not too far-fetched to visualize countless bands appearing as a cohesive force on stage, but off stage, they're nothing more than strangers wrapped in animosity. They brawl or simply loathe one another with a murderous passion. That's precisely the path we found ourselves veering down. Hating each other's guts on a road to ruin.

Despite everything, Japan was out there waiting for us. No matter the emotions that whirled around, we were pumped, ready to hop on that flight destined for Narita, with a pit stop in Helsinki. The journey ahead promised to be a wild one, and we were more than ready to dive headfirst into it.

Just when the stage looked set and failure seemed an improbable visitor, it was Murphy who decided to play the uninvited guest. We had a four-gig agenda on the books. The sale of tickets was in full swing, and before we knew it, they were all snapped up. Calls for additional shows started coming in and there was talk of taking our show on the road, beyond the confines of Tokyo, all the way to Osaka. Everything was humming along just fine - in fact, it was better than fine. It was phenomenal. But then, placing a call to NY threw a wrench in the works. The sun seemed to ice over, and in an instant, the warmth was sucked out, replaced by a bone-chilling freeze.

"*No way, I'm not going to pull it off. The Misfits have gigs lined up, and I need to hit the road right after my return. Plus, I'm only locked in for three performances. Advise them to scrap the first one. I've got another gig on that same day, and the pay is higher, so to hell with Japan*". His words took me by surprise. We had discussed this thoroughly. We'd made solid commitments and just a fortnight before our takeoff, Marky tossed our plans into chaos. "*Have you lost your marbles, you retard fuck?*" I pondered but held my tongue. Provoking his pea-sized brain could have led to a meltdown, and knowing his erratic nature, the remaining three shows could have easily dwindled down to none. I had learned to keep my mouth shut. Swallow my words and nod in agreement. I developed an intolerance for this crappy bullshit attitude, wondering if there was any medication that could cure it. I was desperately in need of some pills since I was going to be the one wiping up his shit. I'd been there before and found myself once more in that familiar predicament. The only snag this time was that I was dealing with individuals with a one-track mind. How on earth was I going to convey this to their autist minds? In Japan, commitment equates to honor. We failed miserably. How could I possibly explain that 'honor' was a foreign concept to Marky? He probably couldn't even spell it correctly.

I loathed my own actions, yet I chose to keep the agent in the dark. Truly, I lacked the courage to spill the beans. My gut told me that confessing now would result in a two-week marathon of playing mediator, striving to appease both parties while achieving nothing. Instead, I chose inertia as my defense, buying time through passive resistance. It's intriguing how one learns to burrow in, hide under a rock, and devise plans for self-preservation. It's likely the least rock-n-roll action imaginable; yet, it was a survival tactic I could not afford to abandon. The last thing I wanted was to witness the building crumbling.

I had made up my mind to ride this storm out until we were just two days away from departure. Then, I would reveal that Marky had fallen sick, and his arrival would be delayed by a day. Illness was an easier pill for them to swallow, and who in their right mind would debate that? I knew they'd hurl curses and swear, but it wouldn't alter the circumstances. They'd just have to suck it up, Booster Dragon. I wasn't about to bend over, put down my pants once again, and take it from the back this time around. The sting from the last encounter still felt sore.

As I had expected, the dragon was livid yet powerless to alter the circumstances. I offered my apologies and bowed my head in a sign of remorse. I was well-versed with this Japanese custom. Regardless, they couldn't afford to lose face just two days before the main event. Sure, we flunked one show, but three more were on the horizon. They somehow managed to jam-pack everyone into the remaining three gigs or reimburse those who couldn't attend. On our end, we Europeans were ready for action. The only thing left was to cross our fingers and hope that Marky would get on the plane and make it on time. And to be fairly honest, my confidence in that was shaky. When you dive headfirst into these chaotic situations, your trust in everything and everyone dwindles until you witness things unfold firsthand. But Jack, Dee, and I were holding up our side of the bargain. Nothing was going to throw us off our course.

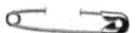

Stepping foot in Narita International Airport was nothing short of a comedy skit. This wasn't my first rodeo and it was familiar territory for me, but for Jack and Dee, it was like stepping into a fresh and unexplored alternate universe. The customs procedure was laughably extraordinary. Our artist visas were under the microscope, and then we were handed a placard that seemed exclusive to artists, filled with images of every conceivable drug – cocaine, marijuana, pills. *"Do you possess any of these*

substances, Sir?" The official queried with a touch of courtesy that could charm even the most notorious drug peddler. But we weren't packing any of these illicit items. Hence, the gates swiftly swung open, and we were greeted with the warm embrace of our Booster Dragon chaperone.

The instant I began engaging with her in the smattering of Japanese I possessed, it became glaringly apparent that she would dictate the boundaries of our autonomy. The perimeter was ironclad. Rigid, incredibly so. Had she slapped on a pair of handcuffs, the sensation wouldn't have been much different. Her roots must have been intertwined with Chinese or maybe even North Korean soil, given her expertise in imposing such a suffocating sense of control. The journey to our accommodation felt more akin to being transported to a penitentiary than anything else.

Our hotel room was reminiscent of a minuscule, overcrowded jail cell. It's a well-known fact that the Japanese have acclimatized to compact living spaces. However, she didn't need to drive home the point so bluntly that we were not going to experience any differently. Her approach was subtle yet - powerful and impossible to ignore. Her oppressive demeanor was unforgettable. Her carefully orchestrated constraints seemed designed to reiterate we weren't going to be treated any differently. Our stint in this city was turning out to be less of a tour and more of a test of survival.

Inside the room were three beds, absent of any closets, with a single hanger perched in front of each. Dee, with his usual swagger, was the first to cross the threshold, making a beeline for the farthest bed while swiping my and Jack's hangers on his way. Jack claimed the middle bunk, a move I was grateful for as he would now serve as a living sound barrier against Dee's notorious snoring.

Our guardian angel for this journey instructed us to remain within the confines of our room to avoid getting lost in the urban labyrinth. Her offer was simple: whatever we needed, we just had to ring her up, and she would swoop in to save the day. If we dared venture out, she warned us to stick close to our temporary home base - our hotel. It was clear that she intended to keep us on a tight leash.

There was no way we were letting ourselves be boxed in. The trio of us had an entirely different agenda, and her face lit up like a stage at a rock concert when I assured her we'd be hibernating to shake off the travel fatigue. This naive young woman, with an innocence of a child's simplicity, fell for my tall tale hook, line, and sinker. After exchanging our farewells, she departed, and we followed suit. A cool ten minutes after her figure disappeared into the horizon, we were stationed in front of the hotel, primed to dive into the city's vibrant pulse. I was all set to play tour guide for my two comrades, but first on our list was refueling our bodies. When it comes to dining options, Tokyo is a culinary cosmos: As Japan's nerve center, it boasts 23 city wards and numerous towns and Tokyo's dining scene is as varied and innumerable as the stars in the universe. The city is home to over 137,000 eateries catering to every food preference imaginable. While most outsiders would default to familiar Western fast-food joints like McDonald's, Wendy's, Burger King, or NY Pizza, I lead my fellow SpeedKings to my cherished fast-food haven - MossBurger. And just like the infectious grub had me hooked during my Japanese sojourn, my bandmates, too, caught onto its irresistible flavor instantaneously. Fortune was playing our favorite track as one was conveniently located a short walk away from our hotel.

The subsequent day, we pulled the same prank on her. I couldn't tell whether she was lacking in perception or just relieved that we weren't a constant pest. But I sensed her unease, cautioning us against any reckless antics. At moments, she reminded me of myself, the grunt who'd be left holding the broom when chaos ensued. Yet our intention was never to land her in a pickle. I adamantly suggested she take a breather before the whirlwind named Marky descended upon us the following day. I was aware she'd require every ounce of vitality she could muster to handle his quirks.

Having one more day to conquer, we plunged into the heart of Tokyo to make our mark from Shibuya to Shinjuku and rubbed elbows with my local comrades. The most electrifying encounter was with Akihiro Takayama. He was poised to orchestrate a photoshoot with us. This dude was Japan's answer to Anton Corbijn, the rock photography maestro. His lens had captured the raw energy of the biggest names in rock - The Ramones, The Police, Paul McCartney, the Rolling Stones and every name

Spacious luxury at the Tokyo Hotel.
It felt more like a high school dormitory.

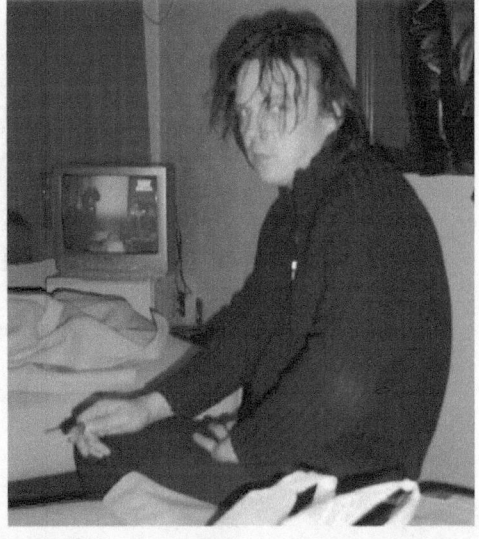

in between. The man was an embodiment of warmth, and getting a chance to collaborate with him was the rare opportunity that comes once in a blue moon.

The day after, our drummer made his appearance, and he was in for a rough ride. Our first gig was scheduled that very night, but I didn't spare him an ounce of sympathy or mercy. He was the author of his own predicament, and all I could do was silently wish for the pain to hit him… hard. Predictably, he played the "I've been incredibly ill" card. If there's one thing he's skilled at, it's navigating these tricky situations with a cunning adaptability. And then some. He went above and beyond, dragging our agency supervisor into this tight spot. He brandished a plastic orange pill bottle before her eyes, *"I desperately need more medication. This is my prescription. Take me to a doctor or pharmacy,"* he implored almost immediately. Anyone with a shred of common sense would realize that this was an unfeasible request, but he seemed to believe that his mere mention of his name would unlock any medicine cabinet. But not in Japan. Our guide was mortified; she was helpless. No matter how much she yearned to assist, it was simply unattainable. He looked like a dark thundercloud before he demanded some "white fish." Somehow, it had become his gastronomic delight, and I had endured this request ad nauseam. Utterly oblivious to time and locale, he always had an appetite for it as if we could snap our fingers and have it on a silver platter, anytime, anywhere.

His spirits dipped and a cloud of silent irritation loomed over him as we drove to our soundcheck location; he hadn't gotten his way. The venue was only a short distance from our hotel, but it felt almost eternal in the car. Navigating Tokyo's congested streets is a nightmare. The gridlock in Tokyo is a total trainwreck, and the underground transportation system is notably more effective.

The backstage was already arranged by our diligent crew. It is standard practice in Japan for each live venue to have its own backline, and luckily for us, they had the Marshall and Fender amps that we'd requested.

Marky's DW Drums had been delivered on schedule, and a representative from the drum company was on-site to greet their endorsee. The representative, a petite woman, was almost lost in the photographs we took; she was hidden in Marky's shadow. The comedic realization that she'd nearly vanished into Marky's armpit.

I hadn't foreseen that the guide chick had a pair of tiny accomplices demanding I surrender all our swag. This was uncharted territory for me, and she clarified that these two sidekicks were going to snag a cut off our profits as their commission. This news didn't go down well with me; we'd never thrown anyone a slice of our earnings before. That merch was our lifeline, our ticket to a few extras. My eyes hadn't yet adjusted to the blinding neon lights of Japan's market rates. The price tag on our merchandise was cranked up to 11. It was a staggering triple of what we were used to charging. But as we calculated our earnings at the end of this wild ride, we found ourselves standing in a shower of gold records. Every last piece was sold, and even after paying the commission, our profit margins looked like they'd been on steroids. It was like selling out Madison Square Garden - everyone was thrilled.

Our three shows were a dynamite explosion of activity, small people but with an energy so large you could feel it shake the ground. The Japanese have a unique brand of zeal, the likes of which you've never seen. Before the show begins, they all sit down in an orderly manner, patiently awaiting the band's entrance on stage. They rise, maintaining their composure until that initial feedback of the guitar fills the air; then, they lose it. They go absolutely apeshit! It's clear that everyone is having the time of their lives. They mouthed along to every one of our songs, in their own charming blend of Japanglish. And when we started playing our rendition of classic Ramones tunes, it was akin to an atomic bomb going off. Takayama-san was backstage, his camera clicking away, capturing stunning live shots and video footage. Post each show, we mingled with our fans and ended up in local restaurants or watering holes where we gorged on countless rounds of drinks, sushi, and skewered yakitori chicken. Marky seemed to have a bottomless appetite for the raw fish.

When the second gig rolled around, Takayama-san escorted us to the pulsing core of Shinjuku for a photo session.

The Kabukichō area is a renowned neighborhood recognized for its thriving entertainment scene and notorious reputation as a red-light district. Tiny clubs, smoky bars, and late-night restaurants are jam-packed into the lantern-lit alleyways of Golden Gai.

It emerges as an epicenter of adult entertainment, carrying the notorious tag of a den of vice. Its labyrinth-like streets house minuscule clubs with their smoke-filled ambiance. This neighborhood, when beheld from Western eyes, slaps your senses with a riot of colors. Its neon signage echoes the clichéd narratives we've all seen in countless documentaries about the city. But when you're fluent in Japanese, the neon allure morphs into a reality. The cryptic Japanese Kanji characters shed light on a different kind of truth. When your eyes catch the phrase "Korean Blowjob," the enchantment quickly fades into grime. This place oozes an insatiable commercialism, where anything and everything seems to have a price tag. Stumbling upon vending machines peddling worn underwear, it's clear that the Japanese have developed some eccentric predilections.

Crack open most manga comics here, and you may be confronted with graphic depictions of rape and sexual violence that make you question the nature of the seemingly polite, robot-like businessmen that throng these streets. Are they really monsters hiding behind a façade of civility? However, contrary to what one might infer from such depictions, sexual violence rates in Japan are significantly lower than in most countries.

Yet, it's impossible to ignore the rampant objectification that seeps into everyday life. The distressing trend of women being harassed in subways has taken on epidemic proportions, indicative of a societal undercurrent where perversion seems to know no bounds.

The most laugh-out-loud incident that occurred during the photo shoot was witnessing Takayama continuously scanning the surroundings for potential hazards. We were standing smack-dab in the middle of a Yakuza hotbed. We'd stumbled into gangland, and he couldn't afford any mishaps. Picture him, camera in hand, inadvertently capturing some mob boss in his lens, only to have him etched forever on a future SpeedKings album cover. It was one of those instances that bordered on the surreal. Japan isn't just another country - it's another planet. Even though Yakuza members prefer to lurk in the shadows, their bare eyebrows make a fashion statement. Buzz is, they even carry their own 'meishi' or business cards, brazenly flaunting 'gangster' as their professional designation.

Classic black leather signature mugshot. The Japanese hairbalm is to be considered the best in the world.

Emiko-san of the Japanese division of DW Drums took great care of the gear we needed for our Tokyo shows.

I 'HEARTBREAK' THE RAMONES

Japan was one wild ride, and we rocked it out as we resonated with the crowd. My best friend, brother-from-another-mother Kazuhiro, was there, a rocker I'd once jammed with in a band we called Salarymen from Hell. Some bonds defy geography and the relentless ticking of the clock. For what felt like forever, I'd been green with envy over his vintage, ivory-toned Gibson Les Paul Custom from the seventies. That's the same axe that Steve Jones of the Sex Pistols shredded on. That guy's got all the luck!

The week ripped by like a jet plane. We flew back just in time to gear up for our impending tour of the American West Coast. It felt like being shot from one cosmic stage to another.

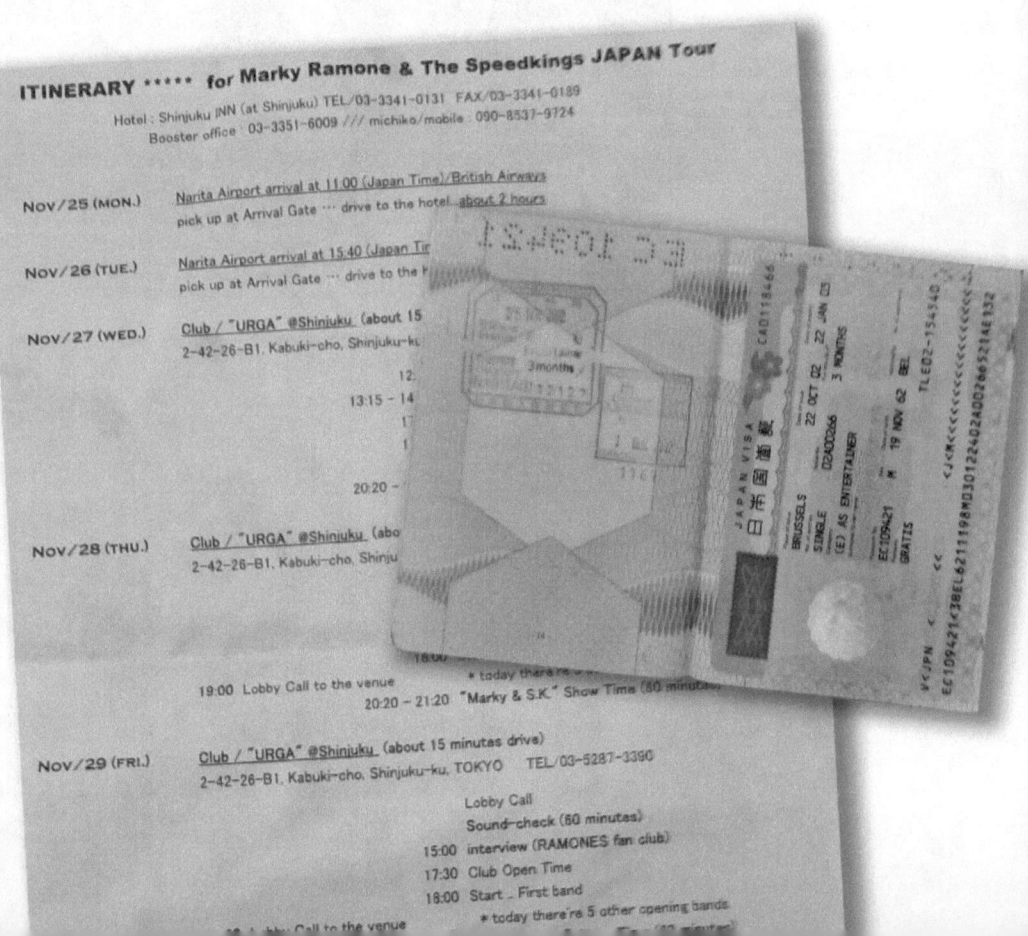

The Shinjuku Station photoshoot.
One of the shots was used for the sleeve of the US Tour Promo 7".

Hanging out with Matsuko and Etsuko Ayukawa of Sheena And The Rokkets.

Akihiro Takayama did the Tokyo photoshoot. In Kabukicho, the red light district, he was constantly checking the area to make sure no Yakuza related matters got in the pictures.

Meeting with Japanese fans after a show at the Urga Club, Shinjuku, Japan

Nightly photoshoot in Kabukicho, Tokyo with Akihiro Takayama

The Japenese Tour announcement.

HI-energy Tokyo action. The crowd loved it and the band couldn't get enough. A pity we missed one of the shows.

Japan Tour
November 28, Urga Livehouse, Shinjuku, Tokyo Japan
Booster Dragon arranged four consequetive shows that all sold out.

The After Show late night sushi
and sake party with our booking agents.

CHAPTER 32
Christmas in LA

"Shooting people and celebrating Christmas: Everything in LA could be done from the comfort of one's vehicle." - Chiara Barzini

On December 24th, 2002, the eve of Christmas, we find ourselves on the brink of embarking on our inaugural US Tour. The anticipation was electric as we awaited the journey ahead. At eight in the morning, Jack pays a visit to the house to signal the start of an eventful day. Our main objective for today was to wrap up a couple of songs in the studio. The clock was ticking as we struggled against time to complete them before our departure. The release of our second album was imminent, and Sanctuary Records eagerly waited for the demos. By nine in the morning, we were at Tony's, our go-to spot for fueling up with caffeine. We settle into the familiar routine of sipping on our coffees while basking in the studio's atmosphere, eagerly awaiting the arrival of Ace, the engineer who was to bring our sound to life.

Jack took on bass duties for four tracks while I stepped up to try my hand at vocals on the three songs that Dee initially recorded for this fresh album. It was an uncharted territory for me, and here I was, depending on the raw, impromptu scratch vocals he laid down. Surprisingly, God was finally at our side. Things turned out even better than we anticipated, and this new material sounded absolutely phenomenal.

I had this grand plan to finish up the session by two in the afternoon, but to my dismay, as we stepped home, the clock reminded us of its cruelty; it was already past five. Time was just ticking away. I still had many things to do – packing, clearing out all the merchandise from the warehouse, and rushing over to my in-laws' place for the Christmas Eve bash. I absolutely must be there before seven-thirty in the evening. Anxiety washed over me and clouded my thoughts. The never-ending pile of emails was waiting for my attention, and the cherry on top, there were many that were waiting to be sent out as well. And it became evidently clear that with passing minute my wish to make it on time was becoming a distant dream.

And if that wasn't sufficient, Marky hits me up while I'm in the midst of my bathroom routine. Just making sure everything's on track. We've got a rendezvous in LA in a couple of days.

The Christmas party was a wild ride. The atmosphere was electric, and the food was scrumptious, but I could only manage to enjoy it halfway. I was in a different universe, a million light-years away. When we finally stumbled home at eleven, there was a mountain of work waiting for me. By one thirty in the morning, I threw myself into the bed, utterly exhausted. However, sleep only evades me, so instead, I was up at four to finish some last-minute tasks. Stitch and Sofie are supposed to pick me up at six. They're my lifeline to the Brussels train station, where I need to catch the high-speed train to Paris Charles de Gaulle Airport, where our crew will embark on a journey to LAX. Of course, they arrived half an hour late. I was not amused, but I suppose we got lucky today. It's Christmas Day, and the highway is as empty as a barren stage during soundcheck. We managed to make it just in the nick of time. Jack was already there; he took the train. As for Dee, well, he's on the wrong platform, lost in his own world. I should have seen that coming from a mile away.

After a round of farewell embraces and kisses, we comfortably settled ourselves in the luxurious first-class compartment, eagerly embarking on our journey towards the enchanting city of Paris. In just under two hours, we were done with the necessary check-in procedures for flight AF062 and stand poised to board the aircraft. The esteemed Delta Airlines gracefully maneuvered this leg of our expedition. As the hours ticked by, eleven in total, we killed our boredom by getting our attention towards the cinematic endeavor by watching a riveting action movie while the tantalizing, hard-to-ignore aroma of a subpar steak filled the air. Finally, we began our descent towards the bustling Los Angeles International Airport, which filled our hearts with anticipation and excitement for the adventures that were ahead of us.

The aftermath of the September 11th tragedy has caused a significant slowdown in immigration processes. And honestly, I can't blame them. Here I am, face to face with an immigration officer, ready to undergo a detailed and rigorous interrogation. The questions kept coming, one after another, with no end in sight. But somehow, I managed to pass this intense examination and hastily made my way to the luggage area.

But it was far from over. We still had to navigate through the customs office. With me I had two suitcases packed to the brim with merchandise which needed to be cleared at all cost. At the same time, I could not afford to take any risks and have all of these things confiscated. It was the last thing I needed. Luckily, the customs officer wasn't the least bit interested in me or my suitcases. Instead, he simply welcomed me to the United States with a casual "Have a nice day." And just like that, we were in. It's as if we've effortlessly breezed through this final hurdle.

In the distance, I spot Jack, whose luck seemed to have taken a turn for the worse. A huge African American woman, wearing in black latex gloves, was rifling through his belongings. I could see the fear in his eyes. The tight grip of those black latex gloves surely had him clenching his buttocks in anxiety. But then something unexpected happened - he bursts into laughter. And it tuned out that another female officer was engaging him in conversation, succumbing to his irresistible rock 'n' roll charm. Before long, we were standing outside, patiently waiting for a taxi.

At 13:25, a sleek black taxicab with the number 1098 cruised down the streets headed towards the vibrant heart of Hollywood. The destination? The Saharan Motor Hotel is a hidden gem that was located on the iconic Sunset Boulevard. With its daily rate of just $59.00, the Courtyard Garden room proved to be an irresistible steal for the three of us embarking on this adventure.

As we approached our temporary oasis, I couldn't help but notice the unmistakable presence of Ralph, affectionately known as Rock'n'roll Ralphs. It was a haven for rockstars and dream-chasers alike, where the air was thick with the electric energy of fame and possibility. A mere stone's throw away laid the legendary Guitar Centre who beckoned us with its siren song of melodic treasures.

The Saharan Motor Hotel stood as a bastion of rock 'n' roll history. The walls echoed with the stories of legends past, who sought solace within its embrace. And now, it was our turn to add our own chapter to this ever-evolving rock 'n' roll epic.

The moment we step foot into our Courtyard Garden room, it was as if time itself has shifted to the rhythm of our beating hearts. The anticipatingly thick air and the promise of adventure.

Christmas in Los Angeles. We decided to get ourselves a mouthwatering burger at Sunset Burger, but our excitement of a warm reception from the booking agency was met with disappointment. We were in an unfamiliar territory, leaving to navigate this journey on our own. No greetings, no phone call to ensure our safe arrival. Could this be an ominous foreshadowing of what lies ahead?

As night fell, we were lost in a world where dreams and reality intertwine. The neon lights of Sunset Boulevard casted an delicate glow upon the streets below, as if summoning us to embrace the electric energy that pulses through this city of dreams. The sounds of laughter and music drift through the air that, seamlessly blended with the distant strum of guitars.

We were not merely guests of the Saharan Motor Hotel. We were part of its story, its legacy. We were the rebellious rockstars on a journey fueled by passion and a thirst for life. It was a beautiful moment. And as we ventured out into the night and readied ourselves to embrace the unknown. We carried with us the spirit of those who came before us - the ones who dared to chase their wildest dreams amidst the chaos and beauty of Hollywood.

The following day, my buddy Tracy Irving showed up at the hotel. He was part of the badass band LA Guns, so he hooked me up with a killer

I 'HEARTBREAK' THE RAMONES

Gibson Firebird and a Flying V for our epic tour. We made our way to Neely's, where they give my guitars a final setup. I was completely geared up and raring to hit the stage. Ready to Rawk!

In the afternoon, Texas Terri rolled up in her 1968 vibrant turquoise Chrysler and took me on a wild ride. She was set to make a special appearance on some of the hottest California shows. Our US Tour single featured the electrifying SpeedKings on the A-side and the fierce Texas Terri Bomb on the B-side. But it's Texxi's anthem, "Dirty Action," that truly stole the show with its raw power and killer vibe on this slab of purple vinyl!

Tex resided close to the iconic Sunset, and we headed over to her place in the legendary Afton Arms apartment building. You might recognize it from the cult classic film "The Boys Next Door." This historic 42-unit building, better known as The Happy Malaga Castle, was originally constructed in 1924 and was designed by none other than Leland Bryant, the brilliant architect behind the iconic Sunset Tower Hotel and the exquisite Romanesque Villa Apartments, which once homed the iconic Marilyn Monroe.

Over the years, Afton Arms become a symbol of fame, infamous for its association with Hollywood's elite. Legend has it that one of its apartments served as a secret rendezvous spot for Joseph Kenney and the renowned actress Gloria Swanson during the roaring 20s. Whether or not this tale holds true remains a mystery, but one thing is certain: Afton Arms has welcomed numerous Tinseltown luminaries and has been witness to its fair share of sinister events and murder.

On June 27, 1988, tragedy struck when Hillel Slovak of the Red Hot Chili Peppers met his untimely demise within the walls of Afton Arms. But let's not dwell on the darkness, for this place is a haven for those who seek adventure and excitement. Just like Texas T, my favorite rebellious rock star, Afton Arms, embodies a spirit of rebellion and daring.

Buckle up and get ready for a Wild West Rock'n'Roll Journey!

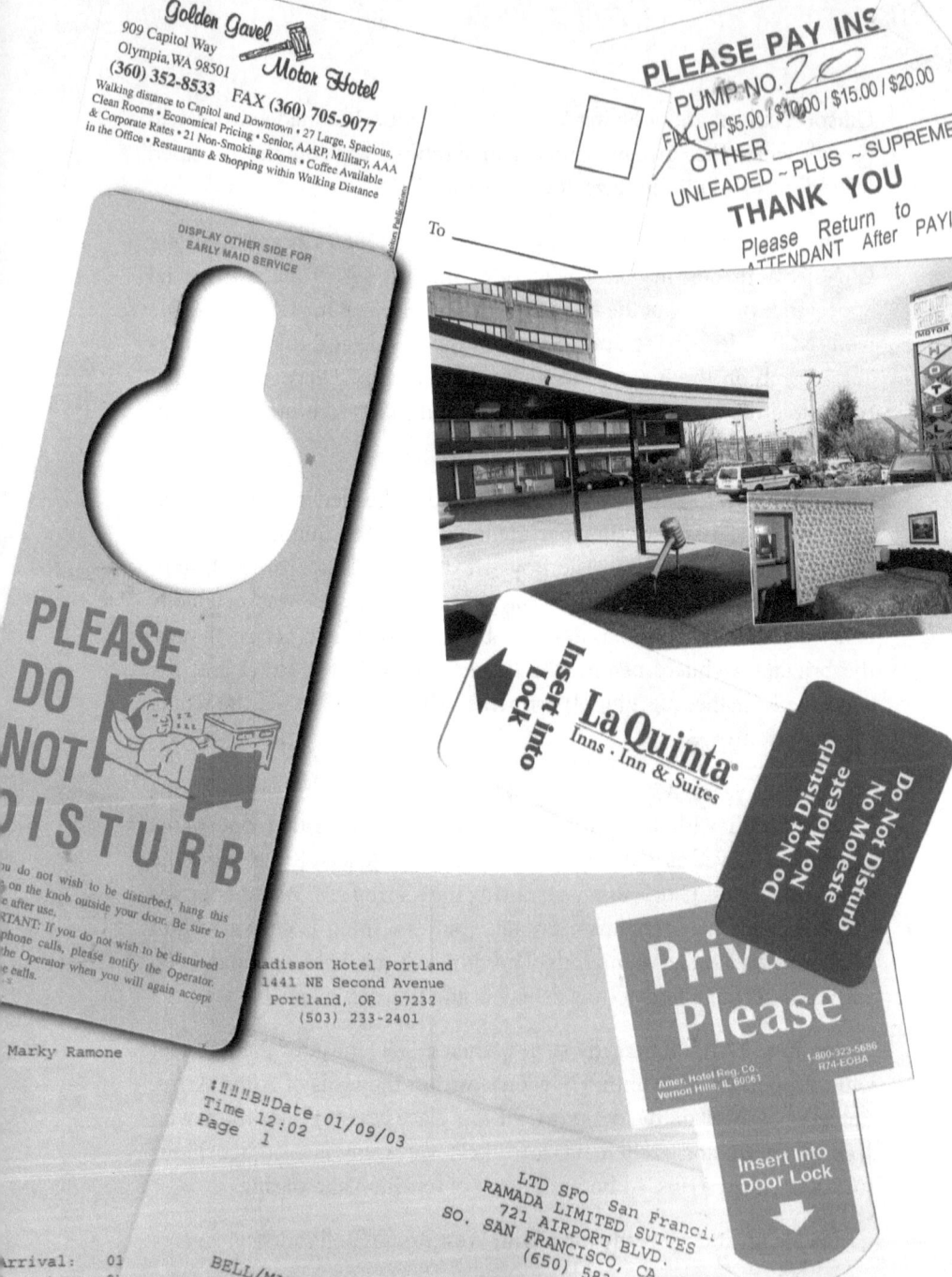

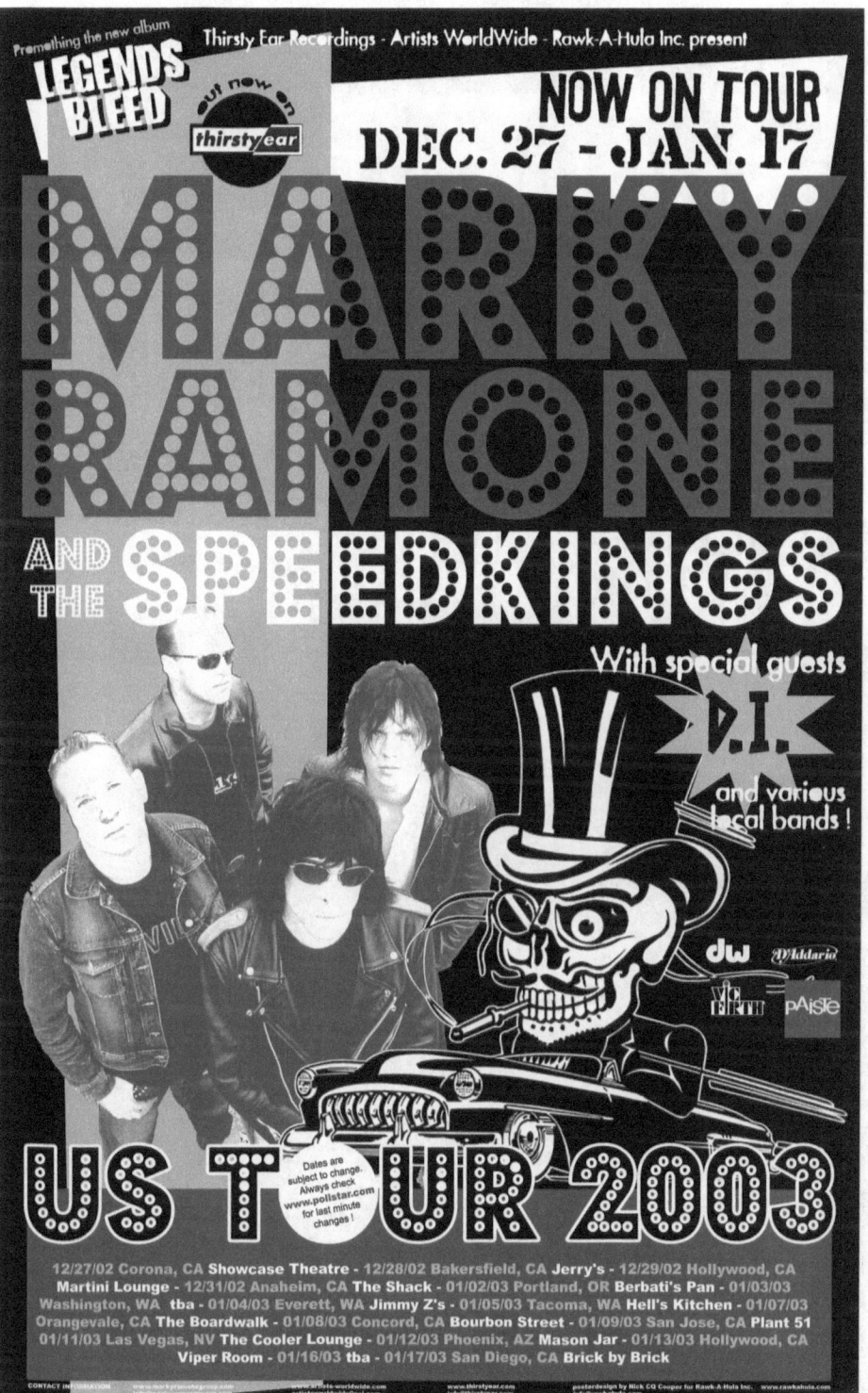

Alternative tour poster for the US West Coast Tour 2003 - Venues were still subject to change.

CHAPTER 33

The Wild Wild West

"Leave me alone and let me go to hell by my own route.
Calamity Jane

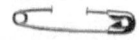

At first, our plan wasn't to set foot in LA, but rather to rock the stage at Don Hill's in NY. But that gig didn't pan out. We're no strangers to such last-minute changes; so it barely raised an eyebrow.

Following our first sun-soaked 48-hour stint plunging ourselves in the rhythm of Sunset Boulevard, Marky sauntered into the Saharan Motel on the morning of the 27th. Next on the To-do list was a trip to the rental place to get our van - our home on wheels for the month-long tour. Then we dashed over to the backline rental. There, we ensured our amps were loaded up in the back of our van, prepped, and primed for the road ahead.

From the get-go, Marky was adamant about collaborating with the booking agency of his preference: Artists Worldwide. This LA-based outfit flaunted a roster of revered bands they were liaising with. The top dog of this operation was Chuck Bernal, who was managing acts such as The Misfits, Dickies, and CJ Ramone, among others. A sense of unease washed over me the instant I encountered him. Devoid of any semblance to the rock'n'roll aesthetic, he shielded his eyes behind sunglasses. He seemed to dote on Marky while treating us like we were the dogshit beneath his shoes. His entire persona reeked of duplicity. The full extent of his true character would eventually be revealed but for now, he and

Marky appeared to be thick as thieves, both adept at swindling. After all, great minds think alike. They had found each other to be scam artists in arms. It wasn't until later that the realization hit me like a freight train - the culprits behind the Japan and European cancellations were none other than Chuck and Marky.

Chuck had lined up a series of 18 gigs. Having no real familiarity with the U.S., I had to relinquish control. For a long stretch, the burden of arranging everything had been solely on my shoulders, so it was a refreshing change to collaborate with a seasoned outfit. Or so I believed at the time. Contracts were sorted out, advances were settled, and we didn't have to fret over anything. All accounts would be settled at the tour's conclusion, and the assurances given were enticing. With time, I've come to realize that when things seem too perfect to be real, they often aren't - but that was a nugget of wisdom I was yet to acquire.

AWW bestowed upon us a tour manager and a sidekick. Landon was to be our guide on this wild journey, but our first meeting on the afternoon of the 27th was far from a harmonious duet. He was the epitome of your typical sun-kissed Californian surfer, bro, with not even a shred of raw, rock-n-roll spirit coursing through his veins. Mike, his accomplice, was so insignificant that I was questioning his purpose in our entourage. Regardless, Landon adopted the supreme air of his leader, looking upon us as if we were mere country hicks. He was there to serve Marky, and we were expected to fall in line with his commands. The shitwork was delegated to us, as if his well-manicured nails were too pristine to be sullied.

Here we were, standing on the hot asphalt of the Saharan, our fingers drumming on guitar cases prepped for the journey. Texas Terri, our secret guest, was all set to ignite the stages across California with us.

Chuck passed us the final roll call of confirmed gigs. The tour was about to strike its first chord:

12/27/2002: Showcase Theatre, Corona, CA (US)
12/28/2002: Jerry's Pizza & Pub, Bakersfield, CA (US)
12/29/2002: Trinity Hall, San Luis Obispo, CA (US)
12/31/2002: The Shack, Anaheim, CA (US)

01/02/2003: Berbati's Pan, Portland, OR (US)
01/03/2003: Hell's Kitchen, Tacoma, WA (US)
01/04/2003: Jimmy Z's, Everett, WA (US)
01/05/2003: 4th Avenue Tavern, Olympia, WA (US)
01/07/2003: The Boardwalk, Sacramento, CA (US)
01/08/2003: The Pound, San Francisco, CA (US)
01/09/2003: Plant 51, San Jose, CA (US)
01/10/2003: Club Voodoo, Reno, NV (US)
01/11/2003: The Cooler Lounge, Las Vegas, NV (US)
01/12/2003: Mason Jar, Phoenix, AZ (US)
01/13/2003: Scrappy's, Tucson, AZ (US)
01/15/2003: Di Piazza's Lava Lounge, Long Beach, CA (US)
01/16/2003: Key Club, Hollywood, CA (US)
01/17/2003: Brick By Brick San Diego, CA(US)

Marky slid into the vehicle alongside Chuck. Of course, his ego as a rock'n'roll icon nudged him to savor the lavish Escalade ride rather than the bumpy ride in the Ford van. Unleashing Chuck and Marky together was like setting up a stage for brewing wicked plots.

We were en route to Corona; our eyes were set on the Showcase Theatre where we'd be doing the opening show later that night. In the middle of the journey, I attempted to follow my usual ritual with Landon. Regardless of personal sentiments, I always harbored this unwavering belief that everyone possessed a spec of goodness. So, this circumstance wasn't any different.

I've never been too arrogant to concede when I'm mistaken, and initially, Landon received all the accolades he was due. His validation was not withheld. It was given freely at the onset.

This band knew the drill all too well, a routine as familiar as breathing: rolling into town, striding into the venue like we owned the place, stashing our personal stuff in the backstage room, hauling in the backline, rigging up the stage, soundcheck, arranging our merchandise booth, fueling up on whatever food was on offer, and then playing the waiting game forever. Waiting for what seemed like an eternity while the opening acts strutted their stuff, trying to prove their worth before we graced the stage. Then, finally, it was showtime. We'd pour our hearts out, give a few encores until we were spent, tear down our hard-earned stage set up, pack our van and hit the road once more.

Throughout all our tours, everyone had their part to play in this dance. Each member had a role they knew inside out, each task was allocated and accepted with a respectful nod. You are as strong as the weakest link. The load was evenly distributed, and like a well-oiled machine, we got the job done. Everyone pulled their weight to lighten the load for the collective. It's a straightforward way of doing things, but hey - sometimes, simplicity is the key.

Yet, the entirety of my routine didn't seem to register well with Landon as his gaze bore into me as if I was spouting the most ludicrous gibberish. *"I'm the tour manager. You lot sort out your own mess, I'll handle mine,"* he spat out in arrogance. I assumed he would at least mean the merchandise stand, but his retort left me stunned: *"I don't think that's part of my job description."* I was utterly dumbfounded. Job description? I was incredulous at what was unfolding. His response felt like a gut punch that catapulted me into a universe where starchy HR folks were conducting some rigid job interviews. Yet, blondie wasn't pulling my leg. His face was painted with seriousness. There went my faith in humanity. Even Texxie fixed me with a bewildered stare that brimmed with questions.

It didn't exactly kick off on a high note. My veins were filled with molten fury. The moment our boots hit the ground, Chuck was in for a face-off, a showdown to straighten things up. When it came to dividing responsibilities on this tour, I was the one cranking up the volume, calling the shots. That was no more than my due, seeing as I was also the one stuck with the messy encore of cleaning up everyone else's shit. That was my bare minimum, my baseline. That initial night, my phrases fell on deaf ears. I was being overly critical, ought to have cut the lads some slack, and ultimately, I came off as an unappreciative jerk, the ungrateful dog. Honestly, I never asked for a tour manager. Why entrust a second-rate asshole with tasks that I could nail a million times better myself? Even more absurd, pay him more than what I pocket and be expected to zip my lips about it. It seemed as if I had landed in a world turned inside out.

The Showcase Theatre was a gem. Dressed in its glory, it was the undisputed king of alternate concert venues in Southern California. Some even hailed it as the CBGB's of the West Coast. Yet, my night spiraled into chaos. A missed chance to witness Buddy Revell, KBH, and Deadman Walking, who warmed up the stage for DxIx and our band. My evening crash-landed into ruins.

Stumbling upon DxIx was a much better encounter. This band, born out of the heart of Fullerton, had been on the scene since 1981. Casey Royer, a veteran of The Adolescents and Social Distortion, was their frontman, hurling them into the underground hall of fame with raging anthems like "Richard Hung Himself" and "Reagan der Führer." To share a tour with them felt like a badge of honor.

Chckn, Clinton, Eddie, and Steve Gee were the kind of guys that you couldn't help but get along with instantly. Luck smiled upon them in the form of tour support from Vans - the famous skate footwear manufacturer. They moved from gig to gig in a generously provided Winnabago motorhome. But even good fortune has its flip side. They were trapped in Vans' most absurd tartan bondage trousers, a fashion disaster that once seemed a fashion statement back in the British '77 punkscene but had faded out even before the punk scene could embrace them. And DxIx was sentenced to wear these trousers every damn day. To amplify the disaster, traditional red tartan came with unsolicited variations of green, blue, and yellow. DI, without a doubt, added a splash of color to this tour. If our tour was a circus act, they were undoubtedly the jesters - although it's worth mentioning the most entertaining clown was part of my band.

At last, the tour had kicked off. Two more gigs in the golden state of California were on the cards, before we'd hit the road northward. For this first night we would return to the Saharan. Clad in their plaid sleepwear, DxIx was performing as if they were the Dead Kennedys' Winnabago warrior, living out their fantasies in their motorhome.

The subsequent morning, our compass pointed towards Bakersfield. We were geared up for a Saturday night at Jerry's Pizza & Pub. The place was an oddity. It was a peculiar blend of the ordinary and the extraordinary. A flashback to 1992, a tenacious Polish immigrant hell-bent on manifesting his American dream claimed a shop on Chester Avenue as his own. He added live music in the basement, quite often with no cover and turned the place into a wildly consistent and successful business. The location felt alien to us. Yet, we were comforted by the certainty of at least one thing - we knew the flavor that would grace our taste buds that night.

That evening, I found myself darting between the stage downstairs and the pizza counter. A perfect blend of music and food. One group of fans, in particular, caught my attention. A mother and her two little sons had come to enjoy the show. As per usual, Jack and I were our authentic selves, always up for a friendly chat with our fans. Before I knew it, I found myself sharing a table and countless slices of delectable pizza with them. Jack whipped out his camera and snapped a shot of us. The image reflected back at me later resembled an all-American punk rock family scene. The mother and her offspring were road trippers who were navigating their way in a motorhome. They would show up at several more gigs later on. Just how rad can a mom get?

The show that was a hit. What made this venue truly mind-blowing was that despite its supposed capacity of 100 people, a staggering 400 enthusiastic kids turned up. It was an absolute madhouse! The moment the show kicked off, it was pure chaos, an explosion of sound and movement that engulfed everyone in its wild embrace.

That night, we stayed at a neighborhood motel, and an indelible memory when I ventured out for an aimless stroll. The Bakersfield Sunday morning was hanging heavy with laziness, and the roads, as if hungover from the previous night's show, lay barren.

As I sauntered, I witnessed tumbleweeds drifting across the thoroughfare. Until that moment, I had dismissed them as mere props embellishing the desolate landscapes of spaghetti westerns. But here they were on Main Street, adding a touch of weird authenticity.

Later that day, we moved on to San Luis Obispo, the destined spot for our gig at Trinity Hall. The event was marketed as an all-ages show, and the venue seemed to be tied to Portuguese influences and steeped in Christian roots. Boasting a capacity of 500, this hall featured an exquisite wooden floor, which hinted that it was a dance hall more than a punk rock venue.

The crowd was overwhelming, and the term "all-ages" took on a literal meaning. It was a sight to behold. I had never witnessed families with toddlers rubbing shoulders with the punk community. They were not just there to soak in the music and enjoy the gig; they had brought some serious cash ready for band merchandise. I'm convinced that was the concert where we sold our highest amount of swag ever. Fathers, their offspring in tow, approached Marky – the musical idol from their own youth – eager to introduce their children to the Ramones legacy. The scene was hilarious, especially seeing tiny tots sporting Misfits-devil locks, resembling pint-sized Jerry Onlys.

That night, we crossed paths with Mario Gomez. The boisterous, afro-haired, bouncer-type Samoan dude decided to remain with us for a couple of gigs as part of our crew. Just before we were on, he jumped the stage and introduced us to the crowd as if we were extraterrestrials.

The term "All ages" was a strange concept to us. Sure, we knew what it meant. "All Ages Show" had been my favorite Dag Nasty tune forever, yet in our European context, age limits on concerts were unheard of. The notion of a distinct rule set was foreign to me. The reality hit me when I attempted to grab a beer from backstage and take it outside for a sip. I was at the back of the venue, no soul in sight, definitely no minors around, yet almost immediately, I was reproached by someone shouting, "Hey, that's a no-go!" I was oblivious to any wrongdoing. Eventually, I found myself ducking into a secluded closet just to knock back a couple of brews. We carried on with our exclusive bash at the Rose Garden Inn hotel deep into the night. A safe distance from any minors trying to sneak in.

Our new friend Mario turned out to be obnoxious company. Not only was he the life of the party, but he couldn't resist sharing the wildest and often most humiliating tales. Mario's masturbation anecdotes proved to be truly out of this world.

Come Monday, it was our first day off, and we were back on Sunset. The year was drawing to a close, with Anaheim NAMM in the midst of preparations. By Tuesday afternoon, Marky would be a guest at the Paiste cymbals stand, showcasing his skills and interacting with fans. As we veered into the artist's parking area, we bumped into Kerry King from Slayer, who was also slated for the exhibition.

New Year's Eve came around, and our band's name was glowing outside the Shack, Bar & Restaurant. It was a mammoth-sized establishment that doubled as a concert hall on the regular. A sprawling parking lot flanked it, and just a stone's throw away was the motel where we were to crash for the night. Our rooms effectively served as personal backstage area.

As the day wore on, the DxIx motorhome became a revolving door for stunning ladies. We were instantly captivated, and with time on our hands, Jack and I concluded their bus was the ideal chill spot. On the other hand, Dee had his sights set elsewhere - or rather on someone else. He set off for LAX airport to retrieve Claudia, who had flown in from Germany. That woman just wouldn't quit making appearances.

Jack and I claimed a captain's chair in the belly of beastly Winnebago, the cool bite of a beer in our grasp as we watched Chckn try his luck with the ladies. We couldn't help but heckle. Their glances flicked towards us, but their dismissal was swift and merciless. We were simply insignificant nobodies to them, inconsequential extras.

Then the call to duty rang out. *"Time for soundcheck, fellas!"* I hollered at DI. That's when one of the women swung into our orbit. *"Oh, you're the crew, right? That's rad!"* she chimed in. Laughter exploded from Jack and me, *"No, darling, we're not just the crew. We're the headliners, and I'm planning to serenade you tonight at the show,"* I corrected her with a grin.

She looked in disbelief, taken aback for a moment. Then, her eyes sparkled with intrigue. She seemed intrigued by the unexpected display of gentlemanly respect. As I leaned closer, my voice dropped to a low croon: *"Keep your eyes on me, sweetheart. I'm gonna do a "Fuck Me" just for you."* A giggle escaped her lips. She laughed it off, thinking it was a joke, but little did she know I was dead serious.

Dee was on the brink of missing the gig, and his contribution to set up had been virtually non-existent. The soundcheck happened without him. His undivided attention was focused on Claudia, and Jack and I were quite relieved that we didn't have to bunk with the love birds. As we rocked out on stage, she performed an exotic, serpent-like dance that captivated him. Her thong, hoisted so high it overran her jeans, left a negligible mystery of where the rest of her attire had disappeared.

The Winnabago gals turned a shade of scarlet that would give any sunset a run for its money each time I dedicated a song with the expletive 'fuck' in it, to them. They were lost on the humor, but it didn't matter; it was New Year's Eve. We quickly approached 2003 and rushed through the encores to kickstart the festivities. The countdown to the new year was drenched in the feedback of my guitar that I had carelessly dropped on stage.

The year didn't exactly kick off on a high note. Our revelry spilled from the venue to the asphalt sea of the parking lot, eventually flooding into our roadside shelter. Landon, his buddy, and some of their dim-witted friends had ditched the show early and sparked chaos in our quarters. As Jack and I walked over to the motel, two police squad cars, their lights flashing, were stationed ominously outside. The motel's proprietor had dialed in the law since Landon and his unruly band were disturbing the peace of the other guests. Consequently, Jack and I, being part of the same entourage, barely escaped getting the boot ourselves. We managed to sweet-talk the officers down from their initial fury and regained control of our rooms - but not without them executing a thorough search for drugs. As for being our tour manager, Landon was doing an abysmal job - he nearly landed us on the cold, hard pavement. My patience with him was wearing thin.

Jack wants to order some more food. We love playing those food places!

> > > **STARKEY** from page 26

Attack of the Ramone

There's no escaping the Ramones, no matter how hard you try. Take Marky Ramone, for instance: Try as he might, he can't bring himself to disassociate himself completely from his former band. His web site (www.markyramonegroup.com) warns visitors "For those of you expecting Ramones-style stuff, this is not what you will find here." And yet he continues to go by the name Marky Ramone, even though his name is Marc Bell. Of course, you can't blame him. Of all the bands he's been in over the years, the Ramones is surely the best known.

Marky (Marc? Bell? Ramone? What should I call him?) started his career at 16 when he recorded two albums with the metal band Dust. The drummer entered the punk scene in the '70s, playing with acts such as Wayne County and the BackstreetBoys (the original BackstreetBoys? Wowza!) and later Richard Hell & the Voidoids. After a two-year stint with the Voidoids, Marky left and was recruited to replace Tommy Ramone, who was leaving the band to become a producer.

Marky joined the band in 1978 and recorded *Road to Ruin*, then starred in "Rock'n'Roll High School," Roger Corman's 1979 cult opus to teenage rebellion. Marky recorded three more albums with the Ramones before leaving the band and being replaced by Richie Ramone. In 1983 Marky joined King Flux and later m-80. Richie quit the Ramones in '87, prompting Marky's return to the Ramones, staying with them until they played their last show on Aug. 6, 1996.

Then came Marky Ramones & the Intruders, then the Marky Ramone Group, which changed its name to Marky's newest incarnation, **Marky Ramone & the Speedkings**, which is who you'll see this **Sunday, Dec. 29** at Trinity Hall in SLO for an all ages 7 p.m. show, featuring opening acts **D.I.** and **Last Call**. Tickets for this Numbskull Productions show are available at Boo Boo's and Ticketweb.com.

ONCE A RAMONE, ALWAYS A RAMONE Marky Ramone & the Speedkings headline a Numbskull Productions show at Trinity Hall in SLO Town Dec. 29.

Dudes on the tour! *'Angry Samoan'* Mario of the Make-Out Boys.
We had quite some fun with him, taking the piss out of the political correct Californians.

The weirdest shit pops up going through the old tour archives.
Artist unknown at The Shack show, Anaheim - New Years eve 2003

CHAPTER 34

Too Far North

"This far north the sun was still up, although very low, riding through the mountains as if looking for something it lost on the ground." - Craig Childs

The dawn of a new year was just another day off for us. This break was absolutely crucial, with the long haul to our upcoming gig in Portland looming large. Before we hit the road, though, I found myself in a serious face-off with Marky, a meeting that felt like a battle council amid war. Landon had royally screwed up, which left our financial operations in utter chaos. Venue payments had been forwarded in advance to AWW, and it was Landon's responsibility to handle the open balance. Out of this amount, it was imperative to settle expenses and hand out the per diems for each band member. Most of the places we played at opted for a food buyout, saving them the trouble of making arrangements. That is, of course, excluding Jerry's Pizza and the Shack Lobster place. Yet Landon had handed us zilch even after pocketing his own fee and per diem along with his minions. Expenses had been charged to my credit card. I was done tolerating his crap.

Marky had been shielding him for a while, always extending the benefit of the doubt, but it was high time this charade ended. No more playing devil's advocate. Enough was enough. Frankly, I couldn't give a flying fuck about Chuck's opinion on the matter. Landon maintained his oblivious and pompous demeanor, arrogantly convinced of his invincibility.

As we hit the brakes for lunch on Highway 1, right on the outskirts of San Francisco, I broke it to Marky that this ride was reaching its finale right there. He had no choice but to nod in agreement, given that even Dee and Jack had had their fill of Landon. Naturally, the privilege of giving the motherfuckers their marching orders fell squarely on my shoulders.

"*Seriously? You actually believe I should tolerate your nonsense? You're such an asshole. Make no mistake, I'm the one dictating terms here!*" Landon's voice was shouting and hurling himself into graves. But I stood my ground. "*Landon, I tried to tell you nicely. This is where the ride ends. Deal with it,*" I responded, my voice steady but my heart pounding against my chest in fury. "*We'll see about that! I'm dialing Chuck. Let's see who gets to stick around,*" he brandished his cellphone menacingly before me.

In a swift, decisive move, I snatched the phone from his grip, and with a rush of adrenaline-fueled strength that felt almost otherworldly, I snapped it cleanly in two. My eyes flashed with unrestrained rage. I tossed the mangled phone onto the concrete and crushed it under my foot, which sent fragments scattered across the ground like shrapnel from an explosion.

"*Marc, Jack, Dee… haul your asses in the van! We're bouncing. These fuckers go home walking!*" My face was probably a heartbeat away from detonation. Even Marky complied. "*Oh yeah, tell Bernal to go fuck himself when you see him!*" I stormed into the van Dee had sparked to life, hammered the door shut, and hit the road. "*Good job!*" Marky praised. I shot him a look that could kill him. I can't stand it when people decide to join your team after they've been playing for the opposition. If people are screwing you over and someone doesn't step up, they might as well be an enemy too. I won't get fooled that easily. For fucks' sake!

We had learned the hard way that life on the road was no place for fair-weather friends, only those you could wager your life on. We'd survived the storm, and now the horizon looked brighter. Marc picked up the phone and dialed Marion's number. His intention was to reach out to Charlie Carpenter, the drum tech he had shared the stage with during his stint with the Ramones. Within the blink of an eye, or so it seemed, Marion was back on the line. Charlie and his Japanese spouse, Naoko Fujita, made a snap decision to lend us a hand for a few gigs. All we needed to do was swing by their San Francisco home and scoop them up. Sometimes it is that easy to get your shit together.

Marky knew them first, but we instantly clicked with them as if we'd known each other for a long time. Both were not only incredibly kind but also unbelievably invaluable. Marky, with his Ramones drum tech at his elbow, seemed to gain a newfound radiance of self-assurance, and our team's proficiency tripled. Regardless of the circumstances, we had always been good at improvising.

Naoko was a revelation. She was a true workhorse as she managed our merchandise booth with an efficiency that left us in awe. She took on so many responsibilities that we found ourselves wishing we had tapped into her resourcefulness sooner. The thought that we would be without her exceptional services in less than a week filled us with a tinge of regret.

At long last, we kissed the Californian borders goodbye and traded them for the verdant expanses of Oregon as we set our sights on Portland. Our journey had taken us from an Italian bistro, to a lobster shack and was now leading us to a Greek joint, Berbati's Pan. The peculiar connection between American rock and roll and dining establishments often baffled me. But hey, I'm not one to grumble. It meant a guaranteed meal at every stop. Back in the UK, I've had my fair share of rough patches, where sustenance seemed to be the last consideration during tours. So, this new experience? It was a downright luxury.

Originally, the joint operated as a restaurant called Berbati's. Still, when the adjacent 24 Hour Church of Elvis moved to a new space in 1994, the owner, Ted Papaioannou, expanded the restaurant into the former location to include a music venue and renamed the business Berbati's Pan. The bar operated with a jukebox and pool tables and the restaurant hosted cabaret shows with belly dancing. The Venue had a large L-shaped dance floor and a couple of hard liquor bars and was described as a "quaint little Greek spot."

Some cool cat whipped up a poster that, in truth, was far more compelling than the actual event. The pinup dames splashed across the promotional materials were conspicuously absent when the night rolled in. More likely than not, they were casualties of the previous evening's raucous cabaret. But we held our own, and for our rookie crew, it was a baptism by fire. Fitting, considering we were rumbling on holy soil - the consecrated turf of the Church of Elvis. To us Europeans, this was an awkward concept, something we could barely wrap our heads around. A Church of Elvis - what kind of lunatic dreams up such a thing?

We blasted off, heading northward, destination - the heart of Washington State, Tacoma. I was entranced, no, ensnared by that city's raw energy. It was the birthplace of something monumental to my existence - the Sonics, pioneers of sixties primal and raw punk. Their music was like an electric shock to my system during my years with Midnight Men. The band that Larry Parypa had crafted had seeped into my veins so deeply that it became inseparable from my identity. Every chord I struck, every lyric I penned was a tribute to these sixties renegades. Their spirit was not just an influence but a defining force that left an indelible imprint on me and every song I would ever write.

The night held promises in Hell's Kitchen - not the one etched on the map of New York City, though. But as I discovered, it didn't need to be inferior. This was a territory where they mopped the floors with stale beer, and the insides bore the mark of burning flames and devilish imagery. They had the reputation of hosting a lot of hard and heavy rockin' acts, and we fell at home the moment we walked in. The gig's poster had boldly scrawled the names of two additional groups set to share the stage with DxIx and us - the Dirty Thieves and the Dimestore Cowboys. Just their names alone were enough to evoke what kind of music we could expect, setting the tone for a night that was gearing up to be nothing short of a loud, fast spectacular.

The show was a riot, but the real showstopper of the night was a voluptuous buxom blonde who positioned herself front and center. We had barely strummed the first chords, and she was already peeling off her top to reveal an ample bosom that could make any Hooters waitress seem like a mere schoolgirl. And this dame was not just about her curves; she was genuinely stunning. Well-endowed babes don't always come with a beautiful face, but this Tacoma bombshell Siren had hit the jackpot in both departments. To say the least, I was distracted so badly that I was struggling to recall the song lineup and lyrics.And it wasn't just me; Dee soon fell under her spell too as his gaze glued to her, while Jack, in his typical style, was shredding his bass guitar with reckless abandon, oblivious to the spectacle before him. He was so submerged in the music that he let the evening slip away, eyes shut tight. When I finally directed Jack's attention to the twin peaks that were practically calling out to us, he was floored. It was as if a swig of her mother's milk had hit him like the most invigorating and potent energy drink known to mankind. For once, our view from the stage comprised more than just grimy punk fan mugs. It was a true sight for sore eyes!

Post-gig, she inevitably became the main event. It's fair to say her appeal was skin-deep, her intellect not quite matching her allure. But she had a sense of humor that made her company enjoyable. To top it off, she was eager to share her number. Now, you might question why this mattered at all. I knew in my bones we wouldn't return to this spot, and her number would eventually be lost on some ragged scrap of paper. Yet, necessity is the mother of innovation, and for reasons unknown, I didn't question it. The real kicker? She wasn't just the owner of one phone number, but two. At the time, it didn't dawn on me that one could be for personal use and the other for work. Instead, the only thought that invaded my mind - her fleshy mountains were so renowned in Tacoma that they each had their own listing in the white pages.

The more we journeyed toward the northern part, the more surreal our experiences became. Seattle was pulling us in, and Dee and Jack had their sights set on the MoPop – the Museum of Pop Culture. They were both undoubtedly captivated by the prospect of catching a glimpse of the grunge movement. My interest, on the other hand, didn't align with theirs. I wasn't particularly drawn to that scene, nor was I an admirer of Kurt Cobain. Quite frankly, I never developed a liking for those who blow their own brains out with a shotgun.

Undoubtedly, the most thrilling part of soaking in Seattle's vibes was our photoshoot at Pike Place Market. The renowned fish market held some iconic significance to me, and one of our shots there eventually found its place as the cover image for our final 7" record release.

But we couldn't hang out forever since we had a date in Everett, where we would play Jimmy Z's. Yet again, another gourmet Pizza and Italian cuisine dive.

Something felt off about the gig at Jimmy Z's, and I couldn't put my finger on it. The main red flag was the glaring absence of the promoter, Ron Rudd. It was standard for promoters to be present during load-in to settle any outstanding balances - their absence usually signaled trouble brewing. The sketchy vibe from the bar staff didn't inspire confidence either. It was like they had materialized out of thin air. Suddenly, Ron's phone details mysteriously vanished, and when we finally got our hands on them, there was nothing but silence on the other end. I hesitated to unload. I was done with playing unpaid gigs, but walking out wasn't a guaranteed payday either.

When we reached out to Chuck, we discovered there had been no deposit. However, Chuck vouched for Ron, saying he had collaborated with him countless times and would stake his reputation on Ron's credibility. Marky bought into it, but I remained wary. The rest of the band shared my reluctance to play. Despite our skepticism, DxIx had already started setting up and was in the middle of their soundcheck. The stage was set for a night of raw music, but the sinking feeling in my gut wouldn't go away.

Truth be told, physically, I was in a bit of a jam. Could it have been something off in my last meal? I'd been battling the age-old war with the constipation blues for the past few days, feeling overly stuffed and uncomfortable. Act or no act, I yearned for the sanctuary of the restroom to finally take a moment for myself while figuring out my next move. Eventually, Lady Luck smiled at me. It was a showdown between push and pull, and in a divine moment of relief, it felt like I had exorcised my entire gut system. It was like I could breathe again, although that's more of a metaphorical expression. The dump I took had been decomposing within me for days. The stench was so overpowering that it nearly knocked the wind out of me. And just then, an unsuspecting soul stumbles into the restroom. "O My God! What the fuck! Did somebody die in here?" he exclaimed before hightailing out of there faster than I

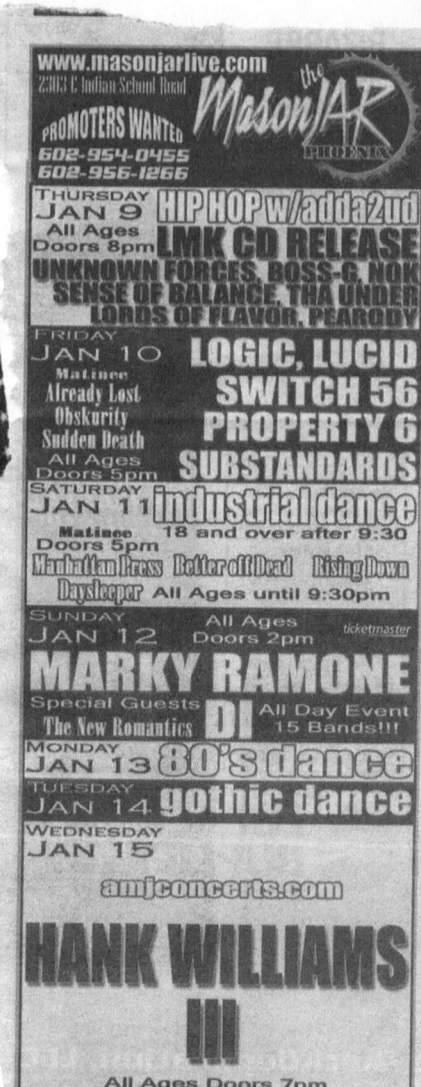

could count. I waited another five minutes, not eager to encounter the hapless guy who thought he'd found a corpse.

Finally, I managed to exorcise those demons. Marky was hell-bent on hitting the stage. He was sure Chuck would dig up the cash. "Ease up on the paranoia," he tried to soothe me, but I could see Jack and Dee's skeptical faces, and even Charlie and Naoko were arching their brows.

I hounded the promoter, but the calls went unanswered. The venue staff sensed the brewing storm, and suddenly, one of them approached us with news that Ron was hurtling towards us. His advice? Start the gig, and Ron will be there shortly. It was the same old song and dance. The oldest trick in the book. We kicked off the performance, and once we hit full throttle, we were nothing short of a runaway train. My eyes kept drifting to the club's entrance, but Ron was likely lost in some godforsaken alleyway. When we wrapped up our set, encores weren't even up for debate. We collected our gear and were about to make a beeline for this dude's residence. Even Marky was beginning to lose his cool.

Despite the fact that our performance was cut short, the crowd was thoroughly enamored. Expressions of regret about the absent encores flooded in when they approached us after the show. These are the times when you could dive into the whys and wherefores, but honestly, I couldn't give a damn. This was something unprecedented. Even Marky started to bug me, hammering on about dialing this asshole's number repeatedly. Thankfully, he read the defiance blazing in my eyes and knew better than to serve up some hackneyed lecture along the lines of, "I hate to say I told you so!"

In the concrete jungle of a parking lot adjacent to Jimmy Z's, I was accosted by a pair of inebriated couples seeking interaction to spice up their night. One of the women, her words slurred with booze, confessed her exhilaration at attending tonight's gig. She gushed with raw emotion, *"I've been a die-hard Ramones fan my whole life, and let me tell you, you've always been my favorite. You're just fantastic! You're Joey, aren't you?"* Clearly, nobody had broken it to her that Joey had bid his farewell to this world a couple of years back.

But then again, considering the Church of Elvis and its beliefs, it didn't seem entirely far-fetched that Joey might've staged a miraculous resurrection and comeback. So, if anyone ever puts you on the spot, assure them that Joey Ramone is still very much alive, now making his home in Everett, Washington. His neighbor, a friendly man named Ron Rudd, helms the Spirit of America Productions. His business card bears the tagline "Local and International Bookings."

Charged and ready, we hit the road heading south until 4th Avenue Tavern in Olympia came into view. Certain experiences can shatter your spirit, casting a dark cloud over your mood for some time. The owner of the club in Olympia and the audience were good folks, treating us as it should be, but we were too shell-shocked to appreciate their kindness. The sucker punch left me questioning my innocence - was I really this gullible? More than likely, it was the feeling of powerlessness that overwhelmed us. I despised that sensation. "I'll handle things with Chuck," Marky tried to reassure me, but by that time, his words rang empty to me. Nothing would be resolved. We played and we lost.

Hanging around all night. Striking stupid poses with new mad friends. Make America fun again!

HELL'S KITCHEN

THU JAN 2 — $3/21+/9pm/$2 wells — DEKREPIT, U.S.K.C.

FRI JAN 3 — $10ADV/21+/9pm — MARKY RAMONE & THE SPEED KINGS, D.I., Dirty Theives, Dollar Store Cowboys

SAT JAN 4 Two shows! — $7/ALL AGES/5pm/Bar w/ID — CLAYMORE, Divinity Of Truth, Severus VS. The World

$5/21+/9pm — KILLING FAIT… and Guests

TUE JAN 7 — $5/21+/9pm — RELEAS… (house, d… with DJs: …

Tix on… and…

2/24

TACOM… 3829 …

…SIC

…nd nightlife jan. 2-8

butler calendar@weeklyvolcano.com

…'s Pub Tacoma. "Hell Night" with Jusdefy, Thaw and guests 9 pm. $5.
Pacific Science Center Seattle. Laser U2 8 pm. Laser Korn 9:15 pm. $5.
The Swiss Downtown. Kry 9 pm.
Tugboat Annies Olympia. Still 9:30 pm.
$5. …the Klassics 6 …

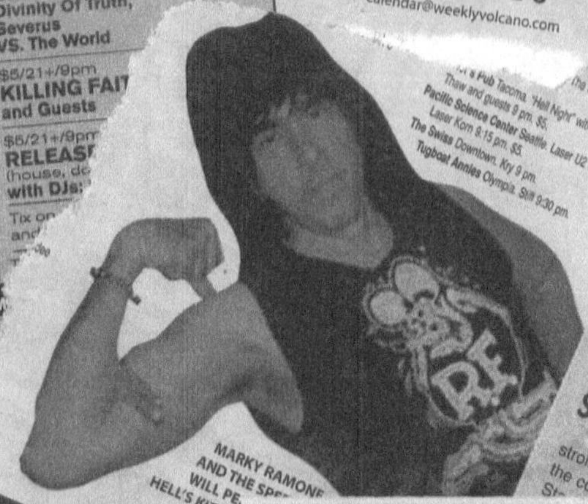

MARKY RAMONE AND THE SPE… WILL PE… HELL'S KITCH… TH…

…fast dev… …est time adhering to his… …t's get on with it:

Friday 3

ON THIS DA… Marvin C. Stone patented the drin… slurp something yu… today.

1,2,3,4! No frills… disco and Electric… poised to homogenize rock… The Ramones arrived like ba… infecting anything that looked r… They used no theatrics, no distra… more than three or four chords to r… genre in under a minute and a half. … did the math: 3 chords + buzzsaw gu… bizarre, opaque lyrics = 2 to 3 minut… fun. They emerged from the shadow… gaudy, over-the-top mid-'70s rock, trans… proclaiming their stripped-down and straigh… tales of fun and disenchantment. Longtime d… mer for the Ramones **MARKY RAMONE** still c… ries the torch — through the South Puget Sou… this week as a matter of fact. Since the Ramon… disbanded in 1996, Marky toured with his band the Intruders in the late '90s, toured with the Belgian punk band The Buckweeds at the turn of the century and now performs with Buckweeds frontman Nick "CQ" Cooper with The Speed Kings. No-frills, loud, fast, punk rock with a Ramone. What else do you greedy knuckleheads need? Jan. 3 with D.I., Dirty Thieves, Dollar Store Cowboys, 9 p.m., $10, Hell's Kitchen, 3829 Sixth Ave., Tacoma, 759-6003; Jan. 5 with D.I., Drunk As Usual, Chief, The Dirty Thieves, 9 p… $8, Fourth Ave. Tavern, 210 Fourth Ave., Olymp… 786-1444.

Saturday 4

strolle… the cou… St…

…EAF MOTORS

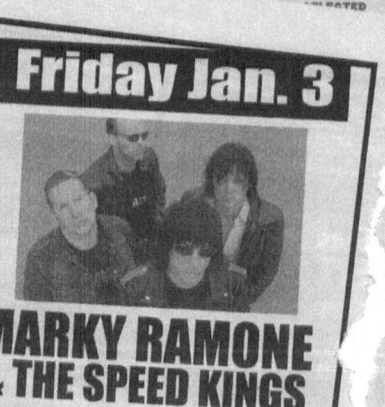

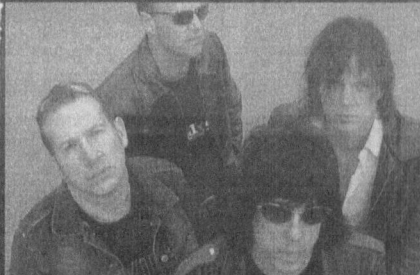

MUSIC CALENDAR

Friday Jan. 3

MARKY RAMONE & THE SPEED KINGS

D.I. • DIRTY THIEVES DOLLARSTORE COWBOYS

$10 cover • 9pm • 21+

tickets available at Mother Records and www.ticketweb.com

Tacoma Reporter · TICKETWEB

HELL'S KITCHEN

www.hellskitchenonline.com

RHYMES WITH SELTZER

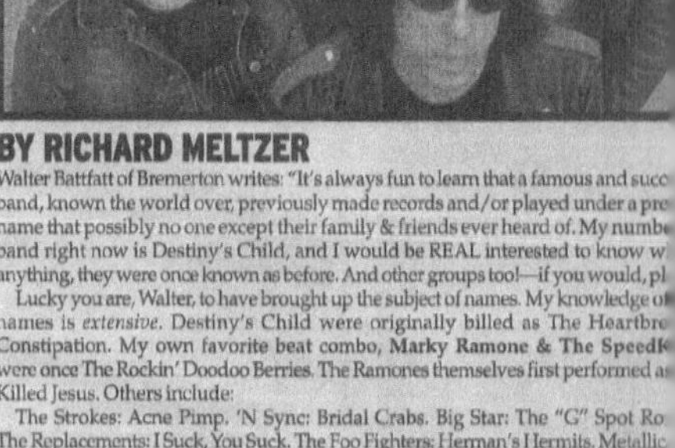

BY RICHARD MELTZER

Walter Battfatt of Bremerton writes: "It's always fun to learn that a famous and succ… band, known the world over, previously made records and/or played under a pre… name that possibly no one except their family & friends ever heard of. My numbe… band right now is Destiny's Child, and I would be REAL interested to know w… anything, they were once known as before. And other groups too!—if you would, pl…

Lucky you are, Walter, to have brought up the subject of names. My knowledge of names is *extensive*. Destiny's Child were originally billed as The Heartbre… Constipation. My own favorite beat combo, **Marky Ramone & The SpeedK…** were once The Rockin' Doodoo Berries. The Ramones themselves first performed a… Killed Jesus. Others include:

The Strokes: Acne Pimp. 'N Sync: Bridal Crabs. Big Star: The "G" Spot Ro… The Replacements: I Suck, You Suck. The Foo Fighters: Herman's Hermits. Metallic… Port-a-Potties. Fugazi: American Coozehounds. Mudhoney: The Scabies L… Radiohead: Of Mice and Poland Water. Guided by Voices: The Knife-Wielding Scum…

Pavement: Cryogenic Pus. Pearl Jam: The Kirk & Michael Douglas Band. Crosby… & Nash: The Reptilians. The Wu-Tang Clan: Beepo. X: Fools' Fucking Folly. The G… Wet Seahag Pee. Yo La Tengo: Penis. Phish: The Handjobs. Ratdog: You Stupid, S… Wuss. Smegma: The Unloved, Featuring Paul McCartney. The Soft Boys: Eight Fat… from Hell.

Marky Ramone & The SpeedKings play Hell's Kitchen in Tacoma at 9 p.m. Fr… 3. $10. They will also perform at Jimmy Z's in Everett at 9 p.m. Sat., Jan. 4. $10.

…time. Kudos to Pedro and the … | Northwest, but their sound is Southern in vibe; cour… …ancient-feeling yet contemporary in its edgine…

CHAPTER 35

Under The Boardwalk

"(Under the boardwalk) We'll be havin' some fun" - The Drifters

The clock was ticking down to the inevitable farewell we had to bid our fresh recruits on the crew, a downer for sure. But this was no surprise as we were aware of it beforehand, and we maxed out on every moment. Their company was pure enjoyment. We basked in moments of unadulterated fun, and in return, they offered us the most remarkable support we could ever dream of. As for the second half of our tour, only time would reveal how we'd navigate it, but for now, we had one hell of a distance to the gap. From Olympia through Salem, Eugene, and Redding, all the way to the heart of Sacramento.

A cool local band, the Secretions, had orchestrated the show in Orangevale. We had been in touch with them for quite a while and were finally about to rendezvous in their hometown, where we were booked at the Boardwalk. This venue was steeped in rich history and it was an honor for us to perform in a place that once echoed with the sounds of Cheap Trick, Social Distortion, and Living Color.

At long last, the drawn-out journey started to chip away at the negativity, shedding it from my shoulders like a worn-out Ramones leather jacket. As we rolled back into California, things began to realign. It's in these moments that you realize the buzz that comes from creating something real, something raw with your mates. If you can't lay your trust on the line for your friends, then who else?

Indeed, The Secretions were ready to do more than just set up a gig. Mickie Rat, their bass guitarist, agreed to tag along and join our band's crew for half a dozen shows. It felt like a divine intervention.

The ride to San Francisco was brief, yet we found ourselves craving it to stretch into infinity. Parting ways with our friends was challenging, but the moment had arrived for a change of the guards, and one of the raddest venues around was ready to welcome our mayhem.

For a good few years, the San Francisco-based haunt, The Pound, was the stomping ground for metalheads and hardcore punk fanatics living in the Bay Area. Occasionally, there would be a fight or accusation of shady business, but it was hands down the place where most punks felt at home. It was nestled in the southeastern industrial district of the city, right next to the notorious Hunters Point projects, this venue was far from a glamour spot. You wouldn't catch a cab or a bus routing close to it; they plainly refused to bring you there. Your only shot at reaching there was with your own wheels.

Painting a picture of The Pound, it was nothing more than a huge shack, bordered by a wire fence, with an adjoining dirt parking lot. However, what truly breathed life into any place were its characters, and The Pound didn't disappoint on that front. Some of them stepped straight out of a comic book.

There was this one staff member who sported an unsightly spider bite on his arm. He found some perverse pleasure in flaunting it to anyone within sight, regardless of their interest or lack thereof. Then there was the "Metal Milf", the smoking hot metal mama who always sported her Hate Eternal jacket. Her beauty was only rivaled by the intimidating size of her boyfriend. Speaking of characters, who could forget the Metal Chef? He'd whip up hot gourmet meals for the bands performing that night.

Marky Ramone & The Speed Kings

TUESDAY, JANUARY 7 @ THE BOARDWALK WITH D.I. AND THE SECRETIONS

It's pretty safe to say **Ramones** are probably one of the five most important rock bands ever. So it's certainly a cause for excitement when given a chance to catch a legend in action. Marky's new band doesn't mine any new ground, but that's not really what anyone wants from **Marky Ramone**. What we want is good, dumb fist-in-the-air punk rock... and the **Speed Kings** deliver! Not only are they performing very Ramone-esque songs, they're even performing a few Ramone faves as well! Yay! Add to that punk rock greats **D.I.**, led by their crazed frontman **Casey Royer**, who still delivers their classics like *"Richard Hung Himself"* and *"Johnny's Got a Problem"*, and can it possibly get any better? Well, if you're familiar with Sacramento's **Secretions** then you know to arrive early, stay late and give your brain a night off. That sounds better to me. —Jerry

The bouncers weren't just muscle but fans, too. They would occasionally ditch their posts to leap into the mosh pit themselves and embody the raw energy this joint thrived on.

We were backed by an army of four local bands - the Fuzz, the Cliftons, Sore Throats, and Leather Pills. A lineup that full is a double-edged sword, really. On the one hand, it's like a lavish buffet for the crowd - more bang for their buck. Some would say that's the silver lining. But from our perspective as the headliner act, it's just another one of those never-ending nights. We're the first to hit the soundcheck and the last to go on stage. Meanwhile, you're sinking into a drunken stupor, sleep deprivation gnawing at your sanity. For the crowd, they're bombarded with a relentless onslaught of decibels until they're dazed and confused. By the time we step onto the stage, it's like a battered boxer entering the final round, his energy sapped, his spirit bruised.

As dawn broke, we found ourselves in San Jose, cast into the industrial complex known as Plant 51. This time around, only one additional band - the Vex - was slated to join the chaos on stage. Plant 51, an unfathomable giant of past industrial might, imprinted itself in my memory, a vague shadow, nothing more. Yet, it couldn't have been a complete disaster. The truly rotten moments have a knack for haunting my mind. The only clear recollection? It was our last night before treading into the wild, unpredictable terrain of Nevada. Our compass was set towards two tantalizing cities where chance ruled, and fortunes were made or lost in minutes: Reno and Las Vegas. The game is open. Place your bets!

From San Jose to Reno, it was merely a few hours of cruising down the highway, but we had to make an unscheduled stop in Sacramento, which was on the way anyway. Mickie had to ensure he had all his essentials with him. Our departure from the Boardwalk gig had been chaotic, and we soon realized he was ill-prepared for the journey ahead. However, blessed with time, we began to relish our drive through the breathtaking expanse of the Tahoe National Forest.

Reno, known as the world's most significant little city, is nestled in the heart of the Great Basin Desert, just across Nevada's border. As we neared, the landscape underwent a dramatic transformation. Club Voodoo, our destination, was tucked away in a somewhat edgier neighborhood, far removed from the dazzling lights of the city's casinos. The club was bathed in an enchanting shade of purple - a color that seemed to perfectly embody its voodoo essence and added to its cabaret lounge allure. The club exuded an irresistible aura that was undeniably cool.

From San Jose to Reno, it was merely a few hours of cruising down the highway, but we had to make an unscheduled detour to Sacramento. The reason? Mickie had to ensure he had all his essentials with him. Our departure from the Boardwalk gig had been chaotic, and we soon realized we were ill-prepared for the journey ahead. However, blessed with time, we began to relish our drive through the breathtaking expanse of the Tahoe National Forest.

Reno is known as the biggest little city in the world which is settled in the Great Basin Desert, just across Nevada's border. As we came close, the landscape underwent a dramatic transformation. Club Voodoo, our destination, was tucked away in a somewhat edgier neighborhood that was far removed from the dazzling lights of the city's casinos. The club was bathed in the shade of purple – it was a color that perfectly embodied its voodoo essence and added to its cabaret lounge allure. The club exuded an irresistible aura that was undeniably cool.

The question of attendance was a lingering curiosity. We had arrived to find our performance touted through posters, only to discover that a neighboring venue was featuring a hardcore gig with Stalag 13. It's an amusing twist of fate, considering that I once produced a limited-edition bootleg 7" for the same band back in the early nineties. My relationship with them began even before their first album release, and I was fortunate enough to own their earliest demo tapes.

Their debut album was a true and undeniable classic in the hardcore scene. What intrigued me beyond their music was their bond with comic artists, the Hernandez Brothers. When I stumbledupon a Stalag 13 live show sketch in Love & Rockets by Jaime Hernandez, I knew instantly that it would make an epic sleeve for the bootleg. The limited-edition release stirred quite a buzz and caught the attention of the likes of Jello Biafra, who reached out personally for his own copy.

Imagine my surprise when I learned that this very band was playing just down the street from our venue. Talk about serendipity! The thought

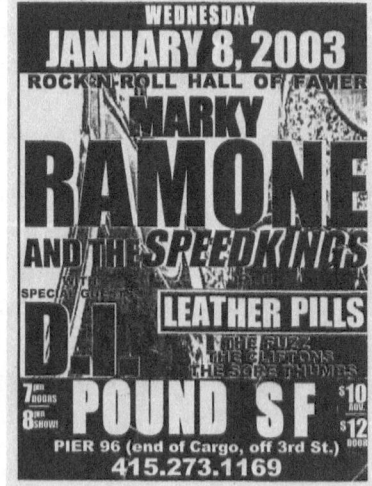

The Pound flyer and poster

West Coast US Tour
January 8, 2003, The Pound, SF, CA

did cross my mind to swing by and catch their performance, but sadly, our own packed timetable wouldn't permit such an indulgence.

Pulling up to the hangout, a pair of youngsters were already there, stationed outside. They'd clearly decided a 'better safe than sorry,' which ensured that they had their tickets in hand well in advance. You could see the shock on their faces when Marky casually hopped out of the van and treated them like old pals. As we began unloading our gear into the club, they seized the opportunity and slipped inside. The elder of the two, a boy, lent a hand, helping us shift some equipment into the venue. The club owner was ready to shoo them out, considering the place wouldn't officially open for a few more hours, but we firmly suggested they be allowed to stay. It would have been a real downer to leave them hanging around on the pavement for another couple of hours.

They were kinda astonished, and it escalated even further when they were privy to an intimate private soundcheck. Their expressions radiated sheer joy. It was as if they were in disbelief of what actually happened. But the best was yet to come after the soundcheck. The owner handed us a menu full of pizzas to choose from for our evening meal. We extended the courtesy to them; they, too, could select a pizza of their liking. The warmth and generosity they experienced left them in awe as we all partook in the pizza feast. The girl's elation was beyond measure. As it turned out, she and her boyfriend hailed from Brazil. The following day brought an unexpected surprise – an email from her brother back home in Brazil sitting in my inbox. Overflowing with gratitude for the kindness we showed his sister, he instantly adopted us as part of their family. It was evident that should we ever play a gig in Brazil, we would be embraced as prodigal brothers.

It doesn't require much to show kindness, and the gratitude received in return is exponentially greater. If there's one trait that defines the SpeedKings, this would be at the forefront of my mind. We were always in it for the kids, and it's mind-blowing to realize that friendships forged in this manner are still going strong, even after more than two decades. If my wealth is measured by this aspect of rock 'n' roll, then indeed, I'm loaded. It's an invaluable bond that no amount of money can procure. This is the kind of richness that resonates on a whole different frequency.

→ www.metroactive.com
metro

Calendar choices by Todd Inoue (TI) and Sarah Quelland

Marky Ramone and the SpeedKings →

PLANT 51
44 S. ALMADEN AVE, SAN JOSE
408.297-5151
THU – 9PM; $10

He's not playing Ramones stuff, so don't ask. Marky Ramone mourned the loss of Joey and Dee Dee, and he is now distancing his music from the Ramones legacy. In his current band, the SpeedKings, he's playing loud, fast, high-octane rock & roll—just what you'd expect from him. D.I. and the Vex also performs. (SQ)

PLANT 51 PRESENTS

MARKY RAMONE

WITH D.I. & THE VEX

January 9th
THURSDAY

& over • $10

www.jambasetickets.com

S Almaden Ave.,
ose 408-297-5151

PLANT 51

THIS WEEK

THU. 1.9 — MARKY RAMONE, D.I., THE VEX $10
FRI. 1.10 — DEKE DICKERSON, THE SHITKICKERS, THE CHOP TOPS $7
SAT. 1.11 — GODSTOMPER, ARACHNIDS, DRUMSHORSE $5
MON 1.13 — ROCKSTARS & BITCHES PRESENTS: DEATH CHANGER, THE RESTITUTION, HIPPY AGGRESSION, DOWNSIDE
MONDAY — CHEAP BOOZE • $2.50 WELL DRINKS & PINTS NO COVER
TUESDAY 9:30–Close — RED ALERT • NO WAVE & ALTERNATIVE NO COVER
WEDNESDAY 9:30–Close — LIMBO LOUNGE W/ DJ ANDY AVERAGE
THURSDAY 6–10PM — DJ CHRIS MITCHUM

UPCOMING
Advance Tickets Available @ www.jambasetickets.com

1/17 — THE DWARVES, THE FORGOTTEN, THE SICK
1/18 — AGENT ORANGE, CLAY WHEELS, LAST SESSION
1/24 — LIFTED, FORTYTHREE, SOUL AGGRESSION, FRICTION
1/25 — BLACK LABEL SKATE VIDEO PREMIERE, DING DANG, THE LONELY HEARTS
1/29 — JESSE DAYTON, THE TREAD ASPHALT
2/8 — REACTION 31, KARATE HIGH SCHOOL, ZEROMIND

44 SOUTH ALMADEN AVENUE | DOWNTOWN SAN JOSE
408.297.5151
UPCOMING EVENTS: www.plant51.net
BOOK ON LINE: booking@plant51.net

There are moments when folks just can't take a hint and cling with a tenacity that borders on relentless. We crossed paths with this maleficent and sinister character who seemed incapable of accepting no for an answer. To add to the fun, he boasted with unabashed pride about how he peddled the finest high-inducing dope this side of the city. Marky found himself unable to shake off this human leech until he passed the buck onto me. *"Give him a free album and a tee"* was Marky's smooth exit strategy, but it left me dealing with the aftermath. My fingers were crossed, hoping he'd be appeased with the swag and make his exit. But no such luck. He suddenly launched into a monologue of appreciation, singing praises about our band's cool vibes and welcoming spirit. I finally managed to disentangle myself from his clutches by accepting a pair of crystal meth packs. *"This one's on the house, buddy,"* he smirked, a devilish glint in his eye, *"You're gonna have a blast!"* And then, just like that, he was gone.

None of us in the group had ever dabbled with the hard stuff, at least not to a serious degree. Sure, we occasionally sparked up a joint and relished in the mellow high of marijuana, but it never became a habit. Both Jack and Dee were more about the booze, and I, too, indulged but with some level of restraint. I aimed to maintain a clear head, at least partially, to ensure our band's affairs were handled efficiently. Yet here I was, in possession of a couple of bags of rock. I had experimented with it in the past. The thought of simply disposing of it seemed wasteful, and I considered that it might offer a distraction from the usual band-related hassles we faced. I wasn't certain how Jack would react. After all, we hadn't ever broached such topics. But we were roommates, and the last thing I wanted was to be driving around with narcotics on me. So, it was going to be used tonight or tossed away.

Our night would be spent in the wild whirl of the Peppermill Casino Resort, a place that thrives on thrills. The check-in counter itself was intoxicating, with slot machines singing and flashing right in your face, ensuring you're drawn into their rhythm even as you wait your turn. The entire setup was meticulously designed to pull the money right out of your pockets from the second your boots hit the floor.

In a world far removed from the shoddy inn rooms we'd been frequenting, Jack and I found ourselves in a standard double suite. Its grandeur was unmatched, an ode to the high-rolling guests the casino aimed to appease. The room was decked out with dual king-sized beds and a monumental television - the very picture of luxury.

As though fate had its hand in our escapade, the moment Jack flicked on the TV, Detroit Rock City - a film featuring Kiss - was just about to roll. It was rock 'n' roll incarnate. When I laid out the stash on the table, instead of recoiling in shock, Jack was mesmerized, his eyes alight. It was crystal clear: we were set for a night of unabashed debauchery.

As Kiss's classics roared from the TV speakers, I started to chase the dragon, Jack eagerly waiting his turn to get a hit. The movie concluded without either of us registering it. As dawn broke over the desert mountains, our supply had run dry. Yet there we were, Jack and I, alert as if we were newborns experiencing life for the first time. Not a wink of sleep had been stolen from us. We'd spent the night in deep conversation, philosophizing about life's profound intricacies.

As we climbed into the van, Marky eyed us with suspicion. *"Did you guys manage to catch enough sleep?"* he asked. We nodded in response and tucked ourselves away in the van's rear. The wave of exhaustion was bound to crash over us soon enough.

JAN 2 - JAN 8

Blazing Trails

The longtime drummer for punk trailblazers the Ramones, Marky Ramone was born Marc Bell in New York City on July 15, 1956. An alumnus of the late '60s band Dust, in 1977 he resurfaced as a member of Richard Hell's Voidoids on their classic *Blank Generation* album. Bell joined the Ramones in time to record 1978's *Road to Ruin*, adopting the name Marky Ramone; he continued with the group through 1983, returning to the lineup four years later and remaining on the roster until they disbanded in 1996.

Following the Ramones' breakup, Marky formed a new band, the Intruders, releasing the album *Answer to Your Problems* in mid-1999. In 2000, Ramone toured Europe with the Belgian punk band The Buckweeds, and later recorded and performed live with The Speed Kings, led by former Buckweeds frontman Nick "CQ" Cooper.

For those expecting flat-out Ramones rehash, however, look elsewhere. The Speed Kings are the first to admit that there was only one band called the Ramones. What they offer is hot, steaming hi-octane rawk, catchy, fast and loud.

Marky Ramone and the Speed Kings are in the midst of their West Coast tour supporting the *Legends Bleed* album, and will be launching a European tour in March. Catch them with D.I., Tacoma's Dirty Theives and others, Friday in Tacoma at Hell's ... Saturday in Olympia at the 4th Ave. Tavern.

Marky Ramone & the Speed Kings

Blazing Trails
Marky Ramone and the Speed Kings, page 13

Tacoma Reporter

News & Entertainment Weekly

VOLUME 8, ISSUE 1 | JAN 2, 2003

FREE

CHAPTER 36

Winner, Winner, Chicken Dinner

"It's like gambling somehow. You go out for a night of drinking and you don't know where your going to end up the next day. It could work out good or it could be disastrous.
It's like the throw of the dice." - Jim Morisson

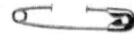

The moment my eyelids lifted, we were already tearing down Highway 95, our sights set on the neon mirage of Las Vegas. With a solid 7 or 8 hours of asphalt before us, it felt like we'd hijacked time itself. Dee was at the wheel, Marky riding shotgun. The road stretched out ahead of us, a barren wasteland as far as the eye could see, until the piercing wail of a siren sliced through the silence. Not long after, we found ourselves flagged down by a law enforcement officer astride a motorcycle bearing the emblem of the Walker River Tribal Police.

Turns out, we were cutting through the Walker River Reservation, and Dee had been pushing the pedal to the metal a bit too much and had blown past the speed limit, which was set at a modest 70 mph. Even on a desolate highway, there was no escaping the long arm of the law. Respect for the rules was universal.

Back in Europe, highway speed limits typically hovered between 75 and 80 mph. That being said, I couldn't deny that Dee had been hammering down the throttle with all the force, easily hitting 90 mph on the speedometer, if not more. And while there might not have been any other souls around to bear witness to our little speed fest, it turns out the law still had its eyes on us.

The native official was as tough as nails. Dee attempted to weave a tale by playing the foreigner card, claiming he didn't have a grasp of the kilometer-to-mile conversion. But the man wasn't falling for any of it. Then Marky had the brilliant idea to jump into the fray. It wasn't unexpected to see him try to pull a stunt. The cop had that look about him that screamed, 'Don't mess with me.' We had been pushing the speed limit. Just confess and take it on the chin, right? But Marky had other plans. He produced a tiny, black leather wallet from his jacket. Inside was a downsized police badge, some sort of proof that he was kin to someone in the force. As if that wasn't enough, tucked into the tiny wallet was a business card belonging to some hotshot district attorney from New York City. As this unfolded, I stood there, merely observing. What on earth was he trying to prove?

It was clear as day that the officer wasn't even close to being entertained, and time was one luxury he had in abundance. On this desolate strip of asphalt, one craved a distraction, a way to dull the monotonous drone of solitude, and we handed him just the right excuse on a silver platter. It was no secret to me that if the charade didn't do the trick, Marky would pull out his tried and tested 'I was in the Ramones' card. It was excruciatingly awkward. The guy didn't even remotely resemble a devotee of the Ramones. All I yearned for was to shut out the world and drift back into oblivion.

Ultimately, we were slapped with a speeding ticket and considered ourselves fortunate that the officer let us off the hook with just that. Dee's attempt was, to be fair, commendable, but the stunts that Marky pulled were simply out of this world. When the local lawman locked eyes with me, I responded with a roll of my own, an attempted silent apology.

The whole fiasco stretched on for what felt like an eternity. The urge to relieve my bladder was unbearable, but I had to make do with the piss bottle. God knows what kind of sacrilege it would have been to desecrate the holy land of the cops' native ancestors.

We had squandered precious time and knew we had to press on but at a lawful pace this time. At last, we reached Beatty, our pitstop for refueling. The detour to the Death Valley Nut & Candy company offered a much-needed reprieve. It was an unrivaled haven for those with a sugar craving, a perfect spot to replenish our cooler and refill our stash of road trip snacks.

Before we realized it, the fringes of Las Vegas stretched out before us. To the European psyche, Las Vegas is synonymous with the Strip. Nothing more, nothing less. It's an unending road, ablaze with neon lights, casinos, and opulent hotels. Yet when we rolled into the parking lot beside the venue, this emblematic vision of the Strip was conspicuously absent.

The Cooler Lounge bore the distinction of being Vegas' most ancient punk bar. To a community of dedicated, long-standing underground music enthusiasts, this bar symbolized more than just a venue for gigs. It was a haven where anarchy could frolic freely. A sanctuary where the authentic spirit of punk continued to thrive in its unadulterated, wild ecstasy. The bar had been a staple for over 20 years, during which it witnessed a cavalcade of chaotic tales. Stories spun from raucous debauchery featuring food battles, baby powder, dwarfs, onstage dumpster diving, inexplicable band brawls, and gruesome black metal performances drenched in blood. This was just the kind of place we'd been seeking.

Regardless of the history of that place, as soon as we stepped foot inside, I was struck by a prickly and coarse aura. It was a completely different feeling from anything we'd encountered before - chilling to the bone and utterly unrefined.

My foreboding sense of something dark coming our way became all too real that night. The venue was teeming with people, uncomfortably so, and there was an undeniable undercurrent of aggression and hostility. DxIx took their spot on the stage, and the OC punks exploded on the scene like a sonic detonator. This only served to fan the flames amongst the crowd. It seemed as though both the band and their audience were squaring up for a showdown. Then, inescapably, chaos broke loose. A man jumped forward from out of nowhere, a broken beer bottle clenched in his fist. He lunged at the stage and savagely slashed and stabbed Eddie, DI's bassist, square in the face. Blood sprayed in every direction. The assailant had vanished before anyone could fully comprehend what had just transpired. Everyone had witnessed the attack, yet no one could provide a detailed description of the perpetrator. Eddie remained frozen to his spot on stage, visibly shell-shocked, with his face marred by a gaping wound. Blood was everywhere. The shattered bottle had narrowly avoided his eyes but left a hole in one side of his nose. If this wasn't hardcore experience, I don't know what is.

It was evident that the gig had reached its abrupt end. While a majority deplored the unfolding events, there was a sickening minority who reveled in the chaos. The spectacle of violence served as some twisted form of amusement despite the harm it caused to human beings.

We were frozen in place as if our feet had merged with the concrete beneath us. The show was barely underway when it came to an unexpected halt. However, it wasn't completely over, as we still had to play. The debate sparked among us - to perform or not. But sometimes, facing your demons is the only way forward. Retreating at this point would signify a victory for that one twisted soul, and we weren't about to grant him that satisfaction. Nevertheless, none of us harbored a desire to be injured. For Marky, the decision was a no-brainer. He safely tucked behind his drum set. Sure, he might take a hit from a stray bottle lobbed onstage, but the rest of us - Jack, Dee, and me - were exposed, like lambs to the slaughter upfront. Canon fodder for the lunatic audience. Fear gripped us all.

Paramedics on the scene had Eddie strapped on a stretcher, and the eerie light from a pair of cop cars parked outside painted an ominous glow over the parking lot. This was not how gigs were supposed to go down.

Ultimately, the call was made to hit the stage. A handful of spare microphone stands were salvaged and bound with duct tape, turning them into crude baseball bat substitutes. Each of us, Dee, Jack, and I possessed one of these cumbersome makeshift clubs, their weight bearing down on the monitors before us.

We stepped into the spotlight, radiating an air of assurance while our nerves screamed for retreat, and we shit our pants. Grasping the microphone, I let my voice roll out low and threatening: *"We are the*

"Cross the line, and you're dead!"
Viva Las Vegas

Eddie Tatar from DxIx, the Cooler Lounge casualty Stabbed in the face with a beerbottle.

SpeedKings, here to rawk your asses off. What happened to Eddie is a goddamn tragedy, fuck you all!" My finger traced an unseen line just shy of the stage edge. Hoisting the impromptu weapon, I extended my arm toward the crowd and bellowed, *"Cross this line... and you're dead!"* Right on cue, Dee fired up the intro, Marky hammered down on the floor tom... The night belonged to the SpeedKings. The mob had received our declaration of war, loud and clear.

I was relieved when the night finally came to an end. I had encountered situations of aggression at shows before, but usually it was confined to the area in front of the stage, among the audience. Occasionally, some asshole would toss garbage onto the stage. Throwing a beer bottle was even rarer. However, I had never witnessed an intentional physical attack aimed at seriously harming a band member on stage. It was something none of us had ever signed up for.

I had long understood that being a band member on stage, elevated above the heads of the audience, gave us a sense of power and control. It put us in a position of authority, even supremacy, and most of the time, that was enough to diffuse any tense situations through loud shouting. But what happened to poor Eddie was beyond anything we could have anticipated.

When it came to ranking the most violent cities in America, Memphis officially topped the list. Surprisingly, Las Vegas didn't even make the top 10. However, this night changed everything for me. It shifted my perspective on city rankings and shattered any preconceived notions.

We were heading out, bidding farewell to Nevada as we set our sights on Arizona. Shortly after we hit the road, nearing Boulder City, we knew the next stop on our journey was the iconic Hoover Dam. Making our way along Nevada State Route 172, just a mile away from reaching the dam, we found ourselves at the security checkpoint. This precautionary measure had been implemented after the tragic events of 9/11. The security at Hoover Dam was tight, and for good reason. The dam stood as a symbol of protection, safeguarding not only the structure itself but also the invaluable water it held behind its walls. Millions of people and farmers relied on this precious resource. Furthermore, the dam played a vital role in producing electrical power for Las Vegas and countless other communities as an integral part of their survival. But it wasn't just about the dam and its immediate surroundings. Downstream communities were at risk, too. In the event of a flood, lives and properties would be in jeopardy. It was a surreal experience, witnessing just how much rested on the shoulders of this one remarkable structure. No longer could terrorists be given any chances. The world had changed, and security measures had to adapt accordingly.

In the midst of our trip across the expansive desert, we stumbled upon Kingman, the heart of Route 66, otherwise known as the revered Mother Road. This town exuded an authentic vintage retro charm with its streets alive with the roar of classic cars and the vibrant glow of neon signs. Regrettably, time seemed to elude us, preventing us from exploring the Route 66 museum. Our path beckoned us forward, urging us to conquer the vast distances that lay ahead.

Marky, not one for indulging in sightseeing ventures, remained indifferent to the prospect of visiting landmarks. Yet, there was an exception. Hidden amidst the desolate expanse of the desert, we chanced upon an old Sherman tank at a peculiar tank stop. Its weathered exterior might have held untold tales of battles fought and victories won. But then again, I didn't really care about the pile of scrap. The Nevada desert greeted us with its relentless waves of scorching sand and searing heat, a stark reminder that this arid landscape was far from welcoming. We were on our way to Phoenix, where we were set to headline a big all-ages festival at the Mason Jar. This legendary venue was established back in 1979 and quickly became one of the hottest clubs in central Phoenix. It had seen the rise of some of alternative rock's biggest names, including Green Day, Guns 'n Roses, and Nirvana. Needless to say, we were stoked to be playing at a place with such a rock 'n roll pedigree. However, as we arrived, we realized that there were way too many small bands on the bill. Now, don't get me wrong, I appreciate the opportunity for up-and-coming acts to showcase their talent. It is always a great experience to share the stage with a cool band, enjoy their killer performance, and maybe even make some new friends along the way. But when the list of support bands seems endless, and the talent is lacking, it starts to feel like we're trapped in a never-ending loop.

After three weeks of non-stop touring, an enduring long drive, and scorching Phoenix heat, all we wanted was some well-deserved rest. But instead, we found ourselves waiting around for what felt like an eternity. What's left of the Mason Jar is mostly a hazy memory, with the realization that we were completely exhausted, and I kept walking in and out of the club to kill time. Walking out because it was too hot inside, walking in because the burning sun outside was unbearable. Tucson was up next on our agenda. The details are a bit fuzzy, but one thing is certain - we were worn out.

Marky understood the importance of getting enough sleep, and since time was often against us, the one thing we needed to prioritize was finding the best possible accommodation. I was relieved when Mickie Rat joined our group to handle these kinds of practicalities, but Marky couldn't bring himself to trust the guy. Not that he was dishonest or whatsoever but more because of Mickie's unconventional hair color. Marky would constantly nag me, warning me not to take any chances: "You go ahead and make the bookings. I don't trust this Mickie character to get us anything but the dirtiest, most terrible rooms they have. I just can't have that. Let him hide in the car until you secure us some decent rooms." Perhaps there was some truth to his remarks.

I reckon the whole of Arizona was a blur. When we hit up Tucson, we rocked out at Skrappy's, this joint run by a bunch of young kids. It's like this kick-ass performing arts and after-school spot that's all about the music and the vibes. Skrappy has been around in some form since '95, founded by Kathy Woolridge. Back in 2002, it was part of Our Family Services, promoting a drug-free, alcohol-free scene where positivity was the name of the game. Jack and I, with our wild shenanigans, would have been met with some serious disapproval here. No wonder I can barely recall our gig; we were too busy dodging the judgmental stares from the squeaky-clean crew at Our Town Family Center. Once again, we are heading in the direction of the sun-drenched state of California, ready to conquer the final leg of our tour. The Saharan Motel stood tall as our trusted sanctuary, providing us with a sense of stability amidst the chaos of life on the road. After a much-needed day of rest, we were back in action, immersing ourselves in the world of culinary rock 'n' roll down in the city of Long Beach. This is also where Mickie Rat said goodbye. Before returning to Sacramento, he would be spending some time with his dad in LA. We were back on our own for the final three shows.

US West Coast Tour
SKRAPPY'S, Tucson, AZ
January 13, 2003

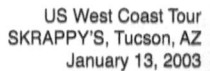

Keeping the Ramones' t[orch]

Marky muses on the past, talks of his present band and other projects

By Theo Douglas
Staff Writer

Marky Ramone: "We (the SpeedKings) don't just do punk, but we do rock."

WITH AN SOBRIQUET LIKE "RAMONE," there's only one band drummer Marc Bell could ever have really been in — and, yep, it's that band.

It, of course, is the Ramones, one of the handful of bands that virtually invented punk — their 1976 debut sparking similar efforts from outfits like the Sex Pistols in England and X out here in Los Angeles.

But time marched on, and like it or not, the Ramones had to march with it. Bell (you might remember him better as Ramones' drummer Marky Ramone) quit the band, then rejoined — then just when things were reaching some sort of public peak, the band called it quits.

Founding members Joey Ramone and Dee Dee both died last year, of lymphomatic cancer and a heroin overdose, respectively, which put the kibosh on any sort of reunion plans ever. And which sort of leaves Marky carrying the torch.

A very loud torch, one suspects. Together with his new band, Marky Ramone & the SpeedKings, he plays tonight at DiPiazza's Restaurant & Lounge in Long Beach.

The Ramones were a fake, albeit charmingly so, band of brothers — Ramone being a surname they all took up. They were deafeningly loud, deadly cool, and bitingly witty.

We spoke last week with the gravelly voiced Marky Ramone, via telephone from New York, to find out what he really thought of the Rock 'n' Roll Hall of Fame, his former bandmates, his current band, the new Ramones tribute and the music he's making now.

Q: Members of your new group, the SpeedKings (which features guitarists Nick 'CQ' Cooper and Dee Jaywalker and bassist Glen Meyer) are European. How did the band come together?

A: Well, yeah, the band's from Europe, and they were friends of mine and I liked the music and I decided to do their first record and I enjoyed the music. Money isn't everything. I made my thing with the Ramones, so I didn't have to do things for the money. We already have a second record (cut) for a future release.

Q: What sort of an audience is the SpeedKings drawing?

A: All ages, from 16 to 21, 22, plus you have older Ramones fans. Curiosity seekers, they want to see Marky Ramone now, and they heard about the Hall of Fame inductee thing, and they're very proud. It's like a continuous party 'cause a lot of these people grew up with me. And the kids who didn't see the Ramones can see me. We're getting a lot of young kids who haven't seen the Ramones, but have seen the Misfits. We don't just do punk, but we do rock.

Q: What are your touring plans?

MARKY RAMONE & THE SPEEDKINGS, WITH THINKING ALOUD, US CRUSH AND AWAKEN

Where: DiPiazza's Restaurant & Lounge, 5205 E. Pacific Coast Highway, Long Beach
When: 9 tonight
Tickets: $10
Information: (562) 498-2461

A: After this bit, I have a day off, and a week and a half later I go to Europe with the Misfits. Then I come back, and I do a Canadian tour with the SpeedKings. Then I come back and deal with the Rock 'n' Roll Hall of Fame Committee to make sure all the people I deal with are OK.

Q: So you're a member of the Rock 'n' Roll Hall of Fame voting committee, and the Ramones were inducted last year. How does that feel for an avowed punk rocker? After all, you might wind up standing next to Phil Collins at some point.

A: There's a lot of good bands in there, like the Beatles, the Rolling Stones, Little Richard, Chuck Berry. It's an honor; you're amongst great company. I really enjoyed the evening we were inducted. I hung out with Phil Spector (creator of the '60s 'Spector sound' and one of our former producers) all night. I love Phil, and I was with Dee Dee a lot, he's one of my best friends. And it's an honor. We're one of the first punk bands in there. It's an honor.

Q: So, what about your current band — how would you describe the music you're making?

A: It's very, very fast, over-the-top speed punk. The term punk really is for the Ramones, the Sex Pistols and the Clash. The Ramones started it in New York and it spread out to Europe. What we do is a little more modernized. It's a lot faster, and the combination of the people makes it interesting. They're from Europe and I'm from New York, and we all put our own originality into it.

Q: And your guitarist plays a hollow-body Gretsch. Don't you need a Fender or a Les Paul to make

this kind of m[usic]

A: No, it ad[...] Everyone [...] Marshall (amp[...] sound like Ra[...] good to be a li[...] there's other t[...]

Q: Now, eve[...] name Ma[...]

A: Well, yo[...] name at [...] world as Mark[...] (back to) my o[...] it's beneficial [...] Ramones) bac[...] keeps the light [...] of new Ramor[...] CDs have bee[...] "Ramones Ar[...] going to come [...]

Q: I hear yo[...] posthume[...]

A: It's 15 ne[...] and I'm [...] the record. Th[...] he was still co[...] hear the demo[...] be producing v[...] secret produce[...]

Q: You're a [...] with the [...]

A: (Bassist) [...] and the M[...] the name goin[...] I'll never be a [...] and it's a lot o[...] music so that's [...]

I respect wh[...] The Misfits ha[...] there's nothing [...] than anyone, s[...] listen to their k[...] of things more [...]

Q: Do you h[...]

A: No, but I [...] crossed r[...] they have to re[...]

Q: Speaking [...] how do y[...] disc that's due [...]

A: It's really [...] but we re[...] had nothing to [...] success, but w[...] very sterile an[...] "Sheena is a P[...] You Remembe[...] there should be[...]

Q: Now, you [...] rejoining [...] there any mor[...]

A: Oh, no, v[...] everybod[...] that Joey and J[...] started drinkin[...] I wanted to ge[...] years later they[...]

Theo Douglas [...] e-mail at theo[...]

CHAPTER 37

The Toast of Hollywood

"Hollywood is a place where they'll pay you a thousand dollars for a kiss and fifty cents for your soul." - Marilyn Monroe

We drove down the East Pacific Highway to Long Beach, craving some more delicious food. Our destination was DiPiazza's Lava Lounge, a renowned restaurant that had been established by the DiPiazza family. This vibrant restaurant offered an array of mouthwatering dishes, including pizza and pasta, and a lively atmosphere with live shows and a fully stocked bar. It was a unique experience for me, as this was the first time I found myself performing in actual restaurants. It felt strange, to say the least. The unfamiliarity of the setting added an extra layer of excitement and anticipation to this tour. It was like stepping into uncharted territory.

A friend who witnessed the gig told me that we absolutely killed it with our intense and high-energy performance, even though this was in the middle of a restaurant. I never apprehended the concept of this. Texas Terri belted out her heart and soul on stage, and after the show, she introduced me to one of her friends. Rebecca turned out to be the mystery name on the guest list. She and Terri were polar opposites. TxT embodied the essence of shock rock, a goddess with her bare breasts adorned with X's over her nipples. Rebecca, on the other hand, was a striking redhead with the most intriguing eyes, full of enigma and intrigue. That night, Terri didn't stick around for long, as she hightailed it back to LA.

Meanwhile, Rebecca and I engaged in a lengthy conversation about her career in the fashion industry, music, films, and everything in between. I mentioned that I had recently acquired a copy of the Mexican road movie, "Y tu mamá también." Just then, Marky approached us and asked Rebecca if she had a car. He wanted to head to the hotel, and true to form, anyone who crossed his path was expected to cater to his every whim like a lowly servant.

In a matter of minutes, we found ourselves inside her 1989 burgundy Chevrolet Monte Carlo. As we pulled up to the hotel, Marky swiftly exited the car and insisted without dialogue that Rebecca and I continue to hang out. It was clear that he had some twisted plan brewing in his mind. I couldn't help but recall a conversation we had once, where he arrogantly declared, *"Why don't I handle the money? Consider yourself lucky. You can have all pussy."* This was accompanied by a sly grin. He took the green and left me with the fur. It felt degrading and demeaning, but honestly, my esteem for the man had long abandoned our relationship.

Rebecca made the decision to head over to her place. She professed to reside in a nearby locale, nestled within a serene community, alongside a few roommates. As we made our way, we happened to pass by Ramona Park. I glanced at the street sign as it swiftly passed, and a smile crept across my face. The synchronicity of the moment was not lost on me - here I was, on tour with a member of the Ramones, driving alongside my very own Ramona, pulling up a driveway on Sunfield Avenue in Lakewood.

I stealthily maneuvered my way through the living room and silently tiptoeing behind her until we reached the back of the house where her room was situated. We boozed, surfed the internet, talked a lot of nonsense, and laughed, all leading up to the moment she decided to play the DVD. The details of the movie escaped me as my focus quickly shifted towards something far more captivating - our passionate embrace. It was an exhilarating and lighthearted experience, a playful combination of teasing and wrestling on the bed while she attempted to capture some candid snapshots. She was undeniably the most stunning creature I had encountered in recent memory, wearing a rad set of racy red lingerie and an alluring push-up bra. However, this was not meant to be a fleeting one-night stand. It was a fun and games adventure fueled by intoxication and weariness.

As I went to the bathroom, I inadvertently stumbled upon some older guy who confronted me with a mix of confusion and irritation and demanded to know who I was. I had the same question for him. For god's sake, you goddamn old grumpy bastard! The unmistakable sounds of laughter emanating from her bedroom provided an answer that required no words. *"I am her father, you jerk!"* "Roommates, my ass!" Well, it's certainly one way to put it.

Our intention had been to stay awake throughout the night, but succumbing to more drugs would have served no purpose. She had an early morning shift in downtown LA, and after catching a few hours of sleep, we hastily departed again, with me being dropped off at the hotel. Marky, who witnessed our arrival, felt like a matchmaker as if he had orchestrated our rendezvous.

I felt a lightness in my head, desperately craving a few hours of sleep. That night, our destination was Sunset Boulevard, where we had a gig scheduled at The Key Club. This was one of those shows that had been on my radar for a while. Any club along Sunset would have been ok, but I had always fantasized about playing at iconic venues like The Whisky A GoGo, the Roxy, or Rainbow Bar & Grill. However, The Key Club held its own legendary status. With a capacity of around 650 people, the show had sold out completely.

As I stepped into The Key Club, it lived up to all my expectations. The interior was enveloped in darkness, creating an atmosphere that could easily be mistaken for the set of an MTV music video. Multiple levels added an intriguing dynamic to the space, and there were even television sets embedded in the floor. It was so cool.

However, I couldn't help but be disappointed with the backline equipment they had set up for us. Thankfully, it didn't take much effort to switch things up and make it just right.

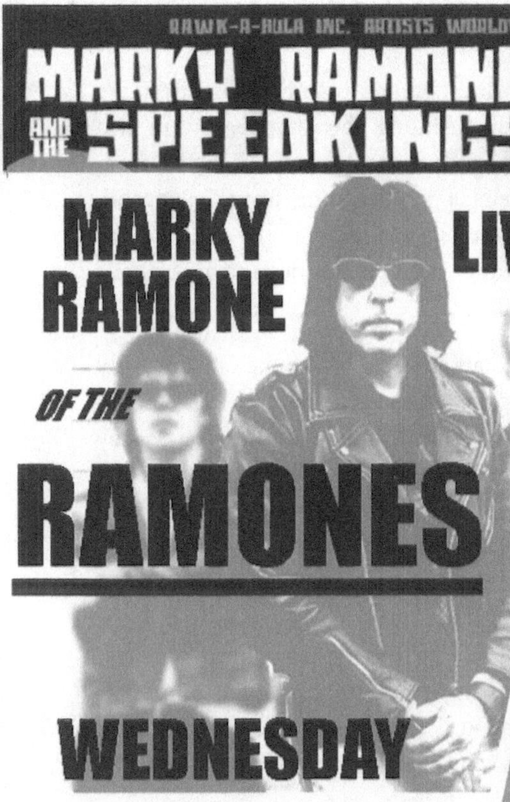

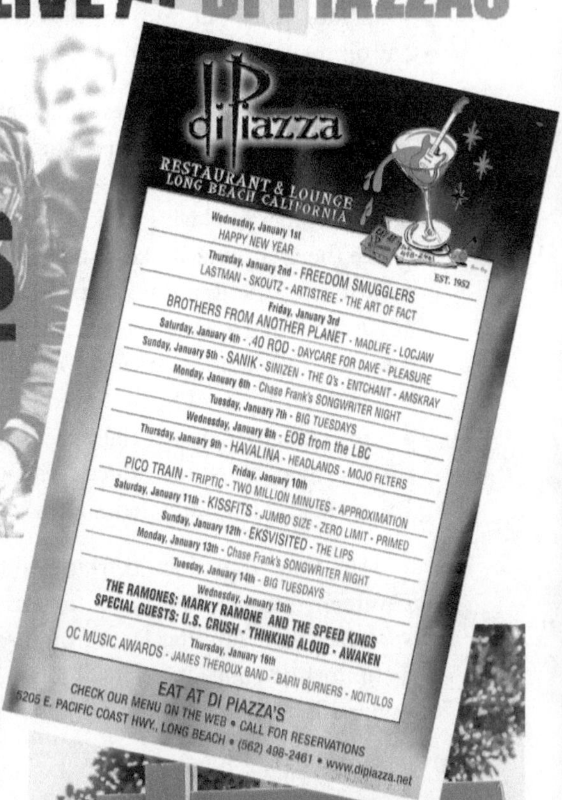

di Piazza

RESTAURANT & LOUNGE
LONG BEACH CALIFORNIA

EST. 1952

Wednesday, January 1st
HAPPY NEW YEAR

Thursday, January 2nd - FREEDOM SMUGGLERS
LASTMAN - SKOUTZ - ARTISTREE - THE ART OF FACT

Friday, January 3rd
BROTHERS FROM ANOTHER PLANET - MADLIFE - LOCJAW

Saturday, January 4th - .40 ROD - DAYCARE FOR DAVE - PLEASURE

Sunday, January 5th - SANIK - SINIZEN - THE Q's - ENTCHANT - AMSKRAY

Monday, January 6th - Chase Frank's SONGWRITER NIGHT

Tuesday, January 7th - BIG TUESDAYS

Wednesday, January 8th - EOB from the LBC

Thursday, January 9th - HAVALINA - HEADLANDS - MOJO FILTERS

Friday, January 10th
PICO TRAIN - TRIPTIC - TWO MILLION MINUTES - APPROXIMATION

Saturday, January 11th - KISSFITS - JUMBO SIZE - ZERO LIMIT - PRIMED

Sunday, January 12th - EKSVISITED - THE LIPS

Monday, January 13th - Chase Frank's SONGWRITER NIGHT

Tuesday, January 14th - BIG TUESDAYS

Wednesday, January 15th
THE RAMONES: MARKY RAMONE AND THE SPEED KINGS
SPECIAL GUESTS: U.S. CRUSH - THINKING ALOUD - AWAKEN

Thursday, January 16th
OC MUSIC AWARDS - JAMES THEROUX BAND - BARN BURNERS - NOITULOS

EAT AT DI PIAZZA'S
CHECK OUR MENU ON THE WEB • CALL FOR RESERVATIONS
5205 E. PACIFIC COAST HWY., LONG BEACH • (562) 498-2461 • www.dipiazza.net

Miss Ramona Park of Long Beach.
The mystery of the stolen Bra after the Di Piazza Show.

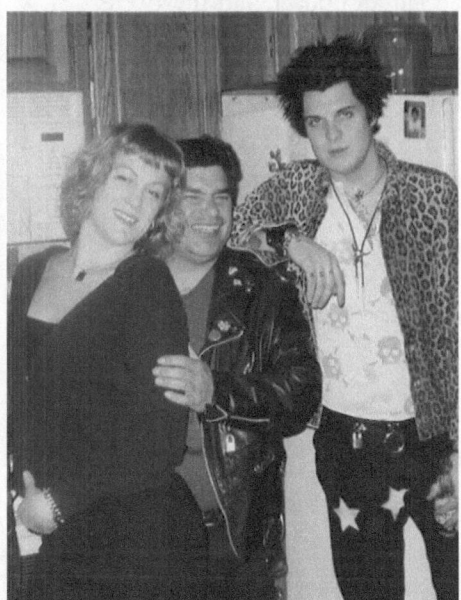

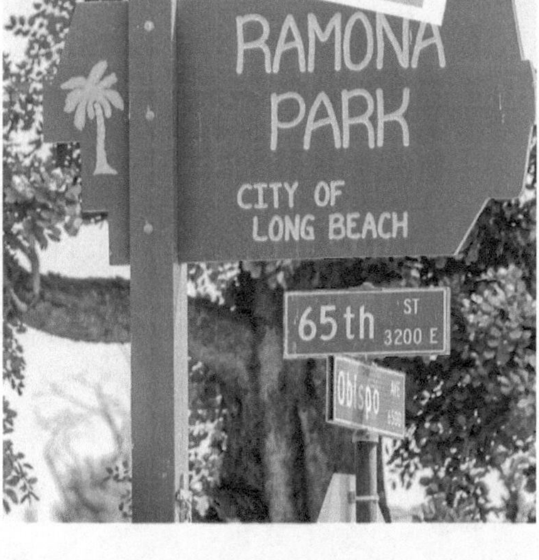

The guestlist overflowed with celebrities, predominantly hailing from the vibrant LA Punk and Metal scene. Among the attendees were two members of GNR, accompanied by their spouses. CC Deville from Poison was also expected, as well as my Ramona from Lakewood. However, to my disappointment, she couldn't make it in the end. She was simply too worn out from the previous night's escapades and an arduous day on the job.

PublicityWhore.com was stoked about the gig: "It's the one and only Marky Ramone and the Speed Kings. The Speed Kings- backed by Marky Ramone's killer drumbeats - are proving that they are the real Macoy when it comes to playing rockabilly punk rock music. I am always stoked to see the OG punk rockers still staying on the scene and playing punk rock music. The Ramones helped start the punk movement back in the 1970s, so being able to see a true legend in punk rock perform is a real blessing. Of course, everyone came for the Ramones tunes, but the original tunes played by the SpeedKings proved they were more than just a Ramones cover band. The SpeedKings have some original tunes that display their ability to produce great punk rock hooks, riffs, and beats. So, I recommend checking them out when they play in a town near you."

And that wasn't too far from reality. We were chilling outside on the pavement when a line began to form, eagerly waiting to get inside. I spotted several familiar faces from previous gigs on this tour, which was a comforting sight. It meant that we had left an impact, and they were hungry for more.

"Coming back to LA was full of surprises. Jack and I decided to grab some food at In & Out Burger, but little did we know that something unexpected would happen. As we were placing our order, a group of kids approached us, recognizing who we were. It felt like a dream, almost unreal. Two guys from Belgium are getting recognized on the streets of Los Angeles. It was incredible. The night couldn't have been any better. Little did we know that the show at the Key Club would exceed all expectations. It turned out to be one of the greatest shows of this tour and perhaps even of all the shows we've ever played." Dee remembers this moment vividly, still basking in the glory of that unforgettable experience.

Finally, we could unleash our demons. "SpeedKings Ride Tonight" took over the venue, and we rode that wave with unbridled passion. Just like the previous night, Txt, the undisputed queen of LA Rawk, ignited the stage, setting it ablaze. The atmosphere was electric, with a volatile energy pulsating through the crowd. It was as if all the highs and lows of our month-long tour were finally released.

Our performance was flawless. We kept pushing forward, never missing a beat. The audience was captivated and completely immersed in the experience. The raw power filled the night like a thunderous roar. As we played, it felt as though time stood still. Each song carried its own story, painting vivid images in the minds of those attending. Obviously, this night would end too soon, so I had no time to waste and just enjoy what came our way.

In the front row, there was this gorgeous girl who had been screaming at me throughout the entire performance. When we reached the encore, she boldly grabbed my feet, and as Dee started a blazing rockabilly solo, I fell on my knees in front of her. Out of nowhere, she tongued me to kingdome come, sending me into a whirlwind of ecstasy. The world seemed to spin around me, and during the final song's explosive feedback, I couldn't contain myself any longer. I threw my SG down, made my way to the edge of the stage, turned my back to the audience, locked eyes with Marky, made the countdown to the end of the song, and let myself fall backward into the awaiting crowd. It felt like landing on a heavenly cloud. As I looked to the side, I spotted CC Deville wearing a big smile at the edge of the stage, as if he were silently saying, *"Enjoy it, buddy!"* We were all filled with euphoria. Undoubtedly, this was the most incredible show of the entire tour, and we only had one more to go. Trying to top this experience would be a tough act to follow.

Since we had been using the equipment provided by the club, packing up was hardly necessary. As I made my way towards the exit, Texas Terri and Mark Diamond caught my attention. They signaled for me to join them for a night out on the town. Just as I was about to leave, the blonde girl who had kissed me earlier bumped into me again. Our lips became entangled in a thrilling game of tongue-twisting. *"My name is Miranda,"* she said, but I was already rushing to catch up with my friends who were heading towards the Kit Kat Club.

What I didn't know was that this iconic rock venue on the Sunset Strip was owned by none other than Slim Jim Phantom of the Stray Cats. It was renowned for its wild, raucous, and stellar jam sessions. It wasn't until TxT took the microphone and the live band began playing "I Wanna Be Your Dog" that I recognized Slim Jim behind the drum kit. This encounter would prove to be significant years later when I found myself handling his merchandise for numerous European tours and getting introduced to his fellow Cats.

Believe it or not, but as soon as I felt a gentle tap on my shoulder, I turned around to find myself staring directly into Miranda's eyes once again. *"You never asked for my number,"* she playfully winked and scribbled it onto the back of my hand. *"We gotta meet soon,"* and she disappeared in the night.

I can't recall the exact moment I found myself stranded in the bed back in the hotel, but I can tell you one thing - I was beyond satisfied. It's possible that I had never experienced such a profound sense of fulfillment before. The little, unassuming Dr. Frog from way back when would have never fathomed the idea of ruling a stage in the heart of Hollywood. And yet, that is where I found myself.

Rebecca was a no-show at the gig, but to my surprise, I discovered a scathing message in my mailbox. "I invited you into my home, believing that I could trust you. But it turns out you're nothing more than a disgusting, thieving, perverted creep! You left and stole my bra! You're a fucking asshole!" Well, that caught me off guard. If I ever had any unconventional fetishes, lingerie certainly wasn't on the list. What the hell would I do with her bra? It wouldn't even fit me.

Fast forward one week later, and she found it resting in her dishevelled, messed-up bed. It brought to mind Mick Jagger's voice belting out those iconic lines, "White girls, they're pretty funny, sometimes they drive me mad." Some girls are just undeniably downright wild and crazy.

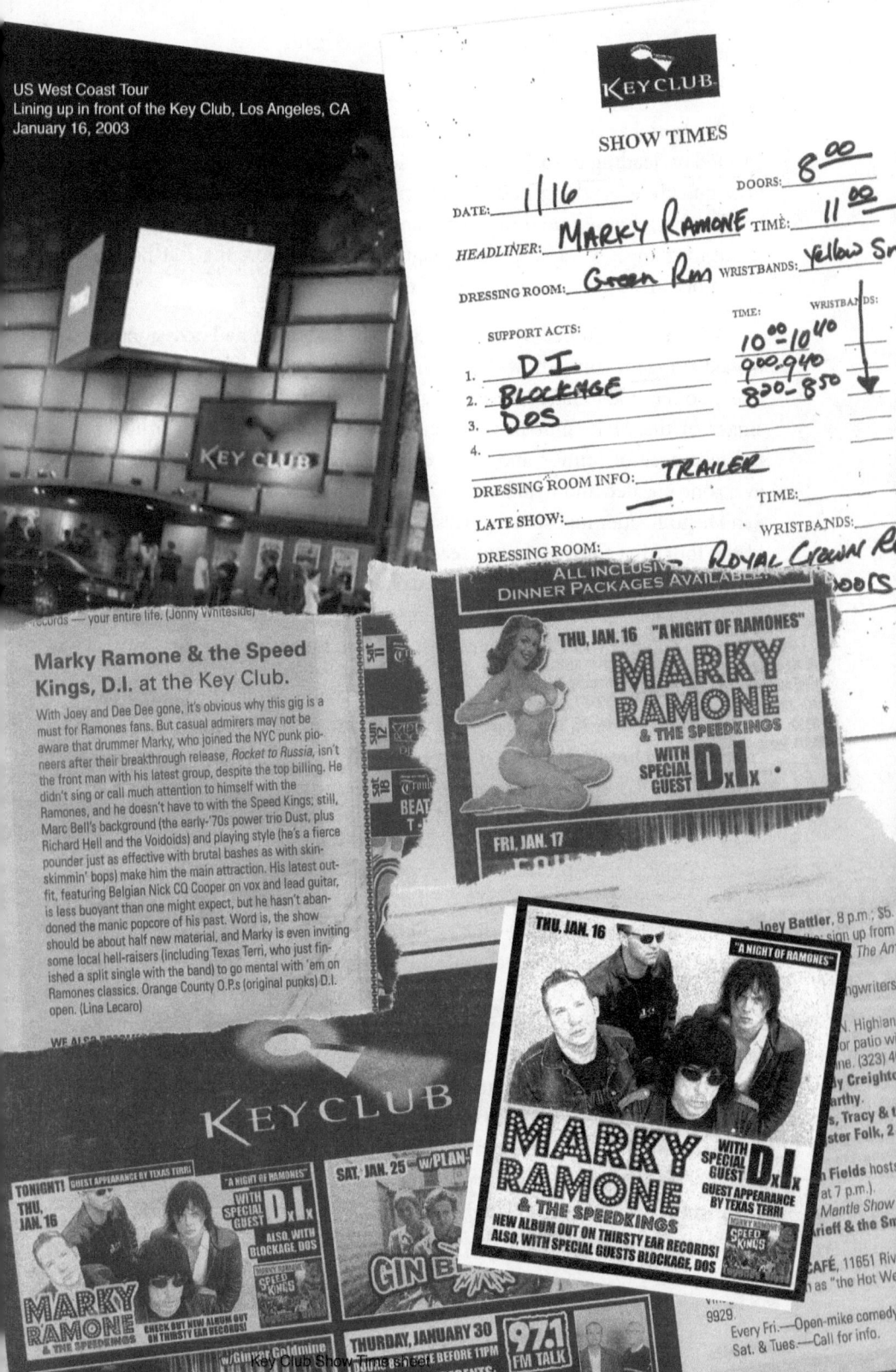

The tour had reached its conclusion. A final journey down south awaited us, leading us to San Diego's Brick by Brick. It was hard to believe how quickly everything had gone by. In just a few days, we would be heading back home, and things would never be the same again. They were about to change in ways beyond imagination. But before that, we had to give it our all and rock the hell out of this place.

Our crew was joined by Mario, a Samoan dude who had occasionally tagged along for some shows. With his dark skin and afro hair, he looked like a comic book character. Interestingly enough, he was also the lead singer of the Make-Out Boys, a seriously kick-ass band. Mario had a twisted sense of humor and often dropped mysterious quotes that left everyone puzzled and wondering what the hell he was talking about. The San Diego Reader had some stories about him years later but at the time of the tour, that future was not set out yet. Despite all that, the moment we arrived in San Diego, the heat hit us hard. After surviving a tour filled with pizza lounges, I was craving something different – some authentic Mexican cuisine and I had no interest in some mediocre fajitas.

Luckily for us, Rich, the frontman of Whole Hog, the incredible rackin' support band, knew exactly where to find the best Mexican food in town. His lovely wife Sheila accompanied us to the nearby taco joint situated just around the corner from the Brick. We ended up at a table under the scorching sun, which only added to the genuine atmosphere.

The final show's promoter was a guy called Nick Peligro. Sulo, who was under Nick's employ, handled all the logistical details, while Vinnie, may he rest in peace, Whole Hog's original bass player, took charge of the sound that evening. Sulo was only 21 years old at the time, and Vinny acted as his mentor, introducing him to a world where money was scarce but rock 'n' roll was abundant. When Peligro secured this gig, Vinny wasted no time in getting Whole Hog on the lineup because he knew Rich was just retarded The Ramones. During the load-in, Sulo stuck around, hoping to greet Marky, but he was ignored. Then, after all the bands had finished performing, Sulo attempted to approach him once more, only to be brushed off again. His disappointment was obvious. Vinny witnessed it all and couldn't help but laugh, saying, *"Don't worry about it, Su… he's not even a real Ramone."*

That night, the stage was being completely demolished by Whole Hog, and I had no choice but to switch to my Gibson Flying V if I wanted to keep up with their mind-blowing performance. These guys were absolutely incredible. But as Rich later explained to me, it went both ways: "After you guys played here, the energy in this place was electric, and it opened up doors for some serious rockin'. Even months later, we could still feel the reverberations of the shockwave you guys instigated."

Here I stood, biding my time at Los Angeles International Airport, awaiting our departure back to Europe. Reluctance coursed through me as I approached the check-in counter. She had assured me on the phone that she would be punctual, yet here I was, left to wait for her. And then, as if by divine intervention, the sliding doors parted, and a radiant beam of light illuminated the entrance hall. In walked Miranda, settling herself in front of me. *"You better come and see me soon,"* she teased, her eyes locked onto mine. With a mischievous flick of her finger, she beckoned me closer, revealing a tantalizing glimpse of what lay just beneath the buckle belt of her jeans. An old-school butterfly tattoo adorned her skin, promising an intoxicating journey towards a land of honey.

Fast forward 12 hours later, and I found myself back home as if the entire experience had been nothing more than a fleeting dream.

Final show of the US West Coast tour.
January 17, 2003 Brick By Brick, San Diego, CA
Support by the great Whole Hog.

A little surprised? Flying V Rawk'n'Roll!

Mickie Rat in the driver seat.
In the van with Marky on our way to LA.

Rock on SpeedKings!

```
SPEEDKINGS RIDE TONIGHT
R&R ASSHOLE
MANUELITA
I DON'T CARE → MARIO
UPS GIRL
SATURDAYNIGHT
FUCK ME
TELEPHONELOVE
SHEENA IS A PUNKROCKER → MARIO
TEENAGE R&R SUICIDE
ROADRAGE
FUCK SHIT UP
BEAT ON THE BRAT → MARIO
SEXPHONEGIRLS
HOTRODS-R-US
CHINESE ROCK
I DON'T CARE ABOUT YOU
WEENIE HAIR
CALIFORNIA SUN
BURNIN' RUBBER
```

Brick By Brick setlist

SpeedKings Ride Tonight!

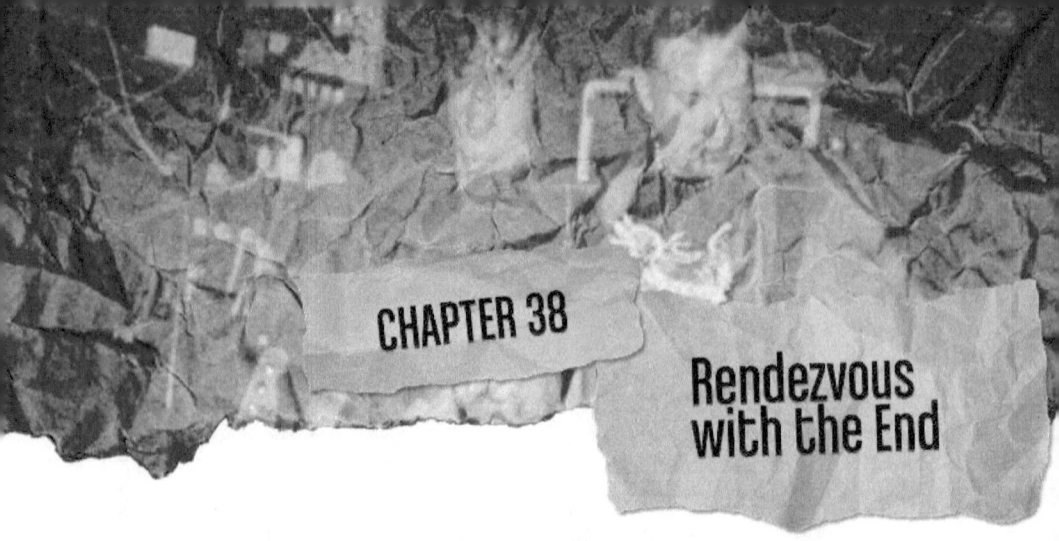

CHAPTER 38
Rendezvous with the End

"Isn't it funny how day by day nothing changes but when you look back everything is different…" - C.S. Lewis

End of January 2003

As January reached its conclusion, I found myself back in my home country after an intense series of eighteen shows that took me all along the enthralling West Coast. It was a whirlwind adventure that spanned across five states: California, Oregon, Washington, Nevada, and Arizona. Touring in the United States is a whole different ballgame compared to Europe. The absence of assistance from our booking agency and the audacious promoters who shamelessly pocketed the door money transformed this chapter into a nerve-racking trial for the SpeedKings.

Dee made the decision to throw in the towel, a move we saw coming from a mile away. It's probably for the best, as he tried to salvage some shred of honor and what is left of his integrity. Although he played a vital role in molding the touch of rockabilly in our unique sound, on a personal level, he just doesn't click with our troop anymore. Our rock-solid friendship crumbled before my very eyes, a harsh reality that I couldn't escape anymore. Despite the confusion and regret it brought, I couldn't compromise my principles and values that felt light years away. At first, Jack and I treated it like a twisted joke, a sick game, but the laughter faded, and it became more of an irritating nuisance. When Dee finally split the beans about his departure, it was like a weight lifted off our shoulders, even though it was far from an ideal situation for the band. Without him, it was like taking a step back, but we would manage somehow and eventually find someone to take his place. As always, we were convinced we would wing it!

In the bustling city of Los Angeles, I stumbled upon an incredible guitar player named Mark Diamond. With his electrifying guitar skills and his role as the guitar slinger for the Dwarves, he immediately captured my attention as a possible replacement. Known by his alter ego, the Fresh Prince of Darkness, Mark possessed the potential to not only fill the void left by Dee but even surpass his guitar prowess. However, before we make any decisions about the future, it's crucial that I sit down with Marky and discuss the next steps. With anticipation building, I can't help but wonder how this new chapter will unfold and what kind of musical endeavors lie ahead.

Lately, *The Man* has been completely consumed by thoughts of the Misfits. Jerry Only, on a mission to rake in some serious cash, has put together a fresh lineup featuring the likes of Robo and Dez Cadena from Black Flag. Also, Keith Morris from Circle Jerks joins in the cash-collecting spree. While I have tremendous respect for the Misfits' legacy, I can't help but feel uneasy about Marky's change in priorities. It's starting to seem like he is becoming nothing more than a puppet in this pseudo-punk-rock cover band for celebrities. He may not realize it, but the SpeedKings set him back on the map and stepped in to fill the void he had found himself in. We were the ones igniting the fire of passion for rock'n'roll. The burning desire is pushing me to seize every opportunity to hit the road and launch yet another thrilling tour.

On the first day of February, I received an unexpected phone call that caught me off guard. It was Marky on the line, currently touring Europe with the Misfits and scheduled to perform in Italy that very day. In just a few days, they would be heading to Holland, specifically to play at the Patronaat in Haarlem, which is close to Amsterdam.

I had been under the impression that we would be left on the Canadian tour in a couple of weeks. However, Marky insisted on meeting up with me in Holland. There were still some matters we needed to discuss. But as our conversation drew to a close, it became clear that our meeting had nothing to do with tour schedules. Marky wanted me to bring him some pills. It was a bizarre request, considering I knew for a fact that he wasn't the kind of person who relied on pills. However, he felt it necessary to have something on hand, just in case.

I could vividly recall the last tour when he was desperately in need of some valium. The challenge we faced in Europe was that prescription drugs were strictly regulated, and even if you had a valid prescription in the US, it didn't automatically apply to the European Union. We tirelessly searched for a solution, visiting countless pharmacists, only to be met with the same disappointing response every time: "No prescription, no pills." That is until we reached France, where we discovered that valium was surprisingly accessible without a prescription. He didn't want us to waste any time rushing to the nearest pharmacy as soon as we crossed the borders. It was as if a weight had been lifted off Marky's shoulders. Interestingly enough, he didn't even end up needing one of the pills. Just having it within reach seemed to calm his restless spirit.

It was obvious that he called me to showcase some of my magic. However, in Belgium and The Netherlands, I couldn't seem to make it happen. "Why don't you ask your mom?" It was a simple question, but I was the one who had to go out and search for it. "Or just drive over to France. You live so close to the border. Get it for me!" It sounded more like a command than a mere request.

Over at my mother's place, I managed to discover a strip of vitamin pills that looked like tranquilizers, in her medicine cabinet. Although the expiration date had long passed, I figured it wouldn't cause much harm.

I hopped in the car with a buddy of mine, and we headed over to the gig in Holland. Thanks to our names on the guestlist, we got quick access to the backstage area. As soon as we stepped into the room, I was greeted by the whole Misfits crew. CBGB's made another appearance. Jerry gave me that nickname because of the shirt I always wore. It was great to see Jerry and Doyle there. Dez was hanging around, too. But when Marky spotted me, he leaped up with the energy of a newborn, pulled me into the hallway, and shoved me into a stall in the men's room. To any unsuspecting onlookers, it would have appeared like a scene straight out of some homoerotic action flick. With an almost desperate tone, he asked, "*Do you have the stuff?*" When I revealed the strip of ersatz medication, it was as if he had received the ultimate birthday gift he had been yearning for his entire life. He disappeared faster than we had entered that stall.

"*Why don't you guys enjoy the show!*" he bellowed with unbridled enthusiasm, directing his words towards me and the friend who accompanied me. Standing at the rear of the venue, we caught a glimpse of a few songs, but it was all too familiar. I yearned for an escape. Little did I know that that fleeting moment would mark the final time my path would physically intertwine with Marky's.

Proposed Canadian Tour 2003

City	Date	Venue	Fee
Clifton, NJ	02/28/03	Connections	$2000
5 hours & 45 to Buffalo, NY	03/01/03	Reservoir	$1200
1 hour & 50 minutes Toronto, Ontario	03/02/03	TBD	
7 hours driving	03/03/03		
7 hours driving	03/04/03		
5 hours to Winnipeg, Manitoba	03/05/03	Pyramid Cabaret	$1300
5 ½ hours to Regina, Sask.	03/06/03	the State	$2000
7 hours driving	03/07/03		
6 hours to Edmonton, BC	03/08/03	the Rev	$2200
7 hours to Calgary, Alberta	03/09/03	McHewen Ballroom	$1800
5 & ½ hours to Saskatoon, Sask.	03/10/03	TBD	$1100
7 1/2 hours driving	03/11/03		
4 1/2 hours to Minneapolis, Mn	03/12/03	TBD	
4 1/2 hours to Milwaukee, Wisconsin	03/13/03	TBD	
1 hour to Elgin, Illinois	03/14/03	Sammy K's	
5 1/2 hours to Cleveland, Ohio	03/15/03	TBD	
6 hours Philadelphia, Pa	03/16/03	TBD	
2 hours to Brooklyn, NY			

All to include 3 double rooms & backline

two weeks 20 K

Canadian Tour
Tour preparation sheet

Band announcement, Edmonton
March 2, 2003

CHAPTER 39
World Falls Apart

"Once you've arrived at the end of the world, it hardly matters which route you took." - Isaac Marion

The US West Coast tour revealed a whole new side of Marky. On his home turf, his true self took center stage, and the difference from his European tours was undeniable. He seemed to be much more preoccupied with his image compared to when he performed overseas. While he had his moments of charm and humor, there were also instances where his irritation, constant whining, and complaining were clearly evident. Even Steve Gee, the drummer from DxIx, couldn't help but laugh as he told me, "Marky is a piece of work." All of these factors contributed to a growing anxiety. It felt like there was a lingering sense of deception that permeated the tour van, involving Chuck from the booking agency and Marky himself - a dubious duo that I can't help but be wary of.

The badass tour lineup has just been unveiled: eight shows spread across a fortnight. Get ready to rock as we conquer seven stages in Canada and one in the US. The moment this news hits me, I burst into action, wasting no time. I swiftly gather up our passport copies and all the necessary documentation for those work visas. Simultaneously, I'm like a wild animal securing an airplane ticket, making sure nothing stands in the way of this rock 'n' roll adventure.

But that's not all. In true rock star fashion, I reach out to Mark Diamond for a potential collaboration that will shake the very foundations of our band. I lay it all out for him, providing every single detail he needs to prepare for this adventure. Setlists are shared, audio files are sent, and even those sacred tabs that hold the key to our SpeedKings magic are handed over to him. Together, we'll create a sonic explosion that will leave Marky begging for more.

The stage is set, and the countdown begins. The high hopes coursing through my veins like a surge of pure adrenaline. The road ahead may be paved with challenges and obstacles, but we are ready. Time to leave our mark on every stage we hit. This is our time to shine, to ignite the fire within and unleash the rawk. The stage is set, and we're about to take it by storm. Rock 'n' roll, my friends. Rock 'n' roll.

As February draws near, the vast expanse of Canada lies just a month ahead. It's that time again when we must prepare ourselves, dotting our i's and crossing our t's, getting the riders in order, and sorting out the backline specifications. And let's not forget about mapping out the route for the schedule, making sure every crack in the road is accounted for.

But amidst all this preparation, there are lingering questions about the tour crew that remain unanswered. It's like a constant itch at the back of my mind, reminding me of the crew issues we encountered during the start of our previous US tour. The memories of that time still haunt me.

I can't help but reminisce about that moment of satisfaction when I convinced Marky and finally decided to part ways with our tour manager and his sidekick. We left them behind at a gas station somewhere between Los Angeles and San Francisco, a symbolic act of liberation. But little did I know, the repercussions of my decision would come back to bite me in the ass later.

Now, those unanswered questions have morphed into doubts and suspicions of potential double-crossing. It's like being caught up in a whirlwind of uncertainty, unsure of who to trust and who might stab me in the back. But hey, that's just the nature of the rock 'n' roll world we live in, isn't it? A constant battle between loyalty and betrayal, where even those closest to us can turn against us in an instant.

As we gear up for another adventure across the Great White North, let's brace ourselves for whatever challenges lie ahead. We may not have all the answers right now, but one thing is for sure: we'll face them head-on, like mercenaries on a rebellious journey.

Our US booking agent and I still struggle to communicate effectively, and there is a lingering feeling of unease between us. It's as if dark clouds constantly hover above, casting a shadow on our interactions. This sense of foreboding deepens when his email arrives, delivering the news that our work permits won't be ready in time. Work permits? Who the hell needs those? I can't help but scoff at the idea of needing work permits. We're a relentless rock'n'roll band, storming stages and leaving no one unscathed. Where the hell has the thrill and danger gone? Suddenly, it feels like our entire crew has transformed into a bunch of obedient cock sucking choirboys. Seriously, what the fuck happened?

CANCELED. March 1, 2003: Underground, ...
CANCELED. March 2, 2003: Healey's, Toronto, ...
CANCELED. March 5, 2003: Pyramid ...
CANCELED. March 6, 2003: The State, Regina, ...
CANCELED. March 8, 2003...
CANCELED. March 9, 2003: MacEwan ...
CANCELED. March 10, 2003: The Odeon, Saskatoon, ...
CANCELED. March 14, 2003: Knights Of Columbus, Indianapolis,

I'm in absolute disbelief at the current situation. Artists Worldwide has managed to screw up yet again. Thanks, Chuck. I should have known better than to trust someone who poses as a booking agent but looks like a Colombian cartel drug dealer driving around in a secretive black Cadillac Escalade. The warning signs were all there. The fact that Marky was getting chummy with Chuck should have been a dead giveaway. Another red flag. But once again, I was too naive to see through their deceit. It feels like a pack of evil vultures sneaking up on me from behind. Once again, I find myself completely messed up, deceived, and left with the evidence etched into my skin like a tattoo. Mark(y)ed with their treachery. No pun intended.

Oh shit! I need to cancel those airplane tickets! *"I am sorry, sir, but your situation does not comply with our cancellation policy."* It's the polite version of "Fuck off, asshole!" Naturally, my buddy Chuck insists that he'll retrieve the cash from the promoter who screwed up our paperwork and sabotaged the work permits. As the weeks go by, Chuck repeatedly assures me that the check is in the mail, so many times that I start worrying the US Postal Service will have to work overtime just to handle all his promises. But not a single one of those supposed checks ever makes it across the vast ocean. It's clear that lying is ingrained in his very DNA.

Just when you believe you've witnessed every imaginable thing, the situation takes a turn for the worse. On the first day of March, Marky launches the Canadian tour, accompanied by Teenage Head, a legendary Canadian punk rock group, serving as his supporting band. Talk about a punch in the gut! Once again, life deals a cruel blow. It's like being a victim of statutory rape if you ask me.

I also got info that the eight shows scheduled in April have vanished into thin air.

04/04/2003 - Faster Club, Torino (IT)
04/05/2003 - Ramones Tribute Festival, Augsburg (DE)
04/06/2003 - Wild At Heart, Berlin (DE)
04/08/2003 - 5 Nutek, Krakow (PL)
04/09/2003 - CDQ, Warsaw (PL)
04/11/2003 - R'nR Highschool Festival, CDK MAI, Moscow (RU)
04/12/2003 - Muha, Moscow (RU)
04/13/2003 - Oralandino, St Petersburg (RU)

Our mission was to venture into the heart of the Iron Curtain and "kill a commie for mommie." We saw the once-divided Berlin as our gateway to Poland and Russia, ready to conquer new territory. However, fate had other plans in store for us. It quickly became apparent to Marky that utilizing local resources and over-eager bands was not only convenient but also a brilliant revenue model. And it served him right. We all have bills to pay and dreams to chase. It's all about minimizing costs and maximizing profits.

But sometimes, you have to remember that you're indebted to others. When you've got even an ounce of respect left in your miserable excuse for a life, you need to show some gratitude. That's when the Russian dudes from Tarkany stepped in. After Teenage Head joined the ranks, they

Candadian Tour
Pyramid Cabaret, Winnipeg, Manitoba
March 5, 2003

became part of our crew, ready to fight alongside Marky in this pinhead army.

I dialed Jack's number, my voice filled with frustration and determination. This charade had reached its breaking point, and I refused to be a part of it any longer. The whole scheme, like a poorly written song, had lost its allure. I was about to cut the cord, severing ties with this deceitful game that had consumed me. I cursed the day I stumbled upon one single Ramones tune. Let them wither away in the depths of hell. I mean it. Every fiber of my being screamed it: **I HATE THE RAMONES!**

I stood there, finally liberated. When you lose everything, it can feel like a weight lifted off your shoulders rather than a loss. You can only deceive yourself for so long. The time had come for me to move on, ready for new endeavors. The whole band experience had been a wild journey, and I had paid my dues. It taught me valuable lessons that would forever be ingrained in my memory. Moreover, it provided me with a network of connections and friends that would prove invaluable in the future.

My passion for graphic design ignited when I took charge of our band's merchandise. Back home, I knew there were opportunities waiting for me, and before I knew it, opportunity came knocking at my door. I established a thriving printing service catering to touring bands. Even though I no longer had to endure endless hours in a smelly van en route to another show, I was still part of the exciting rock and roll circus. And I got to witness incredible performances for free while delivering the goods. Every band greeted me with excitement when I walked in with the merchandise. After all, I was the one bringing in the items that would generate revenue and that the band heavily relied on.

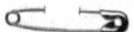

Marky was in hiding, a silent refuge from the fallout of the band's split that had yet to be formalized. As far as I knew, we were still on speaking terms, but the air between us was heavy with unspoken tension. In relationships, sometimes things happen that lead partners to go their separate ways. It doesn't always have to end in a messy divorce.

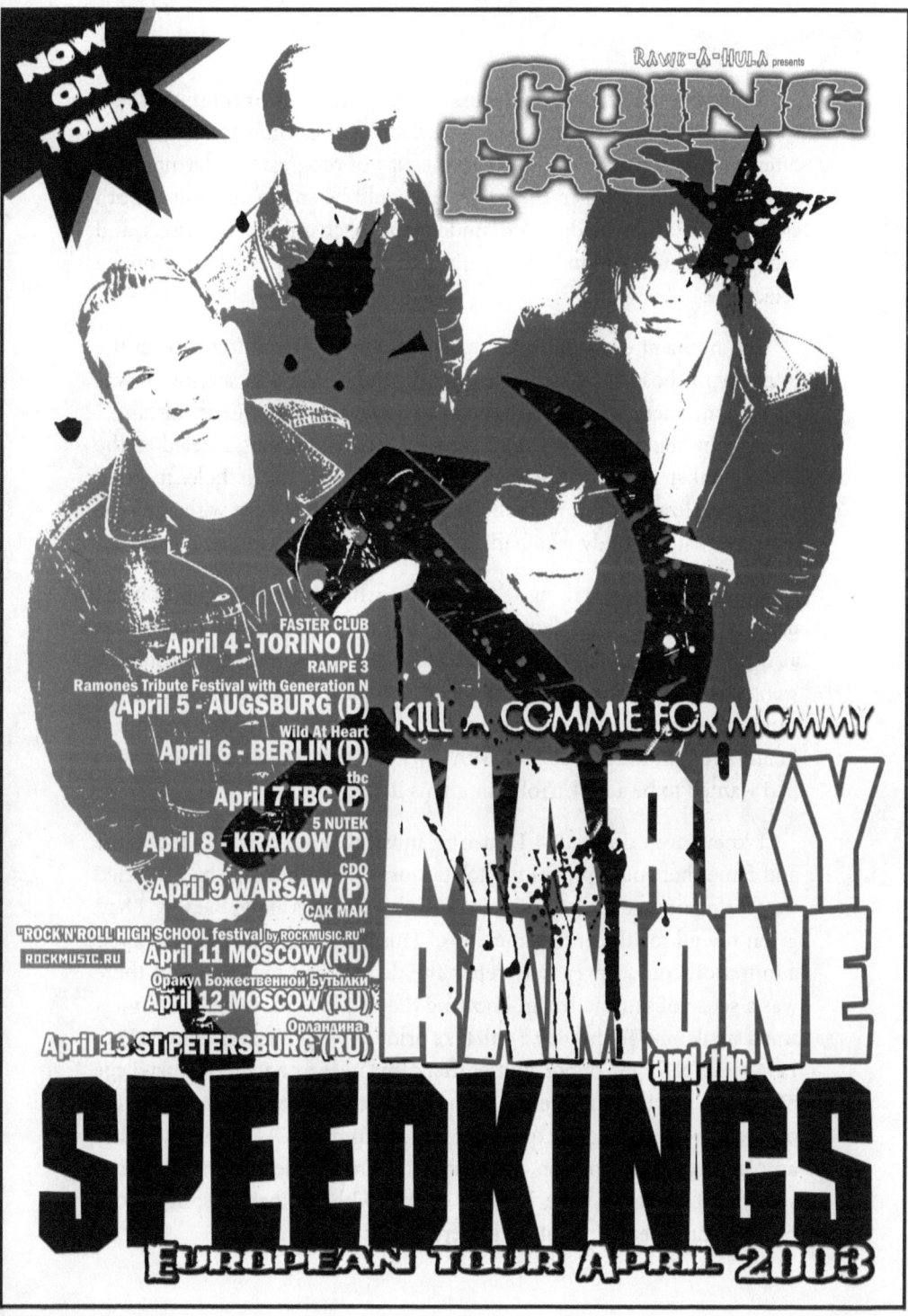

Sometimes, both parties possess enough wisdom and common sense to recognize that parting ways can be a blessing. Unfortunately, more often than not, people's egos get in the way of progress, hindering them from moving forward in their lives. It would be so much easier if both sides could acknowledge and understand each other's emotions and aspirations, but that kind of empathy is a rare gift bestowed upon only a select few.

The moment everything fell apart was when I dared to question the integrity of those I had dedicated my time and efforts to serving. It was also the moment when I demanded to settle the score. In an instant, I went from being a trusted member of the team to being labeled as the troublemaker, the thorn in their side. Here I was, the asshole. It was a painful realization, but it finally brought me face to face with my true identity: just a nobody who had always dreamed of becoming a rockstar.

The moment everything fell apart was when I dared to question the integrity of those I had dedicated my time and efforts to serving. It was also the moment when I demanded to settle the score. In an instant, I went from being a trusted member of the team to being labeled as the troublemaker, the thorn in their side. It was a painful realization, but it finally brought me face to face with my true identity: just a nobody who had wanted to be a rock'n'roll star all his life…

I knew deep down that I wasn't a musical genius, lacking the name and fame that could propel me to stardom. Nevertheless, I had traveled the world and written a few decent and classic songs along the way. I had given my all for the entertainment of fans, knowing full well that their admiration could never fully repay the debts I had incurred. But there was a sense of satisfaction in knowing that I had left my mark, even if it was a small one. To this day, I still take pride in what I have accomplished. I am grateful for the opportunities that came my way and for the privilege of making music alongside one of the greatest musicians in the world. No one can ever take those experiences away from me. As for all the other accolades and recognition, they have become irrelevant in the grand scheme of things. I have learned to live without them. I came from nowhere and went straight back there. It was my salvation!

The SpeedKings name was used although the band never played the show. Punk Rock Fest Mexico City, 2003.

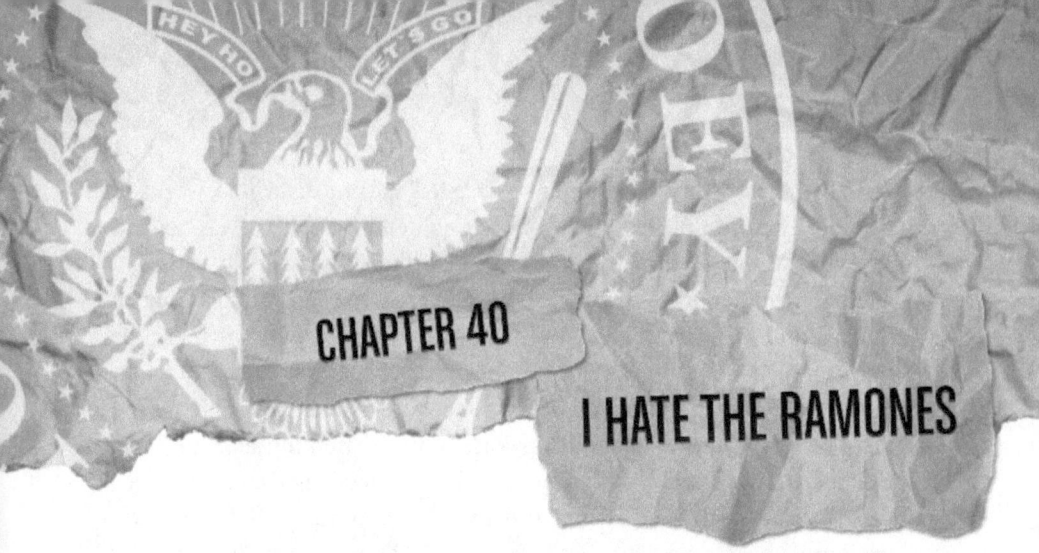

CHAPTER 40
I HATE THE RAMONES

"The man of knowledge must be able not only to love his enemies but also to hate his friends." - Friedrich Nietzsche

Here I stand, right back at the starting point, back at square one. The tale has concluded. Perhaps prematurely, maybe not in the manner we had anticipated, but undeniably in the way it was destined to conclude. It did not transpire as a love story, nor did it culminate in a blissful ending. However, it was not entirely abysmal either. Ultimately, it served as a reminder of reality, the perspective that most of us must embrace. Reaching for the stars is a lofty pursuit, but attaining the pinnacle of success in rock and roll is an arduous journey. It's a long way to the top if you wanna rock and roll. This brings to mind AC/DC. Angus Young held no fondness for the Ramones. He recalls: "The Ramones, I only heard them once; I heard a song, and it did nothing. It seemed to me like the first band I was ever in, and I'm sure even that was better – and was when I was 12".

I have to confess I've been an AC/DC enthusiast for as long as I can remember. It all started back in the mid-seventies when I first crossed paths with Bon Scott. But the Ramones have got a special place in my heart, too. What I adore about them is their unique blend of bubblegum punk tunes, effortlessly played with a touch of that groovy sixties melodic vibe and harmonious twist. It's like a musical fusion that hits all the right notes and keeps me hooked.

On the flip side, the Ramones dragged me into a whole world of trouble. They completely transformed my life in a way that was beyond my wildest imagination. When I crossed paths with Marky, it felt like a fateful encounter. It was the pivotal moment that twisted and distorted all the love and admiration I had for them. And that's precisely why I declare my vehement hatred for the Ramones, not as a mere band but as an unwavering institution. If you dare utter a word against them, it's akin to blasphemy. In the eyes of countless fans, they were nothing short of Gods. But deep down, I know that some of them were lesser gods. However, it's time for me to move on from this bitterness, although it lingers as a profound heartache. But let's face it, people eventually get over heartbreaks.

What is way more important is that this one's for all the badass kids out there, past, present, and future, who've ever longed to be rock stars.

Many will try, but only a select few will be chosen. Yet, don't let that stop you. Keep chasing those dreams with every ounce of your being. Because let me tell you, those dreams may not be worth much in the grand scheme of things, but oh, the ride is something else.

I've been there, just like you. Maybe we don't have an abundance of raw talent, but that doesn't matter in the end. The crazy adventures, the wild experiences - they're all worth it. And who knows? Amongst you fearless dreamers, one might just rise to stardom. So go on, my friends. Embrace the madness and rock it like there's no tomorrow. Go for it and give it your all!

Look at me now. I wanted to be a rockstar all my life… But truth be told, I never really put in the effort to become a master musician, and most probably, I even lacked the natural talent. However, fate smiled upon me, and I got a taste of the rock'n'roll lifestyle. It wasn't a complete sex and drugs frenzy, but I went deeper into that world than most people ever will.

It's funny how people underestimate what it's really like. They only see the glamorous side, the wild parties, and the endless fun. But being in a band, going on tour, and playing night after night is really hard work. Those intensive tours with hardly any days off take their toll. Sure, you can choose to party all night long, but after a few days, exhaustion sets in, and your performance suffers. And if you decide to dabble in drugs, it might seem cool at first, but it slowly wears down your body and mind until you're a wreck. And as for those dreams of endless sex orgies, well, the reality is you rarely have the time to charm all those ladies into your bed.

But that doesn't mean nothing happens. You just have to go with the flow and embrace the mystery of what's coming next. Life on the road is full of surprises and unexpected twists. It's like riding a wave, never knowing where it will take you. It's about living in the moment, taking risks, and embracing the chaos. The road may be tough, but it's also thrilling and exhilarating. It's like being on stage, feeling the adrenaline surge through your veins as you connect with an audience who shares your love for music.

Rocking out isn't all glitz and glamour. It's a wild ride filled with highs and lows, struggles and triumphs. It's about embracing the rawness of life and channeling it into every note you play. It's about pushing boundaries and defying expectations. And even though it may not always be easy, there's something magical about being part of a world fueled by the power of rock'n'roll.

The greatest thrill of being part of a rock 'n' roll band is the exhilarating kick and surge of adrenaline that courses through your veins when you take the stage, witnessing the crowd revel in your music. It's an indescribable feeling of fulfillment to witness the wild, passionate gaze in the eyes of your fans as they passionately sing and shout along to every song.

But just like that, it's all over. Not a single regret in sight. I've experienced it all and lived through every moment. There comes a time when you realize that you have savoured every ounce of joy that this journey has to offer, and it's time to move on. It's better to burn out than to fade away.

In the years following my time with the SpeedKings, I started a few other bands, but I couldn't bring myself to dive back into the whirlwind of touring. The Starlet Motherfuckers, P.O.G.O.Z, The Electric Thunder Syndicate, The Sonic Salvations, and The Suicide City Bluesbreakers provided their own moments of fun, but they never quite matched the sheer satisfaction I had once felt. Deep down, I knew it was time to pass the torch onto a new generation, allowing them to carry on the legacy.

It's high time to move on. If you embrace the suck, you move the fuck forward! Lately, I can't get the words of Stiv Bators out of my head. They're swirling around in my mind, and I find comfort in what he said: *"If I could do it all over again… I wouldn't…"*

CHAPTER 41

COMING OF AGE

"Well, my misery's without company
My partners in crime have been taken from me
We used to laugh about our legacy...
...I'd hate to think it's a conspiracy
No one's left who makes sense to me....
And the scum lives on
All my friends are gone
Why they gotta die so young
And the scum lives on"

THE SCUM LIVES ON - DEMOLITION 23 - 1994

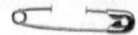

This is my coming of age. According to the odds, I can confidently declare that I have surpassed the halfway point of my existence. As I reflect on the remarkable first half of my life, I am filled with a sense of awe. With each passing year, I become increasingly cognizant of the preciousness of life, recognizing that not everyone is fortunate enough to receive this invaluable gift. It is often said that "the good die young," and sadly, many of my dear friends from yesteryears have become nothing more than cherished memories. However, I aspire to keep their memory alive, ensuring that they are not consigned to oblivion. Although none of us are destined to live forever, let alone etched into the collective consciousness, I am grateful for this fact, for our minds are already brimming with thoughts and experiences.

I ain't one to forget easily. The arteries in my brain are still rockin' and rollin'. Cracking open those old boxes filled with faded photographs, newspaper clippings, and random trinkets that were once treasured but now gather dust, they bring back memories that have long been tucked away. And let me tell ya, it's crystal clear that I've always marched to the beat of my own drum. I did it my way, and I have no regrets. See, I've always believed in embracing the things I've done rather than dwelling on the things I haven't. There are moments in my life that fall under the category of "irresistible urges." I couldn't resist them even though I knew deep down they were bound to crash and burn or not amount to anything significant.

I've encountered this predicament countless times, and it has consistently overwhelmed me. It led me on a global journey, taking me to every corner of the world. I worked on various continents and I rocked on so many stages, pouring my heart and soul into my music. Did it bring me any tangible benefits? Well, experiential, it definitely did. Emotionally, however, the scars on my soul tell a different story. As for material wealth, I can't say it made me financially wealthy. But true riches lie in other realms.

The common saying goes that good health is the ultimate treasure. I won't argue with that. I'm not here to whine about adding another year to my age. Instead, I'm thankful for being given the chance to celebrate another trip around the sun. Many of my peers and companions weren't fortunate enough to have that privilege.

The ones responsible for my wealth are my children. They possess an abundance of affection and a plethora of life lessons. Witnessing your offspring, who can sometimes be cunning like snakes, mature and flourish is the most precious gift one can receive. Kids, one must do what is necessary, not necessarily what one desires. This aspect is crucial to the overall journey. However, nothing compares to the satisfaction of knowing that they are thriving and have discovered their purpose in this chaotic world.

At the end of the day, my wealth stems from the incredible individuals who surround me and whom I cherish wholeheartedly. My emotional bank account for relationships was deeply in debt for a prolonged period. One after another, my romantic endeavors crumbled. While I presented myself as a pillar of strength for my children, there remained an insatiable longing for the perfect partner. A companion who embodied both love and desire in equal measure. However, every time I clung stubbornly to my preconceived notions of who this soulmate should be, it ultimately ended in disappointment. It was only when I mustered the courage to discard all preconceived ideals and embrace change that she unexpectedly appeared. And she remains by my side, an unwavering presence in my life. Together, we flourish in abundance.

Have I always been, for everyone, a righteous individual? I cannot claim to be on the path to beatification or canonization. Quite the opposite, actually! My journey as a person who contributes to relationships has been arduous and lengthy. It has been a process of trial and error spanning decades. I must acknowledge my role in the suffering and anguish experienced by others. I do not anticipate forgiveness or oblivion. That is the course I am destined to follow. That's my fate. It was never intended, yet it materialized. I refuse to absolve myself for allowing this to occur. If it were possible, I'd reverse the course of events, but what's done is done. However, it has served as a valuable lesson, urging me to strive for improvement and be a superior version of myself.

After unlocking the door to relational complexity, my life took on a whole new light. The intricate web of existence suddenly became more straightforward, offering me a sense of tranquility and a clear understanding of my priorities.

A crucial aspect of true wealth is the freedom from the compulsion to do anything. It's not about being obligated but rather having the ability to choose. It's about finding the serenity to let go of certain things, knowing that you have the power to pursue them if you so desire.

The place I find myself in today is not solely a result of my own efforts but largely due to the individuals I choose to have in my life. They have created an atmosphere and ambiance that has allowed me to grow and flourish. These are the people who hold a special place in my heart, whom

I deeply value and respect and would go to great lengths to support. I am confident that they would do the same for me.

Throughout my life, I've held a special place in my heart for my friends. However, it's important to recognize that not all friends are created equal. Some friendships go beyond the realm of the heart and tap into the depths of my mind, becoming my trusted confidants and sounding boards.

These extraordinary individuals become more than just companions; they become interlocutors of my innermost thoughts and emotions. They possess the ability to engage in deep conversations that stimulate my intellectual curiosity and challenge my perspectives. We delve into topics that ignite a fire within me, pushing the boundaries of conventional thinking.

These friends, the ones who connect with me on a mental level, are a rarity. They are the ones who truly understand the complexities of my mind and appreciate the intricate layers that make me who I am. With them, I can explore the depths of my thoughts and share my deepest fears and aspirations without judgment or hesitation.

In a world where superficial connections often prevail, finding these extraordinary friends is like discovering a hidden gem in a vast desert. They bring color and vibrancy to my life, injecting it with excitement and adventure. With them by my side, I feel invincible, ready to take on any challenge that comes my way.

As for everyone else, well, they are nothing more than insignificant scum. And unfortunately, the scum lives on.

I've been the stepping stone for all the "scum," the leeches who love to ride on my momentum for far too long. I used to be naive enough to expect gratitude in return. But that couldn't be further from the truth. Most people are stingy when it comes to recognition and paying back their debts. They prefer to attribute everything to their own abilities. And if it ended there, I might still find it in my heart to forgive them. But these types of individuals have the audacity to not only claim credit for themselves but also have the nerve to make others believe that I'm the ungrateful mutt they generously helped.

Some individuals seize the opportunity when circumstances align perfectly, finding themselves in the right place at the right time and effortlessly riding the wave of their momentum. It baffles me how some people can be so self-absorbed, completely oblivious to the needs and feelings of others.

Sometimes, it's the little, absurd things that reveal so much. Other times, it's a blatant display of excess, a true embodiment of greed and indulgence in certain individuals. Either way, it speaks volumes about them, not me. You see, these individuals are like a broken record, stuck in a repetitive loop of consumption and self-gratification. They dance to the beat of their own gluttony, oblivious to the consequences of their actions. It's as if they've become slaves to their own desires.

In the end, their gluttony is their own burden to bear. It may define them in the eyes of others, but it holds no power over me.

These so-called friends who thrive on exploiting kindness are the epitome of betrayal. It's sad to see them act this way, but at the same time, I'm grateful because their actions have revealed their true colors. I know exactly who they are now. Once they realize that you see right through their façade, they distance themselves from you. And you know what? That act of shunning is actually a blessing in disguise. It protects you from further exploitation. So, thank you for that.

In the end, it all boils down to striking a harmonious chord between the beats of your heart and the thoughts in your mind. There's this saying that often floats around, claiming that if you're young and lean toward the left, you lack rationality, while if you're older and lean toward the right, you lack compassion. But the truth is, the world isn't simply a binary choice between left and right. The key lies in finding that delicate equilibrium between the fiery passion in your heart and the logical reasoning of your mind. This delicate balance is what defines my integrity.

Sometimes, I find myself yearning to embody a little more of the audacious spirit of JR Ewing from the legendary TV series Dallas. He once uttered these words, "Once you up on integrity, everything becomes easy." Yet, as much as I might admire his brazenness, I find it impossible to follow in his footsteps. Every single day, when I gaze into the mirror, I am confronted with the unwavering presence of the person I see staring back at me. There's no escaping him. So, rather than fighting against this reflection, I choose to embrace it. As disheartening as it may be at times, I've come to realize that aligning myself with my own reflection is the only viable option.

Finding the sweet spot where my heart and mind converge allows me to navigate through life with authenticity and integrity. It's a constant dance between passion and reason, a tightrope walk between emotions and logic.

So, let the world debate about left and right, right and wrong; I'll be right here, reveling in the exquisite balance between my heart's wild rhythm and my mind's calculated melodies. In this symphony of self-discovery, I'll continue to embrace the person I see in the mirror, for he is my unwavering guide.

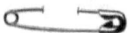

I have absorbed wisdom and knowledge from various avenues, absorbing their essence and infusing it into my own unique artistic vision. This journey has taught me that true fulfillment lies in pursuing what sets your soul ablaze. Throughout it all, my mantra has remained unwavering: "Follow your passion, and success will effortlessly follow suit."

Life's twists and turns may have led me down an unconventional path, but I have embraced the ride with open arms. Now, armed with a renewed sense of purpose and an unwavering commitment, I will continue to dance to the beat of my own drum.

The beginning of the latter half has just commenced, and I can't help but feel a sense of anticipation for what lies ahead. This farmer, weary from the toils of the past, has now found solace in unfamiliar terrain.

Perched upon the crest of this quaint Tuscan village, I envision myself as the reigning monarch of this domain, the King of the Hill.

The older I get, the more I realize the real luxuries in life are time, slow mornings, and the freedom to choose whatever I want to do.

"The nicest thing about coming of age is that I can do whatever I like." - **Cilla Black**

"For me it's about the music, and it always has been. Maybe for some other it's more about the money."
Ace Frehley - KISS

POSTSCRIPT

While penning down this book, my life took a dramatic twist. A year ago, my father came to live with us, but he was no longer the towering figure of strength and pride that I had always known. Dementia had taken hold of him, robbing him of his former self. Some things in life are beyond our control, and when the weight of dementia settles on your shoulders, there is no escape. All you can hope for is a nurturing and caring environment to support you through it all.

The relationship I shared with my father had its fair share of ups and downs. He could be tough on me, imposing strict rules and expectations. However, amidst the clashes and disagreements, he always respected the choices I made. We may have argued over trivial matters, but despite our divergent viewpoints in the past, our bond today is unbreakable.

I vividly recall the day he placed a picture of a band on his dresser. It was a symbol of his understanding that being in a band was my way of finding joy and fulfillment in life. Just as I cherished my own musical journey, he found solace in his own passions. And now, as he faces the challenges brought on by dementia, I am by his side, offering comfort and support every step of the way.

Life's twists and turns have led me to this point, where I find myself navigating the complexities of my father's condition. Spoon-feeding my father is undoubtedly more challenging for me than it is for him. This experience has not only humbled me but has also forced me to reevaluate my true priorities in life. We all face heartbreaks of varying magnitudes, and we each bear our own burdens. Life may be challenging, but it has bestowed upon me invaluable lessons about humility, empathy, and the importance of embracing life's hardships. It has taught me to appreciate the simple yet profound pleasures that can be found in caring for another human being. And ultimately, it has shaped me into a stronger, more compassionate individual, ready to face whatever obstacles may come my way.

It is a journey that requires strength and resilience but also compassion and love. As I walk on this path alongside my father, I am reminded of the power of family and the unwavering bonds that hold us together.

> *Walking through the crossfire heart*
> *Feeling heavy and hopeless*
> *And wonderin' how I ever will*
> *See through this darkness.*
> *Every drop of blood can*
> *Be so beautiful*
> *And I sure was bleedin' the drops by the bucketful.*
>
> *I have the strength to endure*
> *And all the love so pure*
>
> *Dee Dee Ramone – Strength to Endure*

ACKNOWLEDGEMENTS

I owe a debt of gratitude to my amazing wife and kids for their unwavering support during the moments when I was hunched over my typewriter or lost in my own world, grappling with memories and weaving them into the fabric of this book. Their patience and understanding have been invaluable.

A big thank you goes out to my friends who have been by my side since the beginning, constantly fueling my inspiration for this book with their endless supply of ideas, captivating stories, and pictures that collected dust for far too long: Jari-Pekka Laitio-Ramone, Kenneth Bergdahl, Andre Dahlman, Stevey Jay, Glen 'Jack' Meyer Rotsaert, Diederik 'Sniper,' Helena Peterson, Steve Gee, Texas Terri Laird, Rebecca Pride, Hannu 'Woimasointu' Jokinen, Jari 'Juki' Lehtola, Fredrik 'Freddy' Eriksson, Rich Travers, Ludo Halsberghe, UxJx Neggörath, Bram van Schaik, Izumi Kazuhiro, Hans 'Vito Jr' Verbeke, Dominiek 'Dee Jaywalker' Decandt, Ed 'Goodlife' Verhaeghe, Martin Vantomme, Thomas Goze, Winny Kas, Stiegermeister Ramone, Damo 'Long Gone Loser', Anna Piella Castells, Alfredo Cordeiro, Celine Moray, Jan Beddies, Leandro Ciocca, Frank Droll, Gaston RamonesForever, Koldo Idigoras, Kurt 'Curtis' Herman, Tony De Block, Patrick Bruneel, Cindy Frey, Monka, Madde. I apologize deeply if I happened to overlook any of your names. The passage of time has also taken its toll on my own memory.

A big thank you to a publishing partner in crime: David Gamage and the Earth Island crew. We do Punk Books! Hell Yeah!

A few kind souls lent their expertise to the technical aspects of this book. Their contribution and dedication made all of this possible.

This tale wouldn't have come to life without the presence of my bandmates Stevey, Vito, Jack, Dee, and our road crew UxJx, Tim Yult, Warren Cohen, Tsepitch, Lode, Stitch, and Sofie.

A big pat on the back for Marky Ramone, drummer extraordinaire! Regardless of what others may assume about my feelings towards Marky Ramone, I raise my glass to him, my dear old companion. He may be an asshole, but damn, he's one hell of a drummer. I'm grateful that we once shared a friendship and a lot of stages. Deep within my soul, I am indebted to this man for the incredible years we spent together. He taught me so much - not only the things I detest but also the fervor for the beat that runs through my veins. Never blame anyone in your life. Good people give you happiness. Bad people give you experience. Worst people give you a lesson and best people give you memories. You gave me a little of everything!

And how could I possibly overlook the most essential of them all... A huge shoutout of gratitude to the devoted fans across the globe and the band that I love to hate: The RAMONES!

In Memory of Adrienne 'Sheena' Manglos (1957-2019) – Gone but not forgotten! I wish you had found the time to write that *"We're not Groupies"* book together with Cee.

PHOTOCREDITS

All photos and illustrations copyright of Nick Cooper except:

    Jari-Pekka Laitio-Ramone – 150, 225, 226, 255
    Bram van Schaik – 206, 289
    Vito D'Agostini – 55, 223, 240
    Dee Jaywalker – 215, 225, 340
    Glen "Jack" Meyer Rotsaert – 369, 383, 399, 405, 418
    Kenneth Bergdahl – 254
    Damo "Long Gone Loser" – 283
    Frank Droll – 242, 257
    Helena Peterson – 256
    Rebecca Pride – 409
    Kurt "Curtis" Herman – 91
    Ronny Wynants – 212
    Diederik "Sniper" Van Der Sype – 287, 289
    John Holmstrom – 266
    Adrienne "Sheena" Manglos – 266
    Eddy Verbruggen – 316, 326, 327, 328
    Akihiro Takayama –346, 347, 349
    Gaston Ramone – 416, 417

    Drawings by Tom de Geeter – 1, 2, 29

Every reasonable effort has been made to trace copyright holders of material reproduced in this book, but if any have been advertently overlooked then publishers will be glad to hear from them.

Special thanks to Willy-Jan van Gemert for the backcover picture of the 2002 ALIVE CD release. Back in the day we never credited him for it so now is the time!

DISCOGRAPHY, PRINTED MATTERS & SHIRT DESIGNS

A comprehensive exploration in the Music and Book releases of Nick Cooper.

Cover of the 1984 cassette album. Less than 20 were produced.
Today this tape and the lyrics fanzine are an impossible find.

A limited edition vinyl album was released in 2023 in yellow and pink vinyl. 100 copies each.

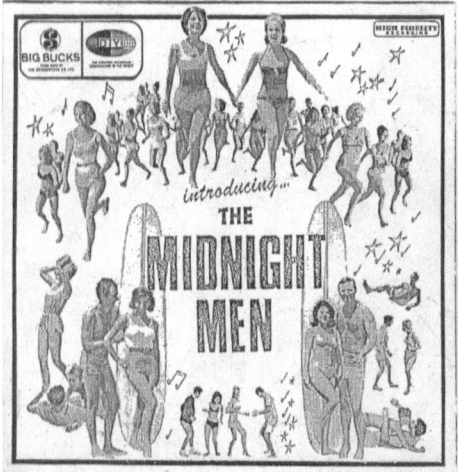

The fake debut 7" that never got pressed.

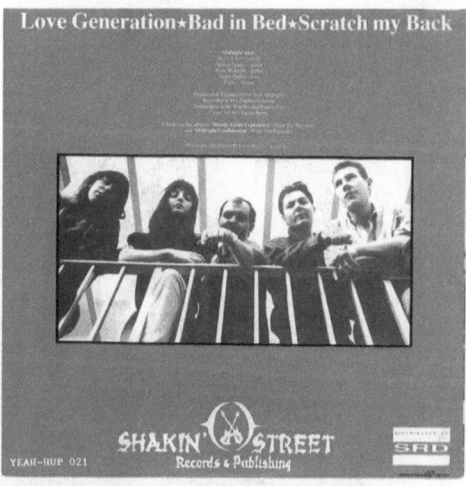

LOVE-INN, KILLIN' 7" on Shakin' Street Records UK. Red vinyl.
The testpressing has the extra track Scratch My Back by The Damned.

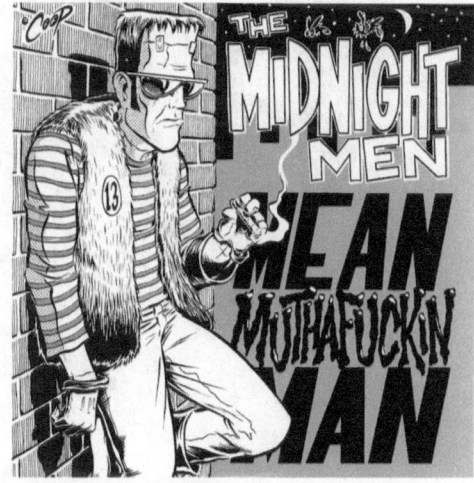

TEENAGE GANGBANG - MEAN MUTHA FUCKIN' MAN 7"
on Sympathy For The Record Industry Records USA on blue and purple vinyl.

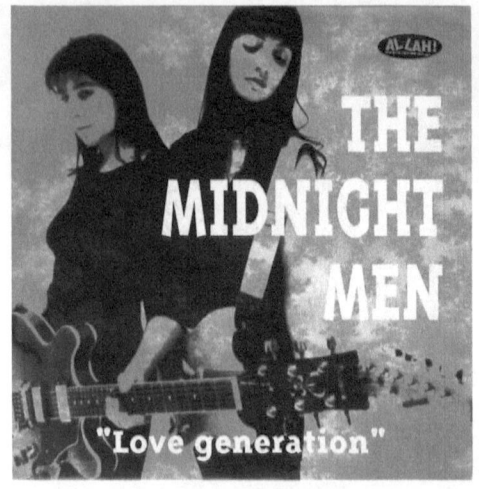

HELLZAPOPPIN' 7"
Freebie with The Thing Magazine - Greece

LOVE GENERATION Promo 7"
Released on ALLAH! Records Belgium

I WANT YOUR BLOOD one sided 12"
White vinyl - 25 copies only - Private pressing.

MONDO TEENO EXPERIENCE

CANDY MAN	WHEN YOU SAY GOODBYE
BAD IN BED	SOMETHING I SAID
INVISIBLE CREATURES	POSSESSED
ANGEL EYES	NIGHT OF THE SADIST
ACID BABY	CALL ME SKY
GIMME	LAST CARESS

THE MIDNIGHT MEN ARE
DIZZY LIZZY (vocals), SPACEY STACEY (guitar, backing vocals), NICK MIDNIGHT (guitar, backing vocals), SUGAR DADDY (bass), CURTIS (drums), RON DA DO RON RON (breakmaster)

additional musicians
VDK DE HAAN (guitar), HAZEL (backing vocals)

Recorded at Mrs Studios, Nov. 1989
Produced by Nick Midnight
Engineered by The Dangerous Brothers

Front cover photography by Ron – Backcover photography by Nol

SEND NO FLOWERS

JOIN THE MIDNIGHT MEN – FANCLUB!
Brug. vennoyeplein 15
B-8980 Kortrijk
BELGIUM
tel 32 (0)56 225694

Midnight Men debut Album MONDO TEENO EXPERIENCE.
Released on Punk Etc Records. Black vinyl only.

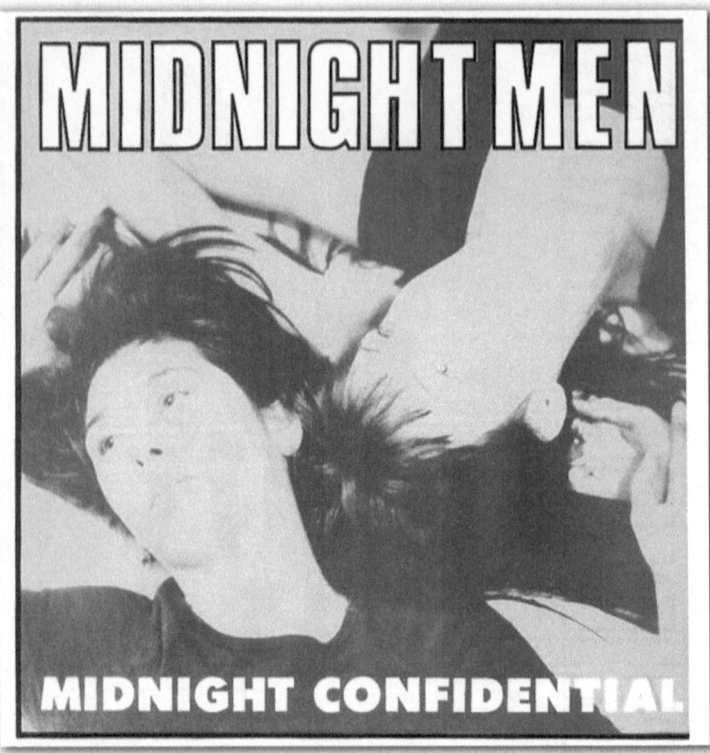

MIDNIGHT CONFIDENTIAL - compilation of odd and rare to find tracks.
Released on Wipe Out Records in Greece. Black vinyl only.

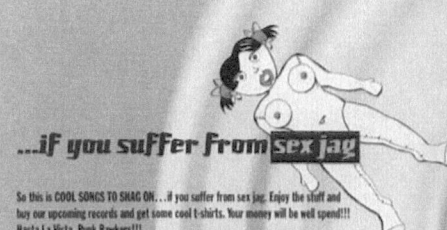

...if you suffer from sex jag

SMOKIN' TROLL RECORDS PRESENTS THE KINGS OF SMUT...
The BUCKWEEDS!
cool songs to shag on

So this is COOL SONGS TO SHAG ON...if you suffer from sex jag. Enjoy the stuff and buy our upcoming records and get some cool t-shirts. Your money will be well spend!!! Hasta La Vista, Punk Rawkers!!!

Get in touch with the Kings of Smut:
The BUCKWEEDS! • Burg. Vercruysselaan 15 • B-8500 Kortrijk • BELGIUM
e-mail: HYPERLINK mail to: sa_cooper@hotmail.com
web site: HYPERLINK http://www.angelfire.com/ny/makemydaypunk

Sleeve design and artwork by Curtis Blow • Photography by Double Duty our loyal roadie

© Smokin' Troll Records - ℗ The Buckweeds!
[All songs written by The Buckweeds! except 'Beat the Meat' by the Riverdales and 'I only Lick Butt' by the Queers.
Lyrics rewritten by the band [Teenage Head Music 1998 [This is a Your Father is an Idiot!" records production]

Recorded at Midas Studios (B) and Studios 195 (NL).
[Produced by The Buckweeds! • Engineered by Paul • Mixed by Tony Midas and Pat 195 • Mastered at Midas]

[WARNING]

This is a horrible platter: if you place it into the CD-player, we guarantee that you will be awe-struck by this vulgar, gross, horrible, blunt, tasteless, naive, onslaught of sentimental trash. And if this isn't enough, the backing to these brattish, nasal renditions of bland rock and roll songs is supplied by the BUCKWEEDS! who have nothing else to offer than their own 'Wall of Sound'; a blitzkrieg of slashing cymbals sitting on top of a vast, primitive horde of thundering bass and guitars.
All together, this makes a vast conglomeration of musical garbage on such an abundant scale, that you can't help but be impressed by it.

If any of you are offended by the contents of this package, we recommend that you place this disc back in it's rack, and forget any queer notions you had of ever buying it or playing it.

THIS AWESOME CD CONTAINS THE FOLLOWING SONGS
- BUCKWEEDS! ARE GO! - The opening song which really is 'Alright' but only a couple of verses are used here as the CD-intro - OKLAHOMA CITY B.A. - An un-'tribute' to white punk Terry McVeigh for damaging federal property. He blew something else than his nose. Don't try this at home! - TEENAGE ROCK'N'ROLL SUICIDE - Eddie Cockring rises from the dead, followed by a little taste of our music hall ambitions is 'Gay-sus Christ Superstof'. Nothing more than stupid, mindless and obnoxious juvenile delinquent fun. If you are bored of wasting your time, waste your life and blow your head off. - SEX PHONE GIRLS - You can find their phone numbers in all kinds of mens magazines. Dirty girls never say no, that is why we love them so. - POWER IS OK! - Hear all about the things that happened in the White House Oval Room. This songs was written before Zippergate became a nationwide sensation. - DOUBLE D CUP - CQ took over the leadvocals and rants about these heavenly female balloons. You actually hear him sing the song without his pants on! - WEENIE HAIR - What would you do if you discovered one morning that all your pubic hair was gone? Break down and cry? Or start a career as the Kojak of the triple X? - ZORRO EL PIMPO - Take a stroll down Tijuana and meet the pimp of all pimps. If you want a girl you better be prepared for the flamenco. - CAPT'N CRUNCH - If you can't get nookie, go for the cookie. This song will probably never make it as a commercial but it would surely beat the hell out of the lame tunes the Capt'n is accompanied by right now. - I ONLY LICK BUTT - It seems the Queers only drink Bud. And hey, who are the Buckweeds! to argue about that? - NYC - If we die, please bury us in the East Coast Scumfuck City. Home of CBGB's, The Ramones and Howard Stern. - JUGS - They're great to suck on, once you held one, you wanna hold a ton! Titty Flashing Galore! - KILL YOUR FAMILY - This is about the family of one of the band's members. Guess who's family it is and you get a free funeral service for yours! - POSSESSED - A cover version of an original by The Midnight Men, a band CQ and Curtis used to be in. Try and find their rare records now. - BEAT THE MEAT - This is originally by The Riverdales, but the Buckweeds! changed the lyrics and have been using it as the opening song for many of their live shows. - CJ JOE - Written for a fan of the band who got involved with some military child molester. Marines are assholes and we all got one in our underpants. - HEAVY MENTAL BIMBO - They're fat, they wear lot's of blueish make-up, short white leather skirts, fishnet stockings and high heeled boots. The only species on this earth who have an IQ that hits rock bottom. - BILL'S GOT A PROB - Zippergate explosion! Paula Jones, you're such a slut, Bill should have stabbed you in the gut! - THERE GOES THE NEIGHBOURHOOD - Do you wanna live next to the Buckweeds!? Yeah, I bet you would, but most of the folks grow grey hair having these guys around. And as concerned citizens, the Buckweeds! don't give a flying fuck. - THIS CD ALSO CONTAINS A LOT OF OTHER CRAP YOU CAN DISCOVER YOURSELF -

THE BUCKWEEDS! WOULD VERY MUCH LIKE TO THANK THE FOLLOWING ALIENS
FOR LETTING US INVADE THIS PLANET
Ourselves for being such a fine bunch of law abiding, politically correct, visiting granny after church on Sundays - kind of guys, Ron Van Winkle and Jim Darky for being there when this band first started out (It's a pity things didn't work out, but hey man, that's life!), Marino Punk appears courtesy of Freedom Records [+ 32 (56) 53 04 58], our devoted (s)crew Double D for managing all the roadstuff and for putting up with all our insults and Peter (Pan) the raving Jousie, Beru at XIII-Records Paris for baby-sitting Manny during the Summerfestivals, Ed Green Leaf Records (and Goodlife), the guy at Fried Chicken Record store for promoting our junk, Byron Ruoka of LameAss Recordz in Canadoh, Aaron Muentz of the Probe Magazine, Ronea Bryant of On the Rag records and Magazine, Setsuko Yoshino for keeping CQ on the right track during his stay in Tokyo, Ken Ishihara for being a good friend and Miki, Ryuta and Taka of Think Tank Pink Poup for sharing the stage with CQ, Love to Megumi of The Nil for lending her guitar, Yamazaki of Jiyuzo (best live house in Tokyo), Nao - chan for being so cute. The Tokyo scene rules! Hi Kazuhiro! Sauri - chan for sticking around!
Remember Wendy O Williams, Heavy Mental Bimbo extra-ordinaire, our ultimate suicide date!
Very special thanks to Pete Troll of Smokin' Troll for believing in us and taking the risk of releasing our sloppy stuff. Mucho thank you to the "Your Father is an Idiot!"-staff Barbie an Tina for some serious backscrubbing...
And let us not forget of the people who told us we sucked... you made us push our barriers of suckerness and sucksex even further ! We are very much obliged !

Get a life and stop being illiterate trash. Dig yourself into some of the books, bands and miscellaneous stuff mentioned here and your miserable life might look a little brighter:
All records by the Queers, Screeching Weasel, Riverdales, Nobodys, Down By Law, Lagwagon, NOFX, Bad Religion, Gits, Fastbacks, Sloppy Seconds, Mr. T Experience, Sarge Abuse, McRackins, Boris the Sprinkler, Connie Bungs, Doomas, Vindictives, Pennywise, Pink Lincolns, Pansy Division, 88 Fingers Louie, Hanson Brothers and all the other Goofballs, Nogoodniks...
Recommended reading: all books from Stewart Home, James Ellroy, C. Bukowski, Hunter S. Thompson, all RE/search stuff, Answer Me!, The Probe, Loaded, Bizarre, Mad Magazine.
Only drink Bud, Corona, Heineken BOB, Ten Dogs, Celis White, Gordon's Gin or Black Death Vodka. Mars bars rule!

COOL SONGS TO SHAG ON debut CD.
Released on Smokin' Troll Records UK - 1998.

DON'T WORRY IT'S ONLY PUNK ROCK Japanese Tour
promo CD on Smokin' Troll Records UK - 1999.

BETWEEN THE COVERS WITH THE BUCKWEEDS 7"..
Smokin' Troll Records UK - 1999 - Black vinyl..

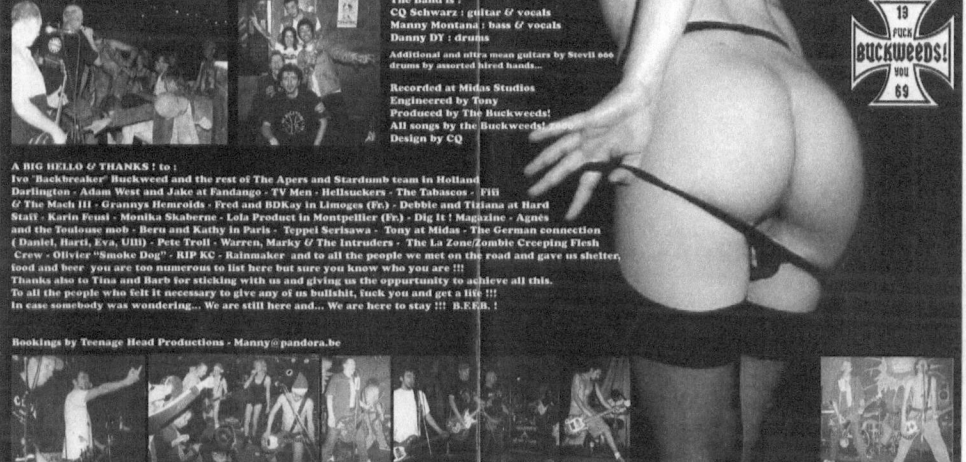

WHAT'S WRONG WITH ATTITUDE CD
Released on Fandago Records USA - 2000.

 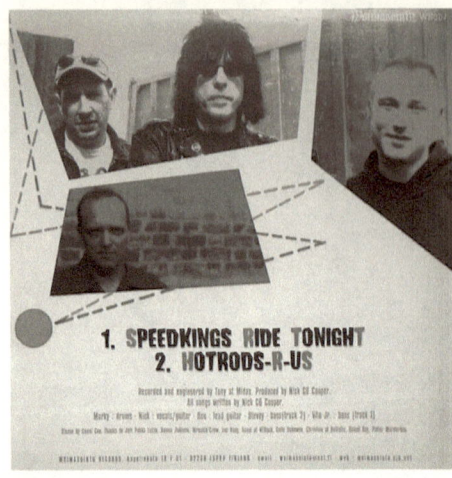

SPEEDKINGS RIDE TONIGHT 7"
Woimasointu Records Finland 2001 - On black, orange, blue, green marbled and red marbled vinyl.

RAWK OVER SCANDINAVIA 7"
Woimasointu Records Finland 2002 - On black, red and blue vinyl.

 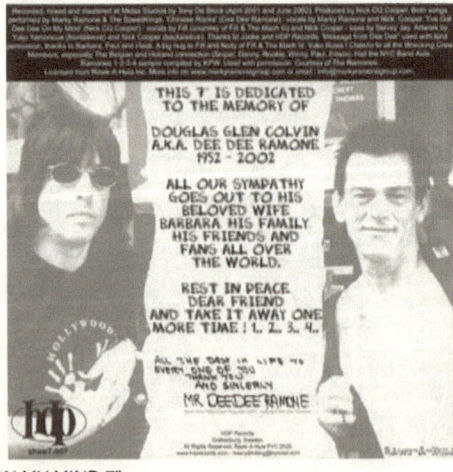

I'VE GOT DEE DEE ON MY MIND 7"
HDP Records Sweden 2002 - On black and brown marbled vinyl.

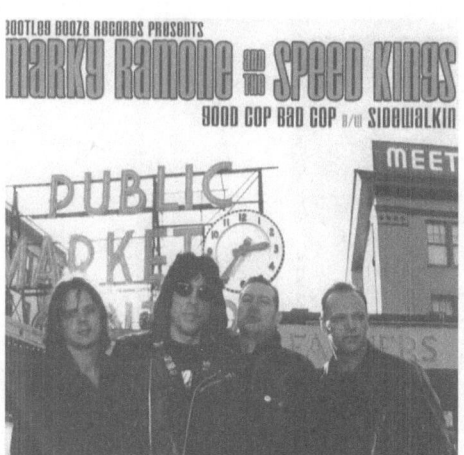

Good Cop Bad Cop
Bootleg Booze Records - 2003 - Black and white vinyl
Limited edition with Tattoo sticker.

Love Hates Me - US Tour promo
Devil's Shitburner Records - 2002 - Black and purple vinyl.

SpeedFins Compilation EP
Woimasointu Records - 2002

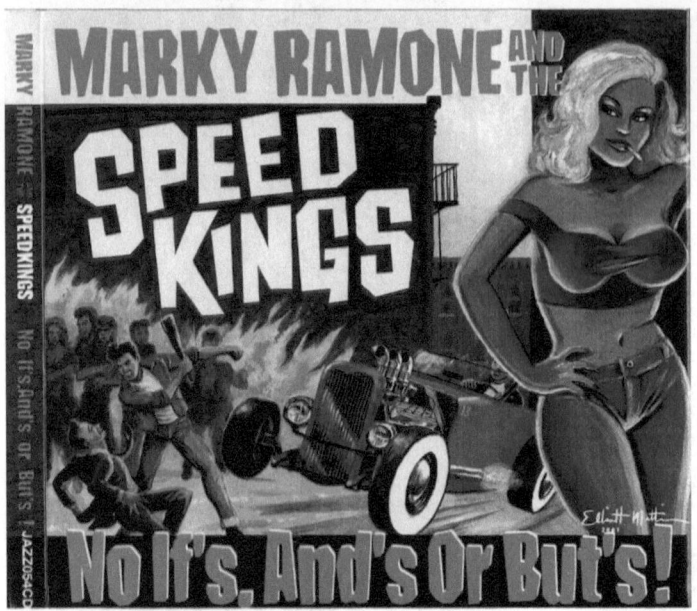

The WHITE JAZZ RECORDS (Sweden) release of the debut album "No If's, And's or But's!". Digipack CD only.

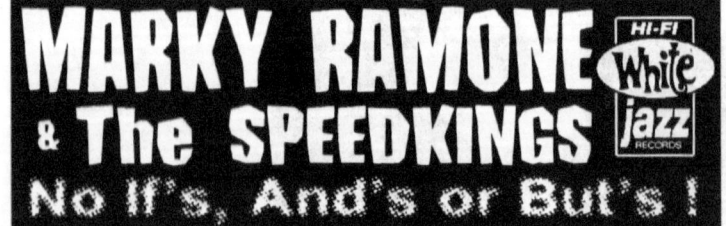

WHITE JAZZ Promo stickers.

Marky Ramone about the SpeedKings: "I liked what I saw, I liked what I heard. Becoming friends with these guys was the start of the new band. It was great to record the album and I am looking forward to perform this stuff live".

The SpeedKings about Marky Ramone: "From the first beat to be played, we knew this was right : an American classic to join the ranks. This band truly is the ideal combination of US and Euro thrash !"

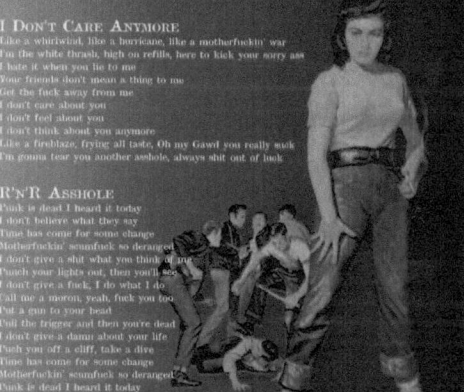

I Don't Care Anymore
Like a whirlwind, like a hurricane, like a motherfuckin' war
I'm the white thrash, high on refills, here to kick your sorry ass
I hate it when you lie to me
Your friends don't mean a thing to me
Get the fuck away from me
I don't care about you
I don't feel about you
I don't think about you anymore
Like a fireblaze, frying all taste, Oh my Gawd you really suck
I'm gonna tear you another asshole, always shit out of luck

R'n'R Asshole
Punk is dead I heard it today
I don't believe what they say
Time has come for some change
Motherfuckin' scumfuck so deranged
I don't give a shit what you think of me
Punch your lights out, then you'll see
I don't give a fuck, I do what I do
Call me a moron, yeah, fuck you too
Put a gun to your head
Pull the trigger and then you're dead
I don't give a damn about your life
Push you off a cliff, take a dive
Time has come for some change
Motherfuckin' scumfuck so deranged
Punk is dead I heard it today
I don't believe what they say

Fuck Shit Up
I hate it when you talk to me
I hate it when you walk with me
I hate it when you're fighting me
I hate it when you're liking me
I hate it when you look at me
I hate it when you're touching me
I hate it when you're asking me
I hate it when you're begging me
I hate it when you're calling me
I hate it when you come to me
I hate it when you're cursing me
I hate it when you're hurting me

Saturday Night
Time and time again, I call you on the phone
But always that machine tells me you ain't home
I've waited all week to see you again
But you're fooling around with just another man
I don't want you near me
I don't want to see you
I don't want to hear you
I don't want to feel you
I'm not gonna take it
You're not gonna break me
But I can't get around you, wasting my... Saturday Night
Now I'm in this place with Sheena on my side
You're giving me that look and you're putting up a fight
Cos is pulling hair and Sheena kicks you out
You're trying to escape in the steaming hot crowd

Girls & Gasoline
I saw you passing
by the custom shop
just the other day
I can't stop thinking of the way,
you looked at me
Your angel eyes are
burning holes
deep inside my soul
The devil told me
I gotta have you
before I take the fall
I was standing there
waiting by the church
Just a Sunday morning
trying to hide my hurt
Your dad came up to me
and told me to get lost
He shouldn't have crossed my
path, now he will pay the cost
Your daddy tells me
I smell of girls and gasoline
But all my heart does
is pumping up adrenaline
Speeding down the Interstate
I try to run from sin
You're riding shotgun,
the law is closing in
There's no escape from here,
this is where it ends
No more running
death is my only friend

HotRods-R-Us
You're all I want, youre all I need
You drive me crazy baby, I just can't breath
Roll the dice, spin the wheel
Buckle up honey, I'll show you how it feels
We're all greased up, we've got nowhere to go
Hot Rods-R-Us
Well, I'm a loser, I'll never learn
Come with me Baby watch me burn
I'm a demon, a speeding ghost
I've got three carburetors, dual exhaust

Sex Phone Girls
Saw your number in a magazine
You're the sluttiest babe I've ever seen
Dial your number, please pick up the phone
But all I hear is the busy tone
I bet you're home
Pick up the phone
I just wanna hear you moan
Bleach blond sluts want it up their ass
Fuck a teen in front of the class
Dial that number, five one on one
Better get ready for some adult fun
But maybe you're a fake, you're a fraud
I must admit it's a scary thought
Fondle your tits while you ride the bike
And you turn out to be an ugly chick

Weenie Hair
Stop looking at me now dude
Don't give me that stupid stare
Seems to me you never saw
A guy without weenie hair
Slap my shoulder, comfort me
Say I shouldn't care
But obviously you're not the one
With the missing Weenie Hair
I get around to find some help
Is anybody out there
I get on my knees and start to beg
Please trade me your spare
I am bald, yes I am naked
All the way down there
I wanna wig of pubic hair
To hide the lack of Weenie Hair
I'm the Kojak of the Triple X
No curlies in my underwear
I'd rather be a normal guy
And look like a grizzly bear
Some jock at school don't think it's fair
I sing about my weenie hair
So make my day if you dare
I'll burn off all your weenie hair

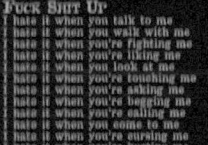

Bornin' Rubber
Double spinnin', dripping gasoline
Satisfaction is guaranteed
Satisfy your and my desire
Just a little push and set it on fire
Hellfire Ada, poison bite
Burning rubber on a summer's night
Living on carbon monoxide
Supersonic turbo suicide
Hey, baby you are all I need
I've got 6 on track mind built for speed

UP's Girl
UPs girl, UPs girl
You make me hard
When you deliver, I start to shiver
You drive me nuts
She's always on time
I wanna make her mine, My UP's girl
Cruising through town
Dressed in sexy brown
My kinda girl
Ups girl, UPs girl
You drive me mad
When we meet again, she's glued to my lips
My UP's girl
I'm doing it again
With her in her van
My UP's girl

Fuck Me
Boyfriend, lovers, daddy's lovers
I don't give a shit... Fuck me
Pimps and hookers,
damn good lookers
I don't give a shit... Fuck me
Hold his hand, wear his ring
Forget about the guy and... Fuck me
Be a cheat, bitch in heat
No one gives a damn... Fuck me

Manuelita
We're coming down to Argentina
We're gonna rock every cantina
Cool dudes and pretty señoritas
And in Brazil we'll rock you all
Playin' hard the rock'n'roll
Slamdancin' till you all fall
Sao Paulo, Rio, Porto Alegre, Mar del Plata
Americana, Curitiba, Buenos Aires, Pelotas
Recife, Mendoza, Cordoba, Belo Horizonte
Limeira, Vitoria, Bahia Blanca, Manaus
Barranquilla

All lyrics printed by permission

"No If's, And's or But's!" CD release on FOGON - Argentina.
CD Jewel Pack with booklet.

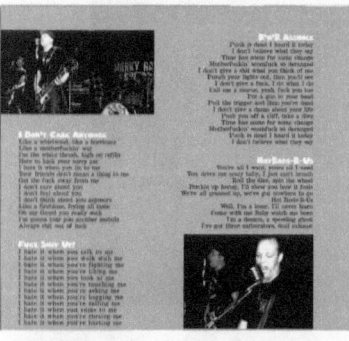

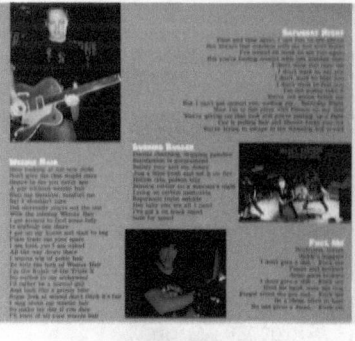

The Japanese release of the Speedkings debut album on JVC Records.

"Legends Bleed" CD release on Thirsty Ear - USA.
CD Jewel Pack with booklet.

The 'ALIVE' CD was released by Rawk-A-Hula Records as a Fanclub Edition in September 2002.
The SpeedQueen album was available with the white Mandy Ellis sleeve and the black Danielle Deville cover.
500 copies pressed.

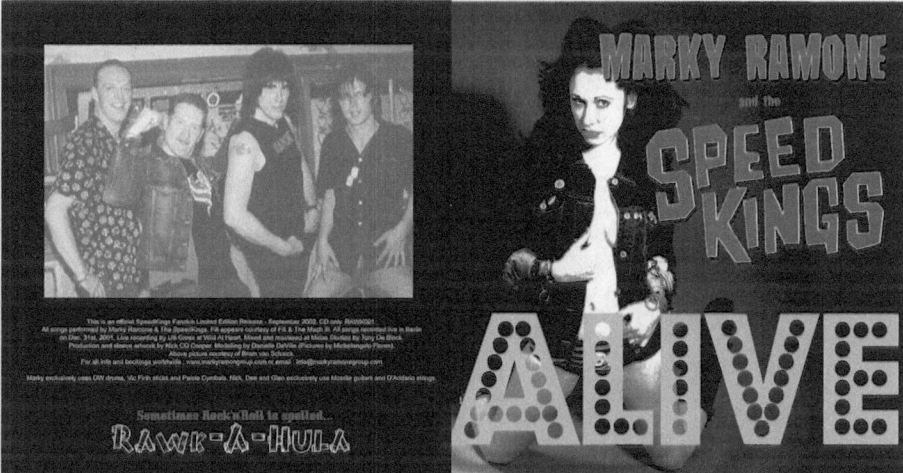

1. SPEEDKINGS RIDE TONIGHT (Nick CQ Cooper)
2. I DON'T CARE (Ramones)
3. SATURDAY NIGHT (Nick CQ Cooper)
4. TELEPHONE LOVE (Marky Ramone/Fred Bell)
5. TEENAGE ROCK'N'ROLL SUICIDE (Nick CQ Cooper)
6. CHINESE ROCKS (Ramones)
7. STAGBOOKS (Marky Ramone/Meyer Rossabi)
8. HOTRODS-R-US (Nick CQ Cooper)
9. CALIFORNIA SUN (Glover/Levy)
10. GIRLS & GASOLINE (Nick CQ Cooper/Stevey Jay)
11. BEAT ON THE BRAT (Ramones)
12. SHEENA IS A PUNKROCKER (Ramones)
13. SCUMFUCKS-R-US (Nick CQ Cooper)

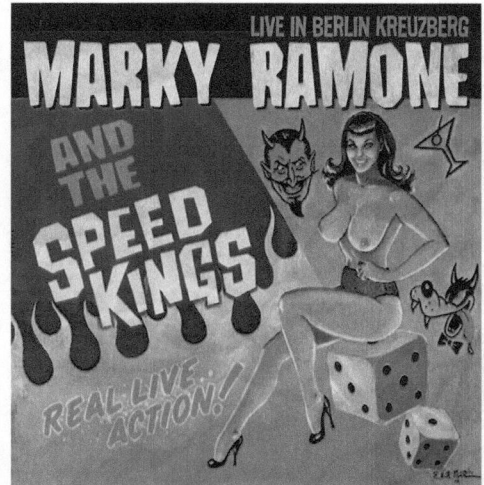

The ALIVE CD was reissued as a vinyl album in 2024. Gatefold sleeve.
Pressed in red, white, blue and gold vinyl and limited to 350 copies only.

BACK SEAT BINGO, the unrealead second album.

The Electric Thunder Syndicate EP
2 song CD on Hitsville Recordings 2006

1965 b/w CRY MYSELF TO SLEEP

THE ELECTRIC THUNDER SYNDICATE
Nick Cooper D (vocals/electric guitar) KPW (electric guitar/backing vocals)
Pip Vreede (electric bass) Geert Ossey (drums)

Recorded at Hitsville Bushforth Mixed and Mastered by Luc Crabbe at Luna Barn Studios
All songs written and produced by Vreede/Perwez/Cooper D
October 2015 Cover design Nick Cooper D Photography by An Sophie Houbroukx & Sarah Baert

Carrera De Los Muertos

Wildfire Custom Hotrods

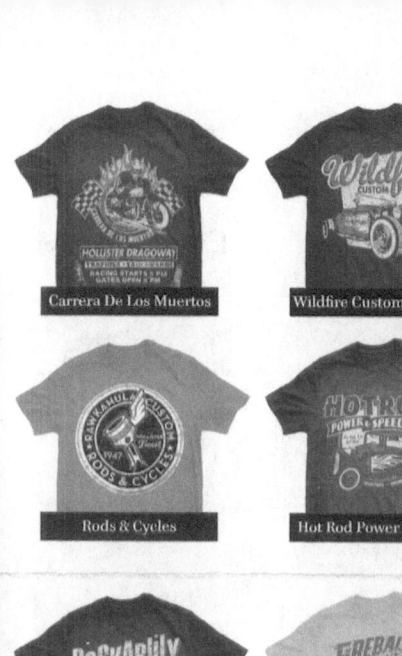

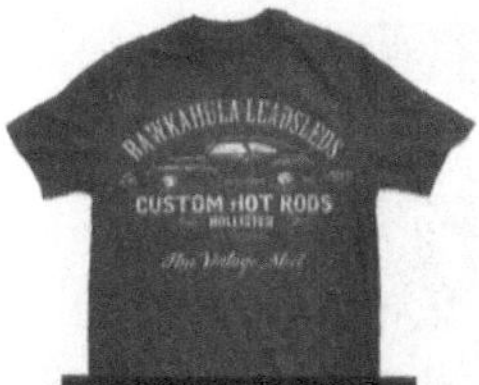

Rawkahula LeadSleds

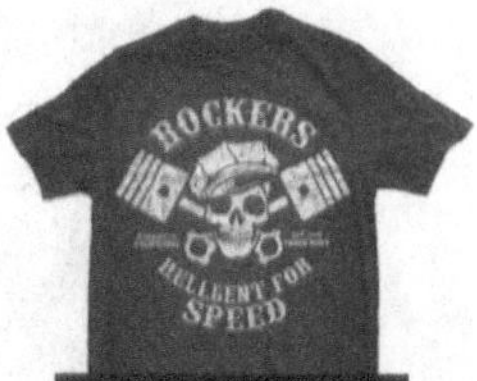

Rockers

Rods & Cycles

Hot Rod Power & Speed

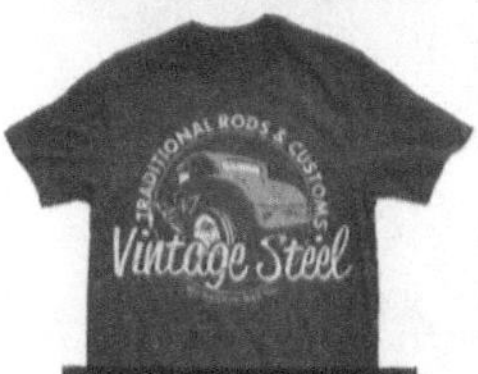

Vintage Steel

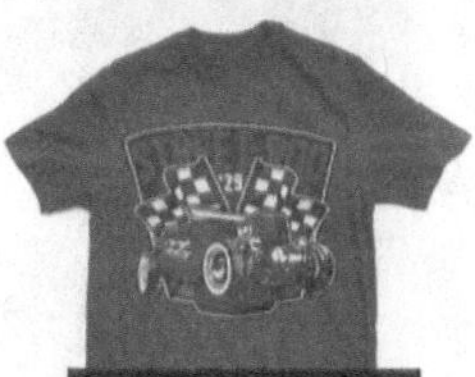
Street Rod '29

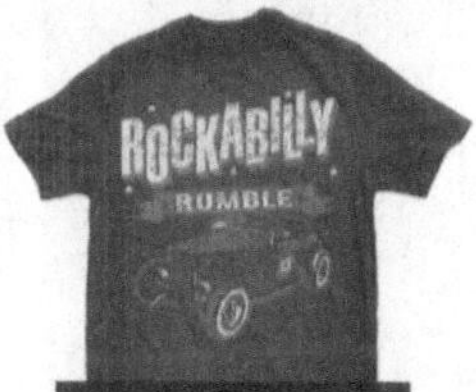

Rockabilly Rumble

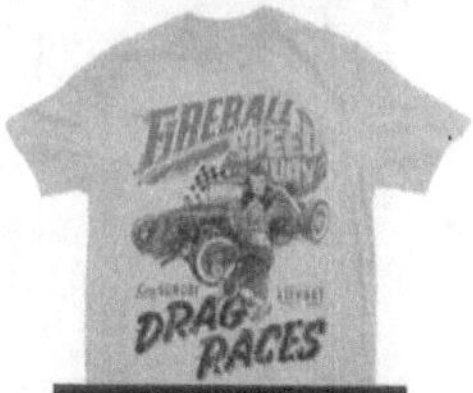

Fireball Drag Races

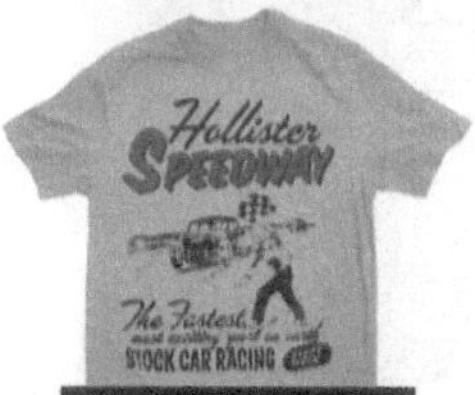

Hollister Speedway

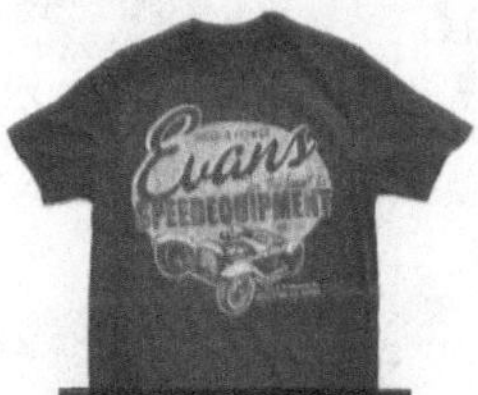

Evans SpeedEquipment

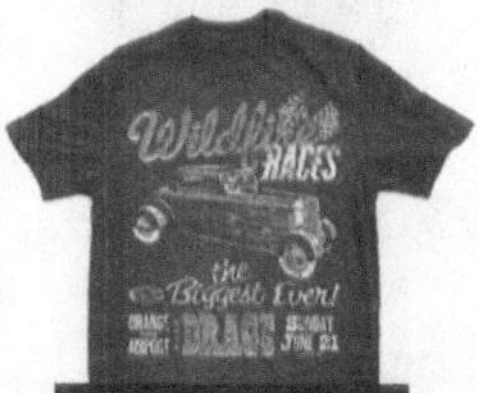

Wildfire Races

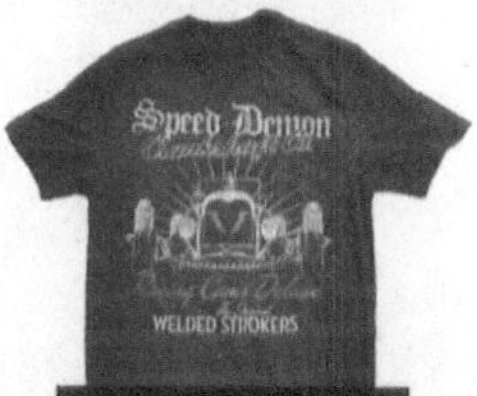

Crankshaft Company

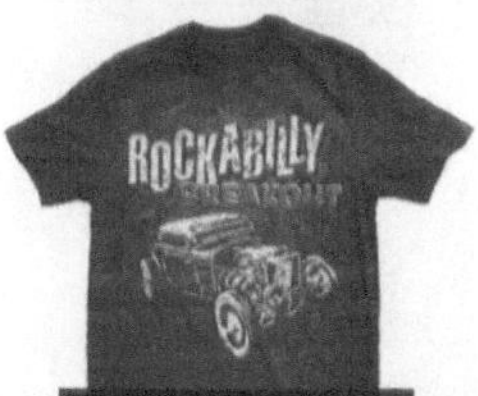

Rockabilly Breakout

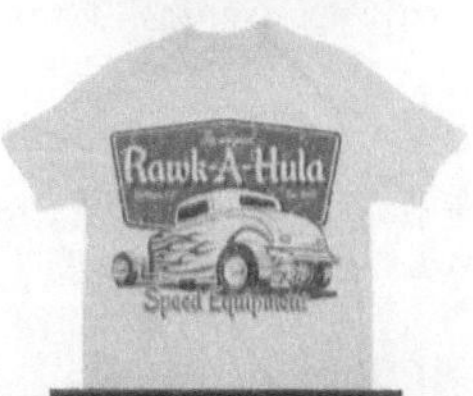

Rawkahula Speed

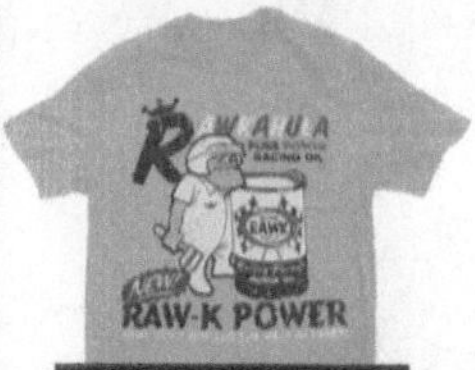

Raw-K Power

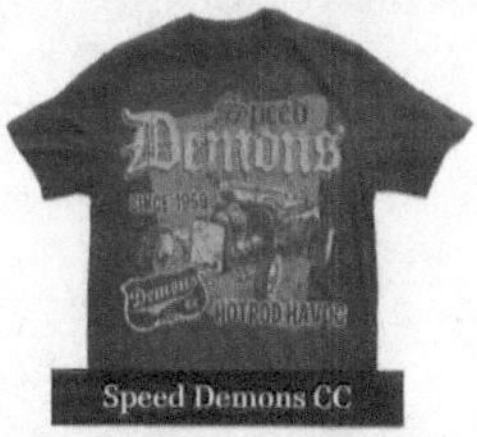

Speed Demons CC

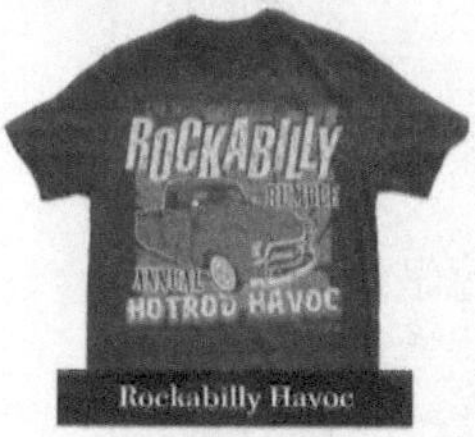

Rockabilly Havoc

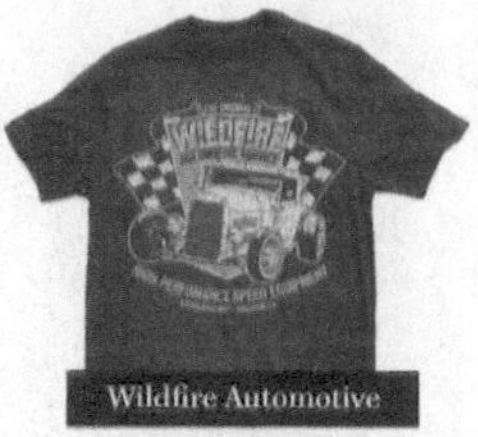
Wildfire Automotive

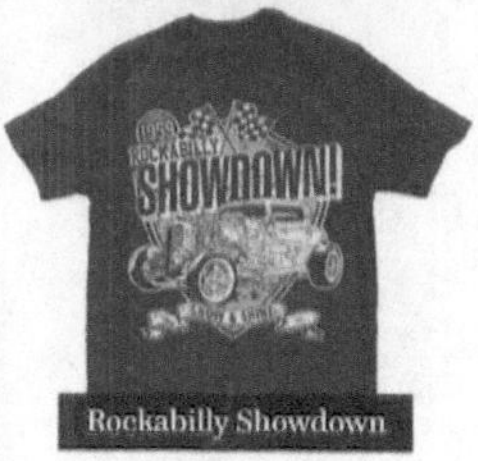

Rockabilly Showdown

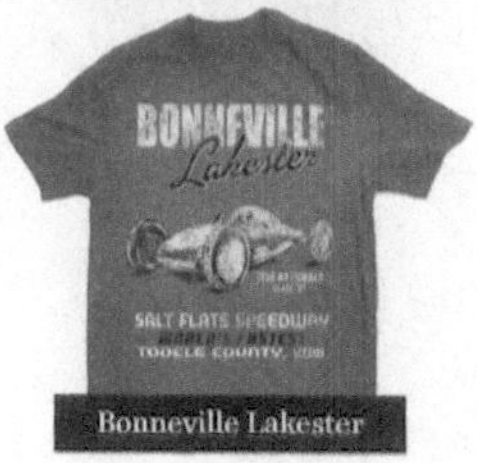

Bonneville Lakester

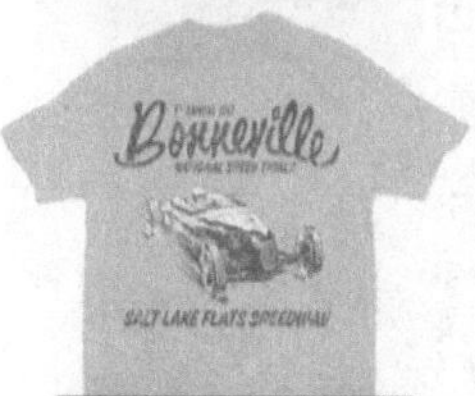

Bonneville Speed Trials

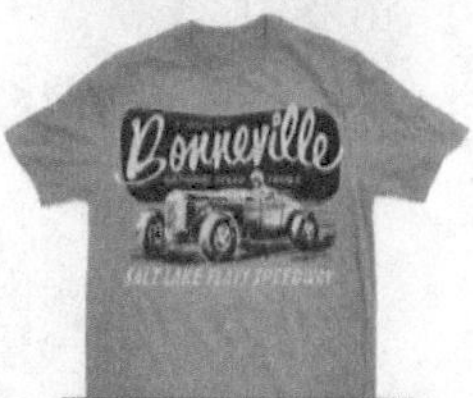

Bonneville 1957

Selection of designs that were produced for
the RAWKAHULA Kustom Kulture Clothing collection - 2010.

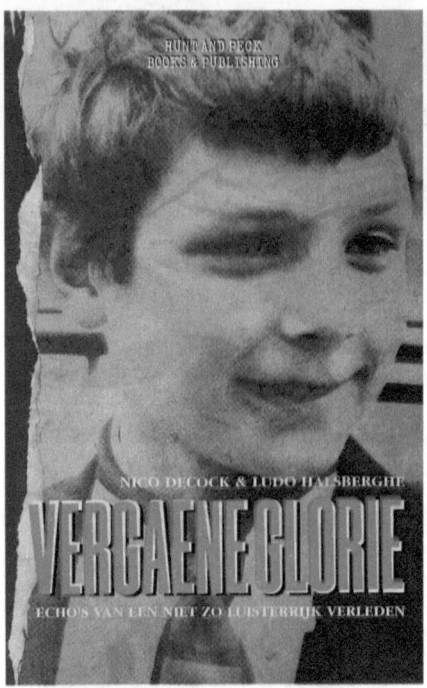

VERGAENE GLORIE (FADED GLORY BOYS)
First print paperback - June 2023

VERGAENE GLORIE (FADED GLORY BOYS)
First print hardcover - June 2023

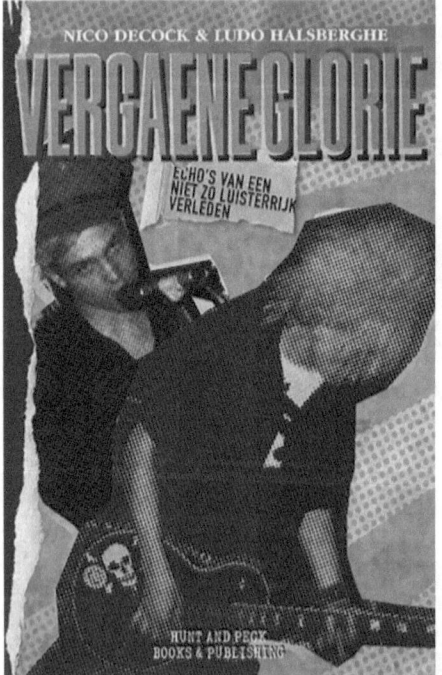

VERGAENE GLORIE (FADED GLORY BOYS)
Second print revised - paperback - Halloween 2023

ANARCHIST ANONYMOUS
First print - paperback - June 2023

INDEX

0

013 147, 175

1

1+2 Records 158

A

AC/DC 57, 58, 77, 280
Adrienne 74, 298, 299
Afton Arms 186
Agent Mulder 114
Akihiro Takayama 168, 299
Alfredo 160, 166, 297
Alien Love 41
American Heartbreak 180
Amsterdam 79, 80, 82, 133, 162, 92, 149, 263
Amsterdamned 78
Amy Winehouse 33
anarcho 76
Andre Dahlman 18, 62, 296
Angels Place 149
Anna 160, 166, 296
Anti-Nowhere League 28
Anton Corbijn 168
Apers 117
aroma therapy 188
Atak 91, 103
Athens 102, 103
Attila The Stockbroker 76
Australia 102, 98

B

Backyard Babies 130
Bad in Bed 102
Bad Religion 30
Badlands 187
Ballistic Bookings 111
Bambix 18
Bar Salamandre 171
Barnhomes 158
Batcave 175
Beat On The Brat 13
Bee Gees 38
Bengtson 64, 65, 66
Bennie 78, 84
Bertrand Sassoye 92
BGK 178
Black Flag 199, 200, 262
Black Sabbath 55, 79, 113
Blitzkrieg Bop 13, 140, 200, 49, 50, 51, 68, 89, 99
Blondie 32
Bon Scott 57, 281
Bonanza 44
Bones 53
Bonnie & Clyde 55
BOOM! Records 101
Booster Dragon 159
Born to be Wild 53
Boys and Vaseline 124
Bram 175, 17, 91, 296, 298

Bram van Schaik 175, 91, 296, 298
Brooklyn 139, 73, 75, 77
B-track Records 78
Buckweeds! 16
Burning Rubber 15
Burriana 130

C

Calle Schewen 10
cannabis 188
Captain Buerk 97, 99
Carabel 135
Carbondale 202
Caril Ann Fugate 187
Carlos 114
Catweazle 44
CBGB's 199, 206, 193, 264
CC Deville 65
CCC 91, 92, 96
Ceausescu 45
Celine 210, 68, 74, 77, 79, 297
Charlie Starkweather 187
Cherry Red Records 83
Chopper bar 59
Chrissie Hynde 65
Christmas 11, 40, 43, 44, 111, 126, 181, 182, 185
Chuck Berry 13
CJ 15, 17, 133, 5, 190
CJ Ramone 15, 16, 17, 190
Clash 159
Claudia 27, 91, 197
Clycke 59
CNN 210, 41, 144
cocaine 41, 149, 165
Coop 102
CQ Cooper 116
Crass 75, 85
Cretins 49, 51, 61
Crossroads Club 163
crystal meth 204, 227
Cunni Cox 116
Curtis Blow 116

D

Damned 69, 102
Damo 98, 99, 101, 296, 299
Dana Scully 114
Daniel 90
Daniel Rey 15, 211, 5, 96
Danielle Deville 81
Dave Stein 210
David Bowie 189
David Cassidy 78
David Kelly 16
David Lynch 116
De Kreun 130, 131
Dead Boys 32
Deborah 54, 55, 56, 57, 58, 59, 64
Dee Dee 10, 14, 15, 16, 131, 182, 212, 5, 21, 58, 73, 74, 295
Dee Dee Ramone 10, 14, 15, 21, 73, 295

Dee Jaywalker 14, 101, 208, 296, 298
Dee Snider 78
Deep Purple 9
Detroit Rock City 56, 228
Devil's Shitburner Records 22
Dez Cadena 199, 262
Didier Chevolet 92
Dig It! Magazine 157
Dirk 131
DIY 31, 62, 83, 84
DOA 128
Dogmeat Records 102
Dolf 81
Dolors Cubero 166
Don Hill's 73, 74, 189
Doyle 199, 264
Dr. Slump 112
Duffers 114, 117

E

Eagles 199
Eddy 144, 145, 146, 147, 148, 149, 150, 151, 299
Edward 100, 13, 98
El Duende Club 130
El Guapo Stuntteam 118, 119
Elliott Mattice 9
EMI 158
Emma 54, 55, 98
Enschede 91, 103
Eskimo girl 66
Estrus 102
Eva 98

F

FADED GLORY BOYS 7, 23
Fandango 117
Filthy 149
Finland 13, 17, 18, 4, 58, 66
Fitzcarraldo 165
Flipside 78
Fogon Distribution 58
Ford Cougar 202
Ford Escort 57
Forest Hills 25
Forest Rangers 43
Frank Droll 22, 297, 299
Fredrik 'Freddy' Eriksson 49, 296
Frites Modern 78
Fuck Me 30, 197
Fuck Shit Up! 15

G

Gamma Club 46
Gang of Nivelles 91
George Tabb 74
Gigant Poppodium 103
Gildas Cosperec 157
Girls and Gasoline 187, 124
Girlschool 41, 113
Girona 160, 11, 44

Gleis22 135
Glen 182, 15, 88, 296
Glen Matlock 182, 15
Gluecifer 10
Goodlife Recordings 13, 98
Göteborg 60
Grafton Hotel 196
Graves 20, 63
Green Day 122, 239
Grolsch 90
Grolschbusters 97
Gruta 77 .... 112, 131

H

Hang on Sloopy 39
Hannu Jokinen 48, 89
Hans 14, 296
Happy Malaga Castle See Afton Arms, See Afton Arms
Hard Rock Cafe 161
Harley Davidson 54
Hazel 100, 101
Hell Suckers 180
Hellacopters 10
Hellfire Booking 114
Hells Angels 163, 165, 39, 146, 147, 149
Henry Rollins 35
Hill Street Blues 115
Hillel Slovak 186
Holidays in The Sun festival 208
Hookers 180
House of Kicks 60
Huntingtons 137, 139, 145, 147, 148, 150, 151, 153, 160, 163, 165, 169, 173, 174, 175, 176

I

I Don't Care Anymore 15, 124
Iggy Pettersson 49
Impotent Sea Snakes 199
Industrial Copera Festival ... 130
Intruders 132

J

Jack 10, 180, 66, 76, 88, 91, 101, 117, 126, 130, 135, 164, 165, 167, 181, 182, 183, 184, 194, 197, 198, 204, 207, 208, 209, 227, 228, 236, 237, 240, 251, 262, 276, 296, 297, 298
Jack Black 180
Jack Kerouac 10
Jadelyn Hunter 201
James Dean 39
James Drescher 80
Jamie Reid 59
Japan 20, 111, 112, 117, 118, 119, 180, 142, 156, 157, 158, 159, 161, 162, 163, 168, 169, 170, 171, 172, 174, 190
Jari 'Juki' Lehtola 49, 296
Jari-Pekka 18, 25, 4, 48, 58, 66, 68, 89, 296, 298
Jari-Pekka Laitio-Ramone 18, 25, 89, 296, 298
Jayne County 74, 79
Jim Darky 115
Jimmy Gestapo 81
Jimyh Anti 115

Joan Jett 33
Joe Queer 147
Joey Ramone 14, 15, 16, 62, 191, 5, 17, 48, 74, 120, 212
John Cafiero 35
John Cooper Clarke 76, 28
John Holmstrom 77, 79
Johnny Chiba 74
Johnny Ramone 14, 17, 161
Johnny Thunders 143
Joke's Koeienverhuurbedrijf ... 78
JP VAN 101
Judas Priest 57
Judy Is A Punk 13
Jux Tap 111, 114
JVC 158, 159, 161

K

K4 126
Kaaos 17
Kay-Lou Courts 203
Keith Morris 200, 262
Kenny Bergdahl 49, 89
Kerrang 11, 42
Key Club 64, 191, 248, 252
Kimmo Aaltonen 67
KISS 56, 57, 58
Knitting Factory 162
Koslow Club 125
KPW 172, 207, 73
Kreun 146, 172
KSET 11, 30, 32
Kulturhuset 60, 65
Kulturzentrum Pelmke 11, 52

L

La Bobilla 146, 158, 159
LA Guns 185
La Zone 118, 119
Lagabbia Club 112
Lea 53
Legends Bleed 14, 58
Lemmy 119, 148, 150
Let's Fuck! 128
Livio 114, 117, 139
Locanda Atlantide 28
Long Gone John 102
Long Gone Loser 98, 296, 299
Lotoma Bookings 60
Lunachicks 74
Lynne Cameron 191

M

Machine à Coudre 146
Mad Louie Biondi 103
Malcolm McLaren 15
Mandy 80, 81
Marc Bell 197, 209
Maryslim 50
Max Cavalera 148
MaximumRocknRoll 78
MC5 33
McCoy's 39
Mephisto club 41
Michael Graves 200
Midnight Confidential 103
Midnight Men. 100, 116, 13, 206
Mike Blank 74
Miranda 64, 253, 260

Misfits 16, 35, 196, 198, 200, 208, 4, 163, 190, 196, 262, 263, 264
Misters 172, 207
Mondo Bizarro 112, 120, 121
Mondo Teeno Experience 101
Morzelpronk 78
Mosrite 112, 161
MossBurger 168
Motörhead 118, 119, 148
MTV 5, 28, 29, 248
Mud 53
Murphy's Law 80
Musikbunker 10, 26

N

Nations on Fire 13, 98
Never Mind The Bollocks 58
New Musical Express 102
New York Dolls 32
Nick 2, 14, 15, 16, 17, 35, 157, 161, 170, 5, 17, 20, 22, 46, 49, 50, 51, 62, 63, 95, 150, 259, 298
Nick Cooper 2, 14, 16, 17, 161, 5, 298
Nicke Borg 130
Nieuwe Koekrand 78
Nitwich 78
No If's, And's, Or But's!" 14
No Picky 129, 135
Nobodys 123
Noisy Neighbours 86
Nomads 10
nomunication 156
Nuggets 100

O

Osaka Popstar 16
Ozzy 54

P

Paard 10, 16, 17
Pabelon Club 135
Palace Theatre 196, 199, 201
Pansy Division 123
Partridge Family 78
Pascale Vandegeerde 92
Patrick Fitzgerald 76
Patti Smith 32
Paul Cook 24
Paul McCartney 168
Pete Steele 78
Phil 90
Phil Carson 77
Pierre Carette 92, 96
Pink Lincolns 123
Poison 65
Poison Girls 75
Pojat 48
Popface 114, 115
Posh Boy 200
punkitude 62, 65, 111

R

Radical Records 73
Radio Blast 124
Ralphs 184
Rattus Riistetyt 17

Rawk over Scandinavia 89
Red Hot Chili Peppers.......... 186
Registrators.............................. 117
Reign in Blood...................... 108
Reservoir Dogs..................... 162
Retarded................................. 176
Revenge 88..............................88
Ribbed for Her Pleasure....... 115
Richie Ramone......14, 15, 16, 17
Rise Above 199, 13, 98
Roadrunner 9, 157, 158
Robert Johnson 182
Robert Williams.................... 102
Robert Wise 39
Rock'n'Roll Hall of Fame 10
Rolling Stones................ 100, 168
Ronettes..................................38
Ronnie James Dio 113
Rot Records 83
Roxy Club 11, 46
Rubettes..................................53
Runaways 32, 33

S

Saharan Motor Hotel.... 184, 185
Sala Magic124, 125, 126, 41, 112, 129
Salmiac 48, 49
Sanctuary Records 181
Santa Claus 44
Santa Sebe Club.................... 134
Satirnine.................................50
Saturday Night15, 200, 29, 68, 75
Schlachthof..................... 11, 30
Schnitzel House............. 173, 174
Scotty 132, 133, 134, 135
Scratch My Back................... 102
Senza Benza 115
Sepultura.............................. 148
Sex Pistols25, 58, 59, 65, 182, 15, 174
Shakin' Street 102
Sheena164, 180, 200, 210, 67, 74, 77, 79, 89, 298
Sheena & The Rokkets.......... 180
Showaddywaddy 53
Shrine 11, 49, 51, 61, 68
Sid Vicious 65, 15
Silver......................................65
Sky Lopez 103
Slade.......................................53
Slaves of Satan 147
Slayer 108
Smokin' Troll Records 116
Snap Her............................... 117
Sniper 90, 296, 299
So What! Club 19
Sofie112, 115, 182, 297
Sommercasino............... 10, 112
Sophocles 51
Sound Pollution 11, 49
Specials 113
Speedealer 138
SpeedKings2, 14, 15, 16, 17, 19, 24, 27, 35, 101, 187, 190, 5, 6, 9, 14, 17, 18, 19, 42, 45, 47, 48, 50, 51, 52, 57, 58, 60, 75, 78, 80, 88, 89, 96, 99, 104, 120, 131, 144, 157, 162, 168, 172, 185, 226, 237, 251, 252, 261, 262, 269, 283, 294

St. Louis 201
stagbook............................. 188
Stardumb 147, 176, 180
Steppenwolf..........................53
Steve Austin 44
Steve Jones 174
Stevey Jay 14, 185, 296
Stitch 112, 182, 297
straight-edge 13, 52, 112
streetwalkers 40, 126
Strollers 50
Suburban Records 16
Subvert! 85
Supa Space Rockets 131
Svatsöx 78
Sympathy For the Record Industry..........................102

T

Tarakany 17
TCB Crew 14
Teen Idols 117, 122
Teenage Gangbang 102
Teenage Head .. 16, 117, 273, 276
Teengenerate 180
Telephone Love 67
terrorism.............. 46, 90, 92, 210
terrorists 46
Terveet Kädet 17
Texas T 186
Texas Terri185, 191, 244, 253, 296
Texas Terri Bomb 185
Texxi.................................. 186
The Ex 78, 80
The First Steps......................83
The Kids...............................34
The Knights of Fuzz 103
The Police 99, 168
The Queers 117, 122, 138, 147
The Salary Men From Hell ... 118
The Six Million Dollar Man ... 44
The Sound of Music 39
The Sweet..............................53
Therapy 68
Thirsty Ear 58
Thomas35, 60, 61, 63, 64, 69, 122, 124, 125, 126, 296
Thomas Goze 35, 122, 296
Thunder Road................112, 139
Tim 13, 14, 28, 31, 33, 79, 297
Timothy Gassen.................. 103
Tina Tuner 30
Tom 70, 74
Tommy Ramone 13
Tony14, 68, 69, 70, 44, 46, 95, 111, 121, 125, 126, 127, 129, 130, 181, 297
Tony De Block...............14, 297
Tony Producionnes 121
Too Tough to Die..................13
Too Tough To Die..................14
Tooraloo Radio 52
Tooth & Nail Records 137
Totem 112, 139
Tracy Irving 185
Travoltas 117, 175
Troubadour 91, 104
Tsepitch................. 14, 28, 297
Tulle146, 169, 171
Turo Ihalainen 67

Twenty-One club............. 60, 208
Twin Peaks 116, 202
Twisted Sister........................78
Type O Negative 74, 78

U

Uli 53
Uncle Bob.............................43
Underground..........146, 174, 272
Uniform Choice 13
Uniform Jantje....................... 13
Urga160
Urrke................................... 64
UxJx12, 13, 14, 28, 31, 33, 296, 297

V

Velvet Club........................ 115
Velvet Rock Club................ 111
Vergaene Glorie.......60, 74, 75, 77, 86
Virgin Records..................... 65
Vito 189, 14, 15, 29, 31, 32, 41, 43, 44, 45, 46, 47, 52, 59, 98, 296, 297, 298

W

Wayne County 102
Wayne Kramer...................... 33
What's Wrong with Attitude? 117
White Jazz Records 5, 9
wig 119, 39, 75, 76, 79
Wild At Heart 11, 273
Winny Kas.................... 90, 296
Wipe Out Records 102, 103
Woimasointu............... 48, 58, 296
Wonderfools 123, 124, 126
World Trade Center............. 210
Wreckin' Crew 90

X

Xevi Zoroa 166
-XXX- 77, 78, 81, 83, 84, 86, 100

Y

Ya Basta 146, 149
Yakuza.............112, 172, 174

Z

Zauberberg.................. 10, 22
Zeke138, 14
Zorro................................... 44
Zounds 85

WWW.PUNKROCKHEARTBREAK.COM
INFO@HUNTANDPECKBOOKS.COM

www.ingramcontent.com/pod-product-compliance
Lightning Source LLC
Chambersburg PA
CBHW021757220426
43662CB00006B/93